Ilan Stavans is one of our foremost and most versatile essayists and cultural critics. This comprehensive anthology, the first to appear in any language, reveals his wide range of interests. *The Essential Ilan Stavans* is divided into five parts: Stavans's writings on Latinos in the United States, his essays on politics and the arts north and south of the Rio Grande, his pieces on Jewish literature, autobiographical writings, and his frequently reprinted stories.

Readers will be compelled by Stavans's essays on influential figures like Gabriel García Márquez, Sandra Cisneros, Subcomandante Marcos, Elias Canetti, Rigoberta Menchú, Mario Vargas Llosa, Cantinflas, Lionel Trilling, Walter Benjamin, and others. His seminal articles on the sounds of Spanglish, kitsch, translation, memory and literature, and the Holocaust are also reprinted.

Stavans was born in Mexico into a Yiddish-language milieu and educated at Columbia University. His work has been translated into half a dozen languages. He has been nominated for the National Book Critics Circle Award and is the recipient of the Latino Literature Prize and a Guggenheim Fellowship. With prose as energetic as it is incisive and cautionary, Stavans displays an appetite for ideas in all their multifaceted complexity.

"Cantankerous and clever, sprightly and serious, Stavans is a voracious thinker. In his writings, life serves to illuminate literature—and vice versa; he is unafraid to court controversy, unsettle opinions, make enemies. In short, Stavans is an old-fashioned intellectual, a brilliant interpreter of his triple heritage—Jewish, Mexican, and American."

—Henry Louis Gates, Jr.

"Ilan Stavans, a Mexican Jew writing in English, has the sharp eye of the internal exile. Writing about the sometimes reluctant reconquista of North America by Spanish-speaking cultures or the development of his own identity, Stavans deals both with the life of the mind and life on the streets. Literary criticism, social essays, stories—this book examines the conflicts and contradictions of that frontier where Kafka meets NAFTA."

—John Sayles

"These reflections where the *you* and *yo*, Anglo and Spanglo, are joined in the richness of one Latino intellectual and artistic tradition make for stimulating reading. Positive, exultant, anti-provincial, and inspiring, Stavans gives the reader the opportunity to celebrate the creation of a new Latino self in which we are not one but many, and the border becomes our 'dream catcher,' the magic web that permits us to re-invent the future."

—Rosario Ferré

"Ilan Stavans is a prodigious reader and listener, and also an acute observer of American ways, in particular those half-hidden literary cultures and subcultures of the southern continent that are so often misread in the United States. He is also a very good writer, and his essay collection— lively and intelligent, eclectic, sharp-tongued yet fair-minded—is a marvelous survey of cultural matters that most of us imagined that we knew about but really didn't."

—Peter Matthiessen

"Ilan Stavans may be our most savvy reader. The 'we' in that sentence provides a space in which many groups can truly identify. He is a brilliant participant and reader of Mexican, Latin, and South American literature and culture. He is an incisive and critical voice in and out of the Jewish world in Hispanic America. He is one of the best critics and interviewers in the North American, Anglophone world. *The Essential Ilan Stavans*— something for everyone and something of true quality."

—Sander L. Gilman

"Stavans is bold, engaging, refreshingly agile as narrator and essayist, and this book is a most impressive accomplishment. Stavans's prose evinces how cultural differences can coexist in one writer and shed ironic light on one another, a curious tension but one familiar from Jewish literature. This is increasingly unavoidable for Latinos who are doubly American by definition (often with dual nationalities). Latino arts will embrace Stavans's challenge of irony and multiple identities, in its parallel with Jewish 'double consciousness' as the normal condition of Diaspora. It's this Diasporic cosmopolitan condition that allows Stavans to move from one position to another, to make connections, and to provoke his admiring readers."

—Doris Sommer

"It is rather infrequent that an intellectual in the United States will occupy himself with the literary currents of Latin America in a manner that is thoroughly conscious and rigorous, demonstrating a sincere and endurable interest in the region. This volume by Ilan Stavans fills a vacuum that has threatened to become both chronic and inexplicable. Each of its entries is a display of absolute devotion and passion. It evinces a singular mastery of the craft of the essay and reaches unexpected levels of depth. English-language readers will come tête-à-tête with the real continent they left unknown for far too long. And of course, the book will be equally enlightening to the Spanish-speaking public who will understand themselves in ways not previously imagined."

—Alvaro Mutis

"More than an anthology, this book is a tribute to the work of a talented writer, with an original vision of contemporary problems, especially those related to cultural identities (Latino, Jewish, American) and pop culture. Writing about Spanglish or Canetti, Jewish gauchos or the Latin phallus, Rigoberta Menchú or Octavio Paz, Cantinflas or García Márquez, Stavans opens to the reader the doors of a world (or several worlds). He is not only a keen essayist, he is also an excellent fiction writer, as demonstrated by the short stories in this volume. In short: Ilan Stavans gives us a comprehensive and affectionate panel of human and intellectual profiles of our times."

—Moacyr Scliar

"Ilan Stavans is the rarest of North American writers—he sees the Americas whole. Not since Octavio Paz has Mexico given us an intellectual so able to violate borders, with learning and grace."

—Richard Rodriguez

Other Books in English by Ilan Stavans

FICTION
*The One-Handed Pianist and Other Stories*

NONFICTION
*The Hispanic Condition*
*Art and Anger*
*Bandido*
*The Riddle of Cantinflas*
*Imagining Columbus*
*Latino U.S.A.: A Cartoon History* (with Lalo López Alcaráz)

EDITED COLLECTIONS
*The Oxford Book of Jewish Stories*
*Tropical Synagogues*
*New World*
*Mutual Impressions*
*The Urban Muse*
*The Oxford Book of Latin American Essays*
*Growing Up Latino* (with Harold Augenbraum)

TRANSLATIONS
*Sentimental Songs/La poesía cursi*, by Felipe Alfau

*The   Essential*

# ILAN STAVANS

Ilan Stavans ∎

ROUTLEDGE

*New York*
*London*

Published in 2000 by

Routledge
29 West 35th Street
New York, NY 10001

Published in Great Britain by
Routledge
11 New Fetter Lane
London EC4P4EE

Routledge is an imprint of the Taylor & Francis Group.

Library of Congress Cataloging-in-Publishing Data
Stavans, Ilan.
    The essential Ilan Stavans / edited by Ilan Stavans.
       p. cm.
    Includes bibliographical references and index.
    ISBN 0-415-92753-6 (hb) — ISBN 0-415-92754-4 (pbk.)

AC8 .S6685 2000
081—dc21                                                          00-022609

# CONTENTS

CONTENTS

## POP CULTURE

**3**

## SOUTHERN EXPOSURE

**4**

## STORIES

**5**

# PLATES

Into

the

Melting

Pot

# LIFE IN THE HYPHEN

What if *yo* were you and *tú fueras* I, Mister?

Born in 1885 in Jalisco, Mexico, the painter Martín Ramírez spent most of his life in a California madhouse, in a pavilion reserved for incurable patients. Since his death in 1960 he has become a symbol in Hispanic immigrant experience and is considered today a leading painter with a permanent place in Chicano visual art. As a young man, Ramírez worked first in the fields and then in a laundry; he later worked as a migrant railroad worker, relocating across the Rio Grande in search of a better life and to escape the dangers of the violent upheaval sweeping his native land. He lost the power to talk around 1915, at the age of thirty, and wandered for many years, until the Los Angeles police picked him up and sent him to Pershing Square, a shelter for the homeless. Diagnosed by doctors as a "deteriorated paranoid schizophrenic" and sent to the Dewitt Hospital, Ramírez never recovered his speech. But in 1945, some fifteen years before his death, he began to draw. Ramírez was fortunate to be discovered by a psychiatrist, Dr. Tarmo Pasto, of the University of California, Sacramento, who, as the legend claims, was visiting the hospital one day with a few pupils when Ramírez approached him, offering a bunch of rolled-up paintings. The doctor was so impressed with Ramírez's work that he made sure the artist had plenty of drawing materials to use. Soon Pasto began collecting Ramírez's work and showed it to a number of artists,

First published in *The Hispanic Condition: Reflections on Culture and Identity in America* (New York: HarperCollins, 1995).

including Jim Nutt, who arranged an exhibit of Ramírez's paintings with an art dealer in Sacramento. Other exhibits soon followed—in New York, Chicago, Sweden, Denmark, Houston, among other places—and Ramírez, the perfect outsider, was a dazzling revelation at the exposition "Outsiders" in London's Hayward Gallery.

In a controversial text written in June 1986 to commemorate an exhibit, "Hispanic Art in the United States: Thirty Contemporary Painters and Sculptors," at the Corcoran Gallery in Washington, DC, Octavio Paz, the 1990 winner of the Nobel Prize in Literature, claimed that Ramírez's pencil-and-crayon drawings are evocations of what Ramírez lived and dreamed during and after the Mexican Revolution. Paz compared the artist to Richard Dadd, a nineteenth-century painter who lost his mind at the end of his life. As Carlos Fuentes, the Mexican novelist and diplomat, claimed in his book *The Buried Mirror*, the mute painter drew his muteness, making it graphic. And Roger Cardinal, the British author of *Figures of Reality*, argued that the artist's achievements should not be minimized as psychotic rambling and categorized him as "a naïf painter." To make sense of Ramírez's odyssey, Dr. Pasto concluded that Ramírez's psychological disturbances were the result of a difficult process of adaptation to a foreign culture. Ramírez had left Mexico at a turbulent, riotous time and arrived in a place where everything was unfamiliar and strange to him.

Ramírez's plight is representative of the entire Hispanic cultural experience in the United States. Neither a diluted Mexican lost in a no-man's land nor a fully rounded citizen, Ramírez symbolizes the voyage of millions of silent itinerant *braceros* and legal middle-class immigrants bewildered by their sudden mobility, furiously trying to make sense of an altogether different environment. But Hispanics are now leaving his frustrated silence behind. Society is beginning to embrace Latinos, from rejects to fashion setters, from outcasts to insider traders. New generations of Spanish speakers are feeling at home in Gringolandia. (Etymologically, *gringo*, according to *Webster's Dictionary,* is derived from *griego*, stranger, but it may have been derived from the Spanish pronunciation of a slang word meaning fast-spender, *green-go*.) Suddenly the crossroad where white and brown meet, where "yo soy" meets "I am," a life in the Spanglish hyphen, is being transformed. Many of us Latinos already have a Yankee look: We either make a conscious effort to look gringo, or we're simply absorbed by the culture's fashion and manners. And what is more exciting is that Anglos are beginning to look just like us—enamored as they are of our bright colors and tropical rhythms, our suffering Frida Kahlo, our legendary Ernesto "Che" Guevara. Martín Ramírez's silence is giving way to a revaluation of things

Hispanic. No more silence, no more isolation. Spanish accents, our *manera peculiar de ser*, have emerged as exotic, fashionable, and even enviable and influential in mainstream American culture.

However, just as Ramírez's art took decades to be understood and appreciated, it will take years to understand the multifaceted and far-reaching implications of this cultural transformation, the move of Hispanics from periphery to center stage. I believe that we are currently witnessing a double-faceted phenomenon: Hispanization of the United States and Anglocization of Hispanics. Adventurers in Hyphenland, explorers of El Dorado, we Hispanics have deliberately and cautiously infiltrated the enemy and now go by the rubric of Latinos in the territories north of the Rio Grande. Delaying full adaptation, our objective is to assimilate Anglos slowly to ourselves.

Indeed, a refreshingly modern concept has emerged before American eyes—to live in the hyphen, to inhabit the borderland—and nowhere is the debate surrounding it more candid, more historically enlightening, than among Hispanics. The American Dream has not yet fully opened its arms to us; the melting pot is still too cold, too uninviting, for a total meltdown. Although the collective character of those immigrating from the Caribbean archipelago and south of the border remains foreign to a large segment of the heterogeneous nation, as "native strangers" within the Anglo-Saxon soil, our impact will prevail sooner, rather than later. Although stereotypes remain commonplace and vices get easily confused with habits, a number of factors, from population growth to a retarded acquisition of a second language and a passionate retentiveness of our original culture, actually suggest that Hispanics in the United States shall not, will not, cannot, and ought not follow paths opened up by previous immigrants.

According to various Chicano legends recounted by the scholar Gutierre Tibón, Aztlan Aztlatlan, the archetypal region where Aztecs, speakers of Nahuatl, originated before their itinerant journey in the fourteenth century in search of a land to settle, was somewhere in the area of New Mexico, California, Nevada, Utah, Arizona, Colorado, Wyoming, Texas, and the Mexican states of Durango and Nayarit, quite far from Tenochtitlán, known today as Mexico City. Once a nomadic tribe, the Aztecs settled and became powerful, subjugating the Haustec to the north and the Mixtec and Zapotec to the south, achieving a composite civilization. Latinos with these mixed ancestries, at least six in every ten in the United States, believe they have an aboriginal claim to the land north of the border. As native Americans, we were in these areas before the Pilgrims of the *Mayflower* and understandably keep a telluric attachment to the land.

Our return by sequential waves of immigration as wetbacks and middle-income entrepreneurs to the lost Canaan, the Promised Land of Milk and Honey, ought be seen as the closing of a historical cycle. Ironically, the revenge of Motecuhzoma II (in modern Spanish: Moctezuma; in its English misspelling: Montezuma) is understood differently in Spanish and English. For Anglos, it refers to the diarrhea a tourist gets after drinking unpurified water or eating chile and arroz con pollo in Latin America and the West Indies; for Hispanics, it describes the unhurried process of the penetration of and exertion of influence on the United States—*la reconquista*, the oppressor's final defeat. Yesterday's victim and tomorrow's conquistadors, we Hispanics, tired of a history full of traumas and undemocratic interruptions, have decided to regain what was taken away from us.

There is no doubt that the attempt to portray Latinos as a homogenous minority and/or ethnic group is rather recent. Within the various minorities, forces have always pulled unionists apart. As Bernardo Vega, a Puerto Rican social activist in New York City, wrote in his *Memoirs* in the 1940s:

When I came to [New York] in 1916 there was little interest in Hispanic culture. For the average citizen, Spain was a country of bullfighters and flamenco dancers. As for Latin America, no one could care less. And Cuba and Puerto Rico were just two islands inhabited by savages whom the Americans had beneficially saved from the clutches of the Iberian lion. Once in a while a Spanish theater company would make an appearance in New York. Their audiences never amounted to more than the small cluster of Spaniards and Latin Americans, along with some university professors who had been crazy enough to learn Spanish. That was it!

The constant growth of the Puerto Rican community gave rise to riots, controversy, hatred. But there is one fact that stands out: at a time when there were no more than half a million of us, our impact on cultural life in the United States was far stronger than that of the 4 million Mexican-Americans. And the reason is clear: though they shared with us the same cultural origins, people of Mexican extraction, involved as they were in agricultural labor, found themselves scattered throughout the American Southwest. The Puerto Ricans, on the other hand, settled in the large urban centers, especially New York, where in spite of everything the circumstances were more conducive to cultural interaction and enrichment, whether we wanted it that way or not.

Until the early eighties, Mexicans, Puerto Ricans, Cubans, Central and South Americans, and even Spaniards were considered independent units in the United States, never part of a unified whole. If culture is defined as the fabric of life of a community, the way its members react in a social context, then Hispanic culture in the United States is many cultures, as many as national groups from Latin America and the Caribbean, linguistically tied together—with Antonio de Nebrija, the first grammarian of the Spanish language, as a paternal figure. After the 1990 U.S. Census, which counted more than 22 million Hispanics—9 percent of the overall population (although at least 3 million wandering illegal immigrants should probably be added to that count)—we emerged as a solid political and social force. Before then our political struggles and social behavior were often associated, in the view of Congress and in governmental offices, with an image of some monstrous creature, inchoate, formless, inconstant, whose metabolism was difficult to define. Assimilation was analyzed according to our independent nationalities: For instance, many Cubans who came to the country after the 1959 Communist Revolution and before the Mariel boat lift in 1980 were educated upper- and middle-class people; consequently, their adaptation acquired a different rhythm from that of Puerto Ricans, who, mostly as *jíbaros* from rural areas near San Juan and elsewhere on their native West Indian island, arrived in the United States illiterate and without a penny. Although not all Cubans were well-off nor all Puerto Ricans miserable, many thought the two subgroups needed to be approached separately and as autonomous units. Things indeed have been reversed. Today the various parts making the Hispanic whole are approached by scholars more or less uniformly, as interdependent screws adding up to a sophisticated, self-contained machinery: Latinos are seen as an assembly of forces, in close contact with their Hispanic siblings under the border.

The discussion on how Hispanics have been assimilated has been greatly influenced by, among others, Juan Gómez-Quiñones, the dean of Chicano hisotry; he wrote the groundbreaking 1977 essay on ethnicity and resistance entitled "On Culture," first published in *Revista Chicano-Riqueña,* as well as studies of Chicano politics and the radical politics of the Mexican anarchist and anticlericalist Ricardo Flores Magón. This discussion has been centered for decades on what theoreticians called "negative assimilation." Immigrants from Spanish-speaking countries—anthropologists, sociologists, and historians believed—were ready to retain their ancestral heritage against all odds and costs; their daily existence in an alien, aggressive milieu provoked a painful chain of belligerent acts against Anglo-Saxon domination. According to this view, Mexicans in East Los Angeles, Puerto Ricans in Upper Manhattan's El Barrio, or Cubans in Key West and Miami's Little Havana silently yet forcefully engaged in a battle against the environment's imposing values. The Anglo, always the enemy, was seen as colonizing and enslaving, a view shared by many south of the Rio Grande since the time of the Spanish-American War. In a tantalizing poem, Lorna Dee Cervantes, a Chicana in California, author of *Emplumada*, wrote about the pilgrimage to a paradise without complete freedom: "I see in the mirror/my reflection: bronzed skin, black hair./I feel I am a captive aboard the refugee ship./The ship that will never dock."

At the end of the 1960s, a confrontational, bold, politically charged era emerged. The Chicano movement, led by César Chávez and the intellectually sophisticated Rodolfo "Corky" González,* which was intimately linked to the Vietnam War and the civil rights era, was, according to many, the apex of such social strife. The term *chicano* embodied the effort to overturn the dire conditions existing within the Chicano communities during the postwar period. And in their activism, Chicanos were joined by Puerto Rican revolutionary nationalists to form such organizations as the Young Lords, who fought for the independence and self-determination of Puerto Rico, equality for women, an end to racism, and better education in Afro-Indian and Spanish cultures. To oppose, to affirm one's own collective tradition, to remain loyal to the immigrant's culture, was considered essential and coherent with the Hispanic nature north of the Rio Grande. Such an attitude would often incorporate apocalyptic overtones. On the aesthetics of resistance, Gómez-Quiñones once wrote: "The forms and ethos of one art must be broken—the art of domination; another art must be rescued and fashioned—the art of resistance. . . . It is art that is not afraid to love or play due to its sense of history and future. It negates the exploitation of the many by the few, art as the expression of the degeneration of values for the few, the corruption of human life, the destruction of the world. At that point art is at the threshold of entering the dimension of politics."

Led by feminists such as Gloria Anzaldúa and Cherríe Moraga, whose work is devoted to analyzing "the mestizo world view" (first used as a racial category by "El Inca" Garcilazo de la Vega, the term

---

* Unfortunately, when Anglicized, Spanish appellations and words often drop their accents. The explanation may be technological: Typewriters and word processors that are used in the United States either exclude them or have complex, laborious commands to bring them forth.

*mestizo,* from the latin *miscére,* to mix, refers to people of combined European and American Indian ancestry), interpreters today are engaged in an altogether different frame of discussion. They suggest that Latinos, living in a universe of cultural contradictions and fragmentary realities, have ceased to be belligerent in the way they typically were during the antiestablishment decade. It is not that combat has disappeared or ceased to be compelling; it has simply acquired a different slant. The fight is no longer from the outside in, but from the inside out. We Latinos in the United States have decided to consciously embrace an ambiguous, labyrinthine identity as a cultural signature, and what is ironic is that, in the need to reinvent our self-image, we seem to be thoroughly enjoying our cultural transactions with the Anglo environment, ethnically heterogeneous as they are. Resistance to the English-speaking environment has been replaced by the notions of transcreation and transculturation, to exist in constant confusion, to be a hybrid, in constant change, eternally divided, much like Dr. Jekyll and Mr. Hyde: a bit like the Anglos and a bit not. Such a characterization, it is not surprising, fits the way in which Hispanics are portrayed by intellectuals in Latin America. Octavio Paz and Julio Cortázar once offered the *axolotl*—a type of Mexican salamander, a lizardlike amphibian with porous skin and four legs that are often weak or rudimentary—as the ad hoc symbol of the Hispanic psyche, always in profound mutation, not the mythical creature capable of withstanding fire, but an eternal mutant. And this metaphor, needless to say, fits perfectly what can be called "the New Latino": a collective image whose reflection is built as the sum of its parts in unrestrained and dynamic metamorphosis, a spirit of acculturation and perpetual translation, linguistic and spiritual, a dense popular identity shaped like one of those perfect spheres imagined by Blaise Pascal: with its diameter everywhere and its center nowhere. We are all to become Latinos *agringados* and/or *gringos hispanizados;* we will never be the owners of a pure, crystalline collective individuality because we are the product of a five-hundred-year-old fiesta of miscegenation that began with our first encounter with the gringo in 1492.

What is applauded in today's multicultural age is a life happily lost and found in Spanglish, which the southern writer and scholar Rolando Hinojosa, the Chicano author of the Klail City saga, calls *el caló pachuco*: a round trip from one linguistic territory and cultural dimension to another, a perpetual bargaining. Bilingual education, which began in the 1960s in Florida in response to a request from Cubans who wished to allow their children to use Spanish in public schools, has reinforced the importance of our first language among

Latinos. The tongue of Spain's Gold Age poets Luis de Góngora and Francisco de Quevedo, rather than fading away, is alive and changing, a crucial player in our bifocal identity. The hyphen as an acceptable in-between is now in fashion; monolingualism, people in the barrios of the Southwest enjoy saying, is curable. One of the best portrayals of Latino assimilation into the melting pot that I know of is found in Tom Shlamme's 1991 television film *Mambo Mouth*, in which the performance artist John Leguizamo (who wrote the original play as well) impersonates a Japanese executive trying to teach Latinos the art of "ethnic crossover." He claims that in corporate America there's no room for "Spiks," and thus elaborates a method by which Latinos can look and become Oriental. In the tradition of satirical comedy, Leguizamo ridicules Hispanic features: dietary and dressing manners, ways of speaking and walking, etc. As the monologue develops, we learn that the Japanese executive himself was once a Latino and that, occasionally, he longs for the *sabor hispano* of his past. Slowly, as in Chekhov's dramatic digressions—indeed, Leguizamo's piece is remarkably similar to Chekhov's tragicomic monologue "On Smoking and Its Dangers"—the character loses his integrity; while speaking, his feet suddenly run wild, dancing a fast-paced salsa rhythm. Obviously, the method for "ethnic crossover" has failed: Wherever we go, as Latinos we will always carry our idiosyncratic self with us.

Even before the publication of Oscar Hijuelos's dazzling novel *The Mambo Kings Play Songs of Love* in 1989 and its subsequent receipt of the Pulitzer Prize, an explosion of Latino arts was overwhelming the country. Young and old, dead and alive—from William Carlos Williams to Joan Baez and Tito Rodríguez, from Gloria Estefan, Piri Thomas, Diego Rivera, Anthony Quinn, and Oscar Lewis to María Conchita Alonso, Celia Cruz, and Cortijo—novelists, poets, filmmakers, painters, and salsa, merengue, plena, rumba, mambo, and cumbia musicians are being reevaluated, and a different approach to the Latino metabolism has been happily promoted. The concept of negative assimilation has been replaced by the idea of a cultural war in which Latinos are soldiers in the battle to change America from within, to reinvent its inner core. Take the fever surrounding Latin America's magical realism, what the Cuban musicologist and novelist Alejo Carpentier first called *lo real maravilloso* after a trip to Haiti in 1943, and what has been used to describe, obtusely, Gabriel García Márquez's fictional coastal town Macondo, with its rain of butterflies and epidemic of insomnia. Incredibly marketable, magical realism exploited the tropics—largely forgotten in the international artistic scene, aside from the surrealist curiosity about primitivism, until after World War II—as an extrinsic geography, full of picturesque landscapes, a banana republic of magisterial proportions where treacherous army officials tortured heroic rebels.

Foreigners' obsession with such images quickly transformed the region into a huge picture postcard, a kitsch stage where everybody was either a dreamer, a harlot, or a corrupt official. After intense abuse and massive commercialization, where Evita Perón was Patti Lupone singing an Andrew Lloyd Webber melody, the image has finally lost its magnetism, eclipsed by another scene: barrio nightclubs and alien urban turf. You don't need to travel to Buenos Aires or Bogotá anymore to feel the Latino beat. Miami, once a retreat for retirees, is now a laboratory where Latinization, as Joan Didion and David Rieff have argued, is already a fact, and where, as the xenophobic media claims, "foreigners," especially Cubans and Brazilians, have taken over. It is *the* frontier city par excellence: It has incorporated 300,000 refugees from Latin America who seem to have come with a vengeance; bilingualism is the rule; there's little pressure to become a citizen of the United States; tourists are besieged and threatened and unhappy Anglos have fled; and huge investments pour in from wealthy entrepreneurs in Venezuela and Argentina, among other places.

Although some stubbornly persist in thinking that the so-called Third World begins and ends in Ciudad Juárez and Matamoros, the neighboring cities south of the Rio Grande, the fact is that Los Angeles, first visited by Spaniards in 1769 and founded as a town a few years later, is Mexico's second capital, a city with more Mexicans than Guadalajara and Monterrey combined. And New York City, originally a Dutch settlement called New Amsterdam, has turned into a huge frying pan, where, since the 1970s, the Puerto Rican identity has been actively revamped into Nuyoricanness, a unique blend of Puerto Ricanness and New Yorkese, and where numerous other Latino groups have proliferated since the 1980s. *Bienvenido,* gringo! Claude Lévi-Strauss's *tristes tropiques* have just been relocated: Hispanics are now in the background, while Latinos, with their Jerome Robbins–choreographed, Stephen Sondheim-lyricized West Side stories, have come forth as protagonists in vogue.

Tonight, tonight,
The world is full of light,
With suns and moons all over the place.
Tonight, tonight,
The world is wild and bright,

Going mad, shooting sparks into space.
Today the world was just an address,
A place for me to live in,
No better than all right,
But here you are,
And what was just a world is a star
Tonight!

In quality and quantity, a different collective spirit is emerging, seasoned with south-of-the border flavors. The new Latino's ideological agenda is personified in the breathtaking prose of Sandra Cisneros and made commercial in the Madonna-like mercantile curiosity, in the Anglo arena, toward veteran musicians Tito Puente and Dámaso Pérez Prado. Again, the objective is to use the mass media, the enemy's tools, to infiltrate the system and to promote a revaluation of things Hispanic. For Hispanics Anglo-Saxon culture is, no doubt, still very much the villain, but the attitude is more condescending, even apologetic. As the poet Taro Laviera wrote in *AmeRícan*, a poem from which I quote two segments:

We gave birth to a new generation,
AmeRícan, broader than lost gold
never touched, hidden inside the
puerto rican mountains.

we gave birth to a new generation,
AmeRícan, it includes everything
imaginable you-name-it-we-got-it
society.

we gave birth to a new generation,
AmeRícan salutes all folklores,
european, indian, black, spanish,
and anything else compatible:

AmeRícan, defining the new America, humane
america, admired america, loved
america, harmonious america, the
world in peace, our energies
collectively invested to find other
civilizations, to touch God, further
and further, to dwell in the spirit of divinity!

AmeRícan, yes, for now, for i love this, my
second land, and i dream to take
the accent from the altercation, and
be proud to call myself american,
in the u.s. sense of the word,
AmeRícan, America!

Our understanding of the evasive concept of borderland—a
never-never land near the rim and ragged edge we call frontier, an
uncertain, indeterminate, adjacent area that everybody can recognize and that, more than ever before, many call our home—has
been adapted, reformulated, and reconsidered. Hyphenated identities become natural in a multiethnic society. After all, democracy,
what Felipe Alfau called the tyranny of the many, asks for a constant revaluation of the nation's history and conviviality. And yet, a
border is no longer only a globally accepted, internationally defined
edge, the legal boundary dividing two or more nations; it is first and
foremost a mental state, an abyss, a cultural hallucination, a fabrication. Latinos, as frontier dwellers, immersed in the multicultural
banquet, can no longer afford to live quietly on the margins, para-
sites of a bygone past. For today's newly arrived immigrant, *la
patria*, one's home nation, what Yiddish-speaking immigrants once
called *der alter heim*, is, as Tato Laviera claimed, whatever one
makes of today's United States. Animosity and resentment are put
on hold, the semiburied past is left behind while the present is
seized.

Our generation is triumphantly ready to reflect on its immediate
and far-reaching assimilation process, and this inevitably leads to a
path of divided loyalty. Indeed, divided we stand, without a sense of
guilt. Gringolandia, after all, is our ambivalent, schizophrenic *hogar*.
We are reconsidering the journey, looking back while wondering:
Who are we? Where did we come from? What have we achieved?
Overall, the resulting hybrid, a mix of English and Spanish, of the
land of leisure and futuristic technology and the Third World, has
ceased to be an elusive utopia. Latin America has invaded the United
States and reversed the process of colonization highlighted by the
Treaty of Guadalupe Hidalgo and the Spanish-American War.
Suddenly, and without much fanfare, the First World has became a
conglomeration of tourists, refugees, and émigrés from what Waldo
Frank once called *la America hispana*, a *sopa de razas e identidades,*
where those who are fully adapted and happily functional are looked
down on.

This metamorphosis includes many losses, of course, for all of us, from alien citizens to full-status citizens: the loss of language; the loss of identity; the loss of self-esteem; and, more important, the loss of tradition. Some are left behind en route, whereas others forget the flavor of home. But less is more, and confusion is being turned into enlightenment. In this nation of imagination and plenty, where newcomers are welcome to reinvent their pasts, loss quickly becomes an asset. The vanishing of a collective identity—Hispanics as eternally oppressed—necessarily implies the creation of a refreshingly different self. Confusion, once recycled, becomes effusion and revision. Among many, Guillermo Gómez-Peña has verbalized this type of cultural hodgepodge, this convoluted sum of parts making up today's Hispanic condition. "I am a child of crisis and cultural syncretism," he argued, "half hippie and half punk."

My generation grew up watching movies about cowboys and science fiction, listening to *cumbias* and tunes from the Moody Blues, constructing altars and filming in Super-8, reading the *Corno Emplumado* and *Artforum,* traveling to Tepoztlán and San Francisco, creating and de-creating myths. We went to Cuba in search of political illumination, to Spain to visit the crazy grandmother and to the U.S. in search of the instantaneous musico-sexual Paradise. We found nothing. Our dreams wound up getting caught in the webs of the border.

Our generation belongs to the world's biggest floating population: the weary travelers, the dislocated, those of us who left because we didn't fit anymore, those of us who still haven't arrived because we don't know where to arrive at, or because we can't go back anymore.

Our deepest generational emotion is that of loss, which comes from our having left. Our loss is total and occurs at multiple levels.

Loss of land and self. By accommodating ourselves to the American Dream, by forcing the United States to acknowledge us as part of its uterus, we are transforming ourselves inside El Dorado and, simultaneously, reevaluating the culture and environment we left behind. Not since the abolition of slavery and the waves of Jewish immigration from Eastern Europe has a group been so capable of turning everybody upside down. If, as W. E. B. Du Bois once claimed, the problem of the twentieth century was meant to be the problem of the color line, the next hundred years will have acculturation and miscegenation as their leitmotif and strife. Multiculturalism will sooner or later fade away and will take with it the need for Latinos to inhabit the hyphen and exist in constant contradiction as eternal *axólotls*. By then the United States will be a radically different country. Meanwhile, we are experiencing a rebirth and are having a festive time deciding to be undecided.

How can one understand the hyphen, the encounter between Anglos and Hispanics, the mix between George Washington and Simón Bolívar? Has the cultural impact of south-of-the-border immigrants in a country that prides itself on its Eurocentric lineage and constantly tries to minimize, even hide, its Spanish and Portuguese backgrounds, been properly analyzed? Where can one begin exploring the Latino hybrid and its multiple links to Hispanic America? To what extent is the battle inside Latinos between two conflicting worldviews, one obsessed with immediate satisfaction and success, the other traumatized by a painful, unresolved past, evident in our art and letters? Should the opposition to the English Only movement, Chicano activism, Cuban exile politics, and the Nuyorican existential dilemma be approached as manifestations of a collective, more-or-less homogeneous psyche? Are Brazilians, Jamaicans, and Haitians—all non-Spanish speakers—our siblings? Is Oscar Hijuelos possible without José Lezama Lima and Guillermo Cabrera Infante? Or is he only a child of Donald Barthelme and Susan Sontag? What does he as a Cuban-American share with Chicana Sandra Cisneros and Dominican-American novelist Julia Alvarez, author of *How the García Girls Lost Their Accents*, other than an amorphous and evasive ethnic background?

Are César Chávez and twentieth-century Mexican anarchist Ricardo Flores Magón ideological cousins? Is Edward Rivera, author of the memoir *Family Installments* and an English writer and professor at City College of New York, in any way related to Eugenio María de Hostos, René Marqués, and José Luis González, Puerto Rico's literary cornerstones in the twentieth century? Is the Mexican-American writer Rudolfo A. Anaya, responsible for *Bless Me, Ultima*, a successor of Juan Rulfo *and* William Faulkner? Ought Richard Rodríguez be seen as a result of a mixed marriage between Alfonso Reyes and John Stuart Mill? Is Arthur Alfonso Schomburg—the so-called Sherlock Holmes of Negro History, whose collection of books on African-American heritage forms the core of the New York Public Library's present-day Schomburg Center for Research on Black Culture—our ancestor, in spite of his disenchantment with his Puerto Ricanness? How do Latinos perceive the odd link between the clock and the crucifix? Is there such a thing as Latin time? Is there a branch of Salvadoran literature in English? What makes gay

Latinos unique? What is the role played by Spanish-language television and printed media in the shaping of a new Latino identity?

In the fashion of the lifelong attempts by Zora Neale Hurston, Arthur A. Schomburg, and the black artists and scholars during the Harlem Renaissance of the 1930s, who fought to disprove once and for all the common misconception that "Negros have no history," our generation ought to demonstrate that we Latinos have an abundance of histories, linked to a common root but with decisively different traditions. At each and every moment, these ancestral histories determine who we are and what we think. As I am sure it can already be perceived, my personal interest is not in the purely political, demographic, and sociological dimensions, but, rather, in the Hispanic American and Latino intellectual and artistic legacies. What attracts me more than actual events are works of fiction and visual art, historiography as a cradle where cultural artifacts are nurtured. Idiosyncratic differences puzzle me: What distinguishes us from Anglo-Saxons and other European immigrants as well as from other minorities (such as blacks and Asians) in the United States? Is there such a thing as a Latino identity? Ought José Martí and Eugenio María de Hostos be considered the forefathers of Latino politics and culture? Need one return to the Alamo to come to terms with the clash between two essentially different psyches, Anglo-Saxon Protestant and Hispanic Catholic? The voyage to what William H. Gass called "the heart of the heart of the country" needs to begin by addressing a crucial issue: the diversity factor. Latinos, no question, are a most difficult community to describe: Is the Cuban from Holguín similar in attitude and culture to someone from Managua, San Salvador, or Santo Domingo? Is the Spanish we all speak, our *lingua franca*, the only unifying factor? How do the various Hispanic subgroups understand the complexities of what it means to be part of the same minority group? Or do we perceive ourselves as a unified whole?

Culture and identity are a parade of anachronistic symbols, larger-than-life abstractions, less a shared set of beliefs and values than the collective strategies by which we organize and make sense of our experience, a complex yet tightly integrated construction in a state of perpetual flux. To begin, it is utterly impossible to examine Latinos without regard to the geography we come from. We are, we recognize ourselves to be, an extremity of Latin America, a diaspora alive and well north of the Rio Grande. For the Yiddish writer Sholem Aleichem's Tevye the milkman, for instance, America was a synonym of redemption, the end of *pogroms*, the solution to earthly matters. Russia, Poland, and the rest of Eastern Europe were lands of suffering. Immigrating to America, where gold grew on trees and could easily be found on sidewalks, was synonymous with entering Paradise. To leave, never to look back and return, was an imperative. Many miles, almost impossible to breach again, divided the old land from the new. We, on the other hand, are just around the corner: Oaxaca, Mexico; Varadero, Cuba; and Santurce, Puerto Rico, are literally next door. We can spend every other month, even every other week, either north or south. Indeed, some among us swear to return home when military dictatorships are finally deposed and more benign regimes come to life, or simply when enough money is saved in a bank account. Meanwhile, we inhabit a home divided, multiplied, neither in the barrio or the besieged ghetto nor across the river or the Gulf of Mexico, a home either here or within hours' distance. José Antonio Villarreal's 1959 novel *Pocho*, for example, called by some critics "a foundational text" and believed to be the first English-written novel by a Chicano, is precisely about the eternal need to return among Chicanos: a return to source, a return to the self. And Pablo Medina's meticulous Cuban-American autobiography *Exiled Memories*, along the same lines, is about the impossibility of returning to childhood, to the mother's soil, to happiness. But return is indeed possible in most cases. Cheap labor comes and goes back and forth to Puebla and San Juan.

One ought never to forget that Hispanics and their siblings north of the border have an intimate, long-standing, love-hate relationship. Latinos are a major source of income for the families they left behind. In Mexico, for instance, money wired by relatives working as pizza delivery boys, domestic servants, and construction workers amounts to a third of the nation's overall revenues. Is this nothing new, when one ponders previous waves of immigration? Perhaps. Others have dreamed of America as paradise on earth, but our arrival in the Promised Land with strings attached underscores troublesome patterns of assimilation. Whereas Germans, Irish, Chinese, and others may have evidenced a certain ambiguity and lack of commitment during their first stage of assimilation in the United States, the proximity of our original soil, both in the geographic and metaphorical sense, is tempting. This thought brings to mind a claim by the Iberian philosopher José Ortega y Gasset, author of *Rebellion of the Masses*, among many other titles, in a 1939 lecture delivered in Buenos Aires. Ortega y Gasset stated that Spaniards assumed the role of the New Man the moment they settled in the New World. Their attitude was the result not of a centuries-long process, but of an immediate and sudden transformation. To this idea the Colombian writer Antonio Sanín Cano once mistakenly added that Hispanics, vis-à-vis other settlers, have a brilliant capacity to assimilate; unlike the British, for instance, who can live for years in a foreign land and never become part of it, we do. What he forgot to add is that we achieve total adaptation at a huge cost to ourselves and others. We become the New Man and Woman carrying along our former environment. Add the fact that we are often approached as traitors in the place once called home: We left, we betrayed our patriotism, we rejected and were rejected by the milieu, we aborted ourselves and spat on the uterus. Cubans in exile are known as *gusanos*, worms, in Havana's eyes. Mainland Puerto Ricans often complain of the lack of support from their original families in the Caribbean and find their cultural ties tenuous and thin. Mexicans have mixed feelings toward *Pachucos, Pochos,* and other types of Chicanos; when possible, Mexico ignores our politics and cultural manifestations, only taking them into account when diplomatic relations with the White House are at stake.

Once in the United States, we are seen in unequal terms. Although England, France, and Spain were the chief nations to establish colonies this side of the Atlantic, the legacy of Iberian conquerors and explorers remains unattended, quasi-forgotten, almost deleted from the nation's memory. The first permanent European settlement in the New World was St. Augustine, Florida, founded by the Spanish in 1565, over forty years before the British established Jamestown in Virginia. Or simply consider things from an onomastic point of view: Los Angeles, Sausalito, San Luis Obispo, and San Diego are all Hispanic names. People know that during the U.S. Civil War, blacks, freed in 1863 from slavery as part of the Emancipation Proclamation (which covered only states in the Confederacy), fought on both sides; what is unknown or perhaps even silenced, what is left unrecognized, is that Hispanics were also active soldiers on the battlefield. When the war began in 1861, more than ten thousand Mexican-Americans served in both the Union and the Confederate armed forces. Indeed, when it comes to Latino history, the official chronology of the United States, from its birth until after World War II, is a sequence of omissions. Between 1910 and 1912, for instance, U.S. railroad companies recruited thousands of Hispanic workers, and nearly two thousand braceros crossed the border every month to work for the railways. Also, Hispanic workers' unions are not a recent invention, and César Chávez was no sudden hero. Many Puerto Rican and Chicano rebellions occurred in the early stages of World War I, and organizers like Bernardo Vega and Jesús Colón were instrumental in shaping a new consciousness before the mythic La Causa movement took shape. For instance, after miners went on strike in Ludlow, Colorado, around the time that the Archduke Francis Ferdinand, heir apparent to the Austro-Hungarian throne, was assassinated in Sarajevo, more than fifty people, many who were Mexican-Americans, were killed by the National Guard. Puerto Rican and Chicano soldiers fought in World War II, and many more participated in the Korean War. Furthermore, Martí, Dr. Ramón Emetrio Betances, Hostos, and other revolutionaries were active in New York and elsewhere in the United States in the late nineteenth century, especially in wake of the Spanish-American War. But very few are acquainted with these facts.

Flowing some 1,880 miles from southwestern Colorado to the Gulf of Mexico, the Rio Grande, the Río Turbio, is the dividing line, the end and the beginning, of the United States and Latin America. The river not only separates the twin cities of El Paso and Ciudad Juárez and of Brownsville and Matamores, but also, and more essentially, is an abyss, a wound, a borderline, a symbolic dividing line between what Alan Riding once forcefully described as "distant neighbors." The flow of water has had different names during several periods and along several different reaches of its course. An incomplete list, offered by Paul Horgan in his monumental Pulitzer Prize–winning book, *Great River: The Rio Grande in North American History*, follows: Gran River, P'osoge, Río Bravo, Río Bravo del Norte, Río Caudaloso, Río de la Concepción, Río de las Palmas, Río de Nuestra Señora, Río de Buenaventura del Norte, Río del Norte, Río del Norte y de Nuevo México, Río Grande, Río Grande del Norte, Río Guadalquivir, River of May, Tiguex River, and (by extension) the Tortilla Curtain. What's in a name? South facing north thinks of it as a stream carrying poisonous water; north facing south prefers to see it as an obstacle to illegal *espaldas mojadas*, a service door to one's backyard. The name game pertains to our deceitful, equivocal, and evasive collective appellation: What are we: Hispanics, *hispanos*, Latinos (and Latinas), Latins, *iberoamericanos*, Spanish, Spanish-speaking people, Hispanic Americans (vis-à-vis the Latin Americans from across the Rio Grande), mestizos (and *mestizas*); or simply, Mexican-Americans, Cuban-Americans, Dominican-Americans, Puerto Ricans on the Mainland, and so forth? And should I add *Spiks* to the list? (Pedro Juan Soto, who taught at the Universidad de Puerto Rico, once tried to trace the word's origins and mutant spelling to *Spigs*, used until 1915 to describe Italians, lovers of *spig-goty*, not *spaghetti*, and from *I no spik inglis*; the term then evolved to *Spics, Spicks,* and currently *Spiks*.)

Encyclopedias, at least until recently, described us as *Hispanic Americans* vis-à-vis the *Latin Americans* from south of the border. The confusion evidently recalls the fashion in which Black, Nigger, Negro, Afro-American, and African-American have been used from before Abraham Lincoln's abolition of slavery to the present. Nowadays the general feeling is that one unifying term addressing everybody is better and less confusing; but would anybody refer to Italian, German, French, and Spanish writers as a single category of European writers? The United States, a mosaic of races and cultures, always needs to speak of its social quilt in generally stereotypical ways. Aren't Asians, blacks, and Jews also seen as homogeneous groups, regardless of the origin of their various members? Nevertheless, in the printed media, on television, out in the streets, and in the privacy of their homes, people hesitate between a couple of favorites: *Hispanic* and *Latino.*

Although these terms might seem interchangeable, an attentive ear senses a difference. Preferred by conservatives, the former is used when the talk is demographics, education, urban development, drugs, and health; the latter, on the other hand, is the choice of liberals and is frequently used to refer to artists, musicians, and movie stars. Ana Castillo is Latina and José Feliciano is Latino, as is Andres Serrano, the controversial photographer, author of *Piss Christ*, who, alongside Robert Mapplethorpe, prompted conservative Senator Jesse Helms and others, in the late 1980s, to consolidate the so-called culture war against obscenity in modern art. Former New York City Schools Chancellor Joseph Fernandez is Hispanic, as are Congressman José Serrano and Bronx Borough President Fernando Ferrer. A sharper difference: Hispanic is used by the federal government to describe the heterogeneous ethnic minority with ancestors across the Rio Grande and in the Caribbean archipelago, but since these citizens are *latinoamericanos*, Latino is acknowledged by liberals in the community as correct. The issue, less transitory than it seems, invites us to travel far and away to wonder what's behind the name Latin America, where the misunderstanding apparently began. During the 1940s and even earlier, *Spanish* was a favorite term used by English speakers to name those from the Iberian peninsula and across the border: Ricardo Montalban was Spanish, as were Pedro Flores, Pedro Carrasquillo, and Poncho Sánchez, although one was Mexican and the others were Cuban and Puerto Rican. In Anglo-Saxon eyes, all were Latin lovers, mambo kings, and spitfires homogenized by a mother tongue. It goes without saying that from the sixteenth to the early nineteenth century, the part of the New World (a term coined by Peter Martyr, an early biographer of Columbus)* known today as Latin America was called Spanish America (and, to some, Iberian America); linguistically, the geography excluded Brazil and the three Guyanas. The term *Hispanic American* (*Hispanic* meaning "citizen of Hispania," the way Romans addressed Spaniards) captured the spotlight in the 1960s, when waves of legal and undocumented immigrants began pouring in from Mexico, Central America, Puerto Rico, and other Third World countries. (The term *Third World* is the abominable creation of Frantz Fanon and was largely promoted by Luis Echeverría Alvarez, a simple-minded Mexican president. Carlos Fuentes, in his volume on Spain and the Americas, *The Buried Mirror*, prefers the term *developing*, rather than *Third World* or *underdeveloped*.) When nationalism emerged as a cohesive force in Latin America, *Spanish-American* lost its value because of its reference to Spain, now considered a foreign, imperialist invader. The Spanish conquistadors were loudly denounced as criminals, a trend inaugurated by Fray Bartolomé de Las Casas centuries before, but until then not legitimized by the powers that be.

As Spanish speakers became a political and economic force, the term *Hispanic* was appropriated by the government and the media. It describes people on the basis of their cultural and verbal heritage. Placed alongside categories like Caucasian, Asian, and black, it proves inaccurate simply because a person (me, for instance) is Hispanic *and* Caucasian, Hispanic *and* black; it ignores a reference to race. After years in circulation, it has already become a weapon, a stereotyping machine. Its synonyms are drug addict, criminal, prison inmate, and out-of-wedlock family. *Latino* has thus become the option, a sign of rebellion, the choice of intellectuals and artists, because it emerges from within this ethnic group and because its etymology simultaneously denounces Anglo and Iberian oppression. But what is truly Latin (Roman, Hellenistic) in it? Nothing, or very little. Columbus and his crew called Cuba, Juana, and Puerto Rico Hispaniola (the latter's capital was San Juan Bautista de Puerto Rico). One of the first West Indies islands they encountered, now divided into the Dominican Republic and Haiti, was known as Española. (later, Saint Domingue and Hispaniola). During colonial times, the region was called Spanish America because of its linguistic preponderance, and then, by the mid-nineteenth century—with Paris the world's cultural center and romanticism at its height—a group of educated Chileans suggested the name *l'Amérique latine*,

---

* See my book *Imagining Columbus: The Literary Voyage* (New York: Twayne-Macmillan, 1993), where I discuss the birth of the Americas in Europe's collective imagination.

which, sadly to say, was favored over Spanish America. The sense of homogeneity that came from a global embrace of Roman constitutional law and the identity shared through the Romance languages (mainly Spanish, but also Portuguese and French) were crucial to the decision. Simón Bolívar, the region's ultimate hero, who was born in Venezuela and fought an ambitious revolution for independence from Iberian dominion in Boyacá in 1819, saw the tem as contributing to the unification of the entire southern hemisphere. Much later, in the late 1930s and early 1940s, Franklin Delano Roosevelt's Good Neighbor Policy also embraced and promoted it. Yet historians and esthetes like Pedro Henríquez Ureña and Luis Alberto Sánchez railed against the designation: perhaps being Hispanic America *and* Portuguese America, but please, never Latin America. Much like the name America is a historical misconception that is used to describe the entire continent—one that originated from the explorer Amerigo Vespucci (after all, Erik the Red, a Viking voyager who set foot on this side of the Atlantic around the year 1000, and even poor, disoriented Cristóbal Colón, arrived first)—Latino makes little sense even if Romance languages in Latin America are true equalizers that resulted from the so-called 1492 discovery. This idea brings to mind a statement made by Aaron Copland after a 1941 tour of nine South American countries. "Latin America as a whole does not exist," he said. "It is a collection of separate countries, each with different traditions. Only as I traveled from country to country did I realize that you must be willing to split the continent up in your mind."

In mammoth urban centers (Los Angeles, Miami, New York), the Spanish-language media—newspapers and television stations—address their constituency as *los hispanos,* but hardly ever as *los latinos.* The deformed adjective *hispano* is used instead of *hispánico,* which is the correct Spanish word; the reason: *hispánico* is too pedantic, too academic, too Iberian. When salsa, meringue, and other rhythms are referred to, *latino* is used. Again, the distinction, artificial and difficult to sustain, is unclear; the Manhattan daily *El Diario,* for example, calls itself the champion of Hispanics, whereas *Impacto,* a national publication that is proud of its sensationalism, has as its subtitle "The Latin News" (notice: *Latin,* not *Latino).* Inevitably, the whole discussion reminds me of the Gershwin song performed on roller skates by Fred Astaire and Ginger Rogers in *Shall We Dance:* I say to-may-to and you say to-mah-to.

From Labrador to the Pampas, from Cape Horn to the Iberian peninsula, from Garcilaso de la Vega and Count Lucanor to Sor Juana Inés de la Cruz and Andrés Bello, the scope of Hispanic civilization—

which began in the caves of Altamira, Buxo, and Tito Bustillo some 25,000 or 30,000 years ago ("the ribs of Spain," as Miguel de Unamuno would call them)—is indeed outstanding. Although I honestly prefer Hispanic as a composite term and would rather not use Latino, is there value in opposing a consensus? Or, as Franz Kafka would ask, Is there any hope in a kingdom where cats chase after a mouse? I herewith suggest using *Latinos* to refer to those citizens from the Spanish-speaking world living *in* the United States and *Hispanics* to refer to those living elsewhere. Which means that, by any account, a Latino is also a Hispanic, but not necessarily vice versa.

As for the pertinent art of Martín Ramírez, the mute Chicano artist whose drawings were shown at the Corcoran Gallery in the late 1980s, an Oliver Sacks–like "disoriented mariner" in an ever-changing galaxy, his quiet vicissitude in Gringolandia's labyrinthine mirrors will become my leitmotif. I am attracted to the striking coherence and color of his three hundred–some paintings. Although produced by a schizophrenic, these images manage to construct a well-rounded, fantastic universe, with figures like trains, beasts, automobiles, women, leopards, deer, *bandidos,* and the Vírgen de Guadalupe; they are characterized by heroism and a mystical approach to life. He is a true original, a visionary we cannot afford to ignore. Indeed, in terms of authenticity, Ramírez, it seems to me, reverses the syndrome of so-called unreal realism, of which the best, most enlightening examples are Chester Seltzer, who took the Hispanic name Amado Muro and pretended to write realist accounts of growing up Latino, and the now infamous Danny Santiago.

When Santiago's admirable first novel, *Famous All Over Town* (prophetically called, while in manuscript form and until its uncorrected galley-proof stage, *My Name Will Follow You Home*) appeared in 1983, reviews praised it as wonderful and hilarious. Chato Medina, its courageous hero, was a denizen of an unlivable barrio in East Los Angeles, the product of a disintegrating family who had a bunch of disoriented friends. The novel received the Richard and Hilda Rosenthal Award of the American Academy and Institute of Arts and Letters and was described as a stunning debut about adolescent initiation among Latinos. The author's biography on the back cover, which appeared without a photograph, stated that he had been raised in California and that many of his stories had appeared in national magazines. The arrival of a talented writer was universally acclaimed. Nevertheless, success soon turned sour. A journalist and ex-friend of Santiago, motivated by personal revenge, announced Santiago's true identity in a piece published in August 1984 in the *New York Review of Books.*

It turned out that Daniel Lewis James, the author's real name, was not a young Chicano, but a septuagenarian Anglo, who was born in 1911 into a well-to-do family in Kansas City, Missouri. A friend of John Steinbeck, James was educated at Andover and graduated from Yale in 1933. He moved to Hollywood and joined the Communist Party, together with his wife Lilith, a ballerina. He worked with Charlie Chaplin, collaborating on *The Great Dictator,* and wrote, together with Sid Herzig and Fred Saridy, a Broadway musical, *Bloomer Girl,* which opened in 1944. During the 1950s, he devoted himself to writing horror movies. He was blacklisted during the McCarthy era, when the House Committee on Un-American Activities was investigating left-wing infiltration of the movie industry. The Lewises began a solid friendship with the East Los Angeles Chicano community, attending fiestas and inviting scores of Chicanos to their Carmel Highlands cliffside mansion. As a result of that relationship, James began to feel close to the Latino psyche, digesting its linguistic and idiosyncratic ways.

Subsequently, Father Alberto Huerta, a scholar who teaches at the University of San Francisco and has devoted a large part of his intellectual endeavors to analyzing the life and times of the outlaw Joaquín Murrieta, defended the beleaguered writer in the journal *The Californians,* accusing trendy Latino writers and New York intellectuals of "brown-listing" a genius. Father Huerta had kept a four-year-long correspondence with Santiago. It originated after the future author of *Famous All Over Town* reacted to one of Huerta's essays on Murrieta. They met at Santiago's Carmel Highlands home in 1984 and became friends. Father Huerta remains Santiago's most ardent defender. He is adamant about the unfair treatment the writer has been subjected to, and when I wrote critically of the controversial novel in 1993, he sent me a cordial but strong letter inviting me to change my opinions.

After the scandal erupted, an open symposium, sponsored by the Berkeley-based Before Columbus Foundation, entitled "Danny Santiago: Art or Fraud," took place in Modern Times Bookstore in San Francisco. The participants were Gary Soto, Rudolfo A. Anaya, and Ishmael Reed. James, of course, is a paradigm. Like the scandalous identity of Forest Carter, the white supremacist responsible for the best-seller *The Education of Little Tree,* and like other authors of buried background, it was an interesting career move to go from being a writer of low-budget movies to the darling of Latino letters. In spite of the aesthetic power of *Famous All Over Town,* Lewis personifies the feverish need in a nation consumed by the wars for identities to transgress. Authenticity and histrionics: In essence,

Ramírez's silence and Danny Santiago's theatrical voice are opposites. They are the bookends of Latino culture.

Which brings me back to the culture itself. In a symbolic poem by Judith Ortíz Cofer titled "The Latin Deli" and published in book form in 1993, Hispanics north of the border are seen as an amorphous hybrid. Sharing heterogeneous backgrounds, they are summed up by an archetypal mature lady. The poet reduces the universe to a kind of curative store, a *bodega* in which customers look for a medicine to their disheartened spirit. This Patroness of Exiles, "a woman of no-age who was never pretty, who spends her days selling canned memories," listens to Puerto Ricans complain about airfares to San Juan, to Cubans "perfecting their speech of a 'glorious return' to Havana—where no one has been allowed to die and nothing to change until then," and to Mexicans "who pass through, talking lyrically of *dólares* be made in El Norte—all waiting the comfort of spoken Spanish." Ortíz Cofer's image, incredibly inviting, is perfect to conclude this chapter. Latinos, while racially diverse and historically heterogeneous, an *ajiaco* (Cuban stew) made of diverse ingredients, by chance or destiny have all been summed up in the same grocery store called America. America, where exile becomes home, where memory is reshaped, reinvented. In the eyes of strangers, our hopes and nightmares, our energy and desperation, our libido, add up to a magnified whole. But who are we really? What do we want? Why are we here? And for how long will the *bodega* be owned by somebody else?

# THE SOUNDS OF SPANGLISH

The Census Bureau has declared that by 2020 Latinos will be the largest minority group in the United States, surpassing blacks and Asians and numbering more than 70 million. One of every four Americans will be of Hispanic descent. This population explosion is likely to transform every aspect of culture and society in the United States, not the least of which is language. In fact, the verbal metamorphosis is rapidly taking place already: Spanish, spoken on this continent since Iberian explorers colonized territories in present-day Florida, New Mexico, Texas, and California, has become ubiquitous in the last few decades. The nation's unofficial second language, it is much in evidence on two twenty-four-hour TV networks and more than 275 radio stations. Bilingual education has expanded knowledge of Spanish in schools nationwide. It is used in 70 percent of Latino households, and on campuses across the country it is the most studied and sought-after "foreign tongue." According to the *Miami Herald*, "Young American professionals in every field seem eager to learn it as fast as possible so as not to feel left behind."

But Spanish is not spreading in pure form north of the Rio Grande. A sign of the "Latin fever" that has swept over the United States since the mid-1980s is the astonishingly creative amalgam spoken by people of Hispanic descent not only in major cities but in rural areas as well: neither Spanish nor English but a hybrid known as Spanglish. The term is controversial, and so is its impact: Has Spanish irrevocably lost its purity as a result of it? Is English becom-

First published in *Hopscotch: A Cultural Review* 1:1 (1999).

ing less "Anglicized" on the tongues of Latinos? Is Spanglish a legitimate language? Should it be endorsed by the intellectual and political establishment? Is it a slang in the process of becoming a dialect? It is likely one day to become a full-fledged language, complete with its literary masterpieces? Who uses it, and why? What are its prospects? The term *Spanglish* has gotten hot as the debate about the use of Ebonics (black English) has burned in schools across the United States and as the English-only movement has picked up steam.

As one might expect, these questions have contributed to an atmosphere of anxiety and fear in both Hispanic and non-Hispanic enclaves. Are we witnessing the Latinization of America? Is the nation at risk of adopting a new tongue? Is it losing its collective identity? On the other side, purists within the fractured Hispanic intelligentsia refuse to endorse Spanglish as a vehicle of communication. They claim that it lacks dignity and an essence of its own. This stand is *una equivocación,* though. It regards speech as stagnant, when in truth it undergoes eternal renovation. For the 28 million Hispanics north of the border, Spanish is the connection to a collective past and English the ticket to success. But Spanglish is *la fuerza del destino,* a signature of uniqueness. It is not taught in the schools, but children and adolescents from coast to coast learn it on a daily basis at the best university available: life itself.

One need only think of Yiddish, used by Eastern European Jews from the thirteenth century on, to realize the potential of Spanglish. Yiddish was born of the disparities between high- and lowbrow segments of Jewish society in and outside the ghetto. It originated in an attempt to separate the sacred from the secular, the intellectual from the worldly. Its linguistic sources were plentiful—Hebrew, German, and Russian, Polish, and other Slavic languages—and the mix was later reinvigorated by other linguistic additives, including Spanish in Buenos Aires, Havana, and Mexico City and Portuguese in São Paulo. At first rabbis and scholars rejected Yiddish as illegitimate. Long centuries passed before it was championed by masters like Sholen Jacob Abramovitsh, Isaac Leib Peretz, S. Ansky, and even Marc Chagall, whose pictorial images are but translations of his shtetl background.[*]

Obviously, the differences between Yiddish and Spanglish are many, and we are not suggesting that they have the same metabolism. Yet their similarities are striking. Latinos are already a prominent

---

[*] Not only Yiddish, but *Yinglish,* as Daniel Bell has suggested, ought to serve as a point of comparison in the analysis of Spanglish. See *Correspondence* 6 (2000): 7–8.

part of the American social quilt. For ivory-tower intellectuals to condemn their tongue as illegitimate seems preposterous to me. It signals the awkwardness of scholars and academics. Who are we, living in campus comfort, to require millions in East Los Angeles and Spanish Harlem to study proper Spanish? Who are we to dictate what is acceptable and what is not? As Maimonides once argued, what is lofty can be said in any language, but what is mean needs a new language.

Protecting Castillian Spanish from the barbarians in the ghettoes of East Los Angeles and Spanish Harlem is futile, for Spanglish is here to stay, and it is time for the nation's intelligentsia to acknowledge it. Language, after all, changes constantly. Borges wrote in an Anglicized Spanish, and Julio Cortázar made his fiction come alive by writing in Spanish with a French twist. Both were condemned at various times in their careers for "polluting" the language. But who would dare to invoke Cervantes's tradition now without them? Writers are, among many other things, harbingers of change. They turn it into a testimony of their era. And rapid change is what we are witnessing in the United States today—social, political, religious, but primarily verbal change. Immigrant lives are brewing in new grammatical and syntactic pots, incredible blends of inventiveness and *amor a la vida*. In them binationalism, biculturalism, and bilingualism go hand in hand. Extraordinary artists and writers are translating this change into works made of words that are neither Cervantes's nor Shakespeare's but are equally legitimate. Ana Lydia Vega from Puerto Rico, for instance, has a memorable short story, "Pollito Chicken," written in Spanglish. Giannina Braschi and Tato Laviera, among many others, have authored poems in it, and Juan Felipe Herrara uses it magically in the novel *Crashboomlove.*

What is at stake here is not the future of Spanglish, already solid and commanding, but broad acceptance of it. English is and no doubt should be the nation's sole official language. But that does not mean that other tongues should not live side by side, as they have done since the arrival of the *Mayflower.* Nothing has ever been pure in this land, especially not the idea of home. Unlike other immigrant groups, Latinos find that their ethnic language has remained alive and well here, 150 years after the Treaty of Guadalupe Hidalgo, which brought an end to the war commonly known as the "trauma of encounter." Other immigrant tongues—German, Italian, even Yiddish—have vanished as popular channels of communication, but not Spanish. In fact, its stamina at this *fin de siglo* is more apparent than ever: on the radio and TV, in music, in the printed word, and especially *en la calle,* on the street. It isn't the Spanish used in the country of origin, nor is it English. Will politicians and academic institutions begin to recognize its huge power? Or will they remain, as they have done for decades, a step behind society? Latinos will unquestionably leave a mark on America in their own tongue. By doing so, they not only will invite the rest of the society to join their verbal celebration but, even more attractively, will change the way it uses its own language.

So the emergence of Spanglish is neither sudden nor new. In one way or another it has been around for decades, even centuries— at least since 1848, and in a more intense form as a result of the Spanish-American War of fifty years later—although since the mid-1980s it has gained not only national attention but a sense of urgency, making its presence felt in rap and rock music, art, and literature. But even though poets and singers are beginning to pen it down, and sections like the classified ads in newspapers and music and sports magazines can't avoid it, it remains, for the most part, an oral code of communication, free in spirit and defying standardization. What follows is a brief lexicon, selected from a pool of over six thousand words. It lists words alphabetically and specifies where they are used, but it offers neither a context for usage nor a brief history of crucial terms, such as *pocho, Nuyorican,* and *YUCA.* It is a work in progress, meant to culminate in a comprehensive dictionary of Spanglish that should be at once historical and morphosyntactical.

A serious lexicon of this hybrid form of communication should, I trust, move in various directions at once: it ought to distinguish between code switching and established words; to reflect the varieties of Spanglish active in the United States by inventorying various pronunciations and their origins; to list common expressions that highlight the crossbreed grammatical nature of Spanglish *(Llamar pa'tras, ¡Qué tenga un buen día!);* to list the Anglicisms and U.S. pop culture terms that have recently entered the Spanish language *(antibaby, kleenex)* and the Hispanicisms that have penetrated English *(piñata, burrito);* and, finally, to incorporate the ubiquitous cyber-Spanglish, the computer and technological language used especially on the Internet.

Needless to say, I am not the first to attempt such a classification. Roberto A. Galván and Richard V. Tescher compiled their *Diccionario del español chicano* in 1989; José Sánchez-Boudy has published his *Diccionario de cubanismos más usuales* since 1982; and Rubén Cobos, a professor at the University of New Mexico, edited *A Dictionary of New Mexico and Southern Colorado Spanish* in 1983.

These are but a few of the valuable, though partial, efforts so far. Their central focus has been the impact of English on Spanish in particular geographic regions and among individualized national groups. Only Bill Cruz, a contributor to the Miami-based magazine *Generation ñ,* has granted autonomy to Spanglish as a verbal code, in his pocket-size guide *Cuban Americanisms* (1996), scheduled to be republished, in an enlarged version, by Fireside as *The Official Spanglish Dictionary.* Unfortunately, Cruz's thesaurus, while rich in appendages, is mostly limited to the lingo of Miami. It is neither official nor, truly, a dictionary, as it lists fewer words than a Spanglish-speaking child uses in an hour—my own two beloved boys included.

## Origins

C = Cubanism
Ch = Chicanism
CS = Cyber-Spanglish
ELA = East Los Angeles
G = general
I = Iberianism
M = Mexicanism
NE = Northeast
NR = Nuyoricanism
PR = Puerto Ricanism
SW = Southwest

### A

**accesar**, v., to access. [CS]
**ace**, n., m., tennis term. [G]
**acid**, n., m., 1. amphetamine. 2. music rhythm. [G]
**aerobics**, n., m., aerobics. [G]
**afterauers,** n., m., after-hours. [I]
**aftersheif**, n., m., aftershave. [G]
**aftersun**, n., m., after-tanning moisturizing lotion. [G]
**aguaplanin**, n., m., outdoor sport in which the athlete slides on water at high speed. [I]
**águate**, interj., beware. [SW]
**airobús**, n., m., airbus. Also known in Puerto Rico as **guagua aérea**. [NR, PR]
**amigoization**, n., f., Mexicanization of the Southwest. [Ch, SW]
**ancorman**, n., m., TV news personality. [I]
**anion**, n., f., onion. [NR]
**antibaby**, n., m., birth control pill. [I]
**anticiclón,** , n., m., high-pressure zone. [NE, PR]

**arme**, n., m., army. [Ch]
**atejanar**, v., to be Texanized. [SW]
**auditear**, v., to audit. [C, M, SW]

# B

**babay**, exp., bye-bye. [G]
**bacup** n., m., reserve computer information. [CS]
**barrio**, n., m., neighborhood. See also **hood**; also **hud**. [Ch, SW]
**bastardiar**, v., 1. to have extramarital sex. 2. to produce bastards. [G]
**batería**, n., f., legal term, from Eng. *battery*. [C]
**baunsiar**, v., to bounce a check. [G]
**beat**, n., m., music rhythm. [G]
**bed-and-brec**, n., m., bed-and-breakfast. [NE]
**beis**, n., m., baseball. [G]
**beseler**, n., m., best-selling item. [G]
**betnic**, n., m., beatnik. [NE]
**biciclo**, n, f., bicycle. [G]
**bife**, n., m., beefsteak. Also **bifstaik**.
**bifstaik**. See **bife**. [G]
**bigban**, n., f., 1. big bang. [G] 2. big band. [NE]
**bildin**, n., m., building. [NR, PR]
**bipiar**, v., to page someone, to use a beeper. [G]
**bipop**, n., f., hip-hop. [NE]
**blakou**, n., m., 1. blackout 2. blockage. [NE, PR]
**blister**, n., m., blister pack. [PR]
**blodimari**, n., m., bloody Mary. [NR]
**blof,** n., m. and f., bluff. [C]
**bluchi**, n., m., blue chip. [CS]
**blumers**, n., f., panties. [M, SW]
**blus**, n., m., blues (music rhythm). [G]
**bluyin**, n., m., blue jeans. [G]
**body**, n., m., body of a dress. [NR, SW]
**bodybildin**, n., m., body building. [G]
**bodybor**, n., m., surfboard. [I, SW]
**boila**, n., f., heating appliance. [NR, PR, SW]
**boiscau**, n., m., Boy Scout. [G]
**bom**, n., m., homeless person. [C]
**bomper**, n., m., car bumper. [NR]
**bopepo**, n., m., boat person. [C]
**borderígena**, n., m. and f., border citizen. [SW]
**borderlain**, n., m. and f., person on the verge of a mental breakdown. [G]
**Borinquén**, n., m., Puerto Rican person. See also **Borinqueño, Portoriqueño, Puerto Rican**. [G]

**Borinqueño,** , n., m.; Borinqueican person. See **Borinquén.** [NR, PR]

**botonbra,** n., m., push-up brassiere. [I]

**botoniarlo,** n., m., the process of fastening buttons. [G]

**boulin,** n., m., bowling. [G]

**brainstormear,** v., to think intently. [CS]

**brainstormin,** n., m. See **brainstormear.** [I]

**break,** n., m., vacation. See also **breka.** [C, NR]

**breikdaun,** n., m., mental collapse. [G]

**breka,** n., m., break. automobile brake. [Ch, SW]

**breque,** n., m. See also **breka.** [NR, PR]

**brifin,** n., m., updating, briefing. [NR, SW]

**brode,** n., m., pal, friend. Also **broder, carnal, guey.** [G]

**broder,** n., m. See **brode.** [G]

**broquer,** n., m., intermediary. [C, NR]

**Bufalo,** n., m. See **Chicano.** [Ch, SW]

**bum,** n., m., explosion. [NR]

**C**

**cachar,** n., m., to catch. [G]

**cacher,** n., m., catcher (baseball). [G]

**cachup,** n., m., ketchup. Different spellings throughout the Americas. [G]

**Califa,** n., m. and f., resident of California. Also **Califeño**; see also **Californio.** [SW]

**Califas,** n., California. See also **Califa.** [SW]

**Califeño,** n., m. and f. See **Califa.** [SW]

**Californio,** n., m. and f., native of California. See also **Califa.** [SW]

**camcorder,** n., m., video recorder. [G]

**carnal,** n., m., brother, friend. See also **brode, broder, güey.** [Ch]

**chale,** interj., 1. expression of disagreement. 2. synonym of *damn.* [Ch]

**Chicano,** n., m. and f., 1. Mexican-American without an Anglicized self-image. 2. politicized Mexican-American. [G]

**chip,** n., m., computer chip. [CS]

**chiriar,** v., to use slick means to obtain something. From Eng. *cheating.* [Ch]

**chirlider,** n., f., cheerleader. [G]

**chiz,** n., m., gossip. From Sp. *chisme.* [C]

**cho,** n., m., show. [C, NR]

**chokear,** v. See **choquear.** [G]

**chomba,** n., f., jumper. Also **chompa.** [NR]

**chompa,** n., f. See **chomba.** [NR]

**choque**, n., m., nervous depression, state of shock. [G]
**choqueado**, adj., surprised, dumbfounded. See also **choque,
    choquear.** [G]
**choquear,** v., to shock. [G]
**chor**, n., m., endeavor. [G]
**chut**, n., m., strong kick (soccer). [G]
**chutar,** v., to shoot (soccer). [G]
**ciber**, adj., m., cybernetic. [CS]
**cibernauta**, n., m. and f., Web navigator. [CS]
**confuso**, adj., in a confused state of mind. [G]
**culísimo**, interj., very cool. [G]


**D**
**dancin**, n., m., dancing space. [NE]
**databais**, n., m., database. [CS]
**databanc**, n., m., data bank. [CS]
**dataglove**, n., m., video game using a glove for sensorial
    activity. [CS]
**dauntau**, n., m., downtown. [C]
**dedlain**, n., m., deadline. [G]
**diler**, n., m. and f., distributor. [G]
**dirísimo**, super. of *dear.* [NE]
**discopob**, n., m., discotheque. [I]
**disquete**, n., m., diskette. [CS]
**dixi**, adj., m., jazz style. [G]
**dogibag**, n., f., doggy bag. [G]
**dolby**, n., m., electronic device for reducing background noise
    from recorded or broadcast sound. From trademark. [G]
**dona**, n., f., doughnut. [G]
**dopar**, v., to dope up. [NE]
**dopear**, v., to drop. [G]
**draftear**, v., to be drafted. [G]
**driblar**, v., to dribble (soccer). See also **dribler.** [G]
**dribler**, n., m., one who dribbles (soccer). See also **driblar.** [G]
**driblin**, n., m., the act of dribbling (soccer). See also **driblar,
    dribler.** [G]
**dril**, v., to drill. [G]
**drinquear**, v., to drink. [C]


**E**
**éjele**, exp., the act of poking fun at someone. [Ch, M]
**elba**, n., m., barber. [Ch]
**escoch**, n., m., Scotch whiskey. [Ch]

**escurer**, n., m., scooter. [Ch]

**Ese**, n., m. and f., friend, pal. See also **brode, broder, carnal, güey**. [Ch, SW]

**esprés**, n., m., espresso. [G]

**esteples**, n., m., staples. [C, Ch]

**estilacho**, n., m., style. [Ch, M]

**estore**, n., f., store. [G]

**estraiquiar**, v., to strike. [C, Ch, NR]

**estroc**, n., m., stroke. [C, Ch]

**estufiear**, v., to sniff drugs. [Ch]

**estulear**, v., to serve as a police informer. [Ch]

**F**

**fail**, n., m., file. [CS]

**faite**, n., m., fight. [G]

**feria**, n., m., money. [Ch]

**firme**, exp., fine, all right. [ELA]

**fletear**, v., to walk the streets. [C]

**fletera**, n., f., female flirt. [C]

**flica,** n., f., movie theater, drive-in. [Ch]

**flipar**, v., to be surprised, shocked. [NR, PR, SW]

**flonquear**, v., to flunk an examination. [G]

**floshear**, v., to flush the toilet. [G]

**foreinmarque**, n., m., foreign market. [G]

**fresco**, n., m., soda. [G]

**fri**, adj., gratis. [G]

**fullear**, v., to be in a hurry. [C, SW]

**G**

**gacho**, exp., what a mess. [M, SW]

**ganga**, n., f., gang. [C, SW]

**gom**, n., m., bubble gum. [C, NE]

**gringo**, n., m. and f., 1. foreigner. 2. gibberish. [G]

**grocerías**, n., f., groceries. [C, NR]

**guachá**, interj., watch out. [SW]

**guachear**, v., to observe. See also **guachá**. [SW]

**guafe**, n., m., wharf. [SW]

**güat**, exp., used to suggest disorientation. From Eng. *what?* [G]

**gué**, n., m., friend. [SW]

**güey**, n., m. See **brode**. [Ch, SW]

**gufeao**, adj., 1. fashionable, excellent. 2. to one's liking. [Ch, SW]

**gufear**, v., to joke, to kid. [Ch, SW]

**guisa**, n., f., attractive woman. [Ch, SW]

# H

**haifenado**, adj., m. and f., having a divided identity. [NE]
**hartón**, n., m. and f., glutton. [Ch]
**hina**, n., f., female. [ELA]
**hipiteca**, n., m., Aztec hippy. [Ch]
**honrón,** , n., m., home run (baseball). [C, Ch, NR, PR]
**hood**, n., m., neighborhood. See also **barrio, hud**. [Ch, SW]
**hooda**, n., f., police. From Sp. *judicial*. [Ch]
**hud**, n., m., neighborhood. See also **barrio, hood**. [Ch, SW]

# I

**Igle**, exp., Eagle Pass, Texas. [SW]
**infilda**, n., m., infielder (baseball). [G]
**inglesado**, adj., m. and f., Anglicized. [G]
**inspectar**, v., to inspect. [G]
**imail**, n., m., e-mail. [CS]
**imailiar**, v., to send e-mail. [CS]
**irrigar**, v., to irrigate. [Ch]
**Istlos**, exp., East Los Angeles. [SW]

# J

**jaina**, n., f., honey, sweetheart. [C]
**jale**, n., m., job. [Ch]
**janguiar**, v., 1. to hang out. 2. to loiter. [C]
**jazzear**, v., to improvise. [C]
**jefa**, n., f., mother. [Ch, M, SW]
**jefe**, n., m., father, boss. [Ch, M, SW]
**Jersi**, n., f., 1. T-shirt. 2. ref. to New Jersey. [C, NE]
**Jersisiti**, ref. to Jersey City. [C, NE]
**jiriola**, n., f., absence from classes. [Ch]
**jit**, n., m., hit (baseball). [G]
**joslear**, v., to steal. [Ch, SW]

# K

**kanseco**, adj., m. and f., native of Kansas. [SW]
**kenedito**, n., m., traitor. From Eng. John F. *Kennedy*. [C]
**kikyándola**, exp., relaxing. [SW]
**kuriosita**, adj., attractive (said of a girl). [Ch, SW]

# L

**laca**, n., f., car lock. [NR, PR]
**leva**, n., m., loser. [Ch, SW]
**liftear**, v., to lift. [NR, PR]

**lina**, n., f., line of cocaine. [G]

**liquear**, v., 1. to bite one's tongue, 2. to leak. [Ch, NR]

**lis**, n., f., lease. [G]

**lobi**, n., m., lobby. [G]

**lodeador**, n., m., data loader. [CS]

**Loisiada**, exp., Lower East Side (New York City). [NE, PR]

**lonche**, n., m., lunch. [G]

**lonchear**, v., to lunch. See also **lonche**. [G]

**Los**, exp., Los Angeles. [SW]

**lurio**, n., m. and f., crazy. [Ch]


**LL**

**llegue**, n., m., hit, punch. [Ch, M, SW]

**llorona**, n., f., police car. [SW]

**llovedera**, n., f., heavy rain. [Ch]


**M**

**madama**, n., f., female pimp. [SW]

**maicrogüey**, n., m., microwave oven. [C, NE]

**malinchi**, n., m. and f., unpatriotic Mexican. From Sp. *Malinche*. Also **malinchista**. [Ch, M]

**malinchista**, adj., m. and f. See **malinchi**. [Ch, M]

**Mallamibish,** exp., Miami Beach. [C, NE]

**mancito**, n., m. and f., youngster. [NE]

**manflor**, n., f., lesbian. [Ch]

**mapear,** v. See **mapiar**.

**mapiar**, v., to mop. Also **mapear, mopear**. [NE, PR]

**margarita**, n., f., tequila drink. [G]

**Marielito**, n., m. and f., a person involved in the 1980 Mariel boatlift. [C]

**marqueta**, n., f., supermarket. See also **super**. [NE, NR, PR]

**mary**, n., f., marijuana. [Ch]

**maula**, adj., m. and f., clever. [Ch]

**maus,** n., m., computer mouse. [CS]

**Mexkimo**, n., m. and f., Mexican residing in Alaska. [SW]

**migra**, n., f., immigration police. [SW]

**Mikimau**, n., m., 1. Mickey Mouse. [C] 2. computer mouse. See also **maus**. [CS]

**misi**, n., f., missus. [G]

**míster**, n., m., mister. [G]

**mojo**, n., m. and f., youngster. [Ch, SW]

**mopa**, n., f., mop. [NR, PR]

**mopear**, v. See **mapiar**.

**mora**, n., f., girl. [Ch, SW]
**morro**, n., m., little brother. [SW]
**mula**, n., f., money. [Ch]

## N

**nacho**, n., m., 1. thick tortilla chip. [G] 2. Disloyal Chicano. [Ch, SW]
**naco** (NA co), n., m. and f., plebe. [Ch, M]
**Neorican**, n., m. and f., Puerto Rican from New York. Also
    **Nuyor(r)ican, Nuyorriqueño**. [NE, PR]
**nerdear**, v., 1. to act like a nerd. 2. to study too hard. [NE]
**nerdio**, n., m., nerd. See also **nerdear**. [NE]
**ñero**, n., m., Mexican-American male. See also **pocho**. [SW]
**net**, n., f., Internet. [CS]
**neta,** exp., sincerely. [C]
**nítido**, adj., to one's liking. [NR, SW]
**nocaút**, n., m., knockout (boxing). [G]
**Norgué**, exp., northwestern section of Miami. See also **Saguesera**. [C]
**Nuyor(r)ican**, n., m. and f. See **Neorican**. [G]
**Nuyorriqueño**, n., m. and f. See **Neorican**. [G]

## O

**oben**, n., m., oven. [Ch]
**okai,** exp., all right. From Eng. *OK*. [G]
**órale**, exp., 1. used to signify agreement. 2. used to attract one's
    attention. [Ch]
**overol**, n., m., overalls. [M, SW]

## P

**pachuco**, n., m., Chicano person in East Los Angeles and in
    California in general. Used in the 1940s and 1950s. [Ch, SW]
**pacoima**, n., m., square. [Ch]
**pankays**, n., m., pancakes. [G]
**pari**, n., f., party. [NE, NR].
**parisear**, v., to hang around parties. [C, NE, NR]
**parisero**, n., m. and f., partygoer. See also **parisear**. [NE, NR]
**parqueo**, n., m., the act of parking a car. [M, NE, SW]
**parquiar**, v., to park a car. [M, NE, SW]
**partain**, n., m., part-time job. [C]
**pedo**, n., m., 1. trouble. 2. drunkenness. [Ch, M]
**pégamelas**, exp., used to welcome someone. From Eng. *to slap
    five.* [Ch, SW]
**peni**, n., f., prison. See also **pinta**. [M, SW]
**performear**, v., to perform. [NE]

**peso**, n., m., dollar. [G]
**pichear**, v., to pitch (baseball). [G]
**pimpo**, n., m., pimp. [NE]
**pinta**, n., f., prison, penitentiary. [ELA]
**piquear**, v., to choose. [NE]
**piruja**, n., f., bitch. [M, SW]
**pirujo**, n., m., clever. [M, SW]
**placa**, n., f., police. [Ch]
**pocho**, n., m., Mexican from the United States. [Ch, M, SW]
**ponchar**, v., 1. to hit. [G] 2. to punch a time card. [C]
**Portoriqueño** , n., m.; **Portoriqueña**, n., f. See **Borinquén**. [G]
**printear**, v., to print. [CS]
**púlover**, n., m., sweatshirt. [G]

## Q

**quebradita** n., f., break, intermission. [Ch]
**queki**, n., m., cake. See also **queque**. [Ch, SW]
**quemadora**, n., f., incinerator. [Ch]
**queque**, n., m., cake. [Ch]
**quequito**, n., m., cupcake. [SW]
**quire**, n., m., kitten. [Ch]
**quit**, n., m., kid. [SW]

## R

**ratón,**, n., m., computer mouse. [CS]
**recor**, n., m., record. [C]
**recortado**, adj., m. and f., short of money. [M, SW]
**recortar**, v., to tighten a budget. [M, SW]
**referí**, n., m., referee. [G]
**relís**, n., m., 1. cliff. 2. release form. [SW]
**rentero**, n., m. and f., renter. [Ch]
**ringuear**, v., to ring. [G]
**rocka**, n., f., crack, drug. [Ch, SW]
**roliar,** v., to roll. [SW]
**rorra**, n., f., beautiful woman. [M, SW]
**rorro**, n., m., handsome male. [M, SW]
**rufa**, n., f., roof. [NE]

## S

**Saguesera**, exp. See **Norgué**. [C]
**sardo**, n., m., sergeant. [Ch]
**simón**, affirmative exp. [Ch]
**singlista**, n., m., singles tennis player. [G]

**sochal**, n., m., 1. Social Security number. 2. monthly check. [C]
**sodonga**, n., f., soda water. [Ch]
**super**, n., m., supermarket. See also **marqueta**. [NE, NR, PR]

# T

**tachar**, v., to touch. [Ch]
**taifa**, n., m., thief. [C]
**taipear**, v., to type. [CS, G]
**teipear**, v., to record with a video or tape recorder. [CS, G]
**tipear**, v., to tip. [G]
**tiquete**, n., m., ticket. [G]
**tiquetero**, n., m., ticket seller. [G]
**tiviri**, adj., m. and f., socially busy. From Eng. *activity*. [C]
**toile**, n., m., toilet. [C]
**trial**, n., m., motorcycling ability. [SW]
**tripi**, n., m., dose of LSD. [G]
**troka**, n., f., truck. Also **troke**. [G]
**troke**, n., m. See **troka**. [G]
**trust**, n., m., conglomerate of workers' unions. [Ch]
**turf**, n., m., racetrack. [Ch, NR]
**twist**, n., m., type of dance. [G]

# U

**ufo**, n., m., unidentified flying object. [G]
**ufología**, n., f., science of UFOs. [G]
**unión**, n., f., workers' union. [G]

# V

**vate**, n., f., water. [C, Ch]
**videoclip**, n., m., music video recording. [G]
**víbora**, n., f., penis. [Ch]
**virula**, n., f., bicycle. [SW]

# W

**wachale**, exp., watch out, look out. See also **wachear**. [Ch, SW]
**wachear**, v., to watch. [Ch, SW]
**wasá**, exp., hello. [Ch, NR, SW]
**windo**, n., f., computer program, as in *Windows 98*. [CS]
**winshiwaipers**, n., m., windshield wipers. [C]

# Y

**yanitor**, n., m., janitor. [C, Ch, NR, PR]
**yarda**, n., backyard, patio. [NR]

**yet**, n., m., jet. [Ch, M]
**yip**, n., m., rip-off. [G]
**yoguear**, v., to jog. [C, M]
**YUCA**, n., m. and f., young urban Cuban American. [C]
**yunier**, n., m. and f., junior. [G]

## Z

**zafo**, exp., may the Lord protect me. [Ch]
**zapeta**, n., f., diaper. [SW]
**zapo**, n., m., shoe. [Ch]
**zeta**, n., m., defender of the oppressed. [SW]

# SANDRA CISNEROS

*Form over Content*

Officially anointed *La Girlfriend* by the English-speaking media, Sandra Cisneros is considered a living classic. She is the most sought-after Latina writer of her generation and a guest impossible to ignore in any multicultural fiesta. The black-and-white photographs used to promote her work are colored by an overwhelming sense of theatricality. They make her look like a sweet light-skinned Indian with a European flair—a natural beauty out of a Sergei Eisenstein film. Her enigmatic smile hides the ancient mysteries of her people, and her cowboy boots, tiny miniskirts, idiosyncratic Mexican shawls, and hairbands inject the needed exoticism into her ethnic roots.*

Her status as the voice of a minority has not befallen by accident. Born in 1954 in a Chicago barrio and educated in the Midwest, Cisneros acquired her distinct *tejano* identity when she settled in San Antonio in the mid-eighties. She has since turned the U.S.–Mexican border into her habitat. She proudly parades around under a hybrid facade, part nativist Spanish and part antiestablishment American. She is constantly asking her audience to approach her as the star of a cross-cultural *bildungsroman* where *mestizas,* ignored and underrepresented for ages, end up baking the cake and eating it all. Indeed, Cisneros describes herself as "nobody's wife and

First published in *Academic Questions* 9, 4 (Fall 1996). Reprinted in *The Riddle of Cantinflas: Essays on Hispanic Popular Culture* (Albuquerque, NM: University of New Mexico Press, 1998).

* I examine Sandra Cisneros in the context of Latino culture in *The Hispanic Condition* (New York: HarperCollins, 1995).

nobody's mother" and "an informal spokeswoman for Latinos." Her imposed profile is that of an eternal sympathizer of lost causes, a loose woman, a south-of-the-border feminist outlaw happily infuriating anyone daring to obstruct her way. "They say I'm a bitch," a poem of hers reads,

> Or witch. I've claimed
> the same and never winced.
> They say I'm a *macha,* hell on wheels,
> *viva-la-vulva,* fire and brimstone
> man-hating, devastating,
> boogey-woman lesbian.
> Not necessarily,
> but I like the compliment.
>
> By all accounts I am
> a danger to society.
> I'm Pancha Villa.
> I break laws
> upset the natural order,
> anguish the Pope and make fathers cry.
> I am beyond the jaw of law.
> I'm *la desperada,* most-wanted public enemy.
> My happy picture grinning from the wall.

Her artistic talents are clear but overemphasized. In fact, what truly attracts readers is not her compact prose, which she perceives as "English with a Spanish sensibility," but her nasty, taboo-breaking attitude. Her works are pamphleteering. They denounce rather than move; they accuse rather than educate.

Responsible for several poetry collections, a children's book, and a couple of volumes of fiction, Cisneros hit high into the firmament with her 1984 novel *The House on Mango Street,* a chain of interrelated vignettes widely read from coast to coast and repeatedly assigned to undergraduates. The plot is unified by the voice of Esperanza Cordero, a preteenage girl coming to terms with her impoverished surroundings and her urge to write her life. Cisneros's second published book, with the imprint of Arte Público Press, a small nonprofit house at the University of Houston devoted to minority literature, *The House on Mango Street* came out just as she was celebrating her thirtieth birthday. The match between writer and publisher seemed ideal: a simple, cliché-filled coming-of-age tale by and about Hispanic women, uncomplicated and unapologetic, with the potential for enchanting a broad audience of young school girls, and a federally funded press whose mandate had been to place in bookshelves the fiction by Latinos that mainstream New York publishers refused to endorse. In a short time both parties benefited greatly, the unknown Cisneros becoming, without any major reviews, an incipient version of the *bandida latina* that would later blossom, and her title turning out to be one of the fastest selling in the house's catalogue.

That all happened when diversity and the politics of inclusion were still in diapers. By the late eighties, multiculturalism had become a national obsession, and a spokesfigure for the brewing Latino minority was urgently needed. Richard Rodriguez, whose autobiography *Hunger of Memory* had appeared in 1982, was already an illustrious presence, but his antibilingualism, often confused for anti-Hispanicism, seemed repugnant and xenophobic to the liberal establishment. Since Rodriguez stood alone, an unopposed male, a right-wing intellectual whose soul not even the devil could buy, a female counterpart was quickly sought. Cisneros seized the opportunity: Susan Bergholz, a Manhattan literary agent making a niche for emerging Latinos literati, took her as a client; soon after, Vintage agreed to reprint *The House on Mango Street* and Random House to publish another collection of stories, *Woman Hollering Creek*. A sudden metamorphosis occurred. Talented and outgoing as she was, Cisneros *la marginal* became Cisneros *la atractiva*. With the help of the right promotional machinery, she moved to center stage, and the applause hasn't stopped: From a Before Columbus American Book Award to a MacArthur Fellowship, she basks in the spotlight, sporting fancy sunglasses to reduce the glare.

But the problem, paraphrasing Gore Vidal, is that Cisneros wants to be not good but great, and so she is neither. Her style shows signs of maturity; her tales are not prepubescent anymore, and her sentimentality has mellowed down. *Woman Hollering Creek*, for instance, offers a gamut of pieces of self-discovery, set primarily in southern Texas and Mexico, often overstyled, on the role of women in our collective psyche: Rachel, narrating "Eleven," tells what it is like being a girl of that age; Ines Alfaro, who in "Eyes of Zapata" runs away with Mexican general Emiliano Zapata, talks about how his machismo destroyed her life; Cleófila Enriqueta de León Hernández, the character at the heart of the title story, follows her husband to the United States, where she realizes the extent of her own oppression—to cite only three among many other "suffering souls." These tales are neither fully original nor groundbreaking. Race and gender are their stuff, which Cisneros, by an act of cultural fiat, recycles with just the right ingredients to call attention to Hispanics as instinctual and exciting and interesting. For what they are worth, a handful are actually commendable, but the public has embraced them with far less ardor than it had *The House on Mango Street,* which isn't a good novel. It is sleek and sentimental, sterile and undemanding. Its seductive flavor, I guess, is to be found in its primitiveness. What Cisneros does is tackle important social issues from a peripheral, condescending angle, drawing her readers to the hardship her female characters experience but failing to offer an insightful examination of who they are and how they respond to their environment.

Since its republication by Vintage, *The House on Mango Street* has sold close to a quarter of a million copies. It might seem fine for seventh graders, but making it required reading in high schools and colleges from coast to coast, where students should have more substantial fare, is saddening. Its impact in the United States, obviously, has resonated worldwide. It has appeared in a dozen translations, including the unrefined Spanish one made by Elena Poniatowska, another one of Susan Bergholz's clients and Mexico's most important *femme de lettres.* Cisneros builds her narrative by means of minuscule literary snapshots, occasionally as short as half a page. Esperanza Cordero, whose name in Spanish means "hope," thinks aloud. She describes what she sees and hears in poetic terms, focusing on the women who surround her and the way they are victimized by men. The image of the house, a ubiquitous motif in so-called Third World fiction, becomes the central leitmotif: Esperanza's poor house embarrasses and pains her; she dreams of a larger, embellished one, a signature of the better times she yearns for for herself and her family. Men in her neighborhood are by nature evil; women, on the other hand, particularly the untraditional ones, are saintly, and she seeks a handful of them (Minerva, Alicia, Aunt Guadalupe) as role models. At one point Esperanza is raped as she accompanies her friend Sally to a carnival. At another, Sally is beaten by her father as punishment for seeing boys. The cast is presented as real folks but, in truth, it is Manichean and buffoonish. Together they introduce a risky rhetoric of virtue that utilizes the powerless victim to advance a critique of the Hispanic idiosyncrasy, but that fails to explore any other of its multiple facets.

Cisneros seasons her plot with the type of "magical realism" readers have grown accustomed to in Latin American masterpieces. This is done to make her work ethnic enough; it validates its authenticity. A witch woman, for instance, reads Esperanza's cards to unravel her destiny, and what she finds is "a home in the heart." Her identity quest is dissociated into alternative selves, all related to the various names she dreams of possessing. But her main concern is with the female body. Her descriptions of Esperanza's nascent sexuality are built upon the recognition of the opposite sex as a bestial monster ready to attack. A distant resemblance can be found between Cisneros's novel and Alice Walker's *The Color Purple.* Clearly Walker is much more concerned with relevant historical issues; she tackles slavery from a female perspective and reaches a level of high melodrama as her protagonist, Celie, undergoes a transformation from passive acceptance to self-assertion and human dignity. The epistolary structure of her book, as well as her use of dialect, give it a depth absent in Cisneros. Nonetheless, both writers resort to the same manipulative devices: Their novels depict men within an ethnic minority as patently evil and detail the psychological development of female characters who, only through conversion, can receive redemption. First you learn to understand the injustices of the environment, and then you become your own master.

Does the book deserve its current status? The answer is no. True enough, Latino fiction in English is still green, but turning *The House on Mango Street* into obligatory reading, presumably because of its accessibility, is wrong. It ratifies the image of Hispanics as sentimental dullards, and, equally worrisome, it celebrates the Latino intellectual as pubescent protester. I do not mean to blame Cisneros for a wrong she is not responsible for. Hers is a first novel, a debutante's first turn around the dance floor. What is disturbing is the uncritical deification that surrounds her book. Scholars date the origins of the genre back to 1959, when José Antonio Villarreal published *Pocho,* a tale of revolution and assimilation, about a young Mexican-American kid facing discrimination and finding his rightful place in America. Since then a lot of what is published today by Latino fiction writers is realistic and semiautobiographical. The field is clearly awaiting a major breakthrough that will push its boundaries from conventional immigrant literature to a more sophisticated world-class writing, the type of transition carried on by Philip Roth and Saul Bellow in Jewish letters in the United States. Whenever such reformulating takes place, a recognition of earlier nontraditional voices will be crucial. Few, for instance, regard the pre-postmodern novelistic exercises by an Iberian, Felipe Alfau's *Locos: A Comedy of Gestures,* published in 1936, as a Latino ancestor, if anything because Alfau was a conservative fellow, unconcerned with ethnic envies, and also because, as a Spaniard, he automatically suits the profile of the oppressor. His novel, though, in the line of Pirandello and Italo Calvino, is light-years ahead of the immigrant-handles-it-all fiction we have grown accustomed to by a considerable segment of the Latino intelligentsia.

But the pantheon is vastly expanding, and high-caliber figures like Oscar Hijuelos, Julia Alvarez, Aristeo Brito, and Cristina García have already delivered commanding and mature novels, at once multifaceted and far-reaching, volumes that go far beyond easy stereotypes. Their understanding of what fiction ought to do—an investigation into the obscure aspects of humanity—makes Cisneros, by comparison, a far less demanding artist. Her messages come in soundbites and often have the taste of stale political sloganeering. She makes social protest the foundation for utopia. Trapped in her condition as Hispanic and woman, her creation, Esperanza, can only rely on her words and imagination to escape. She vows not to grow up tame, which makes her perceive poetry as the door out—her way of escape to an alternative life, her device to reject the ugliness of the outside world. So what type of literary model is *La Girlfriend?* Confrontational yet wholeheartedly anti-intellectual, her pen is just a weapon to incriminate. Nothing new in this, of course; after all, Cisneros is part, indirectly at least, of the illustrious genealogy of Latin American writers qua opponents to the system, from José Martí to Rosario Castellanos and Elena Poniatowska herself. But her ready-made U.S. odyssey, her "making it" in the American Dream, is curiously harmless. Hers is a domesticated form of belligerence. Rather than position herself as opponent to the powers that be, she courts them, feeds them with the dose of animosity they need, and in turn is fed lavishly by them on a diet of awards and prizes. Her forte lies in her articulation of words, not in her display and knowledge of ideas. She offers neither surprises nor profound explorations of the human spirit. The ethnocentrism that gives her legitimacy transforms her complaints into bourgeois mannerisms—transitory temper tantrums that society is ready to accept simply because they present no real subversive threat. Her tales are flat and unoriginal and thrive on revising moribund stereotypes.

In short, the acclaim granted by the liberal establishment to *The House on Mango Street,* and to this nineties version of the flamboyant Mexican artist Frida Kahlo, as the classic Latina writer of her generation, is, to me at least, a form of collective nearsightedness and one more evidence of how exoticism pays its dues. What forces us to give simplistic, overly accessible novels, fiction cum caricature, to the young? Are they allergic to more complex readings? Or could it be that our research into the archives of Latino literature has not gone far enough? By endorsing Cisneros's attitude and no one else's, the risk of falsifying the role of Latino intellectuals is quite high. All serious literature, by definition, is subversive, but in our MTV age, not all of it needs to be foul-mouthed and lightweight.

# AGAINST THE OSTRICH SYNDROME

I've often heard people use the metaphor of the ostrich to describe the Latin American intelligentsia in the United States, particularly that portion of it that sought asylum in el Norte during the sixties and seventies. It is easy to understand why: An ostrich's feathers are beautiful but utterly useless, and this large swiftly running bird is reputed to bury its head in sand when confronted. Self-delusion is indeed the chief characteristic of this intelligentsia. What I want to address in this brief essay is the unfortunate impact of such thinking. I am hardly the first person to call this phenomenon to wide attention: Mario Vargas Llosa did so at some depth in his political memoir *A Fish in the Water,* and more recently in *Making Waves,* a collection of his essays. The political analysts Jorge Castañeda in his book *Utopia Unarmed* and Octavio Paz in his meditations on Marxism in the southern hemisphere both address the subject. Their examination of the Latin American intelligentsia looked northward from south of the border. Mine is an attempt to look inward, for I have moved across the Rio Grande to a pulpit at a comfortable New England college. Necessarily, my arguments differ from theirs. I am not interested, for example, in the awkward patterns of behavior of émigré Latin American intellectuals in an Anglo-Saxon habitat, but rather how certain postures, certain attitudes, play themselves out within the academic world—and in particular, in Spanish departments. What has been their attitude toward the profound ethnic and verbal transformation shaking the texture of American society

First published in *Academic Questions* 11, 1 (Winter 1997–98).

today? How do they respond to the pressures of Spanglish and of Latinos moving from the periphery of American culture to the mainstream?

Often sidestepped by their respective administrations, Spanish departments are at the center of a heated debate today, one mirroring the social upheaval that surrounds them. It has been announced that by the year 2020, Hispanics will become the largest minority in the country; and by 2050, one out of every four Americans will be of Hispanic descent—an impressive datum, signaling what I've called elsewhere "the *latinoamericanización* of the U.S." Their tongue is the unofficial alternative language in many major urban centers. And it is certainly the most popular foreign language studied on campus, drawing students who look south for the future. These departments have also grown in popularity because a remapping of foreign policy is under way and Latin America has inevitably become a primary focus of attention among Washington politicians and pundits. Not only is the area one of the most visible and promising in terms of economic growth, but the democratic fever sweeping it makes it attractive for short- and long-term investment. This attractiveness is not free of drawbacks, of course. The region bristles with drug traffickers and cartels, whose tentacles are spreading ever more widely from their home bases. One can witness this in the way Hollywood villains have ceased to be Soviet spies to become Colombian and Mexican drug kings. All this is clear evidence of an inevitable new marriage. Looser restrictions on the commerce in human and natural resources create multitudes of new links between Latin America and the United States at the dusk of the century.

As a result of the post–Cold War political landscape, most European languages—especially Russian and French—have experienced a sharp decline in student enrollment. Even German, which after reunification soared temporarily in popularity, is also traveling down a slippery enrollment slope. However, Spanish has become highly fashionable and will continue to be so, not only because of the popularity of Latin America, but also because, from the early sixties onward, bilingual education, willy-nilly, has elbowed the way for Spanish into the public school classroom and thus legitimized it. On the other hand, the contentious English Only movement has raised the political profile of Spanish as a somewhat subversive influence. What is unquestionable, however, is that Spanish is not fading away like other immigrant languages in the past—Yiddish, Italian, German, and Gaelic. Instead, it is forcing itself into the nation's consciousness at an incredible speed. As time goes by, not to be conversant in Spanish north of the border will become an impediment.

Obviously, the Spanish departments are not the only ones responsible for teachings on Latin America, its people and culture. Special wings in other academic fields, from political science and history to sociology, share the burden. But, since language and culture are the laboratory where collective identity is shaped, what takes place in the Spanish departments is essential to a student's understanding of Hispanic civilization as a whole. It sets the tone for other areas of study. Because Spanish departments play (or ought to play) a pivotal role, it is essential that we understand what is right and wrong in their pedagogy.

With all the excitement surrounding the Spanish language and its environment, one is likely to think these academic bastions would be galvanized—entranced by their good fortune. In fact, they are deeply fractured, submerged in an ancient bloody battle between two quarrelsome factions: *los peninsularistas,* devoted to Iberian linguistic and literary traditions, and *los latinoamericanistas,* fostering scholarship in colonial and modern Hispanic America. So antagonistic is their animosity that both often forget that their role is to teach language and culture, past and present, from our contemporary vantage point. Their internecine struggles are bewildering to students, who end up acquiring biased tools with which to tackle their subject matter. The *peninsularistas* desperately hold on to the last vestiges of power long since lost to Spain. Their Latin American colleagues still approach the Hispanic world with colonial eyes: the oppressor versus the oppressed. The result is depressing. Little is done, for instance, to reflect on the current social and verbal changes affecting Latinos in the United States. This represents an abdication of leadership, whose main repercussion is the appropriation of the subject by other departments, say, English or American Studies. Worse, the view one gets of Hispanic civilization from the courses offered in many Spanish departments is one of rigidity and contentiousness. The teachers are imprisoned in a premodern mentality, misanthropic in nature, alienated, reacting rather than acting.

These departments are not to be blamed solely for this disheartening viewpoint. The study of Latin America began in the mid-nineteenth century with the works of William Prescott and other eminent historians. From early on, their attitude was mostly condescending, due in large measure to the poor standing the Iberian peninsula had had since the eighteenth century with respect to the European continent and in the American imagination. Those historians approached Mexico and South America as provinces where brutality and barbarism reigned. Ever since the Spanish empire began to lose control of its North American territories—its settlements in

Florida and the Southwest—Iberians were perceived as ill mannered and avaricious if not uncivilized. By the time the Spanish-American War took place, this view was already a stereotype, useful in giving vent to anger against the enemy.

Its echoes are surely still around, but this vilification ceased to be feasible in the sixties. Signs of change first came with the Cuban Revolution of 1958–1959. Fidel Castro, Ernesto "Ché" Guevara, and the other compañeros of the Sierra Maestra portrayed themselves as a David against the fearsome Goliath up north, which sponsored the loathed Batista dictatorship. Castro's initial triumph and the institutionalization of his policies in the sixties brought along a fever of hope among Latin American intellectuals: Imperialism could be challenged, even by a tiny Caribbean island with few military resources. Many an acolyte on both sides of the Rio Grande embraced the Cuban revolution as a sign of rebirth of the whole continent. And rebirth meant a refreshing sense of self-confidence. The region was no longer a congregation of Banana Republics. Overnight it had become a field of redemptive dreams.

The impact of Castro's ascendency was immediate on campuses in the United States: to a large extent, departments of history and political science became active supporters of his communist policies. American schools hired many south-of-the-border intellectuals, Havana sympathizers unsuccessfully trying to implement similar strategies in their military-ruled countries. Those new hires went predominantly into Spanish departments. It was a bizarre yet obvious asylum. Among them were writers and pamphleteers famous in their own countries, with limited English proficiency, seeking a quiet environment where they might live in peace, yet where they still could be politically active at home—politically *engagé* but by remote control. The United States might have been "the ugly monster," but its First Amendment and the promise of tenure and economic security made the terrain too tempting to reject. Ironically, as Washington-sponsored military governments were hunting for left-wing agitators in Latin America, U.S. colleges and universities were opening doors to them.

The refugees moving north had a very clear vision. While they would live inside the belly of the beast, they would *never* adopt the American Dream. This meant becoming pariahs rather than active participants in the internal intellectual debate; it meant an outright rejection of their students' values and worldview. These émigré intellectuals persisted in attacking the United States for imperialism, accusing it of stereotyping Hispanics in general and Latin Americans in particular. What they have never acknowledged is that it was in their hands to dislodge stereotypes through knowledge and spirited discussion. This backwardness became evident during the civil rights movement, when César Chávez and the United Farm Workers boycotted the grape industry and staged a strike against "internal colonialism." Almost in unison, the Puerto Rican Young Lords manifested their unhappiness with the status of Spanish-speaking Caribbeans on the East Coast, mostly in New York. Many of the Latin American intellectuals bunkered in American campuses, though, watched the uproar silently from afar, scared of participating in a struggle that, by definition, was theirs as well. And when they did participate, it was only to support the black struggle, not that of Chicanos and Puerto Ricans. Their passivity was explainable: In Latin America, people accused those who had left of treason and refused to recognize Hispanic culture within the United States as legitimate. Mexicans have a poor opinion of Chicanos. So do Puerto Ricans on the island of their siblings in the mainland. Cubans disdain Cuban-Americans. The response of Latin American intellectuals followed the same pattern. Ideologically, the émigrés had never made the trip to America.

This refusal to adapt has precedents. Until recently, the left-wing Hispanic intelligentsia was not only well known for its intransigence, it was also seen as impulsive, unreflecting, and irresponsible. It employed a rigid and uncreative Marxism to explain class struggle south of the Rio Grande, and the best answer it had to oppression was an endorsement of violence. In Marxist eyes, the world was all-too-easily divided into "good guys" and "bad guys," the latter being the foreigners. On campuses north of the Rio Grande, their characteristic response was an automatic *No.* When pressured for an explanation, what they usually came up with were squalid, unqualified reformulations of their original response. In short, their behavior in the United States became notorious for what has come to be known as "the ostrich syndrome." They paraded pompously, flapping ideological wings that never took them off the ground. Rather than openly engage in debate, they preferred to hide their heads in the sand, disappearing intellectually even as they remained palpably there—a facade hiding dreams of self-delusion.

This intelligentsia used the classroom not only to advance its Marxist views but also to misrepresent an entire civilization. Latin America was a land left unfinished by God; it lived in a state of perpetual suffering. Mass culture, American and European influence, and foreign economic investment were all evil. What the region needed was a form of redemption that could easily be understood as "a process of purification," of elevation to a higher stratum by purging all external influence.

Anyone in his right senses agrees that poverty in Latin America was—and still is—rampant and that corruption runs far deeper than any democratic change can fathom. But, endorsing violence and purification as the solution to these problems was deceptive at best. Still, the views of newly appointed Spanish-speaking faculty were not only tolerated but often applauded by left-wing administrators. After the Cuban revolution, America seemed to discover its neighbors down south, and in the late sixties Latin American literature began to proliferate in English translation, and readers were eager to find out more about the authors—Gabriel García Márquez and his entourage. Early on, many of these were Marxist, although the most visionary of them began to renounce extremist or egalitarian views as soon as they realized what Fidel Castro was truly after. This change of heart took time to reach American readers; until it was fully understood, Marxism distressingly reigned as the sole intellectual ideology to interpret the region.

The arrival of left-wing *latinoamericanistas,* and the support they received by their sympathizing American-born colleagues, resulted in clashes with the *peninsularistas,* who quickly came to resent the popularity of Latin America among students. In several cases the struggle for power between the two camps ended in fist fights and even law suits. Administrations turned a blind eye to the struggles because internal warring is a symptom of the entire Hispanic culture. But is it? Is Latin America really as contemptuous of Spain as its left-wing intelligentsia wants us to believe today? And, is the Iberian peninsula so openly envious of the culture in its former colonies across the Atlantic? I contend that these fraternal battlings were more the product of academic hysteria.

Indeed, it is very much a hysteria in the teacups of the intelligentsia. Events in the larger Hispanic world have overtaken the rarified concerns that generate parochial squabbles. Since the late seventies, Spain and Latin America—Cuba included—have entered a new era of political and cultural exchange. The dialogue between the two sides is multifaceted and quite promising, but it seems completely to have been overlooked in many Spanish departments. So, a badly needed reexamination of the new dynamics is taking too long to be implemented. Hispanics, as Alfonso Reyes once put it, have owned "the right to universal citizenship." That ought to be acknowledged in the academy, and an emerging generation of scholars would be the ones to do it. But, this generation is hampered somewhat because the wisdom that has been imparted to them is based on a stagnant and largely falsified view of the world.

In many corners of Latin America left-wing groups are finally replacing the hand grenade with the ballot box, moving from a position of antagonism to one of civil participation in the political debate. Simultaneously, as the twentieth century draws to a close, the response to Fidel Castro's rhetoric has gone from enthusiasm to ridicule. And, the foreign policy in the region also has a new attire: FBI spies and assaulting soldiers are giving way to merchandising and the assumption that a free market economy can bring forth an atmosphere conducive to healthy ideological debate. Unfortunately, the exiled intellectuals barricaded in Spanish departments hardly feel these changes. For one thing, the anachronistic radicalism of the Cuban Revolution still governs. Many schools continue to assign pro-Castro literature and send their students to Havana. Not that this literature should be suppressed. On the contrary, it should continue to be read with the exact same voracity. What must change is the context in which such study is placed. It is the context, as I said, that requires reexamination.

This isn't the only problem today, though. The new generation of teachers that is moving into Spanish departments is brighter and more dynamic. It is also influenced by mass culture and has a less caustic view of America's foreign policy. The old guard, however, is holding these departments hostage. For one thing, it is refusing fully to acknowledge the new class of students raised in Hispanic households within the United States. These Latino students do not really come from a homogenized group. They come from various ethnic backgrounds—Mexican-American, Puerto Rican in the mainland, Cuban-American, Dominican-American, and so on. What distinguishes them from their predecessors is the realization that, as a minority, they are no longer at the fringes of American society, but instead are moving toward the center with an impetus that can only gain momentum. "Empowerment" is the fashionable word: Latinos are being empowered as a function of numerical growth—the more there are, the larger their influence will be. This is as it should be and Spanish departments must accept the new reality. That doesn't mean their curricula should completely reflect the needs and desires of these students. Departments are not in the business of pandering to students but of expanding their horizons. Learning, however, is not done in a vacuum; to be successful, it must acknowledge who these students are.

So, who are they? The new class of Hispanic students is often bilingual, but its Spanish is not fully developed. It is aware of its roots in Latin America, and its members gravitate to Spanish departments seeking verbal fluency and a wider understanding of their ancestry. The first response they receive is that their Spanish is "deficient," which it is, although hardly any recognition is given to the stamina of Spanglish as a burgeoning dialect. In terms of courses, these students are offered a rigid travelogue through the Iberian Golden Age, Cervantes, the Generación del '98, and the Spanish Civil War, as well as through Colonial Latin America, *modernismo*, and the artistic movements of the twentieth century in the Americas. This list is commendable, although, once again, the context surrounding it is deficient to the core, thus crippling the student with a distorted view of Hispanic civilization. These masters— Góngora, Quevedo, Unamuno, Sor Juana Inés de la Cruz, Rubén Darío, et al.—matter still today because they speak to our internal fears, our self-referential thirst, our modern angst. They ought to be studied in ways that highlight their own artistic condition and how it related to the present times. What I'm advocating, then, is a reframing of the issues. I do not want to replace them with others more ad hoc to the times. Teachers ought to make these Iberian and Latin American classics come alive, the way Shakespeare and Henry James can come alive through refreshing pedagogical strategies. Otherwise, they cannot help but be stiff, dusty, and antiquated. It's all a matter of perspective, for Quevedo, Cervantes, and Sor Juana, to name only three, seem to me much more urgent than a considerable portion of what is written today in Spanish.

The emerging generation of scholars and teachers in Spanish departments has gradually made room in recent years for new writing from Spain and the Americas. The films of Pedro Almodóvar and the culture of *la movida,* the feminist literature from south of the border, and detective and science fiction novels are increasingly welcomed in courses. Sadly, what is hardly provided in these departments is an examination of the immediate background of the new generation of students—Latino culture. As a result of the contempt felt toward Hispanics north of the Rio Grande by those who stayed at home, this area of study is left to other departments. When Latinos are studied, say, in the departments of English, American studies, or sociology, the academic approach to them narrows as if blinders shut out emanations from beyond the border. A lot is lost if Hispanics are just another ethnic group in the domestic multicultural arena. By the same token, the view from outside the melting pot of a Hispanic civilization is incomplete when it constructs some isolated enclave of Latin America living in the United States. By itself, neither of these perspectives is enough. Only by summing themselves together do they provide a full, comprehensive view of Latino life.

Hispanic civilization is vital and energetic. After English and Mandarin, Spanish is spoken most widely. The Hispanic world has redefined itself thoroughly in the last hundred years—at least since 1898. It has ceased to be an economic empire orbiting around a centralized crown and is now composed of distinct spheres, each with its own peculiarities yet all unified by a common language. This fragmentation means that there isn't one Spanish, really, but many, and Spain no longer holds control of what is and isn't verbally acceptable. Constant migrations and cross-pollinations continually reshape Hispanic culture and result in a magisterial verbal multiplicity.

How to address this fascinating diversity and fragmentation is obviously a challenge to the whole U.S. academic establishment, but particularly to Spanish departments. For old-fashioned, dogmatic faculty members to remain fixed on the lost glory of the Iberian peninsula is to lose touch with reality. Similarly, to simplify Latin America into some toy-soldier battleground where "internal" and "external" forces confront each other will only nurture the obsolete and cartoonish view provided since the Cuban Revolution. It is obscene and outright tragic thus to reduce and compartmentalize Hispanic civilization, fostering the sense that few communicating vessels ply the seas between Spain and Latin America and none put in to other ports of call.

Currently, there is insufficient academic interest in the status of Spanglish. Should a subject in which students are frequently more knowledgeable and versatile than their teachers be studied in the classroom? Or should the scholarly world continue to ignore it, in spite of the fact that it is becoming "the newest form" of Spanish around? And, is there one Spanglish or many, as many as the backgrounds of various segments of the Latino community? My own inclination is to be inclusive rather than exclusive—to move at the pace of society, making room for verbal recreation. The language of Latinos can no longer be denied the intellectual scrutiny it deserves. Who are we scholars to withhold its legitimacy when millions are using it on a daily basis?

By the same token, though, I emphatically reject the replacement of Castilian Spanish with Spanglish. Spanish is and will always be the language of Hispanic civilization. As such, it must be taught uniformly as a paradigm in Spanish departments across the country. And along with it, its major practitioners and keepers, the masters of the language, from Cervantes to Borges, from Sor Juana to Camilo José Cela, must remain an irreplaceable part of the curriculum. But Spanish, like any other language, isn't static. It is in constant change, and the United States is unquestionably the habitat where that change is occurring most rapidly. We can no longer afford to ignore and minimize the impact of Spanglish, not only on our students and in our society at large, but also on Latin America. Its vitality is immense, and its impact promises to be far-reaching. Spanish-speaking television shows made north of the Rio Grande but reaching a Latin American audience—*Sábado Gigante, El Show de Cristina, Noticiero Univisión,* many of which regularly use Spanglish terms and patterns—establish patterns of linguistic behavior that are modifying the spoken and written language in countries like Puerto Rico, Mexico, Chile, and Colombia. People commonly use *parquear* instead of *estacionarse* for "to park," *aplicar* for "to apply to a certain program" rather than *inscribirse,* even *roofa* for "roof" instead of *techo.* And this is but a random list that says little about deep syntactical changes. It is time for scholars and academics to pay serious attention to these mutations, bringing them into the classroom as an honorable subject of debate and study.

Some might argue that academia ought not simply fall into a trap of numbers. The Latino population is growing at an incredible speed, but that, they contend, doesn't necessarily mean that the language of Latinos and the literature they produce is worthy of serious scholarly notice. This view is regrettable. It reminds me of the way Yiddish was treated by eighteenth- and early nineteenth-century "enlightened" Jews in Eastern Europe—the *maskilim.* Since its inception at least four hundred years earlier, Yiddish, the "unworthy Jewish jargon," the "bastard tongue" used mostly by women and approached irreverently by rabbis and Talmudists, was seen by highbrow Jewish intellectuals as an aberration, an obscenity, even when poetry, liturgy, folktales, theater, and popularizing biblical interpretation were written in it. It wasn't until the second half of the nineteenth century that it was legitimized by world-class literati enamored with it.[*] They made it acceptable by writing "serious" novels, stories, and essays in it. Spanglish, in my eyes, is the Yiddish of today. The two tongues are dissimilar in many ways, but they also have plenty in common: They are both hybrids, and their legitimacy has been viciously fought by the intellectual elite.

True, Spanglish is not yet a language. Indeed, some even doubt that it has acquired the status of a dialect. We are far from having standardized its grammatical and syntactical rules. In fact, we don't

---

[*] I explore the ambivalence toward Yiddish in my introduction to *The Oxford Book of Jewish Stories* (New York and London: Oxford University Press, 1998): 3–25.

even have an English/Spanglish dictionary. But only someone totally blind to reality would deny its power and vibrancy. It is used, in one way or another, by millions. Popular Latino music is a record of its nuances, and novels, poetry, and plays, not to mention movies, cement its new usages in the popular lexicon. Spanglish is quickly becoming essential in today's America. Will it survive into the twenty-first century? Is it likely to produce literary masterpieces on the order of Sholem Aleichem's *Tevye the Dairyman* or Israel Joshua Singer's *The Brothers Ashkenazi*? It is too early to tell. For the time being, we already have a plentiful supply of high-caliber literary works, if not in Spanglish, at least in either English or Spanish, written by Latinos emerging from the ebullient Hispanic culture in the United States. Many of these works will no doubt be forgotten in the future; much is second-rate. So-called ethnic publishers like Arte Público Press devote themselves exclusively to Latino writers who have long been marginalized. In doing so they put representation way ahead of quality. Still, the wider outlook is quite promising. Landmarks by Hispanics writing in English include Felipe Alfau's *Locos: A Comedy of Gestures,* Aristeo Brito's *The Devil in Texas,* Oscar Hijuelos's *The Mambo Kings Play Songs of Love,* Julia Alvarez's *In the Time of the Butterflies,* to name a few. (And this list doesn't include works originally written in English by Latin American writers like Borges, Carlos Fuentes, Manuel Puig, and Guillermo Cabrera Infante.) The inclusion of these, of course, makes it easier to distinguish and exclude the trash. Many Yiddish novels of the late nineteenth and early twentieth centuries are now forgotten, but many others are for the ages, just as some early works in the burgeoning shelf of Latino letters are likely to last. (Some do have a long posterity: Alfau's *Locos* was written in 1928 and first published in 1936.) Isn't it time for the Hispanic *maskilim* of today, academics in Spanish departments, to acknowledge what lay readers have already realized? Hasn't the moment come for them to stop delegating the study of these works to other departments, and at least to acknowledge the existence of Spanglish? Shouldn't the curriculum in these departments make room?

Spanish departments need revitalization badly. How long must the ostrich remain a symbol of the self-concealment practiced by this intelligentsia? In order to approach the complex vibrant civilization that justifies their departments, scholars of Hispanic matters must show signs of life. Do not mistake my intentions. What I advocate is not only a matter of numbers but a matter of maturity and responsibility. Separating Spanish studies by specific geographical areas is a manifestation of ideological stagnation. Many young professors won't accept it, and they are beginning to offer courses in which Iberian, Latin American, Spanish-speaking Caribbean, and Latino themes intertwine. Josep Pla once argued that Herbert Marcuse contributed with his immense talent to the confusion of our times. The mysterious process by which Hispanic civilization keeps reinventing itself is indeed confusing, and it cries out for more than the simplistic interpretations offered by those on one side or the other of the chasm that splits contemporary Spanish scholarship and teaching.

# JULIA ALVAREZ

## Las Mariposas

Not long ago, I heard Julia Alvarez call attention to an intriguing linguistic tic in her native Dominican culture: When you ask somebody what's up and no easy reply can be found, people are likely to say, *Entre Lucas y Juan Mejía.* "Between the devil and the deep blue sea" isn't the right equivalent in English, Alvarez added, "because you aren't describing the sensation of being caught between a pair of bad alternatives."

> "So-so" isn't the meaning either, because the Dominican expression isn't at all meant to suggest bland stasis, mediocrity. It's much more intriguing than that. "How are you doing?" "I'm between Lucas and Juan Mejía." And who are these guys? . . . The very story that inspired the saying is gone. So . . . you have to go on and tell the tale of why you feel the way you do. What are the forces you're caught between? How did you get there? And how does it feel to be there?

Alvarez's *oeuvre* is precisely about this type of crisis—the identity of the in-betweens—and about why she feels the way she does in somebody else's country and language (she immigrated to the United States with her family when she was ten). Although this subject is ubiquitous in ethnic literature in general, her pen lends it an

---

First published in *The Nation* 259, 15 (November 7, 1994). Reprinted in *Art and Anger: Essays on Politics and the Imagination* (Albuquerque, NM: University of New Mexico Press, 1996).

authenticity and sense of urgency seldom found elsewhere. In fact, in the current wave of Latina novelists she strikes me as among the least theatrical and vociferous, the one listening most closely to the subtleties of her own artistic call. She stands apart stylistically, a psychological novelist who uses language skillfully to depict complex inner lives for her fictional creations.

Alvarez's journey from Spanish into English, from Santo Domingo to New York City, from Lucas to Juan Mejía, was the topic of *How the García Girls Lost Their Accents*, a set of loosely connected autobiographical stories published in book form in 1991, about well-off Dominican sisters exiled in *el norte*. The critical reception was mixed, though readers whole-heartedly embraced the book as charming and compassionate—a sort of minor echo of Laura Esquivel's *Like Water for Chocolate*—and it was welcomed with the type of jubilation often granted to works by suddenly emergent minorities. After all, Dominican literature, in Spanish or English, is hardly represented in bookstores and college courses in the United States. Indeed, not since the early twentieth-century larger-than-life scholar and essayist Pedro Henríquez Ureña delivered the Charles Eliot Norton lectures at Harvard University in 1940–1941, on the topic of literary currents in Hispanic America, had a writer from the Dominican Republic been the target of such admiration here.

In spite of Alvarez's fairly conservative, yet semi-experimental approach to literature, what makes her a peculiar, nontraditional Dominican writer is her divided identity. "I am a Dominican, hyphen, American," she once said. "As a fiction writer, I find that the most exciting things happen in the realm of that hyphen—the place where two worlds collide or blend together."

Alvarez's novelistic debut evidenced a writer whose control of her craft was sharp but less than complete. Some of the autonomous segments of *García Girls* were not knit together well, for example, leaving the reader holding several frustratingly loose ends. Now, three years later, such shortcomings have been largely erased, as her haunting second novel easily surpasses her earlier achievement. And while this vista of the political turmoil left behind by émigrés like the García girls still may not be proportional to her talents, it is extraordinary in that it exhibits quick, solid maturing as an artist. In spite of its title, *In the Time of the Butterflies* is not crowded with magic realist scenes à la Gabriel García Márquez and Isabel Allende. Instead, it's a fictional study of a tragic event in Dominican history, when, on November 25, 1960, three outspoken Mirabal sisters, active opponents of the dictatorship of Rafael Leónidas Trujillo, were found dead near their wrecked Jeep, at the bottom of a fifteen-foot cliff in the northern part of the country. Today the Mirabals are known throughout the Caribbean the The Butterflies—Las Mariposas. Alvarez uses her novel to explore their tragic odyssey and, metaphorically, to bring them back to life.

The novel's three hundred–plus pages are full of pathos and passion, with beautifully crafted anecdotes interstitched to create a patchwork quilt of memory and ideology. We see the sisters as teens, fighting with Papá, marrying, leading double lives, commenting on the Cuban Revolution, becoming rebels themselves, going on to bury husbands and sons. The organization is symmetrical: The book's major parts are laid out in four sections, one devoted to each of the three murdered sisters and one to the fourth sister, who escaped their fate. We have thus a quatrain of novellas, only one of which doesn't end in tragedy. Here's how Alvarez has Dedé, the surviving Mirabal sister, remark on the assassination:

> It seems that at first the Jeep was following the truck up the mountain. Then as the truck slowed for the grade, the Jeep passed and sped away, around some curves, out of sight. Then it seems that the truck came upon the ambush. A blue-and-white Austin had blocked part of the road; the Jeep had been forced to a stop; the women were being led away peaceably, so the truck driver said, *peaceably* to the car.

While the Mirabal incident might seem a bit obscure to American readers (most of Dominican history, perhaps even the U.S. invasion, does), it offers an amazing array of creative opportunities to reflect on the labyrinthine paths of the Hispanic psyche. Others in the Dominican Republic have used this historical episode as a springboard to reflect on freedom and ideology, among them Pedro Mir in his poem "Amén de Mariposas" and Ramón Alberto Ferreras in his book *Las Mirabal*. Alvarez takes a decidedly unique approach: She examines the martyrdom of these three Dominican women as a gender battlefield—three brave, subversive wives crushed by a phallocentric regime. In an openly misogynistic society, the Mirabals are initially dealt with by the government in a delicate, somewhat condescending fashion, which of course doesn't exclude the oppressive power from annihilating them in the end.

The official newspaper of the Trujillo regime, *El Caribe,* treated the deaths of Minerva, Patria, and María Teresa Mirabal and their driver, Rufino de la Cruz, all between twenty-five and thirty-seven years of age, as an accident. Not only did it report the incident without much explanation, it failed to mention the sisters' anti-Trujillo activities. Nor did it acknowledge that a fourth sister wasn't among the victims and had thus survived. Assuming her role as historian and marionetteer, Alvarez fills in the gaps. She didn't know the sisters personally, and she laments at the end of her volume that the reluctance of people in the Dominican Republic to speak out or open up to strangers, as well as the chaotic state of affairs in the nation's libraries and research centers, made it difficult for her to gather historical data. But her task was hardly biographical. "I wanted to immerse my readers in an epoch in the life of the Dominican Republic that I believe can only finally be understood by fiction, only finally be redeemed by the imagination," she writes. "A novel is not, after all, a historical document, but a way to travel through the human heart."

Alvarez writes, for instance, that Trujillo himself had a crush on Minerva, who responded publicly by slapping him in the face. She also analyzes the religious education María Teresa received and later metamorphosed into anti-authoritarian animosity. Much in the *Butterflies* novel resembles *How the García Girls Lost Their Accents*: Hispanic domesticity is at center stage, analyzed in light of the intricate partnerships and rivalries of the four sisters. The male chauvinism that dominates the Hispanic family is meant to mirror and complement Trujillo's own machismo, with home and country approached as micro- and macrocosms. The style is deliberately fragmentary and openly Faulknerian. Alvarez's pages made me think, time and again, of the Israeli writer A. B. Yehoshua: By intertwining disparate literary forms (journals, first-person accounts, correspondence, drawings, etc.) Alvarez allows each Mirabal to acquire her own voice. Pasted together, their voices provide a sense that Truth is a collective invention.

Unlike many Latino writers of her generation, Alvarez abandons the United States in theme and scenario to analyze the role of women under dictatorships in the Southern Hemisphere. Trujillo's presence is felt from afar, as an overwhelming shadow controlling and destroying human happiness—so overarching is the dictator, in fact, that it seems to me he becomes the central character. The Mirabal sisters fight *el líder* as both a real and a ghostlike figure. Their opposition is also an attack against phallocentrism as an accepted way of life in Hispanic societies. In this respect, *In the Time of Butterflies* ought to be equated with a number of Latin American works about dictators (known in Spanish as *novelas del dictador*), including Miguel Angel Asturias's *El Señor Presidente* and Augusto Roa Bastos's *I, the Supreme*. And it is a first-rate addition to the shelf of works by Latina literary artists who write about chauvinism, from Delmira Agustini to Rosario Ferré. In her Postscript, Alvarez writes:

During [Trujillo's] terrifying thirty-one-year regime, any hint of disagreement ultimately resulted in death for the dissenter and often for members of his or her family. Yet the Mirabals had risked their lives. I kept asking myself, What gave them that special courage? It was to understand that question that I began this story.

Fiction as an instrument to decodify a tyranny's hidden and manifest tentacles. Fiction as a tool of journalism and vice versa. Fiction as a device to reclaim a stolen aspect of history. Ironically, it is precisely at this level that Alvarez's volume is simultaneously invigorating and curiously disappointing. The author herself appears at the beginning of the plot: It is 1994 and, as an American woman with broken Spanish, she is eager to interview Dedé. Dedé offers much data about her sisters' journey, from their convent education to their first love affairs and subsequent marriages to high-profile activists in the fifties. Indeed, Dedé serves as the backbone to the entire story. But Alvarez leaves reaction to the Mirabals' assassination to a twenty-page epilogue, in which we find out about public outrage and the spectacular, media-oriented trial of their murderers, which took place a year after Trujillo was killed in 1961. Interleaving news clips, court testimony, interviews, and other paraphernalia throughout her narrative might have helped—anything to insert the Mirabals more firmly in the flux of Dominican memory.

Notwithstanding this structural handicap, *In the Time of the Butterflies* is enchanting, a novel only a female, English-speaking Hispanic could have written. By inserting herself in the cast as *la gringa norteamericana*, Alvarez links the old and the new. At a time when many Latino writers seem so easily satisfied exploring the ghetto, in fictional terms of drugs, crime, and videotape, Alvarez, a writer on a different kind of edge, calls attention to the Latin American foundations of Hispanic fiction in English and dares once again to turn the novel into a political artifact. The inside covers of her book are illustrated with typography listing women and men assassinated by Trujillo. Recalling the Vietnam Memorial in Washington, DC, the names seem endless, an homage to patriotic anonymity. Alvarez pays tribute to only three of these names, but the rest are also evoked in her lucid pages. Her novel is a wonderful examination of how it feels to be a survivor, how it feels to come from a society where justice and freedom are unwelcome and where the answer to the question "How are you?" often has to be, *Entre Lucas y Juan Mejía.*

# READING CÉSAR

*Once upon a time there were duels; nowadays there are clashes and pitched battles.*

—Michel de Montaigne, "On Cowardice"

"The rich have money—and the poor have time." Those were the words of César Chávez in 1991, two years before his death. Is it sheer fancy to suggest that this sentence alone summarizes the dominant concerns of his life? Chávez's life was defined by patience. Patience was his weapon against the grape owners and the Teamsters, against the abuse of the downcast. He had plenty of patience, much more than a normal person, and it was proven in his nonviolent marches, fasts, and petitions. "We don't have to win this year or next year or even the year after that," he told his followers. "We'll just keep plugging away, day after day. . . . We will never give up. We have nothing else to do with our lives except to continue in this nonviolent fight."

Of course, there is such a thing as too much patience. How long will it take for Chávez's message to penetrate the American psyche? He's been dead for almost a decade. His name and face adorn schools and public parks. He pops up in advertisements for Macintosh computers, along with John Lennon and the Dalai Lama—"Think Different"! But these ghostlike appearances are empty of all ideological significance, it's a tame Chávez, not the quixotic knight he was; a brand name, as disposable as any celebrity in Hollywood.

First published in *Transition* 82 (Fall 2000). Reprinted as Introduction to *Sal Si Puedes* by Peter Matthiessen (Berkeley: University of California Press, 2000).

My generation is too young to have witnessed Chávez's odyssey from obscurity to legend. My appreciation for his courage and forbearance came indirectly. I learned about him from books, documentaries, and schoolteachers. Every reference to him was cloaked in an aura of sanctity. But as with most saints, it was hard to figure out exactly what he had done on the road to beatitude. No doubt Chávez was the most important Hispanic-American political figure of the twentieth century. But for someone like me, born at the apex of his career, outside the United States, it was almost impossible to lift him from the junk box where icons are stored away and reinsert him into history. Somehow Chávez the man had become Chávez the statue: pigeons sat motionless on his nose and hands, his beautiful bronze skin corroded by the passing of time.

How can he be rescued from this eclipse? Do his words still have an echo? Have we lost the capacity to appreciate not just a fighter but a true duelist, a crusader capable of reevaluating our preconceptions of the world? What is meaningful about him today? Can his message still speak to us? Americans are obsessed with the radicalism of the 1960s, as epitomized by Malcolm X and the Black Panthers. This obsession is concurrent with a Latin boom, a sudden embrace of Latino music and culture north of the Río Grande. And yet most Americans couldn't care less about Chávez—especially Latinos. The new Hispanic pride is a profoundly middle-class artifact. It replaces radical politics with consumerism, the gun with the Gap, fasts with Taco Bell. Chávez's face on a billboard goes down easier than any of his injunctions about courage, resilience, commitment. Chávez is not alone: other Latino activists have been shelved as well, from Bernardo Vega and Jesús Colón to Dolores Huerta, Rudolfo "Corky" González, and Reies López Tijerina. Even Arthur Alfonso Schomburg, the black historian whose Puerto Rican identity was crucial to his work and life remains a forgotten oddity.

But none of these figures is more emblematic than Chávez. Rumors of a full-length biography surface and then disappear. Very few of his countless speeches have been transcribed, and his occasional writings remain scattered, lost in remote, often inaccessible corners of libraries. Why has no one published a *Portable César Chávez*? Are his politics still too dangerous? Or are they simply irrelevant?

Chávez came from a humble background. He was born in Yuma, Arizona, in 1927, and his family lived on a 160-acre farm not far from town. His grandfather was from Hacienda del Carmen, in Chihuahua, Mexico. He had a slavelike life under authoritarian landowners close to dictator Porfirio Diaz. He was rebellious. The fate of those workers unwilling to cooperate was the draft. But Papa Chayo ran away and crossed the border in El Paso, Texas, eventually moving to the North Gila Valley along the Colorado River. Chávez never quite spelled out his relationship with Mexico, but it's clear that it wasn't colored by nostalgia. Arizona was his home. His father was a businessman. The second of five children and his Dad's right hand, Chávez helped in the crops, chopped wood, and helped with the animals. As he recounted his childhood in the early 1970s, it was a life of hard work, under pressure from heavy taxes. The family was a close niche. But things turned for the worse when Chávez's father lost his holdings during the Depression.

Like many other families, the Chávezes eventually moved to California in search of better opportunities, only to find jobs picking cotton, grapes, and carrots, following the sun and the season from one migrant camp to another. Chávez never finished high school. Segregation was a fixture in the landscape. He once recalled:

> We went this one time to a diner. There was a sign on the door "White Trade Only" but we went anyway. We had heard that they had these big hamburgers, and we wanted one. There was a blond, blue-eyed girl behind the counter, a beauty. She asked what we wanted—real though you know?—and when we ordered a hamburger, she said, "We don't sell to Mexicans," and she laughed when she said it. She enjoyed doing that, laughing at us. We went out, but I was real mad. Enraged. It had to do with my manhood.

The education he got was unstable because of the itinerant life that field labor carried with it. He once said he attended some sixty-five elementary schools, some "for a day, a week, or a few months." At the age of nineteen, he joined the Agricultural Workers' Union. The Union existed in name only—the organizing drive to create it was unsuccessful—but the struggle gave him a taste of the challenges ahead. After a couple of years in the Navy during World War II, Chávez returned to California, where he married Helen, whom he met in Delano—her parents had come from Mexico and one of them had fought in the revolution of 1910—and with whom he eventually had eight children. He returned to the migrant's life but also found the time to read about historical figures. It was around 1952 that he met and was inspired by the work of organizer Fred Ross, a leader of the Community Services Organization, which was supported by the Chicago-based Saul Alinsky. Ross and Alinsky channeled important ideas and concepts to Chávez, from which he developed his own philosophy of struggle. Many had already tried to organize the Mexican migrant workers to improve their miserable working conditions. But it took Chávez's charisma—*su simpatía*—to move mountains. By the time he was 33, he was organizing families in the grape fields and persuading growers to increase wages. His strategy was simple: straight talk and honesty. If he was to become a spokesman for the workers, he would also be a model for them. And role models require commitment and sacrifice.

The National Farm Workers Union was created in 1962, with Chávez as its president. It was the year of the Cuban Missile Crisis, and U.S.–Latin American relations were in peril. The organization grew quickly and changed its name a few times in the 1960s before christening itself the United Farm Workers. Chávez solidified the organization's Chicano base, opened up membership to the Filipino community, and forged links with other like-minded groups, most notably the small community of black farm workers. By the mid-sixties, he had become a beloved folk hero to the poor and to the boisterous student movement, and public enemy number one to conservative California businessmen and politicians—especially Governor Ronald Reagan. Unlike many other leaders of the civil rights era, Chávez combined activism with environmentalism—a combination that would make him a darling of the contemporary environmentalist movement, if only they cared. His struggle to improve labor conditions was also a fight against pesticides.

It has often been said that Chávez wasn't a rhetorician: unlike Martin Luther King Jr. or Julian Bond, Chávez had little talent for highbrow oratory. Still, he had an astonishing ability to redefine audiences, to make them act in a different way. He had an inspired message, a clear vision of his place in history, and faithful listeners to whom he gave a sense of shared history. With the listeners he embarked on a crusade idealistic yet practical that attempted to redefine labor relations in America. He lived life spontaneously, and he responded to every occasion with speeches and responses that were neither preconceived nor sophisticated. Yet he was eloquent, precisely because his improvisational, pragmatic mind always found what was needed. "[You] are looking for a miracle, a leader who will do everything for us," he once said. "It doesn't happen. People have to do the work." Elsewhere, he said, "Nothing changes until the individual changes." And indeed, Chávez was an astonishing teacher, a true role model of the kind that comes along only once in a generation.

Chávez's strategic approach to leadership was symbolized by his confrontation with the Teamsters. The Teamsters and the UFW had forged an uneasy peace: in 1970, they signed a pact that gave Chávez jurisdiction over the fields, while the teamsters had control over the packing sheds. But in 1973, when Chávez was at the height of his powers, the liaison collapsed: the teamsters signed a contract with growers for lower wages in the field. It was a major blow to the Chicano leader; his support fell precipitously, from some fifty thousand followers to fewer than fifteen thousand. Suddenly, Chávez's simple, honest speeches seemed empty. There was talk of financial mismanagement; conventional wisdom held that the UFW was finished. Chávez himself was losing hope—he referred to those years as "the worst of our times." But he was nothing if not determined. The smaller UFW continued to march, and the grape boycott began to make an impact. Within a few years, Jerry Brown was the progressive governor of California, and Chávez was again a hero.

Chávez's patient heroism struck a chord in America, a nation that loves underdogs. He once received a telegram from Martin Luther King Jr.: "As brothers in the fight for equality," it read in part, "I extend the hands of fellowship and good will and wish continuing success to your and your members. . . . We are together with you in spirit and in determination that our dreams for a better tomorrow will be realized." But Chávez's heroism did not win him much of a following in Mexico, where militancy of any sort makes the government nervous. Of course, Mexicans love revolutionaries, and there were those among the left-wing intelligentsia who idolized Chávez. They saw him as a guerrilla leader on the order of Emiliano Zapata, a man of the people, a prophet—North America's Mahatma Gandhi. But most Mexicans—especially those in the middle and upper classes—never thought much about Chávez; the UFW was simply irrelevant, a footnote in the history books. No attempt was made to reclaim him as a Mexican. Chávez was a leader of the Chicano movement of the 1960s, the first sustained bout of Hispanic activism in American history, but Mexicans have never really identified with Chicanos. Chicanos are traitors; they are the Mexicans who left and never looked back, the ones that put themselves, their ambitions, before everyone else. (This attitude toward Chicanos is hypocritical—Mexico's economy depends heavily on its emigrants. Where would the country be without that endless flow of precious U.S. dollars?)

Why didn't we embrace him? It wasn't just apathy; the rise of Chávez on the world stage coincided with the rise of the Mexican counterculture—and the government's fumbling yet brutal attempts to subdue it. In 1968 thousands of students massacred in Tlatelolco Square. The American civil rights movements, black *and* brown, received an icy reception from official Mexico. As for the Mexican people, our attention was focused locally, on the events that were tearing our own country apart.

It was only in my early twenties, after I came to the United States, that I began to understand Chávez's urge to change the world. In streets and public schools along the Southwest, his name was ubiquitous—a legend, a myth. I wanted to get to know him, to recognize the scope and nature of his revolution. I read everything about him I could find. Sometimes, I saw myself in the pages, and sometimes I found myself overwhelmed by a sense of detachment. An outsider looking in, a north-bound Spanish-speaking Caucasian. Could I see myself reflected in Chávez's eyes? Or was he an icon for another Mexico, another me? Why hadn't I learned more about him in school?

I was glad to find that the story of Chávez and La Causa, as his movement became known, had been chronicled dozens of times, by any number of interpreters. But many of these books felt disjoined, even apathetic. Several authors scrutinized the Chicano leader with academic tools that turned him into an artifact. Then there was John Gregory Dunne's *Delano: The Story of the California Grape Strike*, a highly informed if somewhat detached portrait; Jacques E. Levy's pastiche of memories and anecdotes, *César Chávez: Autobiography of La Causa*; and Richard B. Taylor's mesmerizing *Chávez and the Farm Workers*. But the book that brought Chávez home to me, the one that allowed me to share his dreams, was Peter Matthiessen's *Sal Si Puedes*—an honest, lucid picture of the internal and external upheaval that marked the Chicano leader in his most influential years. In later accounts of La Causa, Matthiessen's journalistic portrait is held in high esteem—panoramic yet finely detailed, knowing, and elegant. Nat Hentoff said the book offered a view of a battlefield where the fight is "not only for the agricultural workers but for the redemption of [the whole] country."

I recently reread *Sal Si Puedes* and felt a sense of exhilaration. The book is a kind of aleph that allows the Chicano movement to come alive again, and it gives Chávez's message a much-needed urgency. Somewhere in its early pages Matthiessen admits that he knew he would be impressed by Chávez, but he didn't foresee how startling their encounter would prove to be. After a few weeks in his company, Matthiessen realized the organizer was also organizing him. The author has the same feelings the reader does: first admiration, then awe.

It was the summer of 1968 when Matthiessen first visited Chávez. They were the same age: forty-one. Matthiessen lived in New York City, and he was introduced to Chávez by a common friend, Ann Israel, who had been helping to organize East Coast farm workers. At one point, Israel asked Matthiessen to edit copy for an advertisement about pesticides—not only what they did to crops, but also what they did to the people who worked in the fields. The ad was for the *New York Times*, and Israel wanted to make sure the English was perfect; she was very pleased with Matthiessen when she saw his draft. They struck up a friendship, and one day, she mentioned César Chávez. Matthiessen said he was a great admirer, so Israel took him to Delano, California, where Matthiessen met the Chicano leader. Chávez's grace and intelligence were seductive. It turned out that both men had been in the army around the same time. They shared many passions, including boxing; they both favored Sugar Ray Leonard. Matthiessen would later write a description of Chávez that has become a landmark:

> The man who has threatened California has an Indian's bow nose and lank black hair, with sad eyes and an open smile that is shy and friendly; at moments he is beautiful, like a dark seraph. He is five feet six inches tall, and, since his twenty-five-day fast the previous winter, has weighed no more than one hundred and fifty pounds. Yet the word "slight" does not properly describe him. There is an effect of being centered in himself so that no energy is wasted, an effect of density; at the same time, he walks as lightly as a fox. One feels immediately that this man does not stumble, and that to get where he is going he will walk all day.

Upon his return to New York, Matthiessen got in touch with William Shawn, the editor at the *New Yorker*, and suggested a profile on Chávez. Shawn had sponsored Matthiessen's earlier trips to South America and Alaska; he was receptive to the idea. Matthiessen returned to California, this time to Sal Si Puedes, the San José barrio where Chávez lived and where his career as a union organizer took off. The result was a two-part article, published on June 21 and 28, 1969. It was one of the first pieces on social justice ever to appear in the *New Yorker*, and one of the first articles in a national magazine about César Chávez and the Farm Workers' movement. When Matthiessen gave his *New Yorker* fee to the UFW, Chávez was deeply grateful.

I felt inspired when I first read Matthiessen. For some years I had been infatuated with the California counterculture of the 1960s—the hippie movement of the Haight Ashbury, Carlos Castañeda's fascination with *peyote* and his quest for Don Juan Matos, the music of the Beach Boys. Through *Sal Si Puedes* I discovered the seething political underground, the world in which César Chávez came into his own. It was a revelation to me: California was not all about alternative states of mind but, more emphatically, about courageous political alternatives and attempts to redefine the social texture, about racial and class struggle. From there, I was able to trace other radical figures in the Chicano community, such as Oscar "Zeta" Acosta, who appears as a three-hundred-pound Samoan in Hunter S. Thompson's *Fear and Loathing in Las Vegas.* Of course, there is a huge gap between Chávez and Zeta. It may even be sacrilegious to invoke the two in unison. Physically and mentally unstable, Zeta was a lawyer and activist, the author of *The Autobiography of a Brown Buffalo* and *The Revolt of the Cockroach People,* a brilliant outlaw, a *forajido* never quite ready to put his cards on the table. He might have done more harm than good to the Chicano movement. Chávez, to whom he paid a personal visit, was a full-fledged revolutionary, the true fountainhead of the Chicano movement.

For César Chávez, patience and sacrifice are siblings. He pairs them in a way that only American prophets can, mixing utopian vision with an enviable sense of practicality. The essayist Richard Rodriguez once described Chávez as "wielding a spiritual authority." It is that spirituality—his use of prayer in marches, the realization that the power of his followers' faith is stronger than anything else—that is so inspiring. When his betrayal by the Teamsters brought him low, Catholics around the country rallied for Chávez; church leaders supported him. What did they see in Chávez? A Christ figure, perhaps; a modest man of overpowering charisma; a man unafraid to speak the truth. In 1974 a reporter for the Christian Century wrote that she was "puzzled at the power of such an uncompromising person to command so much loyalty from so many." The entire quest for social justice and commitment, for patience and honesty, cannot but be seen in these terms. Chávez came from a devout Catholic background and he often invoked Christ in his speeches. "I can't ask people to sacrifice if I don't sacrifice myself," he said. Or, "Fighting for social justice is one of the profoundest ways in which man can say yes to man's dignity, and that really means sacrifice. There is no way on this earth in which you can say yes to man's dignity and know that you're going to be spared some sacrifice."

That Chávez allowed a perfect stranger like Peter Matthiessen to enter his life for a period of almost three years—making room at his own dinner table, bringing him along to union meetings, introducing him to friends—is proof of his generosity. But there was also self-interest: Chávez saw an opportunity to compound his notoriety and consolidate his power. Matthiessen did not disappoint. He portrays Chávez critically but responsibly; the leader is seen as enterprising, the owner of an unadultered vitality, capable of minor lapses but overall a prophet ahead of his time.

More than thirty years later, *Sal Si Puedes* is less reportage than living history; a whole era comes alive in its pages: Black Power, backlash, the antiwar movement, the browning of the labor movement, the greening of the browns. Taken with Joan Didion's *The White Album*, it's an indispensable guide to the 1960s, when America was changed forever. The 1900s were difficult for Chávez. He had grown weary and depressed. The media alternately ignored him and attacked him. He still lived in the Gila River Valley. The grape strike and the confrontation with the Teamsters were buried deep in the past. People in general had grown impatient with activism. His home was with the migrant workers, to whom he had devoted his life. But the heyday of the labor movement was over, overwhelmed by the conservative avalanche that brought Reagan and Bush to power. Scholars such as John C. Hammerback and Richard J. Jensen define that last period as "the unfinished last boycott." The cultural climate was different. Chávez, like a chameleon, ceased to be a leader speaking to his constituency and assumed the role of lecturer. In speeches given in the college circuit, he emphasized the power of teaching and amplified his message so as to encompass not only Chicanos in the Southwest but people from all racial backgrounds anywhere in the country. In doing so, though, he watered down the message. "How could we progress as a people," he claimed in a 1984 speech, "even if we lived in the cities, while farm workers—men and women of colors—were condemned to a life without pride?"

From Chicano to *men and women of color*, the politics of language was actually more treacherous. A growing Latino middle class—what historian Rudolfo Acuña, in his book *Occupied America*, defined as "the brokers"—embraced ambivalence as its worldview. It got closer to Spanglish and began to see itself as the owner of a hyphenated identity, a life in between. The shift was perceived as a ticket toward assimilation. This middle class, eager to cross over, started to be courted by savvy politicians and by a merchandise-oriented society. It was clear that the mainstream was ready to open its arms only if Chicanos were ready to define themselves elastically enough so as to become "Hispanics," the rubric that predeceases "Latinos," large enough to also encompass those hailing from Puerto Rico, Cuba, Ecuador, and El Salvador, for example.

But as time went by this polycephalic minority ceased to be acquainted with César Chávez. It no longer recognized the leader's struggles as its own. One comes to America dreaming of a better world, it was announced loud and clear, and in the process, one learns to consume and be consumed. I once heard a friend of Chávez say that he'd had "the fortunate misfortune" to have avoided martyrdom. Unlike Martin Luther King Jr. or Malcolm X, he had outlived himself, outlived his message. His exuberance and self-confidence were replaced by a strange silence. Rumors from within the U.F.W. described him as sectarian. Those that had not stayed and fought were received with indifference; Matthiessen felt some of that reticence when he told Chávez that he was thinking of writing a sequel to *Sal Si Puedes*. Chávez's response was ambiguous, even reluctant. The effort went nowhere. Perhaps we should feel fortunate that it didn't, for the best of Chávez had already been recorded.

Survival, sacrifice. When Chávez died in 1993, thousands gathered at his funeral. It was a clear sign of how beloved a figure he had been, how significant his life had been. President Bill Clinton spoke of him as "an authentic hero to millions of people throughout the world," and described him as "an inspiring fighter." And Jerry Brown called him a visionary who sought "a more cooperative society." In the media Chávez was portrayed as "a national metaphor for justice, humanity, equality, and freedom." Matthiessen himself wrote an obituary for the *New Yorker*. "A man so unswayed by money," he wrote, "a man who (despite many death threats) refused to let his bodyguards go armed, and who offered his entire life to the service of others, [is] not to be judged by the same standards of some self-serving labor leader or politician. . . . Anger was a part of Chávez, and so was a transparent love for humankind."

It is left to us, though, his successors, those who never had the privilege to meet him, the millions of Latinos capable of realizing that middle-class life ought not be a form of blindness, to ponder his legacy. Yes, the rise of consumerism and the disenfranchisement of reformism might have pushed Chávez to the fringes. At first sight his ethos in the field might have little to say to our angst, the one that colors the way we zigzag ourselves through Hispanic history in the United States. But it is an outright mistake to let our class differences obliterate the bridges between us. It is true that toward the end of his sixty-five-year-long career, César Chávez and America parted ways. Yet it is the leader valiant enough to redefine his roots, devoted to make America more pliant, that we most reread and thereafter reclaim, a dreamer that proved that wealth and a formal education aren't everything, that humankind is not about getting ahead of everyone else but getting ahead together. Not Chávez the myth but Chávez the ordinary man—neither the name nor the face but the message, "Let's enable common people to do uncommon things"—awaits attention. In the attempt to agglutinate us all under a single rubric, his Chicano self must be opened up to embrace all Americans, particularly all of those with diverse Hispanic backgrounds. Perhaps it was diversity that killed him. But we can reassess his message, for plurality is inspiring only when the whole doesn't devour the parts. The fact that Chávez was Mexican is significant but not confining; his Mexicanness, he showed us—and now I see—is a lesson in universality.

Toward the end of *Sal Si Puedes*, Matthiessen records a few lines told to him by a black migrant farm worker: "But you know what I— what I really think? You know what I really think? I really think that one day the world will be great. I really believe the world gonna be great one day." This was Chávez's own view as well: a better world, built one step at a time, without exclusionary laws, one harmonious enough for every person. He believed democracy to be the best political system of government, a view he learned to appreciate not from his ancestral Mexico but from and in the United States. He was a great advocate of it, even though his foes at times portrayed him as anti-democratic. What he learned about democracy he learned in the hard way—through punches and clashes. But he was patient. In order for democracy to work, Chávez liked to say, "People must want it to." And he added, "To make it work [for us all], we have to work at it full time."

# AUTOBIOGRAPHICAL ESSAY

*My heart is in the East and I am at the edge of the West. Then how can I taste what I eat, how can I enjoy it? How can I fulfill my vows and pledges while Zion is in the domain of Edom, and I am in the bonds of Arabia?*

—Judah Halevi

*Work of good prose has three steps: a musical stage when it is composed, an architectonic one when it is built, and a textile one when it is woven.*

—Walter Benjamin

I was born in Mexico City, April 7, 1961, on a cloudy day without major historical events. I am a descendant of Jews from Russia and Poland, businessmen and rabbis, who arrived by sheer chance in Veracruz, on the Atlantic coast next to the Yucatán peninsula. I am a sum of parts and thus lack purity of blood (what proud Renaissance Iberians called *la pureza de sangre*): white Caucasian with a Mediterranean twist, much like the Enlightenment philosopher Moses Mendelssohn and only marginally like the Aztec poet Ollin Yollistli. My idols, not surprisingly, are Spinoza and Kafka, two exiles in their own land who chose universal languages (Portuguese and Hebrew to Latin, Czech to German) in order to elevate them-

First published in *Massachusetts Review*, XXXIV, 4 (Winter 1993–94). Reprinted in *The One-Handed Pianist and Other Stories* (Albuquerque, NM: University of New Mexico Press, 1996).

selves to a higher order, and who, relentlessly, investigated their own spirituality beyond the reach of orthodox religion and routine. Ralph Waldo Emerson, in *Essays: Second Series* (1844), says that the reason we feel one man's presence and not another's is as simple as gravity. I have traveled from Spanish into Yiddish, Hebrew, and English; from my native home south of the Rio Grande far and away—to Europe, the Middle East, the United States, the Bahamas, and South America—always in search of the ultimate clue to the mysteries of my divided identity. What I found is doubt.

I grew up in an intellectually sophisticated middle class, in a secure, self-imposed Jewish ghetto (a treasure island) where gentiles hardly existed. Money, and comfort, books, theater, and art. Since early on I was sent to Yiddish day school, Colegio Israelita de México in Colonia Navarete, where the heroes were Sholom Aleichem and Theodor Herzl, while people like José Joaquín Fernández de Lizardi, Agustín Yañez, Juan Rulfo, and Octavio Paz were almost unknown; that is, we lived in an oasis completely uninvolved with things Mexican. In fact, when it came to knowledge of the outside world, students were far better off talking about U.S. products (Hollywood, TV, junk food, technology) than about matters native—an artificial capsule, our ghetto, much like the magical sphere imagined by Blaise Pascal: its diameter everywhere and its center nowhere.

Mother tongue. The expression crashed into my mind at age twenty, perhaps a bit later. The father tongue, I assumed, was the adopted alternative and illegitimate language (Henry James preferred the term "wife tongue"), whereas the mother tongue is genuine and authentic—a uterus: the original source. I was educated in (into) four idioms: Spanish, Yiddish, Hebrew, and English. Spanish was the public venue; Hebrew was a channel toward Zionism and not toward the sacredness of the synagogue; Yiddish symbolized the Holocaust and past struggles of the Eastern European labor movement; and English was the entrance door to redemption: the United States. Abba Eban said it better: Jews are like everybody else except a little bit more. A polyglot, of course, has as many loyalties as homes. Spanish is my right eye, English my left; Yiddish my background and Hebrew my conscience. Or better, each of the four represents a different set of spectacles (nearsighted, bifocal, light-reading, etc.) through which the universe is seen.

## THE ABUNDANCE OF SELF

This multifarious (is there such a word?) upbringing often brought me difficulties. Around the neighborhood, I was always *el güerito* and *el ruso*. Annoyingly, my complete name is Ilan Stavchansky

Slomianski; nobody, except for Yiddish teachers, knew how to pronounce it. (I get mail addressed to Ivan Starlominsky, Isvan Estafchansky, and Allen Stevens.) After graduating from high school, most of my friends, members of richer families, were sent abroad, to the U.S. or Israel, to study. Those that remained, including me, were forced to go to college at home to face Mexico tête-à-tête. The shock was tremendous. Suddenly, I (we) recognized the artificiality of our oasis. What to do? I, for one, rejected my background; I felt Judaism made me a pariah. I wanted to be an authentic Mexican and thus foolishly joined the Communist cause but the result wasn't pleasing. Among the *camaradas*, I was also "the blondy" and "the Jew." No hope, no escape. So I decided to investigate my ethnic and religious past obsessively and made it my duty to really understand guys like Maimonides, Arthur Koestler, Mendelssohn, Judah Halevi, Hasdai Crescas, Spinoza, Walter Benjamin, Gershom Scholem, Martin Buber, Franz Rosenzweig, Abraham Joshua Heschel. It helped, at least temporarily—nothing lasts forever.

Years later, while teaching medieval philosophy at Universidad Iberoamericana, a Jesuit college in downtown Mexico City, during the 1982 Lebanon invasion, a group of Palestinian sympathizers threw rotten tomatoes at me and my students (99 percent gentiles). Eager to manifest their anger, and protest, they had to find an easy target and I was the closest link to Israel around. The whole thing reminded me of a scene that took place at age fourteen, while sitting in Yiddish class at Colegio Israelita. Mr. Lockler, the teacher, was reading from I. J. Singer's *The Family Carnovsky*—a story of three generations in a German-Jewish family enchanted with the nineteenth-century Enlightenment, slowly but surely becoming assimilated into German society until the tragic rise of Nazism brought unthinkable consequences. The monotonous rhythm of the recitations was boring and nobody was paying much attention. Suddenly, a segment of the story truly captivated me: the moment when Jegor, eldest son of Dr. David Carnovsky's mixed marriage to Teresa Holbeck, is ridiculed in class by Professor Kirchenmeier, a newly appointed principal at the Goethe Gymnasium in Berlin. Singer describes the event meticulously. Nazism is on the rise: The aristocracy, and more specifically the Jews, are anxious to know the overall outcome of the violent acts taking place daily on the city street. Racial theories are being discussed and Aryans glorified. Feverishly anti-Jewish, Kirchenmeier, while delivering a lecture, calls Jegor to the front to use him as a guinea pig in illustrating his theories. With a compass and calipers, he measures the length and width of the boy's skull, writing the figures on the board. He then measures the distance from ear to ear, from the

top of the head to the chin, and the length of the nose. A packed auditorium is silently watching. Jegor is then asked to undress. He is terrified and hesitates, of course; he is ashamed and feels conspicuous
because of his circumcision. Eventually other students, persuaded by
Kirchenmeier, help undress the Jew, and the teacher proceeds to
show in the "inferior" Jewish strain the marks of the rib structure. He
finishes by calling attention to Jegor's genitals whose premature
development shows "the degenerate sexuality of the Semitic race."

Astonishment. What troubled me most was Jegor's inaction. I
suppose it was natural to be petrified in such a situation, but I
refused to justify his immobility. So I interrupted Mr. Lockler to ask
why didn't the boy escape. A deadly silence invaded the classroom.
It was clear I had disturbed the other students' sleep and the
teacher's rhythm. "Because he couldn't, he simply couldn't," was the
answer I got. "Because that's the way lives are written." I don't know
or care what happened next. As years went by I came to understand
that concept, the almighty Author of Authors, as intriguing, and the
scene in Yiddish class as an allegory of myself and Mexican Jews as
an easy and palatable target of animosity. At the Jesuit college almost
a decade later, I was the marionette-holder's Jegor Carnovsky—God's
joy and toy: the Jew.

## KALEIDOSCOPE

Bizarre combination—Mexican Jews: some 60,000 frontier dwellers
and hyphen people like Dr. Jekyll and Mr. Hyde, a sum of sums of
parts, a multiplicity of multiplicities. Although settlers from Germany
began to arrive in "Aztec Country" around 1830, the very first synagogue was not built in the nation's capital until some fifty-five years
later. From then on, waves of Jewish immigrants came from Russia
and Central and Eastern Europe—Ashkenazim whose goal was to
make it big in New York (the Golden Land), but since an immigration
quota was imposed in the United States in 1924, a little detour places
them in Cuba, Puerto Rico, or the Gulf of Mexico (the Rotten Land).
Most were Yiddish-speaking Bundists: hardworking peasants, businessmen, and teachers, nonreligious and entrepreneurial, escaping
Church-sponsored pogroms and government persecution whose primary dream was never Palestine. Hardly anything physical or ideological differentiated them from the relatives that did make it north, to
Chicago, Detroit, Pittsburgh, and the Lower East Side—except, of
course, the fact that they, disoriented immigrants, couldn't settle
where they pleased. And this sense of displacement colored our future.

Migration and its discontents: I have often imagined the Culture
Shock, surely not too drastic, my forefathers experienced at their

arrival: from *mujik* to *campesino*, similar types in a different milieu. Mexico was packed with colonial monasteries where fanatical nuns prayed day and night. Around 1910 Emiliano Zapata and Pancho Villa were making their Socialist Revolution, and an anti-Church feeling (known in Mexico as La Cristiada and masterfully examined in Graham Greene's *The Power and the Glory*) was rampant. Aztecs, the legend claims, once sacrificed daughters to their idols in sky-high pyramids, and perhaps were cannibals. Undoubtedly this was to be a transitory stop, it had to. It was humid, and at least in the nation's capital, nature remained an eternal autumn. I must confess never to have learned to love Mexico. I was taught to retain a sense of foreignness—as a tourist without a home. The best literature I know about Mexico is by Europeans and U.S. writers: Italo Calvino, André Breton, Jack Kerouac, Greene, Joseph Brodsky, Antonin Artaud, Katherine Anne Porter, Malcolm Lowry, Harriet Doerr . . . I only love my country when I am far away. Elsewhere—that's where I belong: the vast diaspora. Nowhere and everywhere. (Am I a name dropper? Me, whose name no one can pronounce?)

## OUT OF THE BASEMENT

When the Mexican edition of *Talia in Heaven* (1989) came out, my publisher, Fernando Valdés, at a reception, talked about the merits of this, my first (and so far only) novel. He applauded this and that ingredient, spoke highly of the innovative style, and congratulated the author for his precocious artistic maturity. Memory has deleted most of his comments. I no longer remember what he liked and why. The only sentence that still sticks in my mind, the one capable of overcoming the passing of time, came at the end of his speech, when he said: "For many centuries, Latin America has had Jews living in the basement, great writers creating out of the shadow. And Ilan Stavans is the one I kept hidden until now." A frightening metaphor.

In the past five hundred years, Jews in the Hispanic world have been forced to convert to Christianity or somehow to mask or feel ashamed of their ancestral faith. Their intellectual contribution, notwithstanding, has been enormous. Spanish letters cannot be understood without Fray Luis de León, Arcipreste de Hita, and Ludovicus Vives, without Fernando de Roja's *La Celestina* and the anti-Semitic poetry of Francisco de Quevedo, author of the infamous sonnet "A man stuck to a nose" (*Erase un hombre a una nariz pegado, érase una nariz superlativa, érase una alquitara medio viva, érase un peje espada mal barbado . . .*). In the Americas, a safe haven for refugees from the Inquisition and later on for Eastern Europeans running away from the Nazis, Jewish writers have been active since 1910, when Alberto

Gerchunoff, a Russian immigrant, published in Spanish his collection of interrelated vignettes, *The Jewish Gauchos of the Pampas*, to commemorate Argentina's independence. He switched from one language to another to seek individual freedom, to validate his democratic spirit, to embrace a dream of plurality and progress: Yiddish, the tongue of Mendel Mokher Sforim and Sholem Aleichem, was left behind; Spanish, Cervantes's vehicle of communication—Gerchunoff was an admirer of *Don Quixote*—became the new tool, the channel to entertain, educate, and redeem the masses. Like Spinoza, Kafka, Nabokov, and Joseph Brodsky, he was the ultimate translator: a bridge between idiosyncrasies. The abyss and the bridge. Many decades later, some fifty astonishing writers from Buenos Aires and Mexico to Lima and Guatemala, including Moacyr Scliar, Clarice Lispector, and Mario Szichman, continue to carry on Gerchunoff's torch, but the world knows little about them. The narrative boom that catapulted Gabriel García Márquez, Carlos Fuentes, and others from south of the Rio Grande to international stardom in the sixties managed to sell a monolithic, suffocatingly uniform image of the entire continent as a Banana Republic crowded with clairvoyant prostitutes and forgotten generals, never a multicultural society. To such a degree were ethnic voices left in the margin that readers today know much more about Brazilians and Argentines thanks to Borges's short stories "Emma Zunz" and "El milagro secreto" ("The Secret Miracle") and Vargas Llosa's novel *The Storyteller,* than to anything written by Gerchunoff and his followers. Sadly and in spite of his anti-Semitic tone, my Mexican publisher was right: In the baroque architecture of Latin American letters, Jews inhabit the basement. And yet, *la pureza de sangre* in the Hispanic world is but an abstraction: native Indians, Jews, Arabs, Africans, Christians . . . the collective identity is always in need of a hyphen. In spite of the "official" image stubbornly promoted by governments from time immemorial, Octavio Paz and Julio Cortázar have convincingly used the salamander, the *axólotl,* as a symbol to describe Latin America's popular soul, always ambiguous and in mutation.

## AMERICA, AMERICA

I honestly never imagined I could one day pick up my suitcases to leave home once and for all. And yet, at twenty-five I moved to New York; I was awarded a scholarship to study for a master's at the Jewish Theological Seminary and, afterwards, perhaps a doctorate at Columbia University or elsewhere. I fled Mexico (and Spanish) mainly because as a secular Jew—what Freud would have called "a psychological Jew"—I felt marginalized, a stereotype. (Little did I know!) A true chameleon, a bit parochial and nearsighted, a nonconformist with big dreams and few possibilities. Like my globe-trotting Hebraic ancestors, I had been raised to build an ivory tower, an individual ghetto. By choosing to leave, I turned my past into remembrance: I left the basement and ceased to be a pariah. *Talia in Heaven* exemplifies that existential dilemma: Its message simultaneously encourages Jews to integrate and openly invites them to escape; it alternates between life and memory. Paraphrasing Lionel Trilling, its cast of characters, victims of an obsessive God (much like the Bible's) who enjoys ridiculing them, are at the bloody crossroad where politics, theology, and literature meet. To be or not to be. The moment I crossed the border, I became somebody else: a new person. In *Chromos: A Parody of Truth,* Felipe Alfau says: "The moment one learns English, complications set in. Try as one may, one cannot elude this conclusion, one must inevitably come back to it." While hoping to master the English language during sleepless nights, I understood James Baldwin, who, already exiled in Paris and quoting Henry James, claimed it is a complex fate to be an American. "America's history," the black author of *Nobody Knows My Name* wrote, "her aspirations, her peculiar triumphs, her even more peculiar defeats, and her position in the world—yesterday and today—are all so profoundly and stubbornly unique that the very word 'America' remains a new, almost completely undefined, and extremely controversial proper noun. No one in the world seems to know exactly what it describes." To be honest, the rise of multiculturalism, which perceives the melting pots, a soup of diverse and at times incompatible backgrounds, has made the word "America" even more troublesome, more evasive and abstract. Is America a compact whole, a unit? Is it a sum of ethnic groups unified by a single language and a handful of patriotic symbols? Is it a Quixotic dream where total assimilation is impossible, where multiculturalism is to lead to disintegration? And Baldwin's statement acquires a totally different connotation when one goes one step beyond, realizing that "America" is not only a nation (a state of mind) but also a vast continent. From Alaska to the Argentine pampa, from Rio de Janeiro to East Los Angeles, the geography Christopher Columbus mistakenly encountered in 1492 and Amerigo Vespucci baptized a few years later is also a linguistic and cultural addition: America the nation and America the continent. America, America: I wanted to find a room of my own in the two; or two rooms, perhaps?

## ON BEING A WHITE HISPANIC AND MORE

Once settled, I suddenly began to be perceived as Hispanic (i.e., Latino)—an identity totally alien to me before. (My knowledge of spoken Latin is minimal.) To make matters worse, my name (once again?), accent, and skin color were exceptions to what gringos had as the "Hispanic prototype." In other words, in Mexico I was perceived as Jewish; and now across the border, I was Mexican. Funny, isn't it? (In fact, according to official papers I qualify as a white Hispanic, an unpleasant term if there was ever one.) Once again, an impostor, an echo. (An impostor, says Ambrose Bierce in *The Devil's Dictionary*, is a rival aspirant to public honors.)

Themselves, myself: Hispanics in the United States—white, black, yellow, green, blue, red . . . twice Americans, once in spite of themselves. They have been in the territories north of the Rio Grande even before the Pilgrims of the *Mayflower*; and with the Guadalupe Hidalgo Treaty signed in 1848, in which Generalísimo Antonio López de Santa Ana gave away and subesequently sold half of Mexico to the White House (why only half?), many of them unexpectedly, even unwillingly, became a part of an Anglo-Saxon, English-speaking reality. Today after decades of neglect and silence, decades of anonymity and ignorance, Latinos are finally receiving the attention they deserve. The second fastest-growing ethnic group after the Asians, their diversity of roots—Caribbean, Mexican, Central and South American, Iberian, and so on—makes them a difficult collectivity to describe. Are the Cuban migrations from Holguín, Matanzas, and Havana similar in their idiosyncratic attitude to those of Managua, San Salvador, and Santo Domingo? Is the Spanish they speak their true lingua franca, the only unifying factor? Is their immigrant experience in any way different from that of previous minorities—Irish, Italian, Jewish, what have you? How do they understand and assimilate the complexities of what it means to be American? And where do I, a white Hispanic, fit in?

Nowhere and everywhere. In 1985 I was assigned by a Spanish magazine to interview Isaac Goldemberg, a famous Jewish-Peruvian novelist who wrote *The Fragmented Life of Don Jacobo Lerner.* When we met at the Hungarian Pastry Shop at Amsterdam Avenue and 110th Street, he told me, among many things, he had been living in New York for over two decades without mastering the English language because he didn't want his Spanish to suffer and ultimately evaporate. Borges says in his short story "The Life of Tadeo Isidoro Cruz (1829–1874)": "Any life, no matter how long or complex it may be, is made up essentially of a single moment—the moment in which a man finds out, once and for all, who he is." That summer day I understood my linguistic future lay in the opposite direction from Goldemberg's: I would perfect my English and thus become a New York Jew, an intellectual animal in the proud tradition celebrated by Alfred Kazin. And I did. In just a single moment I understood who I could be.

## THE DOUBLE

To write is to make sense of conditions in and around. Didn't some-body already say this? Jean Genet, John Updike? I am a copy, an instant replay, a shadow, an impostor. Everything is an echo. To live is to plagiarize, to imitate, to steal. I have always had the feeling of living somebody else's life. When I first read Felipe Alfau's *Locos: A Comedy of Gestures,* I was possessed by the idea that, had I been born in 1902 in Barcelona, as had its author, I would have written his book. The exact same sensation was repeated when discovering Pinhas Der Nister Kahanovitch's *The Family Mashber,* a masterpiece of Soviet Jewish fiction by a writer who died in a Russian hospital in 1950 as a result of Stalin's purges. And my mother keeps a yellowish school photograph I once gave her. It was taken when I was eight or nine: Although smiling, I really don't look happy; and in the back it has a brief line written: "With love from a non-existent twin brother." Furthermore, I am often sure I am being observed by an omniscient Creature (with a capital "C"), who enjoys inflicting pain and laughs at the sorrow of His creatures. I cannot but equate the act of writing to God's impact on Nature: He is simultaneously absent and present in His creation, granting birth and death—the Absolute Novelist, a marionette-holder with a vivid imagination and a bad sense of humor (even if I-He laughs).

## "TOTAL FORGETERY"

Acting was my father's trade.

As I was growing up, I remember feeling amazed by his incredible talent. I adored him. Watching his performances, I would be pushed to what Søren Kierkegaard regarded as "an existential vacuum— a mystery." Was he really the man I knew or, instead, a mask-carrier? I was particularly fond of him taking me along on Sunday after-noons. We would leave home alone after lunch. While driving an old Rambler, he would ask me about school and friends, about ideas and books, masturbation and a girl's sexuality. He was a hero, a man of integrity like few others, the only guy I knew who was actually happy, very happy, a few minutes every day: on stage. Then, as my father would park the car, I would begin noticing a slow change of attitude, a metamorphosis, as if a veil, an abyss was now setting us apart. Another self would graciously descend to possess him, to take the man I knew and loved away from me. A few minutes later, I would witness how, without shame, he would undress in front of a mirror, put on a bathrobe, and begin to hide his face in cosmetics. He was becoming somebody else, a stranger, a ghost: today a hotel owner, next season a boxer, a cancer patient, a Jewish prisoner in

Germany. His breathtaking masks were infallible: They always hid my dad's true self, deformed it. As a result of that transformation, I felt totally alone.

Alone and lonely. The whole phenomenon inspired in me mixed feelings: I was astonished by the magic and frightened at the same time; I hated the whole thing and yet would literally do anything to return tomorrow and witness it anew. My father would then ask a handyman to seat me behind the stage, next to a curtain, in order for me to watch the show. And that, oh God, was his and my greatest moment on earth, the one we awaited even more eagerly than the facial and physical change he underwent to become a character. With a difference: In front of an audience, he was happy; I, on the other hand, was scared to death—invaded by the kind of fear that simultaneously generates joy and sorrow. What did others think of his "new" self? Could they recognize the true face behind the mask? Was he an impostor?

Alone and lonely and full of envy, I would feel an overwhelming sense of profound and disturbing jealousy toward the audience. They received all of his attention, which, in normal circumstances, I would keep for my own or, at most, share with my brother and sister. They would be manipulated, seduced by his talents. Why was he so eager to become other people and take a rest from himself? And hide behind a mask? Even more suspiciously, why did the viewers pay to have him taken away from me? How could people pay for my father to cease being himself? The Author of Authors, the Impostor of Impostors: God as playwright. In my eyes the entire universe was a vast and mysterious theater in which he (Yahweh, Adonai, Elohim, the Holy Spirit, the Father of Fathers) would capriciously establish what people, the actors, are to do, to say, to think, to hope. My dad's actual stage was a microcosmos that inspired me to philosophize about religion and eschatology, about freedom and determinism. I wondered: While acting, was my father free to refuse pronouncing a certain line of the script? Could he talk to me at least once during the performance? (Through his real and unimported self?) I also wondered if I, Ilan Stavans (aka Ilan Stavchansky Slomianski), was free to stop being his son? Could I also become other people—like Shakespeare, be one and many? To answer these questions, I became a novelist. To write is to make sense of confusion in and around. (It was me who said that.)

To write, perchance to dream. (Or vice versa?) Not long ago an interviewer asked me why I didn't follow his footsteps and enter the stage. My response was short and somewhat condescending. Deep inside, I dislike actors. I find their vulnerability, their trendiness and exhibitionism disturbing. I would rather live in the shadow than in the spotlight. I love the theater of the mind and have a terrible fear of dying. It might sound absurd, but I see literature as brother to memory and theater as symbol of the ephemeral present. I write in order to remember and be remembered. Death is the absence of recollection—what Luis G. Rodríguez calls "total forgetery." Theater, on the other hand, is *performance art,* a transitory game. It is only alive during a night show, afterward it's gone . . . forever. Nothing remains, nothing. Except perhaps a handful of yellowish photos and (luck permitting) an award or two. And if the theater is like a vanishing photograph, writing is signing one's name on concrete: a proof of existence ("I was here . . ."). But, incorporating past and present images, a narrative plays with Time (with a capital "T") in an astonishing fashion: It makes reality eternal. Marcel's desire for his mother's goodnight kiss in Proust's *Remembrance of Things Past* is not a pre–World War I scene alone but unquestionably an image for the ages. When death turns me into a ghost, at least something, one ingenious thought or a breath of life, will remain a written page like those of Virgil, Dante, and Cervantes. Perhaps and perhaps not. The only certainty is that a library is a triumph over nothingness. And yet, the warm human contact my dad encounters while performing is always reinvigorating. Literature, on the other hand, is a secluded activity. Isolation, silence, detachment, escape. You hope someone will read you someday, although nothing (not even the timing of God's laughter) is certain. Thus decades away from those Sunday afternoons when my father would take me along to his show, I still confess I feel envy: He can be happy, I cannot. I honestly wish I could at times take vacations from myself—like him, have another self. It must be refreshing. Isolation, silence.

Before death and after. Literature, I'm perfectly sure, is no palliative to cure spirit's suffering. The day I die, people will not interrupt their routines, why should they? They will make love, eat, defecate, smoke, and read. They will smile and cry and kiss and hate. It will matter to no one (not even my dearest ones, really) that my life has ceased to be and all is over. The show will go on. Grief—a strange and dishonest feeling. When Calvino and Danilo Kiš, two mentors, died, did I cry? (Albert Camus's protagonist in *The Stranger* is incarcerated for not crying during his mother's funeral.) I did pray for their souls and after that . . . nothing. Only through literature, I feel, can I transcend myself. To write is to overcome the imperfections of nature. I do it every day, every day, every day, every . . . otherwise, I sense that a day's 86,400 seconds are meaningless and in vain.

# THINGS TO COME

A future encyclopedia, to be published in Brussels in 2087, states that at age thirty-one I wrote a book, *Imagining Columbus*, about the Genoese admiral's fifth and final voyage of discovery, one not across the Atlantic but through the human imagination. That I was the author of a controversial reflection on the identity of Hispanics in the United States and a volume of early short stories, collectively called, in English, *The One-Handed Pianist*. It mentions the fact that sometime after 1995, I published a novel about a Belgian actor of Jewish descent, who has trouble distinguishing where reality ends and fantasy begins (poor Konstantin Stanislavsky! Or is it Konstantin Stavchansky?)—inspired, obviously, by his dad's trade; translated into numerous languages, the volume was enthusiastically received by critics and readers. Afterward, I wrote another novel, this one in the style of Vargas Llosa, about the exiled family of a Latin American dictator, after which I won numerous grants and prizes, was internationally applauded and commemorated.

It discusses my multilingualism. After a literary beginning as a Yiddish playwright and short fiction writer, I moved first into Spanish and then into English, translating and reinventing myself. (Although I wrote English with ease and distinction, I spoke like a tourist.) If, as Nabokov once claimed, our existence is but a brief crack of light between two eternities of darkness, why not take advantage and be two writers at once? The entry also states that I left an echo, an echo, an echo. Critics praised my oeuvre, comparing it to precursors and successors like Kafka, Spinoza, and Borges. Because of my dual identity, in Mexico, I was considered a "bad citizen." My themes always dealt with God as manipulator of human conscience, and my existential journey could be reduced to a verse by the Nicaraguan *modernista* poet Rubén Darío: "To be and not to know. . . ." My style is very precise and direct, akin to religious insights. Cyril Connolly says in *Unquiet Grave:* "The more books we read, the sooner we perceive that the only function of a writer is to produce a masterpiece. No other task is of any consequence." The encyclopedia claims that toward the end of life, I wrote extraordinarily lasting short stories, as if everything that preceded them was a prophecy. Finally, it states that I died on August 18, 2033, with some twenty-two original books to my credit. After a consuming sickness, I contemplated suicide but a sudden attack impeded me from arriving at a nearby New York hospital and nothingness took over. That was also a rainy day without major historical events. God witnessed my death and pretended to suffer, although His was of course an actor's gesture. In fact, He laughed: I was (am) his joy and toy.

The

Jewish

Self

# NOVELIZING THE HOLOCAUST?

---

A shameless moral theft has taken place: A Holocaust survivor's voice is being silenced by a Jesuit ex-priest in Ecuador.

A cogent memoir by a survivor, Salomón Isacovici, entitled *Man of Ashes,* about death and endurance at Auschwitz, Gross Rosen, Javorsno, and other camps, was scheduled to appear in 1995, in an English translation, by the University of Nebraska Press. But it has been postponed indefinitely because, as the Press's director, Daniel J. J. Ross, puts it, Juan Manuel Rodríguez, the book's co-author, an Iberian immigrant to Ecuador and an academic who has taught at Kalamazoo College and is Chancellor of Quito's Universidad San Francisco, "is arguing that he, and not Isacovici, should be featured as its primary author."

Isacovici emigrated to Quito in 1948. He died of cancer last February, at the age of seventy-two, deeply troubled by the whole affair. In a letter of 1995, he wrote: "I, Salomón Isacovici, am the legitimare author of [*Man of Ashes*]. After all, it is my autobiography. And I hired Mr. Rodríguez after [the manuscript] was written, in order to help me with the literary and structural parts of the book. I paid him for his work, and agreed in a contract that, should it be published, he would receive his share of the profits."

"My father survived the Holocaust to tell the world his haunting odyssey," Ricardo Isacovici, Salomón's son and a textile engineer in Chicago, told me in a phone conversation, "only to be deprived of it

---

First published in *Hopscotch: A Cultural Review* 1:2 (1999).

by a self-promoting paranoid." Ricardo adds: "We are dealing with an anti Semite who not only wants to boycott the publication of a testimony of the Holocaust but . . . wants to appropriate the father's life for himself."

As a cathartic event in Jewish history, the Holocaust had little impact in Latin America. A small number of refugees made it to its shores just before World War II, and the total number of survivors seeking shelter in the region prior to and after 1945—to Bolivia and the Dominican Republic, especially—is even smaller. As far as I know, less than half a dozen Holocaust memoirs have been published. More famous, of course, are the account about the spotting and arresting of ex-Nazis in Argentina, Paraguay, and Brazil, especially Adolf Eichmann and Dr. Josef Mengele. This alone makes *Man of Ashes* unique. But its uniqueness goes beyond. Isacovici is a native of Sighet, Rumania, Elie Wiesel's home town. (A classmate of Isacovici's younger brother, Wiesel, in fact, is well aware of *Man of Ashes* and has even offered to endorse its English edition—that is, if the legal battles are ever overcome.) After spending time in Auschwitz and loosing his parents and four siblings, he wandered around Europe after the war, looking for his lost relatives. He joined a Zionist group from *Hashomer Hatzair* and almost emigrated to Palestine but remained in Europe before he followed his sweetheart to Ecuador, where he performed menial jobs before becoming a successful entrepreneur.

With a lyrical style, *Man of Ashes* is filled with sharp insights into human suffering. Isacovici frames the plot by beginning and ending with the visitation of death at a 1975 multiple bypass and vault replacement operation he underwent in Boston. Sighet is presented as bucolic, as are sights in Ecuador such as Riobamba and the surroundings of Mount Chimborazo. In fact, only two of a total of twenty chapters—plus a passing passage in the earlier part of the volume—take place in Ecuador. In these segments Ecuador's Indian population—abused, persecuted by the Spanish conquistadors—is compared to the Jews under Hitler. "My father had much more to say on the subject," Ricardo claims, "but Rodríguez persuaded him to shorten it because these sections painted the Iberian treatment of the natives negatively and he wanted to safeguard, as much as possible, Spain's reputation in the Americas."

I first heard about *A7393: Hombre de cenizas*—its Spanish title— when it appeared in 1990, in Mexico, under the aegis of Editorial Diana, a trade publisher. The book was widely distributed and received positive critical and commercial responses. A year later it received the Fernando Jeno Prize from Mexico's Jewish Community. But it was suddenly taken out of circulation and its contract voided when Rodríguez, the author of several novels and collections of stories in Spanish, began to harass the publisher by claiming that Isacovici had not given him proper credit for having written it. According to various sources, Rodríguez claimed the book was really his.

I became curious but lacked details. Then, about a month ago I heard about its English translation and the legal problems surrounding it. I began to make an inquiry. I quickly realized that the collaboration between Salomón Isacovici and Juan Manuel Rodríguez to complete the Spanish-language manuscript was nothing but a mine field. Had a clear-cut contract establishing Rodríguez's role as a ghost writer been executed, all present legal meandering would not exist. Isacovici, of course, can no longer be asked to explain this fault, but his son Ricardo recognized his father had made a mistake. "A contract does exist, in which the two parties appear as co-authors. But Rodríguez takes that to mean that the tragedy of the Holocaust is the mere apparel of his literary talents."

I reached Rodríguez by e-mail and asked him to walk me through the editorial process. He told me only a hundred double-spaced pages, with extra space between paragraphs, had been written by Isacovici, in a laconic style. "The total would have amounted to about forty printed pages," he told me. An agreement was signed between the two parties, whereby Rodríguez was to be paid $4 per finished page. The total amount was around $5,000. I have seen a number of Isacovici's checks. In any case, no financial discord ever aroused. What is at the heart of the matter is Rodríguez's own biased description of the endeavor. "I wrote the book," he claims. "Salomón is my novel's protagonist, I am his author." "The novel has value because Isacovici had an interesting life and the Holocaust as a topic always has readers." But Rodríguez adds: "I achieved a rare success: to become my own protagonist through a variety of novelistic devices. . . . That is because Salomón and I share common experiences.

Born in Bilbao, Spain, in 1945, Juan Manuel Rodríguez spent his childhood and adolescence under Franquismo. "I, too, lost my father at age eleven, left my home at eighteen, and so on. I transposed many of my philosophical views to Salomón. My philosophical formation helped achieve the transplant and succeeded in turning the book from a sheer [Holocaust] account to a novel of ideas." Since *Man of Ashes* is not about ideas but anecdotes, I assume Rodríguez means insights. "[Salomón] simply wanted me to put his experiences in regular Spanish, so that he could keep the memoir for himself and his family. I refused on the ground that I am not a corrector, e.g., a spell- and style-checker. He didn't accept my view. I asked to borrow the first few pages and in a single night I turned them into part of the first chapter, which came out almost without need of revision. When I showed it to him, Salomón realized the material had potential. We thus started to work. I wrote the entire work, its title included, in six months, basing myself in his manu- script and in mutual conversations." He describes the editorial process as a transubstantiation. "I would use my memories in the Iberian countryside as inspiration," he adds. "When I would show Salomón the result, he would be amazed at how much I knew about his past. To the point that I invented passages and details and after- ward he believed he had lived through them. For him the book is an autobiography; for me it is a charming novel."

A recurrent word in Rodríguez's argument is his description of *Man of Ashes* as a novel. Curiously, the word is never mentioned in the Spanish edition. Instead, the publisher uses the term *testimonio* in the cover to describe the volume's content: "El testimonio crudo y fiel de los campos nazis de concentración"—the cruel and truthful testimony of the Nazi concentration camps. (In 1990 Editorial Diana also released a novel by Rodríguez, *El espantapájaro.*) This attempt to "fictionalize" the book aggravates the Isacovici heirs: "A novel?" Ricardo wonders, bewildered. "Everything in it is absolutely true. Not a single iota is fiction. . . . Rodríguez, while drafting what my father would tell him in long hours of conversations, had a tendency to overwrite and fantasize. But Papá would bring him to his senses, eliminating all embellishments."

By the time Rodríguez had finished his job, a manuscript of more than three hundred pages was in store. A couple of publish- ers—Grijalbo and Emecé—rejected it, but Editorial Diana brought it out in Mexico. The names of Salomón Isacovici and Juan Manuel Rodríguez are equally prominent in its cover. This, Rodríguez assured me, is the result of his efforts. "Salomón was ready to leave me out. . . ." He had other ideas in mind, though, and the relation- ship turned between the two men quickly turned sour. He first signed a letter, together with Salomón Isacovici, authorizing Dick Gerdes, then a professor at the University of New Mexico, in Albuquerque, to translate *Man of Ashes* and present it to any pub- lisher he might consider appropriate. But when Nebraska acquired it, he retracted. He argued his name should appear more promi- nently than Isacovici's, pushed to eliminate an introduction by

Gerdes mentioning him only in passing, and asked to have his American-born, Stanford-educated wife appear as an "assistant in the translation" after she submitted a list of corrections. "Clearly, he wants to appear as the book's creator, which is ludicrous," Ricardo told me. "In publicity and future editions, he insists on being the author and my father as a mere prop."

Needless to say, the whole affair is but a symptom of a larger malady affecting all Latin America. Since colonial times, as crypto-Jews sought shelter from the Holy Inquisition, the hemisphere has never quite been comfortable with its Jews. And the Catholic Church, a most powerful institution, has been instrumental in aggravating this discomfort as if benefits from portraying them as aliens. Ecuador has a Jewish community of approximately two thousand members. All in all, less than half a million Jews make their home in Latin America. They have risen economically and socially, and in countries like Argentina and Brazil, also politically. But they remain strangers in a strange land. This in small part is their own making; in truth, the region's deeply rooted xenophobia is the main factor keeping them as "illegitimate" citizens. The bitterness surrounding *Man of Ashes* is yet another aspect of this delegitimization: Jewish suffering is trivialized as a Holocaust survivor's autobiography becomes an excuse for an ex-priest to seek personal recognition.

Daniel Ross, director of University of Nebraska Press, who inherited the project from his predecessor, judges most of Rodríguez's solicitations to be unsound and even offensive. He has been ready to release *Man of Ashes* more than once, but the University of Nebraska lawyers, fearing Rodríguez's legal action, have advised him to the contrary. "He is censoring Isacovici's voice in the United States and benefiting personally from the interest in the Holocaust," Ross told me. "The university lawyers' advice is that we publish the memoir only if the Isacovici family allocates $25,000 in an escrow account. The money will be used solely to pay legal fees, should Rodríguez's lawsuit occur. . . . As you see, this man has literally handcuffed us."

Has he really? Have the University of Nebraska lawyers not unconsciously become partners in Rodríguez's effort to censor a Holocaust survivor's voice? Reports of the ex-priest's increasing obsession with *Man of Ashes* abound, and he himself is ready to corroborate many of them. In Quito, for instance, during a party to launch the book, Rodríguez apparently said—in the presence of Ecuador's vice president—that Isacovici was "the novel's mother and I its father." And during a class at the American High School, also in Ecuador's capital, he let out his feelings of anti-Semitism while discussing his collaboration with Isacovici.

When I confronted Rodríguez with why *Man of Ashes* in Spanish had never been promoted as a novel, he replied succinctly: "That is besides the point." But it isn't. In fact, the question itself is the very heart of the matter: As a novel, the volume is predictable and unimaginative; as a memoir, instead, it is not only harrowing but essential. The real problem, though, is that Rodríguez, in all his shameless demands, has succeeded in injecting a degree of doubt and uncertainty into the book, one unlikely ever to disappear: is *Man of Ashes* Salomón Isacovici's authentic tale of survival and redemption? Or is it the product of a farfetched ex-priest?

Of course, it should be for us readers to decide. But in its English translation, the book sits voiceless in a warehouse, its future uncertain. At forty-five and a husband and father, Ricardo Isacovici cannot afford the money the University of Nebraska Press solicits from him. "Mamá died of cancer. . . . I, too, had cancer. And the bills after Papá's death were quite high. He didn't have an insurance. The family is broke. I don't have $25,000 and neither do my siblings. . . . The only tangible asset Papá left us is his memoir."

# OF JEWS AND CANONS

Samuel Johnson said that we are less in need of discovering new truths than of remembering old ones. He, of course, was the quintessential canonizer, a major force in the drive to systematize what is memorable in English literature. He spent his days not only codifying the language of his day but also scrutinizing the authors who mattered, from Shakespeare to Milton and onward to his own contemporaries, Dryden and Pope. But Dr. Johnson lived in a less skeptical age than ours, one in which Truth, undeniable and absolute, was written with a capital T. That is no longer the case, and today, canons (from the Greek *kanön*, meaning rule) are seen as tricky strategies. They are under heavy artillery attack, particularly in liberal circles, relentlessly portrayed by the press and by academics as capricious and authoritarian. Canon-makers are perceived as fools with flair, self-promoters, no better than the anthologist for whom literature is a limitless river in desperate need of a cut-and-paste job. Who on earth gives them the right to endorse and obliterate?

I must confess to being one of those fools myself, guilty of constantly telling people what is or isn't good in literature, and also guilty of generating "portable mini-libraries," as I often find myself describing anthologies. In the past few years, though, I've come to believe that this fanciful urge of mine—to judge books to be the most precious objects in the universe, and to be certain that among them only a handful are worthy of sacrifice—is genetic, a hand-me-

First published in *The Forward*, January 28, 2000.

down, easily traceable to remote times. It makes me smile that nowadays, in academic debates about the canon, there are always more than enough Jews to make a *minyan*. But why aren't they debating the formation of a Jewish literary canon?

Many of these thoughts sprang into my mind not long ago as a result of a happy coincidence. In a secondhand bookstore, I stumbled upon a copy of *Sefer Ha-Aggadah*, an anthology co-edited by Hayyim Nahman Bialik, the poet of the Hebrew renaissance. I acquired it along with another volume that is more easily accessible: Harold Bloom's *The Western Canon*. As I delved into them, more or less simultaneously, I realized how interconnected they are in their overall message. Bialik was a fervent Zionist, but his dream was not only the physical relocation of the Jews to the Promised Land. He also sought their spiritual and cultural rebirth, and his anthology of rabbinic legend and lore, originally published in Odessa from 1908 to 1911, was part of that project. He was helped by Yehoshua Hana Ravnitzky, another early Zionist and a founder of modern Hebrew journalism. The volume was but a part, albeit a magisterial one, of a larger project that Bialik had in mind. He called it *kinus*, the "ingathering" of a Jewish literature that was dispersed over centuries of Diaspora life. That library, much like its readers, needed to be centralized in a single, particular place, Israel, and in a single tongue, Hebrew—a centripetal canon.

Bloom, on the other hand, sees literature as centrifugal. He doesn't reach out to other cultures; instead, he waits for those other cultures to reach him. His book, more than 500 pages in length, is made up of erudite disquisitions on twenty-six classic authors and on the schools that shaped them, from John Milton to Samuel Beckett, with Shakespeare at the heart of it. A successor to Matthew Arnold (and one of his stronger promoters these days), Bloom doesn't see the canon as a nationalistic heritage, but rather as a universal one. This is a trick, of course. Days after I finished the book, I found on the website amazon.com a reaction from a reader in Madrid: "This isn't the Western canon," it said, "but an English-language one." And it's true: in the table of contents, the British, Irish, and Americans listed total 13, half of Bloom's library for the ages.

Bialik's concept of *kinus* suggests that at some point in its development, Israel would produce a real library of Jewish classics in inexpensive editions, just like the paperbacks of *Hamlet, Middlemarch,* and *Ulysses,* which are easily available in bookstores across America. But such a publishing enterprise hasn't yet been implemented. Sholom Aleichem, Isaac Babel, and Saul Bellow, who have all been translated into Hebrew at some point, remain inaccessible in popular formats for Israeli readers. They are either out of print or in editions that aren't quite suitable to the educational market. The truce between Zionism and the diaspora is still being forged. Israelis are only now recognizing, half a century into their history, that Jews elsewhere on the globe live fruitful lives and that most aren't about to make *aliyah*. As a result, much of the literature produced in gentile milieus, especially from the Enlightenment on, has yet to be digested.

What is puzzling, though, is that no such library exists in English either, and English is the *lingua franca* of the Jews at the dawn of the third millennium of the common era, exactly as Aramaic was in Palestine and Babylonia in late antiquity. And just as they were in antiquity, Jews in America today are undergoing a tremendous intellectual revival. The reading list, however, is frighteningly insular, intra-Ashkenazic and monolinguistic. It starts with the Bible and then jumps haphazardly to the Yiddish masters, Abramovitch, Sholom Aleichem, and Peretz, only to focus its attention on New York immigrants such as Abraham Cahan and Anzia Yezierska, Holocaust writers such as Paul Celan and Primo Levi, and contemporary voices like that of Philip Roth. Medieval Spain doesn't exist at all, and neither does France, let alone a place as peripheral—i.e., barbaric—as Brazil.

The experience of reading Bloom and Bialik together was nothing short of enlightening. It led me to ponder the identity of Jews as canon-makers of Western civilization and their utter avoidance of the task of shaping a Jewish canon for themselves, one that is truly international. Why shape other people's libraries and not our own? Have we not reached a time in which the universalist and particularist trends can be reconciled? What unites secular Jews the world over, especially at a time when a considerable portion of them is non-affiliated? The answer, I often hear, is moral values or a common heritage. Freud spoke of the "psychological Jew" as an entity with a clear moral code and a reservoir of intellect. But how common is that heritage in the global village? What links us together when in one corner of the world the work of someone such as the German-writing Sephardic master Elias Canetti or the French philosopher Edmond Jabès is cardinal yet in another one it is utterly unknown?

*Kanön* plus *kinus*—Bialik envisioned the canon as an instrument for harvesting the universal elements in his own people, to help them along on the road to normalizing their national status. Almost a century later, the same instrument ought to be recast for the intellectual consciousness of a Diaspora that no longer has any boundaries. The duty of our generation is to shape a balanced canon that transcends time and place, first and foremost in English but also in other Diaspora languages and in Hebrew—the finest, most influential of our books, available to everyone in affordable editions. Its main criterion ought to be the power to make the particular universal and vice versa. And its purpose should be the ingathering of the Jews, at home in the world.

# MEMORY AND LITERATURE

*Memory is always problematic, usually deceptive, sometimes treacherous. Proust knew this and the English reader is deprived of the full force of his title which conveys, not the blandly reassuring* Remembrance of Things Past *of the Moncrieff translation, but an initially darker and more anxious search for a time that has been lost. In the ensorcelled film of Alain Resnais the heroine quickly discovers that she cannot even be certain of what transpired last year at Marienbad. We ourselves are periodically aware that memory is among the most fragile and capricious of our faculties.*

—Yosef Hayim Yerushalmi

Where does history end and literature begin? Or is it that they are one and the same, different versions of those chores that are as inevitable as they are impossible, that of remembering and being remembered? Six years ago, I learned of the existence of Yosef Hayim Yerushalmi through a commentary by Moshe Idel on *Zakhor: Jewish Memory and Jewish History*. I bought the book but was sidetracked by a handful of pressing responsibilities. After several attempted readings, I abandoned the project. At this point in my career as reader, I have no doubt that each work we read is successful only if it comes at the right time; otherwise, we tend to put the piece aside regardless of its inherent value. Something like that happened to me with Yerushalmi. My enthusiasm for history and

---

First published as Introduction to *Cuentistas judíos* (Mexico City, Mexico: Editorial Porrúa, 1994). In English it appeared in *AGNI* 48 (Fall 1998). Translated by Brian G. Sheehy.

enormous interest in the subject (the duties of the historian and the vicissitudes of the Jewish Diaspora) clashed with other obligations. I put the book away until recently, when a commentary on another book by the author, *Freud's Moses: Judaism Terminable and Interminable,* published by Yale University Press, reawakened my curiosity. I read this newer title with passion and returned, thank God, to the one that originally attracted me. What happened to me was similar to what happened to Octavio Paz when he discovered the work of Claude Lévi-Strauss in the seventies: I was totally over-whelmed. My reading was full of suggestions, mostly literary though also anthropological and religious, which I shall proceed to discuss.

Between the fruitless first attempt and the second, an intellectual journey made me aware of parallel themes. In mid 1990, at the request of the editor of *Mester* at the University of California in Los Angeles, I wrote an essay on the art of memory, which appeared near the end of that same year. The text opened with a pair of epigraphs, one by Frederick C. Bartlett, the other from Luis Buñuel's *My Last Sight*; my goal was to examine a handful of short stories, novels, and scientific documents whose main protagonist was an individual gifted with prodigious mnemonic faculties. I focused on two: "Funes the Memorious," by Borges, and *The Mind of a Mnemonist (A Little Book About a Vast Memory)*, by Russian researcher A. R. Luria, one of the most intelligent men of the twentieth century, whom I became acquainted with through a passing recommendation from Oliver Sacks. (A small aside: When gathering material for this essay, I real-ized that Yerushalmi, in his epilogue to *Zakhor*, talks about Luria and his book, as well as another complementary work, *The Man with a Shattered World: History of a Brain Wound*.) I also made a cursory study of related themes in Turgeniev, Bruce Chatwin, Pirandello, Leonardo Sciascia, Danilo Kiš, Milan Kundera, and Marguerite Yourcenar, but the first two titles took up almost all available space. A pair of tan-gential readings led me to another fundamental and striking book: *The Art of Memory*, written in 1966 by English scholar Frances Yates. In it she discusses, among other subjects, the *fantastic* theories—in the unreal sense of the term—of Giulio Camillo Delminio and Robert Fludd on the so-called Theater of Memory. Both Renaissance thinkers described our mnemonic faculties using a stage complete with orchestral seats, theatrical curtains, actors, and all. Yates developed an ambitious study of these small-scale stages, exploring the intellec-tual adventures Delminio and Fludd underwent to understand their implications and, also, the resistance they encountered from their readership. In addition, at that time I read the treatises of Israel Rosenfeld, Piranesi, and Sacks himself on remembrance and forgetting as mental faculties. My restlessness did not end here. The writing of the *Mester* essay inspired a long story (or perhaps a novella): *The Invention of Memory*. It was included in the collection *The One-Handed Pianist,* released in Spanish in 1991 and in English in 1996 in a translation by Dick Gerdes. Its protagonist, Zdenek Stavchansky, is a Czech Jew who has an almost total recall. He works in cabarets and circuses and is manipulated by the Communist Party in Prague. In the middle of the story, he receives some bad news; Stavchansky is diagnosed with Wernicke's Affliction, a strange degenerative disease that promises to destroy his mnemonic abilities.

Zdenek travels to Europe, England, and later settles in Mexico, his mother's birthplace, to lose his memory. Thus, this piece of fiction is another attempt to describe the strange marriage between memory and literature; it is also, to a large extent, the product of my reading of Yerushalmi, Luria, Yates, and Borges. The reader might forgive me for having dedicated so much space to the recounting of my journey, but I'm sure that without these ups and downs and moments of excitement the present text would not exist. I have submerged myself again in Yerushalmi's book and my wish here, in addition to summarizing my impression, is to articulate a vision of a solid link between memory and literature inspired by its pages. It occurs to me that each and every one of my attempts from 1990 to the present are chapters in a larger volume in progress that I will finish some day and that already signals an insatiable critical obsession: Is the library not the most perfect and distilled symbol of memory? Can writing and memory be understood as one and the same action?

The main thesis in *Zakhor,* which by the way has an introduction by Harold Bloom and which Yerushalmi himself describes as "a small book, part history, part confession and creed," originated in an article entitled *Clio and the Jews: Reflections on Jewish Historiography in the Sixteenth Century.* The ideas are present in embryonic form, as if they were the seed from which a strong and robust tree would someday grow. The central argument is easy to synthesize. The Jewish people, Yerushalmi claims, has preoccupied itself with preserving the collective memory since time immemorial; this appears to be its prime directive: to remember and to be remembered. In fact, the collective identity is linked to this duty of remembering, of stopping time from erasing the details of the past.

Only through remembering, starting with a dialogue between an ancient and primitive past and an unknown but promising future, is it possible to carve a permanent place in history. History, therefore, is the living manifestation of memory, its theater, and each Jew is a link in a chain, an actor, evidence of an atemporal promise made on Mount

Sinai between heaven and earth that is not, nor ever will be, forgotten. Generations intertwine, establish their similarities and differences, and delineate their breaks and their continuations, all thanks to this unavoidable necessity: the self-knowledge of their role as vessels of an infinite memory, which transforms each and every member of the Jewish people into essential and indispensable links in an immortal tradition. Through the very process of remembering, the Jew swears loyalty to his ancestors and successors and inscribes himself in the flow of history: He is, inasmuch as he remembers who he is and where he is from. His obsession with the Bible, the testament of his promise to God, is therefore symbolic: The book contains the scenes of the past, and the key lies in periodic rereadings to keep the promise alive. The synagogue is the only religious temple where the object of adoration is a text, a written document that affirms and confirms that the past is not a mere invention but divine and earthly truth deposited in history.

It must be acknowledged that Yerushalmi does not subscribe to the ideas of C. G. Jung; that is to say, he does not believe that the collective subconscious is synonymous with collective memory: two distinct entities—one natural, the other artificial. Contrary to what was believed in the eighteenth and nineteenth centuries, Yerushalmi also rejects the idea that a Jewish *enfant savage*, abandoned by the edge of a jungle, would spontaneously learn to speak Hebrew or would know that Abraham traveled from Ur to Canaan and that Moses received the Tablets of the Law in the desert. His vision, as a result, is completely modern (and based to a large extent on the theories of Maurice Halbwachs): He knows, or desires to know, that the collective memory of the Israeli tribe is the product of social interaction and that the child receives knowledge from his parents and the parents of his parents, with only a minimal percentage coming from genetics; this implies that education and daily family interaction are determining factors: According to Yerushalmi, a Jew is not born but made. To remember is to participate in a series of religious and social rituals; it is also to join a congregation and convert oneself in a thorough reading of the Book of Books.

The word *zakhor* means "to remember." But the Jewish imperative to participate in an infinite line of memories, according to Yerushalmi, contains in its heart a duality that is impossible to resolve. The Bible leaves no doubt in assuring that only through this type of activity can a link be established between God and the Jewish people. The verb *zakhor* appears no less than 169 times in the text and has a punitive counterpart: forgetting. Not remembering is to detour from the perfect path, to lose faith and to live in a universe of lies and sins. Forgetting, in a way, approaches paganism and idolatry:

*Remember, oh Israel, that this is your God, the only one*; the rest are alternate deities and wrong turns. Thus, Israel's duty to remember is tempered by its terrible opposite: forever forgetting who one is and what the individual alone and in group is meant to achieve in History.

This gives place to two questions: What should a Jew remember? And through what means? Yerushalmi tries to respond by situating his study in many times and places: the Biblical and the rabbinical; the medieval; during the expulsion of the Jewish people from the Iberian peninsula in 1492—Yerushalmi's expertise is on this historical period; and in the modern era. The oral and written traditions started the moment Moses received the Bible from God on Mount Sinai and gave it to Joshua; he in turn gave it to the wise men, and they, to prophets; and they, to the leaders of the synagogues and so on to the most humble member of society. Reading was coupled with discussion and interpretation of the scenes invoked in the text: reading and speaking, speaking and reading. But one ought to be careful: Yerushalmi never suggests that the Jews have a prodigious memory; but simply, that they are ready to receive and retransmit the past in new versions, sometimes corrected or increased. Each age approaches the problem of how to live in the present while reliving the past in another way, depending on the historical conditions and the adaptations of the tribe of Israel to the surrounding reality. Therefore, even though the art of memory is the same, the remembrance varies according to the dimensions of time and space.

Basing his argument on Plato—nothing new in this Jewish borrowing from a Greek philosopher; it started with Philo and thereafter becomes omnipresent—Yerushalmi is forced to establish a clear-cut, essential difference between memory (*mneme*) and remembrance (*anamnesis*): The first describes the infinite chain that never breaks; the second, the act of invoking what has been forgotten. The Talmud assures us that at some point before birth, the embryo already has perfect knowledge of each and every Biblical passage. However, moments before delivery, an angel hits the fetus in the mouth (in other versions, he kisses him) and makes him forget, erasing these memories. From there all knowledge is based on anamnesis: We remember that which we forget. But the memory to which Yerushalmi refers is *mneme* inasmuch as what is remembered is ancestral and unforgettable. This has little to do with the person and more to do with his ancestors: The individual does not remember personal scenes but foreign ones; and more than remember, he invents them. For this reason, imagination and memory are mental faculties that are closely linked: To remember is to re-create. Remembering is not a return to the past but the adaptation of a past event to the circumstances of the present; it is a reorganization and the giving of new meaning to what was lost.

The disjunction most difficult to deconstruct, which later becomes obsession, the central *leitmotif* in Yerushalmi's excellent book, emerges from the clash and confluence of historiography and memory. The author responds with assurance to questions such as "what the Jew should remember," by stating that the Bible and all Hebrew texts demand that the believer (i.e., the reader) remember an archaic, immortal, and mythic time rather than a historic time. That is to say, the chronology offered by the Bible is neither methodical nor factual; our dates are doubtful and our objectivity imperfect. It is understood that the purpose of its scribes is not to offer a true account of Jewish vicissitudes, but to censure and remodel what has been lived in order to enhance the significance of God and faith. *Zakhor,* therefore, has no other option but to question the work of all Jewish historians. The vision of the past that memory proposes is far from a scientific product; just the opposite occurs with history. If the facts have been reformulated at the convenience of wise rabbis, eliminated and reinvented, the historian must be committed to rearticulating and reworking these facts, basing himself on other historiographic instruments—the archaeological work, the deciphering of parallel texts, the analysis of recovered utensils, etc. Without going farther, Yerushalmi's theory applies to the very act of the creation of the universe just as it is described in *Genesis*: a cumulative process from Nothing to Everything that took place in seven days and nights; man as king and lord of nature and women as vessels; the omnipotent power of God as orchestrator of order and enemy of chaos; and so on. Such description, needless to say, is very different from the alternative offered by biology, astronomy, and evolutionary genetics. And from there on, the sequence of generations, emperors, and battles adjusts itself to the message which the scribes of the Bible wished to pass on: Israel as God's wayward but correctable creation. The main interest, it can be deduced, is not to relive the past, but to charge it with meaning; not to preserve an important fact just as it occurred, but to inject it with symbolic value in order to make it precious.

Although History—with Herodotus as its father and the Greeks as its founders—is linked to memory, it is a radically distinct phenomenon. The Greeks' main goal was not to develop a "universal history" that would reach all four corners of the globe (a misconception produced, to a large extent, by romanticism in the nineteenth century), but instead, in the words of Herodotus, to prevent erosion, to preserve the work of humankind and to keep the glory of Greece from being erased from the face of the earth. One element is essential: objectivity. From the Greek historian to the present, all scientific investigators of the past dreamed about re-creating the events, reducing the subjectivity of the observer to a minimum and eliminating whatever personal tinge the collector of the facts might have introduced. This desire, of course, is a chimera that Freud and the Surrealists have made us reconsider: Objectivity does not exist, everything is imprinted in the mind of the observer and narrator. But even so, the historian tries to minimize the margin of the private in his work. His wish is to allow history to "speak for itself, beyond intrusive eyes."

The two proposals, one Jewish and the other Greek, could not be more different: Both fight to save memory from being forgotten, but their understanding of what exactly should be saved from time's erosion is diametrically opposed. One salvages the myth, the other the truth. The former discards objectivity and is not ashamed to recognize that the only thing of interest in the historic moment is its meaning; the latter eliminates all artificial and contingent meanings and wishes to re-create the past just as it was. What the Jew remembers (or should remember) is very different from what the Greek aspires to recover: One corrals the archetypal past, the other inveterate happenings. And how does the Jew go about fulfilling his duty? Through oral tradition, religious rites, moral and educational duties, and a discussion of the "new" meanings that emerge from past events (i.e., the *ad infinitum* interpretation of texts and legends). And thus, it is easy to agree with Yerushalmi: The Jewish historian is a contradiction in terms. By subscribing to the tradition of Herodotus, he aspires to quantify a past whose very quantification is both unnecessary and inconvenient.

What ought to be said about the link between literature and memory? Before I offer a response, I should clarify a point that perhaps was not evident in the preceding paragraphs. Although Yerushalmi's inquiries devote themselves to Jewish historiography (after all, he is a professor of Jewish History at Columbia University and president of the Leo Back Institute of New York), his work is generally relevant to any ethnic, national, or religious group. Each society establishes its communion with history through a handful of symbols and collective ties (a flag, an anthem, a land, a language) but, most importantly, through a shared mythic past whose veracity historians refuse to refute. The Aztec foundation of Tenochtitlán, known today as Ciudad de México, for example, with its heavenly lakes and prophecy of an eagle perched on a cactus devouring a serpent as an indication of tellurian belonging, announces a historic unreality. According to Miguel León-Portilla, the event upon which Tenochtitlán is founded on elements truth but is doubtless a legend, a mythological sketch crucial to establishing the link between the Mexican and his geography. We could refute it, but what would that accomplish? The opposition between myth and history is impossible to resolve, and in the modern world each community needs both to survive. We drink from both memories and stand divided.

Even though Yerushalmi does not submerge himself in the subject, it can be deduced from his thesis that the author also has a divided heart. Sometimes preferring myth and sometimes history, his imagination oscillates between a fabulous but meaningful past and a re-creation of quantifiable epochs and actions. Two examples: Isaac Babel and Franz Kafka, who could be seen as polar opposites, as possibilities of literary action. The first, a Russian born in 1894 and shot in a Stalinist concentration camp in the beginning of the forties (some give 1939 as the fatal date), limited his literary work to a personalized narrative of his infancy in Odessa and his participation in General Budenny's regiment, the so-called Red Cavalry, in Poland during the civil war after the Bolshevik Revolution. His fictions, part autobiography, part invention, part history, have a very precise context of action: They are abstractions that clarify how people thought and acted during the first decades of this century. Similar to Tolstoy's *War and Peace,* they are not scientific documents: It would be absurd to re-create the actions of the past using this information, but they borrow dates and characters from history. Babel is less interested in extracting meanings than in describing the cruel times in which he lived. His narrative method, which oscillates between the styles of Maupassant and Gorki, feeds itself from journalism and story: It is simultaneously a re-creation of a pain-filled and fragile life ("a human porcelain") and an analysis of the external forces that shape us as individuals. Kafka, on the other hand, prefers allegory and discards history. His characters are figments of the imagination asking to be deciphered, a message encased in ancestral paradoxes. His castle, his trial, his metamorphosis, his report to an academy, are scenes from a psychological life: reflections on God, on redemption, on guilt and the bureaucracy from the point of view of a tormented Eastern European. There is nothing in his work that is historical; the absence of dates, of concrete signposts, is overwhelming and even unbearable. It is for this reason that Harold Bloom and others see Kafka—along with Freud and Gershom Scholem, the scholar of Kabbalah—not only as novelist but as exegete: an interpreter of archaic truths. Babel understands fiction as a recounting of the immediate historic past; Kafka, as the analysis of a mythic past. One looks down, the other looks up. Both are tips of the iceberg: Since their legacy was established, every writer is, in some way, a successor of either one or the other. In other words, there is no other way but to write literature either like Kafka or like Babel.

When thinking about literature, the art of imagining and transcribing alternate realities, two obvious but pressing questions present themselves: What function does it serve? What does it intend? Western man hungers for reflection and entertainment. We confront mortality and wish to dominate the universe via the powers of the mind and through discovery. But we do not want to go without leaving behind traces of who we were and are and even what we dream. These two veins, the epistemological and the historiographic, are intimately linked. When writing and reading a poem or story or novel, we transform ourselves into inhabitants of time: We search the dreams of the past for the answer to existential hunger and, in passing, we fight boredom. Knowledge, amusement, and shivering go hand in hand. This vision of narrative art, its obsession for leaving tracks of its vicissitudes in fantasies that are rarely recorded by the scientific historian, although they are by the collective memory, is the product of the nineteenth century, in which, after the French Revolution and as a result of the Enlightenment, the book forever abandoned ecclesiastic enclosures and became popular and democratic. Its tentacles reached the middle class and made literature ubiquitous and accessible in price. The novels of Samuel Richardson, Henry Fielding, Daniel Defoe, and Laurence Sterne, and the knowledge of the French encyclopedists Voltaire, Rousseau, and Diderot, cleared the way for a massive literature that reached its climax in our century with the proliferation of useless and transitory books and the dissemination of any single book in thousands of disposable paperback editions. While written knowledge, reflection, and amusement belonged to only a few, today they are everywhere without recognizing (or appearing to recognize) any limit.

Education and curiosity are the doors to the world of imagination and epistemology. Susan Sontag explained this very lucidly (*Against Interpretation*): The movement of literature from the elite to general society must be seen as a particular function of postwar change (especially in the fifties), which explains who a writer is and where he is from. Otherwise, the impact of middle-class and marginalized voices on modern literature could not be accounted for. If in the Middle Ages and the Renaissance, intellectual labor was reserved for a handful of initiates in ecclesiastical and academic posts, the multiplicity of the printed word, and the entrance of a humble social class to universities and other places of knowledge have generated a drastic change: Perhaps starting with the nineteenth-century Russian novelists (with the obvious exception of Tolstoy) and their counterpart Edgar Allan

Poe, narrative art springs from a class with a fragile economic balance. Questions like, "What does literature accomplish?" and "What does it attempt?" must be answered in two ways: First, writing attempts to compile a map of our dreams in order to, in the style of Herodotus, save them from the erosion of time and preserve them for the future; and second, each generation and epoch reflects and metamorphoses its environment through its dreams.

Memory and literature are hence closely linked. The printed page has the talent of making fantasy eternal and changing it into a historic document. The delicate movement of each pen echoes more than the immediate context: It impacts, transforms, decides. These two characteristics, eternity and omnipresence, are decisive, thanks to the translator's work and the impatience of the popular press. Unlike the majority of other arts and before television and commercial photography, literature already possessed an enviable property: ubiquity and immortality, not unlike Pascal's sphere, the possibility of being everywhere at all times. For this reason, every writer competes for the audience's attention—not only against his contemporaries but also against his precursors. Thus the library is the architecture of literary eternity: On its shelves writers of different languages, geographies, and ages coexist: Sophocles and Milton and Whitman, Shakespeare and Ram only against his contemporaries but also against his precursos eternal, to be at all times, to live out of time.

It must be added that the composition of a narrative text is a mnemonic act by the very fact that it involves *mneme* and *anamnesis*: It includes immediate and ancestral records, both innate and acquired. But the act of invoking what has been forgotten and what is remembered from education and family traditions, unlike Yerushalmi's history and collective memory, does not have an iota of objectivity: It nourishes itself from intoxicating impartiality. Objectivity does not, nor will it ever, exist in literature. Simply think of *Madame Bovary* as an example: In his correspondence, Flaubert elaborated his theory of the writer who, similar to God, absents himself and lets his creations act of their own accord. The writing of his novel took years: The patience in every phrase and stylistic turn is amazing. The French novelist of *le mot juste* dreamed of giving birth to a perfect book, the Total Book. But nobody would be surprised if the book was as imperfect as any written by Arthur Conan Doyle: the result of human, rather than divine, labor. Nevertheless, Emma Bovary has attributes that are both individual and collective: She is a perfectly sketched creature and for that same reason she becomes an archetype. Without wishing to, through her, Flaubert described each and every feminine attitude caused by frivolity. One gets the impression that his work is closer to Yerushalmi's vision of Jewish memory than to a Western historiography: Through his text, the narrator or poet seeks to interpret, to inject meaning into a person or scene; by doing so, the subject becomes an allegory, a Platonic item whose characteristics are not destroyed by time—a symbol. But that creation, in surging forth from a specific time and space, is also a historic document. To write is to remember and to remember is to transcribe. Kundera once said that literature is a struggle against forgetting. To forget is to limit epistemological curiosity to the discontinuous present and to let dreams steal away and perish. The fight against forgetting seeks to recount the acts in an individual manner, not institutional nor official, making them tangible and concrete. To remember is to install our imagination into History and fight against the erosion that annihilates all human labor; to forget is to deprive the future of the joys of the present. Could anything be more selfish?

I began this essay by describing my discovery of *Zakhor: Jewish History and Jewish Memory*. I said that I arrived at the book after a long intellectual journey from which emerged two texts: an essay on "Funes el memorioso" and on the Russian doctor A. R. Luria and a long story on death and the loss of memory, which are one and the same. I have tried to discuss in the present text the communicating vessels between the act of writing and the collective memory. Upon rereading it, I've realized that I have suggested a type of continuity between the narrative dimension and the religious one. I am not sorry. I have believed for a long time that God is the Writer of Writers—what is the universe if not an infinite inconclusive novel, at once melodramatic and incredibly sensible, and one from which modern literature inherited the feeling of sacredness from the past: Through its pages we improve ourselves, we shiver, and we escape from this stubborn reality; and thanks to her we are, and want to be, less imperfect. Writing and praying are not separate activities. If in Western civilization the Book of Books to which every writer aspires is the Bible, praising it is at once an acknowledgment and an homage. Yerushalmi is right: Memory is the most fragile and problematic of our faculties. If stripping history of all subjectivity is an aggression, shaking literary art of its theological components is to reduce it to a mere transitory and forgettable activity. *Zakhor*: "to remember, to record, to reinvent oneself"—a link between the past and the future, the search of significance in time. The historian and the writer are sculptors of memory, but their approximations are opposing: One quantifies while the other diminishes and reinvents; one makes it flat and the other emphasizes its anachronisms. Greece and Jerusalem, objectivity and subjectivity.

# ON LIONEL TRILLING

Lionel Trilling (1905–1975), once the doyen of literary critics, is undergoing a slow but effective resurgence. It is too early to tell what the implications are, but everything suggests that both his persona and his oeuvre are attracting a young generation of scholars eager to understand his echoes, present and future.

Indeed, the signs of the resurgence are adding up: Six book-length studies of Trilling's oeuvre are already available, not including Susanne Klingenstein's study of his legacy in *Jews in the American Academy* and *Enlarging America;* at least three biographies are underway; Diana Trilling's *The Beginning of the Journey*, a tickling memoir of her marriage to Trilling released in 1993, refuses to go out of print; and Leon Wieseltier of *The New Republic* is editing a volume of Trilling's selected essays. To harmonize it all, John Rodden of the University of Texas-Austin has just released a handsome *rezeptionsgeschichte*, an chronological survey of reviews and essays on Trilling's writings, from his study of Matthew Arnold to *Literary Criticism: An Introductory Reader* and beyond.

Rodden's book is the sharpest, most sophisticated tool so far through which to comprehend Trilling as a Jew, a man of letters, and a public figure. It includes a series of assessments and extensive explanatory notes that offer information readers today might need in identifying a name, title, or movement. The introduction places Trilling in New York, "the undisputed intellectual capital of the nation," and defines, in a nutshell, the "opposing views" that still

First published in *The Forward*, October 29, 1999.

surround him. His detractors accuse him of being averse to ideology to the point of even foreswearing the art of the polemic; for them, Trilling was of the type that never says straight out what he means. His supporters, however, portray him, as Morris Dickstein argues, as an essayist "at once tentative and definitive, transparent and inexhaustible." They celebrate his ambivalent character and the genuinely dialectical movement of his mind, a quality that allowed him to approach literature and politics as "a dark and bloody crossroads" but not to favor one at the expense of the other. These polarities are explored, one at a time, by numerous authors: Edmund Wilson, Harry Levin, Stephen Spender, George Steiner, F. R. Leavis, Jacques Barzun, Robert Penn Warren.

Especially enlightening in Rodden's volume is the way critics have looked at Trilling's "reluctant" Jewishness over the years. He was the first Jew to be granted tenure in Columbia University's English department, a famously difficult victory that was achieved not without pain. But even though he contributed to the *Menorah Journal* and later was close to the founders of *Commentary,* Trilling never openly addressed Jewish topics in his work, nor did he fully acknowledge in public the influence of his heritage on his life. This ambivalence inspires some to vilify him as dishonest and others to describe his half-hearted way through the labyrinth of identity as a veil that in some way "solved his own diasporic dilemma." Morris Dickstein writes in the foreword: "The mask that made Trilling so elusive as a person lent exceptional interest to his essays. He was a reactive critic, attuned to each occasion, whose work cohered around shifting polarities rather than a single point of view."

In London last year, I reread *The Liberal Imagination* (1950), arguably Trilling's most popular book, and found it as flaccid as when I first came across it in the mid-eighties. Its prose, when compared to those of the totemic Edmund Wilson, the owner of an enviable transparency I can't admire enough, as well as those of Irving Howe, Alfred Kazin, and even Isaac Rosenfeld, Delmore Schwartz, and Leslie Fiedler, strikes me as obscure, circuitous, infelicitous in the way it approaches argument. Wilson, whom Trilling admired, praised him as early as 1939, when Trilling's revised doctoral dissertation on Matthew Arnold was published by W. W. Norton. Wilson described his style as escaping the great vice of his generation: "the addiction of obfuscatory terminology." That addiction, of course, has gotten far worse, to the point of total illegibility of academic prose. Trilling does really have a perfect pitch in prose. His gift is to be found in the way he landscapes his theme, more than in the way he surveys each of his paragraphs. No big deal, perhaps; Cervantes, too, was a nefarious stylist, and so were Montaigne and Dostoyevsky. Still, clarity means one thing in a novelist and another altogether different in a critic whose job is to define and contrast ideas. The essays on literature and society in *The Liberal Imagination,* such as his introductions to Henry James's *The Princess Casamassina* and Mark Twain's *Huckleberry Finn,* are limpid in my opinion but also far too serene, too unexciting. The reader is not overwhelmed with needless pyrotechnics but neither is he surprised. Surely some entries in the volume have withstood the passage of time better than others. Trilling's piece titled "The Function of the Little Magazine," which opened *The Partisan Reader: Ten Years of Partisan Review, 1933–1944,* is as enchanting as when it first appeared in 1946 and remains a superior lesson on the juxtaposition between the highbrow intellectual elite and the mass audience in a democracy. And his piece on manners, morals, and the novel, with its broad ethical overview of Cervantes, Flaubert, Proust, and E. M. Foster, remains timely. But his studies on Freud and literature, art and neurosis, are stale, both at the level of content and form.

And yet, my interest was picqued, so I read for the first time Trilling's failed semi-autobiographical novel *The Middle of the Journey* (1947), a quiet yet intense novel of ideas about the left-wing intellectual life in the thirties, and his late *Sincerity and Authenticity* (1972), which was a revised version of his Charles Eliot Norton Lectures at Harvard University. The novel received mixed reviews. Fiedler, in *Kenyon Review,* said it "promises too much" and fails to deliver but upon its reissue; John Bayley, in the *Times Literary Supplement,* described it as "something of a masterpiece," in my view a far too inflated noun. Again like Wilson, Trilling's talents in fiction didn't quite equal his sharp critical eye. The novel fails precisely because the ideas are taken far too seriously, unlike the characters. At its heart is not a plot per se but a debate. Trilling's nonfiction volume, on the other hand, is far more interesting: While it leaps and wanders and is infuriatingly inconclusive, it is also incredibly stimulating in its debate of honesty and the genuine. It also seems quite pertinent for our current climate of treacherous political correctness, in which what is said is often not what is meant and vice versa.

I am in no way trying to undermine, let alone sabotage, Trilling's resurrection. My praise for him, even if restricted, is too strong, for, when appreciated not as a stylist but as a door-opener and path-breaker, he stands as a paradigmatic public intellectual, a truly endangered species if there ever was one that is threatened to evaporate in all if precursors such as he are not calibered properly. When Howe died in 1993, the consensus in the media was that "the last of the New York intellectuals" was gone. The same rhetoric was used when Kazin passed away last year. Truth is, the age in which ideas matter is long gone, and with it the responsibility of intellectuals to verbalize, to ponder, to force upon people's consciousness those ideas. Science and technology advance at such speed today that the arts and social sciences seem to have a difficult time keeping up with the changes. Changing society through pamphlets and marches has been replaced by the philosophy of "small, personal acts of kindness." As a result, the role of the public intellectual as such—and of those of Jewish background, in particular—is under unavoidable siege. Not a de facto member of the New York Jewish bunch, although many in that bunch and beyond (from Norman Podhoretz and Gertrude Himmelfarb up to Morris Dickstein himself) saw him as a teacher and mentor, Trilling managed a balancing act between the scholar and the critic. But colleges and universities abduct the young and promising through tenure and comfort, and what society is left with is a factory of academics whose language is unfathomable and whose voice fails to reach a large audience. Obviously, I'm not speaking about specialist; of those we have too many, people that know more and more about less and less. What I'm referring to is the generalist, the polymath whose function it is to travel from one discipline to another in search for the moral, ideological, philosophical code that unites them all and makes us human.

This might seem a trifle in a universe where attention span is just a bit longer than the time it takes to send an e-mail. But the resurrection of Trilling, I think, signals a desire to look for alternatives, to reinvent the role of public intellectuals that address larger issues in a way that is not only comprehensible but convincing. News of the death of the book has been largely exaggerated. Literature, as far as I can judge, matters today as much as ever. But its true worth is only esteemed when the critic does his job: to serve as an intermediary between the text and the context, to explain in nondidactic form why the word and the characters built through it are our mirror. No democracy can survive without criticism, but only a criticism that is not handcuffed, that is free to speak its mind, can make art and culture find their true place in democracy. Trilling, by being simply himself, by using the academic pulpit not to seek personal comfort but to read novels aloud, for everyone, helped understand that role.

A return to his vision is preposterous. Aside from his unelectrifying style, Trilling failed in a number of ways, not the least important of which was his incapacity to sympathize with the student uprising of the 1960s at Columbia University and in other campuses. He spoke about morality, but the rapid changes of our moral code seemed to have passed him over. Multiculturalism, rather than unite use, has divided us more. Public intellectuals today belong to a specific ethnic turf, speaking mostly to their restricted constituency. Trilling's Jewishness was a platform to dwell on larger, global, cosmopolitan issues. He and his immediate pupils emerged at a time when Jews of a second generation moved away from the immigrant mentality and into the Melting Pot. Today Jews are perhaps the most successful of all immigrant stories in America, but they find themselves intellectually voiceless. A young, refreshing generation of novelists is emerging, but where in the public sphere are the critics to digest their fiction, to make it sit comfortably in our worldview?

For all this, I find John Rodden's *Lionel Trilling and the Critics* immensely useful. The picture that emerges of Trilling is of a fallible yet portentous Jew, professor and public intellectual hesitant about his own talents yet assured that his mission—to tackle ideas and literature seriously, exploring their moral and political implications—had to be accomplished. Rodden's volume thus ought to serve as an invitation: to use Trilling's odyssey to explore the ways in which criticism ought to oscillate from the dispensable to the indispensable.

# WALTER BENJAMIN

## *The Demon of Inspiration*

A common assumption in interpreting the oeuvre of Walter Benjamin (1892–1940), the luminous German cultural critic, is that his heart was ripped in half, pulling him dramatically into opposite ends: toward an explorative, nondogmatic Marxism on one side, and toward the study of Hebrew and his emigration to Palestine on the other. His polar friendships with theater innovator Bertold Brecht and Gershom Sholem, the scholar of Jewish mysticism, as reflected in his assiduous correspondence with the latter, where his peripatetic odyssey is wholesomely displayed, testify to his divided self. Of course, the fact that in the end Benjamin procrastinated his *aliyah* and spend inspiring months in Denmark with Brecht and then returned to Germany while the ghost of fascism was sweeping over announces the resolution he gave to his dilemma—a tragic one, no doubt, for he finally decided to leave Berlin when it was already too late, and his suicide in Spain, en route to America, brought redemption to an abrupt end.

Doomed he was, and from the beginning. Benjamin once said of his idol Franz Kafka: "To do justice to a figure like [him] in its purity and its peculiar beauty, one must never lose sight of one thing: it is the purity and beauty of a failure. . . . One is tempted to say: once he was certain of eventual failure, everything worked out for him en route as in a dream." That same, indeed, applies to him: Failure is his trademark, a failure that strives from his existence as an outcast,

First published in *The Forward*, September 10, 1999.

perpetually alienated from his surroundings, at odds with the intellectual trends of his time, committed in impossible enterprises ultimately abandoned. A substantial amount of what he left us with is what in other authors might be seen as debris—outlines, proposals, diary entries filled with dreams and snapshots of larger plans, all colored by frustration and despair—but not in him, for the magnificence and durability of Benjamin's oeuvre lay precisely there: in his triumphant failure. His indecision to follow his heart in full, to make a truce between his disputing selves, made him a wanderer not only physically but spiritually and intellectually, and his legacy is that of a traveler with one too many destinations in sight.

So to approach Benjamin as a battlefield of opposites is simplistic. The approach fails to convey the expansiveness of his talent in all its splendor. That expansiveness, as Volume 2 of his *Selected Writings*, released by Harvard University Press and edited by Michael W. Jennings and others, testifies, made him a model polymath, equally versatile in history and sociology, politics and literature, highbrow and popular art—a polymath that begs to be approach like a jigsaw puzzle. Yes, the magnetism that Brecht and Scholem exerted over him is important, but only on the surface. Benjamin was, at his core, only at home in the habitat of his mind. Settling in Palestine could not have cured his existential pain, and neither could have a more open, democratic Germany. He appeared to be stuck between the West and Levant, but in truth, he was hostage of a more complex dilemma: the either/or of wanting to conceptualize too much. Viewed against the Greek poet Archilochus's famous line, which Isaiah Berlin made use of in a 1951 essay—"The fox knows many things, but the hedgehog knows one big thing"—he was a fox: eclectic, elastic, heterogeneous. Not a man divided in two but broken into multiple parts.

Surely the heftiness of the seven-tome German edition of Benjamin's *Gesammelte Schriften*, published in Frankfurt between 1972 and 1989, ordered generically (essays, reviews, diaries, radio talks, fragments, etc.), makes one wonder if he was ever asleep. His inquisitiveness is always in motion, hypothesizing about Mickey Mouse and children toys, Goethe, Paris, the Lisbon earthquake of 1755, Kant, kitsch, fingerprinting, the publishing industry, astrology, the mentally ill. . . . It is an inquisitiveness obsessed and possessed by the features of the universe, anxious to find patterns and explanations everywhere but also humble enough to recognize that, in spite of all attempts by human reason, accident is the supreme law of Nature.

My own personal admiration for him is profound. It emanates from his conception that criticism is an essential, irreplaceable aspect of intellectual life, a key to unravel who we are and how we understand ourselves as crucial as fiction. But criticism ought to be approached coherently and systematically, free of pedantisms, something hard to do since the Romantics consummated the marriage between literature and individualism and gave an autonomy to fiction it never enjoyed before. So much of what passes today for "unprejudiced" book reviewing is basically uninteresting and unimportant. What is urgently needed—as needed as when Benjamin was active—is a sharp, consistent viewpoint that "has its own logic and its own integrity." In academic circles this approach is often confused by a jingoism that rather than throw light, it obscures and repels. "Annihilatory criticism must retrieve its good conscience," Benjamin once wrote, and in a fragment entitled "Program for Literary Criticism," published sometime between 1929 and 1930, he developed forty thesis to the topic. "There is fine art in giving praise," he claimed, but it is also "a fine art to bring out the importance of something apparently peripheral" through negative comments. The reader must learn to trust the critic not through pyrotechnics of speech but through judgment. Erudition should play a major role but it ought not be used to hypnotize. The critic should build bridges, make connections, venture explanations that, when put together, have a inner logic. Even if he is wrong, he should build a *weltanshauung* as sophisticated as any produced through fictional devices. Finally, surprise and spontaneity must be always in store: The reader is always thankful when the critic is not a parrot. Annihilatory, fearless criticism that is also daring.

The years 1927–34 marked the final decline of the Weimar Republic and the rise of Adolf Hitler into power. As he divorces his wife Dora, leaving her behind with their young child, Benjamin struggles to make ends meet by freelancing as a nonaffiliated critic and lecturer. He is invariably broke. Europe is dying, but an offer to teach at Hebrew University is postponed time and again. Instead, he moves to Paris, hoping to find respite. He writes to Sholem: "I have hardly ever been as lonely as I am here. . . . In these times, when my imagination is preoccupied with the most unworthy problems between sunrise and sunset, I experience at night, more and more often, its emancipation in dreams, which nearly always have a political subject." Previously he was known as a literary theorist; in this period he ventures into new territory, especially popular culture—as Jennings rightly argues, "a discipline he virtually created." Some of Benjamin's best many-sided work is produced in this period of starvation, and it is featured in Volume 2 of *Selected Writings*. It catches what Rudyard Kipling called "the Demon of Inspiration" in ascent while his social life is in steep decline. Benjamin's extraordinary personal essays, "Unpacking My Library" and "Hashish in Marseilles," appear in it, as does his outstanding "Little History of Photography" and his "Berlin Chronicle." Each of these pieces ought to be read at least twice in a single sitting, once to grasp their content, the other to study Benjamin's lucid, unremitting train of thought. Included in the volume as well are pieces on Charlie Chaplin, Stefan George, Karl Kaus, epic theater, contemporary French literature, Søren Kierkegaard, a conversation with Andre Gide, and a couple of by-now classic pieces on Kafka, including one Benjamin wrote in 1934—at a time when he was interested also in Shmuel Josef Agnon—which, in his own words, "brought me to a crossroads in my thoughts and reflections." In it the Czech author of "The Metamorphosis," he argues, "was pushed to the limits of understanding at every turn, and he liked to push others to them as well." Again, the judgment suits Benjamin to perfection, and therein is why the essay is so precious: It is deceitfully autobiographical even if the pronoun "I" is almost totally absent.

Benjamin is the ultimate Jewish critic: the indispensable interpreter of a culture and era that chose to eject him. He once imagined embarking on a book made fully out of other people's quotations. And, also, on a history of dreams. That he never completed these enterprises is, I repeat, the secret of his appeal, for an original intellect stamps its imprimatur in numerous ways, not the least important of which is its minutia. (I confess to be tempted often to take up where he left off on the latter idea, which is nowhere.) Volume 2 of the Harvard edition—a welcome project I cannot praise enough—is filled with astonishingly "annihilating trivia," as astonishing, I dare say, as Benjamin's half a dozen totally realized monographs. Thanks to it, his luminosity, on the eve of the sixtieth anniversary of his premature death, is happily on focus, a luminosity made of a thousand tonalities. Happily, I say, for what else ought criticism be about if not light?

# ALBERTO GERCHUNOFF'S JEWISH GAUCHOS

*L'art est un anti-destin.*

—André Malraux

Up until very recently, Spanish resisted embracing the Jewish sensibility. This becomes clear in a sentence found in the 1974 edition of the *Encyclopædia Judaica,* in which *The Jewish Gauchos* of the Pampas is described as "the first work of literary value to be written in Spanish by a Jew in modern times." The astonishing implication is that roughly between 1492 and 1910, when Alberto Gerchunoff, a Russian émigré to Argentina, compiled his twenty-six interrelated fictional vignettes on life in Moisésville and Rajil, agricultural communities in South America in the late nineteenth century sponsored by Baron Maurice de Hirsch, into a hymn to transculturation in the Pampas, not a single literary item of merit appeared in the language. Prior to the expulsion from the Iberian peninsula, Jews prayed in Hebrew and wrote in Aramaic and Latin, but mostly communicated in Ladino (i.e., Spanioli or Judeo-Spanish), a hybrid blend of Castilian, Hebrew, Turkish, Arabic, and other verbal elements. Which means that the only literature by Jews in Spanish before *The Jewish Gauchos* is a product of *marranos,* crypto-Jews, and new Christians and, by definition, that it falsifies and misrepresents, it denies its Jewishness.

No wonder Gerchunoff is such a quixotic figure: His lifelong project, to turn Spanish into a home for the Jews, to acclimate the language not only to Hebraisms and Yiddishisms but to a *weltanshauung* totally alien to it, went against the currents of history. In

First published as Introduction to *The Jewish Gauchos of the Pampas*, by Alberto Gerchunoff (Albuquerque, NM: University of New Mexico Press, 1997).

fact, he was not only a modern literateur, as the *Encyclopædia Judaica* describes him, but more importantly, was part of the modernista generation that renewed Hispanic American letters between 1885 and 1915. It did it by drawing heavily upon Parnassianism and Symbolism and by establishing a new crystalline and harmonious Spanish syntax based on restraint and precision, a new language musically elegant and spiritedly metaphorical. Gerchunoff befriended Rubén Darío, Leopoldo Lugones, and Delmira Agustini—a Nicaraguan, an Argentine, and an Uruguayan, respectively, all four pillars of the modernista revolution. But his struggle went beyond: Born into Yiddish, he appropriated Quevedo's tongue, making it his own, and dreamed of inserting Spanish-speaking Jews into the twentieth century by building a three-way bridge between renaissance Spain, nineteenth-century Russia and Eastern Europe, and modern Hispanic America. An authentic polyglot (aside from Yiddish and Spanish, he was fluent in Italian, French, English, Portuguese, and Russian), his heroes were Spinoza and Heinrich Heine, both uprooted speakers and "alien guests," as well as Sholem Aleichem and Cervantes, whose verbal talent and florid imagination explain the two facades of Gerchunoff: his Jewish side and his Hispanic side. Not surprisingly, Miguel de Unamuno once described him as "the cosmopolitan man of letters sine qua non."

His enterprise wasn't easy, though; it often clashed against insurmountable obstacles within and without his milieu: scattered outbursts of anti-Semitism and an occasional pogrom in Argentina and the extermination of his direct ancestry in Europe. His views on socialism and democracy, on freedom and Jewish morality, often pushed him against his people, turning him into an outcast. In his twenties, for instance, Gerchunoff portrayed Argentina as a *país de advenimiento,* a Promised Land, the real Palestine where Jews could thrive in total harmony with gentiles. But his hope quickly tuned sour in 1919 with the *semana trágica,* an explosion of xenophobia that amounted to a full-blown pogrom in Buenos Aires. By then he had already been a member of the Partido Socialista and had switched to the Partido Demócrata Progresista, had been incarcerated for a brief period for siding with Cuba during the Spanish-American War, had fought against the right-wing "radicalism" of President Hipólito Irigoyen, and after a visit to Germany had actively campaigned against its anti-Jewish sentiments. All this pushed Gerchunoff inward: He became more introspective and mystical, less hopeful of earthly utopias. He was often accused of being too slow to recognize and publicly denounce the existence of anti-Semitism. His strategy was to put the best face on Jewish-Gentile relations, and this relentlessly positive outlook cut down on his ability to criticize evil tendencies in society. Still, he never lost his militant edge: A couple of decades later, in an unpopular stand at home, he was active gathering support against Hitler and became the most prominent Hispanic-American intellectual to tackle "the Jewish problem"; and then, between 1945 and his death, already suffering from a heart condition, he traveled within Argentina and beyond—to Brazil, Chile, and Peru—to harvest political support for Zionism. Eliezer ben Yehudah had metamorphosed Hebrew into the Promised Land—but Gerchunoff was already too old to master it. The zeitgeist of history had taken him to the wrong Palestine, and he was forced to recognize Spanish as another diasporic home for the Jewish people, not the center stage he had believed it to be.

In this introduction I'm considerably less interested in his end than in his beginnings. According to his passport, Gerchunoff was born in Proskuroff, Russia, on January 1, 1883; his mother dissented, though (and scholars concur): it was in 1884, she claimed, "and into the Yiddish language." Yiddish, indeed, was in the milk he drank and the early Talmudic lessons he got, to the point that, when he switched to Spanish around 1894, thanks to a Sephardic teacher Don Moisés Urquijo de Abenoim, traces of his Yiddish background could be found, as Gerchunoff himself says it in an article compiled in his posthumous collection *The Pine and the Palm Tree*, "in the verbal choices and sentence structures I made." He remained loyal to his mother tongue until his death, using it in his mature age to deliver speeches and lectures at the Sociedad Hebráica in Buenos Aires, a distinguished Jewish community association he helped found. Actually, one might be able to go as far as to say that *The Jewish Gauchos* was thought out in Yiddish, yet written in Spanish: Its pages have a unique syntax, in part due to Gerchunoff's purist modernista approach, for which he became widely known as editorialist, and in part to his Yiddish ascendancy, and they are seasoned with transliterations from the Hebrew pronounced with a heavy Yiddish accent. This magnificent act of tongue-switching highlights Gerchunoff's need of belonging. The characters in his book, stationed as they are in a southern agricultural milieu, are natural descendants of Mendele Mokher Sforim, Sholem Aleichem, and Isaac Leib Peretz. The narrator admits this via such indications as "the woman answered *en judío*—in Jewish." And yet, he favors Sephardic references over Eastern European. Gerchunoff probably considered Yiddish not lofty and august enough to embrace it as his literary vehicle, yet he keeps it alive in his reader's unconscious by modifying his stylized Spanish to invoke its rhythm and cadence. Isn't this further proof that the written word always means more than it says?

Proskuroff was a small shtetl and, as such, it was inhabited solely by lower-class Jews with a modicum of self-sufficiency. In 1886 the Gerchunoffs moved to Tulchin, where "In the Beginning," the opening chapter of *The Jewish Gauchos,* takes place, a "sordid and sad" city, he wrote, where the family stayed several months. Cossack attacks were in the air, "crushing the old walls of the synagogues and the ancient sanctuaries on whose pinnacle the double triangle of Solomon stood shining" and burning "the sacred books of the city's leading synagogue," when Baron de Hirsch, thinking that Zion could well be established in Argentina, appeared from heaven above as a messiah. They began hearing about de Hirsch's Jewish Colonization Association and an envoy was sent to Paris to discuss possible resettlements. He returned with happy news: "Baron de Hirsch—may God bless him!—has promised to save us." With his help the Gerchunoffs traveled first to Berlin and then to Dresden; later on they took the ship *Pampa,* crossing the Atlantic; finally, after a month-long stay at the Hotel de Inmigrantes, a transit post in Buenos Aires, they arrive in Moisésville, an agricultural colony in the Santa Fé province (named after Baron de Hirsch's deceased son, Moisés), chanting:

To Palestine, to the Argentine,
We'll go—to sow;
To live as friends and brothers;
To be free!

Latin America enjoyed relative stability during the last quarter of the nineteenth century. Eager to open its provinces to entrepreneurial settlers to populate the immense, labor-scarce nation, Argentina, up until World War I, attracted a huge number of immigrants, some from the Ottoman Empire but most of them from Eastern Europe and Russia. (From the latter 158,167 Jews alone entered between 1889 and 1914.) Many settled in the provinces of Sante Fé and Entre Ríos, touching off the greatest social change on the Pampa. Argentine statesmen favored the European newcomers, often called gringos by the gauchos: Juan Bautista Alberdi, for instance, was responsible for the famous dictum: "To govern is to populate"; Domingo Faustino Sarmiento, responsible for the classic *Civilization and Barbarism: Life of Don Facundo Quiroga,* saw them as an influx of "civilized" life in a vastly barbaric landscape. Gringos and gauchos seldom competed directly for employment because the former were farmers and the latter herdsmen.

The definitive social origin of the gaucho in the southern hemisphere still lies shrouded in ambiguity: Some emphasize his

Andalusian and Arabic roots; others call attention to his mestizo heritage—a racial and cultural blending of Indian and Iberian components—and believe the term comes either from the Guarani *huachó* or *huachú*, or from the Quechua *huak-cha*. What is unquestionable is that, since the gaucho's appearance around 1745, his costumes and habits changes substantially, always at a slower speed than the negative sentiments against him, which ultimately improved around 1872, when José Hernández published his poetic defense, *The Gaucho Martín Fierro*, now held as a national treasure. Before then, the gaucho was approached as "pastoral people," "ignorant and cruel," "oppressed" and "in an incipient stage of civilization," an antipathy resulting from the clash between urban and rural populations. But Hernández's revolution came too late: As a result of a juggernaut of changes forcing him to abandon his tradition, the gaucho ceased to exist as an identifiable social type during the last third of the nineteenth century. Interestingly, his last sights coincided with Gerchunoff's arrival in Moisésville.

This is symptomatic. All in all, Gerchunoff spent a total of five years as a *gaucho judío*, from the ages of six to eleven. In Moisésville he began attending school, where he learned mathematics, Argentine history and geography, and the rules and grammar of Spanish. In 1891 a tragic event, metamorphosed in the section "The Death of Elder Saul" of *The Jewish Gauchos*, made them tremble: his father, a businessman and Talmudist who "spoke very little Spanish but he spoke energetically," was killed by a vengeful gaucho. Profoundly saddened, Gerchunoff's mother decided to move the family to Rajil, another agricultural settlement where the future writer "learned the stanzas of the national anthem"; and, in 1895, they all settled in Buenos Aires, where Gerchunoff got his first job in a matzoh bakery.

Moisésville and Rajil were small and somewhat isolated, but they were not shtetls in the strict sense of the word: Jews didn't inhabit an isolated island; natives lived in near proximity, constantly interacting with them to the point of transculturation. In the chapter "The Poet," for example, Favel Duglach, a lazy but well-regarded colonist with an artistic twist, "could feel the native Argentine epics of bravery with the same exaltation he experienced when telling some story from the Bible to a tense, expectant group in the synagogue." Gerchunoff describes Duglach as "an original-looking man. A hooked nose dominated his face, and his long beard was balanced by long locks of hair at the back of his head. He wore the loose gaucho trousers, the *bombachas*, under his traditional Jewish cassock, that was belted in his case. It was a fantastic getup, but Favel explained the absurdities by stating: 'I'm a Jewish Gaucho!'" Other similar intercourses abound: In

the Entre Ríos of Gerchunoff, Jews attend *cuadreras* (i.e., rodeos), listen to gaucho stories with biblical undertones around the warming
*fogata,* and fall in love with Gentile *boyeros* while singing beautifully
sad songs, known as *vidalitas.* They both admire the gaucho and fear
him, conceiving "his life as a thrilling amalgam of heroism and barbarism," and wanting to be like him—but with reservations: They perceive themselves as Jews, and their success in the new land depends
on the balancing of an ancestral tradition and the exposure to a form
of cowboy life previously unknown to them.

This description was called an oxymoron by Jorge Luis Borges. "It
is less a truthful historical document than a testimonial of nostalgia,"
he argued. He published several important essays and edited several
anthologies on the gaucho in Argentine culture. In a lecture delivered
at the Colegio Libre de Estudios Superiores in Buenos Aires (*Discusión,*
2nd. ed., 1955) he established the difference between *poesía de los gauchos* and *poesía gauchesca:* the first is a gathering of popular voices
from the Pampas, whereas the second is made of the "artificial" works
of urban writers interested in the gaucho. By definition, the *gauchesco*
writers pervert and falsify and although Borges never acknowledged
Gerchunoff by name (his immense admiration for his Jewish friend
precluded any attacks), his portrayal of the Jewish gaucho falls, in
Borges's eyes, into this category. Indeed, Borges thought that Jews
were farmers and businessmen, merchants and shopkeepers but
never cowboys; since the age of the horseman in the Pampas preceded, and almost concluded before the Jewish immigration,
Gerchunoff's characters, in Borges's eyes, should be addressed as
*chacareros,* small-time farmers descending from the gauchos. The
assessment is part of an ongoing controversy. The literary tradition
that has the gaucho as protagonist enjoys enormous attention in
Argentina. Its highlights in poetry are works by, among others,
Bartolomé Hidalgo, Hilario Ascasubi, Estanislao del Campo, and also
José Hernández; in nonfiction, it had achieved eminence in numerous books, including a handful written by Sarmiento, William Henry
Hudson, Paul Groussac, Leopoldo Lugones, Ricardo Rojas, and Borges;
and in novelized form it was a favorite of Benito Lynch and Ricardo
Güiraldes. Most of these literati, if not all, were urban dwellers whose
knowledge of gaucho life was reduced to sporadic stays on the Pampa.
They glorified this type as a quintessential national idol, a courageous
peasant everywhere carrying his guitar, his poncho, and his vengeful
spirit, which stands in contrast to Gerchunoff's subdued cast: His *gauchos judíos* are not loners but family-oriented breadwinners; they are
neither malicious nor rancorous but loyal to their biblical code of
ethics. Also, in the works of poets like Hidalgo and Hernández the

narrator is often the gaucho himself, but the prose writers often found strategies to distance themselves from their protagonist; *The Jewish Gauchos,* instead, uses a mix of first- and third-person narration, as well as an omniscient voice serving as an ethnographer with a literary joie de vivre: At times the Jewish orphan Jacobo serves as chronicler of the various episodes; but an anonymous "we" occasionally interrupts him, and so does an observer *sub specie aeternitatis.* The result is nostalgic and enchantingly lyrical, but isn't *gauchesco.*

In appropriating not only the Spanish language but also this most Argentine literary tradition in which to insert himself, Gerchunoff had a clear agenda in mind. Several segments of *The Jewish Gauchos* first appeared, from 1908 on, in the literary supplement of the prestigious newspaper *La Nación,* where Gerchunoff's friend Roberto J. Payró had invited him to work. He was twenty-four years old and when later on he turned the various segments into a book-long narrative interconnected by its theme and the occasional reappearance of a small set of idiosyncratic characters, he dedicated the whole product "to the revered memory of Baron Maurice de Hirsch. . . . His was the first bread that my people ate on American soil."

According to the Hebrew calendar, its publication in La Plata under the aegis of J. Sasé took place on Passover of 5670. It coincided with the first centennial of Argentina's independence in 1910. Lugones was the person in charge of the cultural part of the national celebration, and apparently it was he who had the idea of turning the scattered reminiscences in *La Nación* into commemorative material. Gerchunoff's enthusiasm was uncontrollable. "As I greet you, my brothers and sisters of the colonies and cities," he writes in the prologue, "the Republic is celebrating its greatest festival—the glorious feast of its liberation! The days are clear and the nights are sweet, as the praise of national heroes are sung. Voices reach towards a sky that is always blue and white, as in the national flag. The meadows are alive with flowers, and the hills are covered with new grass. Do you remember how, back in Russia, you laid the ritual tables for our Passover's glory? This is a greater Passover." *The Jewish Gauchos,* hence, was meant to be an homage to the national democratic spirit, a wholehearted display of gratitude.

Several Argentine literary works published at the time reflected strong xenophobic sentiments. For example, *Juan Moreira,* an 1880 novel by Eduardo Gutiérrez, portrayed foreigners negatively; and José María Miró (aka Julián Martel) and Juan Alsina, the latter an important immigration official, were openly anti-Semitic: In their works they criticized Jews in the Pampa for not assimilating. The fear is that separatism would ultimately create a nation made of tribes, abysmally fractured. Gerchunoff wisely inserted himself in this debate by using a double edge: He was neither in favor of separatism, nor of total assimilation; in his eyes, Jews on the Pampa were both in and out: They could integrate (the word was his motto) by maintaining their religious faith and tradition but also adopt Argentine national values. And indeed, his argument proved to be successful: Before *The Jewish Gauchos,* immigrants in Argentine letters had been portrayed as outsiders—Cervantes's tongue a foreign soil, unfriendly and uninviting; after it they became insiders and Spanish became their new habitat.

The issue of belonging to the Spanish language is explored by Gerchunoff in a variety of ways. Early in the book, as the Jews of Tulchin discuss their fate, the possibility emerges of a return to the Iberian peninsula. "Spain would be a wonderful country for us to go to," the Rabbi of Tolno says, "if it were not for the curse of the Synagogue that still lingers over it." At which point the Dain, the dean of rabbis, shrugs indignantly, and says in Hebrew: "*Yemach Shemam Vizichrom!,* May Spain sink in the sea! May she break into pieces! May her memory be obliterated!" Indictments such as this reappear, and while the Jewish colonists invoke Jehuda Halevi, Maimonides, and other luminaries of Spanish Jewry before 1498, while they relate to Galicians and other Spaniards farming the land north of their colonies, their link to España is sour: As a character puts it, "I can never think of Spain without having the blood rush to my eyes in anger and my soul fill with hate."

But Spanish was also the home of Cervantes, Gerchunoff's idol, and that for him was sufficient to reevaluate the ancient Jewish ties to his tongue. His strategy was oblique: He abstracted him from his milieu and turned him into a unique genius above human affairs. Curiously, he managed to establish a fascinating connection between him and Sholem Aleichem, his other idol. He saw them as an inseparable pair. While humor is not one of Gerchunoff's strengths, his prologue to a 1942 Spanish translation by scholar and lexicographer Salomón Resnick of Sholen Aleichem's *The Old Country,* and a profile of him included in *The Pine and the Palm Tree,* exalt the artistic qualities the Argentine admired most and which he emulated in *The Jewish Gauchos:* the accurate, affectionate description of impoverished popular types. Cervantes, on the other hand, symbolized the very first attempt to make the novel a modern genre, as well as a man of letters devoting to illustrating, by means of plots and action, existential dilemmas. For Gerchunoff, Tevye the Dairyman was a Yiddish reincarnation of Don Quixote: a humble man whose understanding of reality is limited, yet whose florid imagination and vast (if farfetched) wisdom allows him to uncover secret truths, an unpretentious figure whose optimism is stronger than the absurdity of life. Both books are mere successions of disjointed episodes but achieve the stature of epics in scope and ambition, a quality Gerchunoff dreamed of achieving as he imagined the multilayered dimensions of the colonies in Entre Ríos.

Actually, Sholem Aleichem and Cervantes are more than idealized models; they are the past and future in between which the author of *The Jewish Gauchos* oscillated. When settling in Buenos Aires, at the age of eleven, Gerchunoff dreamed of applying to the Colegio Nacional, of earning a Doctorate in Letters. His early Spanish readings included *Don Quixote*, handed to him by a journalist friend, as well as books in translation, like *The Thousand and One Nights* and Victor Hugo's novels. References to Cervantes, referred to as "our gracious Master," abound in the twenty-six vignettes and continue in all of Gerchunoff's oeuvre, from the first book he published after *The Jewish Gauchos*, entitled *Our Master Don Quixote*, to the one he was in the process of drafting when he died and appeared posthumously: *Return to Don Quixote*. Yiddish was the tongue of his ancestors, the language of departure and heritage—*der alter shprach;* Spanish, instead, was *la lengua nueva*—the language of the new century, representing renewal but also return. In Gerchunoff's view, Cervantes's masterpiece was the most enduring legacy of renaissance Spain, a chain linking him to the Iberian peninsula just as the Jews were aborted from its conflicted territory; Sholem Aleichem, on the other hand, was the voice of his people in a more immediate past. Why didn't he choose Yiddish as his literary vehicle? Or perhaps Russian, another tongue important in his childhood? Because he considered himself a citizen of Argentina and wanted his fellow Jews to experience a similar feeling of loyalty; because he was a Spanish-speaking Jew in a new land of opportunity.

Prudencio de Pereda's English translation, with an introduction by philosopher León Dujovne, appeared in the United States in 1955 under the aegis of Abelard-Schuman, half a decade after Gerchunoff's death at the age of sixty-six. In spite of being "the first work of literary value to be written in Spanish by a Jew in modern times," it received almost no critical notice. This comes as no suprise: It appeared while the Holocaust and the establishment of the State of Israel were fresh in the mind of its readers, becoming central to the reshaping of an American Jewish identity. The Hispanic world hardly commands any attention from Jewish readers in Europe and north of the Río Grande. Aside from a few stories by Sholem Aleichen, Leib Malach, Isaac Bashevis Singer, and a few other Yiddish writers set in Argentina, the region is considered peripheral and is all but forgotten, even today, in the Jewish collective imagination. Jewish history, like all Western histories, travels from east to west, hardly from north to south. Russia,

Central Europe, the Middle East, and the United States are center stage. With half a million Jews on its soil (the fifth largest concentration after the United States, the former Soviet Union, Israel, and France), Latin America was then a minor appendix in Jewish history, a hemisphere of Banana Republics where caudillos fought chaotic revolutions and where Jewish culture remained in diappers. In spite of Gerchunoff's lifelong struggle, American Jews found his endeavors almost inconsequential. This icy reception is in sharp contrast to the enthusiasm with which Gerchunoff's original Spanish edition, under the imprint of Joaquín Sesé and with an introduction by the folklorist Martiniano Leguizamón, was greeted with enthusiasm in Argentina. The applause was wide and clear: The writer was seen as a "brilliant interpreter of the provinces," a master crafter whose prose "makes us appreciate nature and man living in total harmony." The book not only has had numerous editions and inspired a 1974 film under the same title, directed by Juan José Jusid; it also inaugurated a literary lineage among Jewish-Hispanic American writers that includes parodies of Gerchunoff by the Argentine novelist Mario Szichman and evocative explorations of utopia in *Comuna Verdad,* a 1995 novel by Gerardo Mario Goloboff about Jewish anarchism in Argentina. These descendants widely expanded the horizons insinuated in *The Jewish Gauchos:* They moved their plots from the province to the city and back to the countryside and continue to investigate the full effect of the marriage between Spanish and the Jewish sensibility.

Which makes Gerchunoff the door-opener and path-finder. A consummate and savvy *conversateur,* his stature is not unlike that of H. L. Mencken, the U.S. newspaperman responsible for founding *The American Mercury;* nor was he too different from Abraham Cahan, the influential editor of the New York daily in Yiddish, *Der Forvert:* He was neither insulting nor tyrannical, but he managed to be both a magisterial man of letters and a meticulous stylist with a passion for verbal quests—not only for the allocutions they exhibited, but for the space they created for new voices; and as such he originated an entirely new type in Hispanic American literature: the tongue-switcher qua guardian of the language. Gerchunoff spent his entire life in front of the typewriter, so much so that, when death surprised him in 1950, he had seventeen distinguished books to his credit, excluding *The Jewish Gauchos;* and his reportage, obituaries, literary essays, and articles of general interest were almost countless. (Actually, in 1976 Miryam Esther Gover de Nasatsky counted close to 1,300.) Which prompted Borges to portray him, in a tribute in the journal *Davar,* as "the perfect friend of the Spanish dictionary"—no small praise for a poor Jewish immigrant from Proskuroff.

# THE VERBAL QUEST

*"We will build our Temple here," said they, simultaneously, and with an indescribable conviction that they had at last found the very spot.*

—Nathaniel Hawthorne, *Twice-Told Tales*

For quite some time I have been interested in the link between language and religion—more specifically, in the search of a primal tongue that precedes all others, one whose virtue is not lessened by time. Can such a proto-language be at once divine and secular? Can its meaning and interpretation be standardized? My interest is also targeted toward translation: Would such a proto-language symbolize, once and for all, the abolition of the act of translation? Such miscellaneous questions rumbled in my mind not long ago, as I was reading two thought-provoking essays, one by the Mexican poet and essayist Octavio Paz: "Edith Piaf among the Pygmies"; the other: "The Ephemerality of Translation" by Ray Harris, an Oxford professor. While both share a common theme—the reaches and limitations of translation—their asymmetrical relationship is fascinating. Paz argues that the job of translating a text from one language to another is simply impossible. He offers as an example a television documentary he once saw about several Pygmies who heard Edith Piaf's voice magically reproduced by a phonograph an ethnologist had turned on for them to hear. Whereas the ethnologists could identify

First published in *Translation Review* 48–49 (1995). Reprinted in *The Oxford Book of Latin American Essays* (New York and London: Oxford University Press, 1997).

with the song by the French pop singer, a song about jealousy and violent love, the Pygmies immediately became quite frightened: They covered their ears and ran away. They fled because they were unable to recognize such passionate groans. What seemed to be an aesthetic experience for the scientists was horrifying to the Pygmies. Inspired by Claude Lévi-Strauss's book *Tristes Tropiques,* Paz explains that, had the ethnologists tried to translate the song, surely the Pygmies would have felt even more repulsed. The Petrarchian concepts of courtly and passionate love in Piaf's lyrics were totally alien to them: unrecognizable, unapproachable. One could argue, of course, that the Pygmies indeed understood Piaf's message; otherwise they would have made it clear, through a subtle gesture of annoyance, that they disapproved of her groans. Precisely because both the content of the lyrics and the musical form in which these were expressed were so aggressive, so passionate, there was a misunderstanding, a loss in the act of translation. They probably could not picture a woman screaming vehemently without knowledge of the context from which such suffering was born. Perhaps they could not understand why the fragile threads that make a relationship between a Western man and a woman become the source of such misery. In short, they simply could not understand. Paz concludes that translating moral, aesthetic, scientific, or magical concepts from one language to another, from one culture to another, is a hopeless task; it requires that the recipient in the translation process stop being himself—which means that each translation, by its very nature, creates an insurmountable abyss between civilizations, one impossible to bridge.

At first sight, Paz's argument might seem too emphatic, a statement against translation, but it isn't. Without translations our world would be even more chaotic than it already is. Translations result from dialogue, communication, encounters between disparate entities. Although much can be, and in fact is, lost in translations, they ultimately emerge as an attempt to unite, a desire to reach out. In other words, the translation act, in spite of cultural abysses, cannot so easily be discharged: It is a necessity the modern world cannot afford to live without; it provides an essential taste our intellectual life has become accustomed to, the seasoning that keeps our cosmopolitan spirit afloat. And yet, translation is framed by time and space. Before beginning the task, each translator knows, consciously or otherwise, who his reader will be. If *The Iliad,* in its original language, can overcome the passing of numerous generations of readers and still be accessible, with translations we tend to have little patience: When a translation loses vitality, when it becomes obscure, impenetrable, we replace it with a new one; that is, whereas the original text is treated as invaluable and of primary importance, translations are disposable.

This is where Harris's thesis becomes relevant. More and more new translations of literary classics are required, he claims, because mass culture, in love with disposable products, is always in need of new commodities, always involved in prefabricating past goods. From 1947 to 1972, at least eleven translations into German of Wilde's *Portrait of a Dorian Gray* were made; and betwen 1949 and 1969, at least eight translations of Flaubert's *Madame Bovary* were cast into English. To make a new translation is to recycle an already appealing product, to commercialize it once again in order to make it accessible to a new readership. Publishers and the academy have found a logic to justify such a multiplication of items on library shelves: Modern translations are needed because the language of the original becomes outdated with the passing of time. History wears language down and erases formal structures. It invents new meanings for old words, it introduces neologisms, it reshapes syntax. Since our present civilization is in the process of eternal renovation, retranslating a text is a form of renewal, a strategy for rediscovering who we are, for once again posing old questions in search of meaningful answers. For obvious reasons, marketing plays a crucial role here: Each translation entering the literary market promises to be even more "perfect," even more faithful to the original—even more accurate. But accuracy is a tricky word: An accurate depiction is one in which a reader fully believes the portrait a writer delivers; that is, his social model is reflected in the literary model. History is made up of a never-ending drive to reinterpret old models, to reevaluate ancient epochs. The fall of the Aztec city of Tenochtitlán, for instance, has been understood quite differently in the seventeenth, nineteenth, and late twentieth centuries: The fall of Tenochtitlán is constant, but the implications of the disaster vary. The same applies to translation. As consumers, we get trapped in the uncontrollable torpedoing of new translations, texts that reproduce old texts, texts that revise well-known texts—which, at the end, do nothing but annihilate the utopian dream of ultimate perfection.

Of course, no translation can ever be perfect: As a human endeavor, each attempt is doomed to fail before it was ever begun; it will be useful to a generation of readers and then, when language changes, a new translation will become necessary and available. Like everything else around us, new translations add up to the never-ending flow of life-and-death cycles generated by nature. Volumes pile up, shelves are constantly expanded, and our poor, disorganized, incoherent, and illegible Western culture remains imperfect despite our strivings for coherence.

Clearly, Paz's and Harris's arguments are two facets of one ample, irresolvable matter: Do translations serve a purpose? Are we only falsifying the original message? I use the verb "to falsify" with some uncertainty and awe; translators, not without reason, thoroughly dislike it. After all, no one proud of his career would want to perceive his livelihood as the treason the famous adage urges: *traduttore, traditore.* * An act of betrayal involves dishonesty and deception; a falsification implies fakery, infidelity, and even misrepresentation. The dedicated translator spends hours, days, perhaps months and years finding *le mot juste,* the perfect equivalent for a simple word, only to be accused later on of betraying the original— no doubt in a display of ingratitude by readers who were expected to respond positively. But translations do carry in themselves a measure of distance from the original text and although, at times, a writer might confess that his text in a certain translation reads better than in the original, the natural flavor has magically disappeared. Hence, by the verb "to falsify" I mean to distance, to pervert, to switch words and meanings so as to make a specific message accessible to a foreign culture. I want to be cautious enough not to inject the translation with negative powers, however. Although translations are falsifications, we desperately need them to communicate, to find each other across borders.

In translations one frequently gets the feeling that while the taste of the translated text is legitimate and even acceptable, it carries in itself a form of removal, a distancing from the source. Cervantes thought that reading a translation was the same as seeing a Turkish tapestry from behind: as a silhouette, a shadow, not the real object. Robert Frost used to say that poetry is what gets lost in translation. And Hayyim Nahman Bialik, the poet of the Hebrew renaissance, felt that approaching a translation is like kissing a bride through the wedding veil: The physical contact is indeed experienced but only through a degree of separation. Paz begins his article in an interesting way. He tells us that the search for a common language, one that could transcend all languages, is a way to resolve the opposition between unity and multiplicity, which does not cease to intrigue the human spirit: He posits one language of languages vis-à-vis a multiplicity of idioms and dialects, the one and the many.

---

* I first wrote about translation in "Octavio Paz and the Kabbalists," published in 1985. The essay appeared under a different title in my book *Prontuario* (Mexico: Joaquín Mortiz, 1992), pp. 19–24.

I suggest that that original tongue could be approached in at least a couple of ways: as silence, the absence of language, which, of course, is also a form of language; and as music, which, according to Plotinus, is the natural rhythm of the celestial spheres. Music, dance, and pictorial art are enviable forms of creativity because they are never in need of translation: The original message can never be lost. But music, what Hegel considered the true language of the soul, has an even more nearly unique quality: Its ceaseless, ephemeral, innate, abstract nature makes it universal. Anywhere, at any time, music seems to contain a religious ingredient: It links the earthly and the heavenly terrain, it elevates nature to a supernatural level. Spoken language, on the other hand, precludes an education: It depends on context, and thus, it carries an equivocal message. As a result, the longing for a universal language reflects a need as ancient as humankind: to eliminate error, to make words indefinite, unconfined, open to everybody. Latin, Sanskrit, Hebrew are tongues injected with sacred universality: In spite of their imperfect metabolism, they are the closest we can get to the musicality of the original proto-language. Music and silence are what human languages long for.

Another way to resolve the conflict between unity and multiplicity, Paz says, is through translations. Before the erection of the Tower of Babel, the Old Testament myth claims that all nations on earth spoke the same sacred tongue, a human version of God's proto-language. Everyone understood each other. Words were less equivocal and thus less poetic. Meanings were standardized. As humans we will always long for that primal language. We will look for it in the dark corners of our creativity. Shelley once wrote, for instance, that all the poems of the past, present, and future are episodes or fragments of a single infinite poem, written by all the poets on earth—a proto-poem in a proto-language. Borges thought that "every man should be capable of all ideas" And in "Poetry and Imagination" Ralph Waldo Emerson wrote:

> Poetry is the perpetual endeavor to express the spirit of the thing, to pass the brute body and search the life and reason which cause it to exist—to see that the object is always flowing away, whilst the spirit or necessity which causes it subsists. Its essential mark is that it betrays in every word instant activity of mind, shows in new uses of every fact and image, in preternatural quickness or perception of relations. All its words are poems.

And we are attached to poetry, with its plurality of meanings, because, as George Steiner has claimed, after Babel human communication became a casualty: It was lost—irrevocably lost in the chaos of translation.

The interpretation given by rabbinical Judaism to the causes and echoes of Babel can be easily summarized: The desire to unravel the enigmas of the universe and the desire to understand (e.g., explain) God's mysteries made the Almighty angry. He exploded by creating a majestic idiomatic rupture in the universe: The resulting fragmentation was His revenge against man's daring to understand the impossible. Consequently, today everyone speaks a different language and no one understands anything at the same time. Unity has given way to multiplicity and interpretation has become a sort of religion: To interpret is to understand and vice versa. Our human temples are built on multiplicity. We inhabit a world where meaning is relative, equivocal, malleable. Which means that we are always in search of a completely meaningful language but will never be able to find it. Interpretations are hence often for sale. After the oceanic confusion at Babel, man's presumptions have been in the open, and human communication has been ruled by our lack of understanding. Since early on, the search for a universal language, a *lingua franca*, a tongue meaningful to all, was a dream dreamt by prophets, necromancers, and apocryphal messiahs: the abolition of interpretation, the unificational meaning, a return to the source. Classical Latin of the Middle Ages, unlike its vulgar counterpart, upheld this inspiration. In the modern era, two attempts can be noted: Esperanto, invented by the Polish linguist Ludovic Zamenhof in 1887; and the so-called International Auxiliary Language Association, which originated in 1951. Paz did not quite develop the theme of universal language; instead, he chose to develop the concept of the art of translation. Nevertheless, the drive for a language of languages has always led us to a dead end: While we long for unity, we will always be surrounded by multiplicity—our religiosity, our most profound philosophical questions emerge from such a fracture of the many from the ultimate one. But his logic also leads Paz to discredit the phenomenon of translation: Edith Piaf will never be understood by the Pygmies, who will always run away from her groans.

When talking about language, meaning, and communication, what Paz leaves out, and what Harris does not attempt to address, is a third aspect, as important as a universal language and translation, polyglotism. In a sense, polyglotism, the plurality of fluency *in* languages in a single speaker, unity *in* multiplicity, is the only possible human triumph of a universal tongue: a speaker capable of many tongues—a multifaceted entity; or better, a speaker, the source of many speeches. Polyglotism, it goes without saying, also carries within itself a high dose of imperfection: It is self-centered and solipsistic, but it is an option that manages to eliminate needless obstacles in the search of an entirely meaningful act of communication—and as such it is a metaphor of God's stream of consciousness—in which speaker and listener are one.

At this juncture, I need to center on the nature of the Hebrew language and to bring to my readers' attention the linguistic plight underscored in the theory and practice of Kabbalah, a system of thought which I studied under Moshe Idel (a successor of Gershom Scholem) at the Jewish Theological Seminary in New York City. Among Jewish mystics in medieval and Renaissance times, and above all in the esoteric texts *Ra'ya mehemmá* and *Ticuné Zohar,* written between 1295 and 1305 by a certain disciple of Moisés de León, the principle author of *Sefer ha-Zohar,* we see the idea that the Law that Moses received at Mount Sinai had been thought out and even written in its entirety in advance by the Almighty; that is, that Moses served only as a confidant, a vehicle through whom God dictated the past, present, and future history. Nothing resulting is random; everything has been predetermined. We are only actors in a multicast epic saga that began on the first day of Genesis, in the first chapter of the Hebrew Bible, and will end when God's text reaches its final line. Divine language, the Kabbalah suggests, is different from human language (*lashon adoni* and *lashon bnei adam*). They are as incompatible as oil and water. Yet in order to make himself understood, the Almighty had to translate Himself, to make His message comprehensive, accessible to earthly creatures, almost mundane. Thus, He communicated with the people of Israel in a human tongue: that is to say, in Hebrew—the sacred language, the universal tongue, the language of the synagogue and holy scriptures and the vehicle that unites heaven and earth—which does not imply that God spoke Hebrew to Himself. The Almighty is most likely beyond words. He chose Hebrew, *lashon bnei adam,* to find a channel of communication with His chosen people. Consequently, to speak biblical Hebrew is to elevate oneself to the linguistic code of heaven, to sanctify oneself. Understandably, Jewish literati in the Diaspora who spend their lives creating in pagan languages—the cases of Kafka, Scholem, Walter Benjamin, Cynthia Ozick, to name a few—often crave a return to the origin, an ascendance to paradise, a desire to master the Hebrew language.

Translation, then, is a synonym of transformation, of alteration and movement. It is not an aftermath of the Babel confusion: It actually precedes the event. It is not simply a human act; it is also a divine activity. But translation does not preclude interpretation; on the contrary, it incorporates the original in its womb: To understand a text, one has to uncover its secret truths, those truths God carefully hides from us: the mysteries and enigmas of the universe. To translate the Bible into Yiddish or into English does not imply simplifying God's word: It implies an interpretation. It serves to disseminate the divine teachings in a partial manner. Whoever would like to learn the original significance should read the Hebrew. Was the communication between God and Israel in Hebrew mutually understood? Probably not. Probably something was lost in translation . . . with a bit of conceit, says the *Sefer ha-Zohar* as well as Maimonides in his mysterious *Guide for the Perplexed.* The meaning behind God's words and actions is, and will always be, hidden, unclear, mysterious. The fabric of the Divine Mind, the secrets of nature, cannot be completely understood by humans—but it can be interpreted. Interpretation is a way to clarify, to adapt, to make accessible to human ears. It is also often the case that Hebrew is spoken only by a handful of sages. During the Diaspora, the 2,000-year exile, Israel has come into contact with numerous nations, and the need to learn new languages also has become an imperative: Russian, German, Ladino, Polish, Yiddish, Arabic, Czech, French, Latin, Greek, Italian, Spanish, English, Portuguese are secular, pagan tongues used to establish earthly communication. But through these languages the rabbis also want to explain the hidden meanings in the Bible. To speak many languages is to exist in different dimensions, to search in vain for the sole evasive meaning: It helps reduce the degree of misunderstanding, although it does not solve the confusion that reigns in human affairs. Like translation, polyglotism is a desire to penetrate what is not ours; but it is a more authentic, less confusing attempt: After all, there is no third player in the game; the bridge, the intermediary between reader and author is the translator. In a multilingual existence, the translator and the receiver can be one and the same. Multilingualism, thus, is the journey to penetrate different cultures without accessories and without the necessity for change. What is written in Hebrew—the Bible above all—is original; everything else is vulgar reproduction. And yet, to attempt a translation, to make a life of interpreting texts, which is what rabbinical existence longs for, is an act worthy of the heavens.

While translation and interpretation are two very different activities, they are also part of the same linguistic process: To translate is to interpret, and, simultaneously, to interpret is to translate. It is true that a diaphanous and integral translation of meanings between cultures is utterly impossible. It is an impossible feat stemming from our fallible and awkward human condition. To create a universal language, a tongue meaningful to all, is also impossible because it could imply the inversion of the Tower of Babel, a return from multiplicity back to unity, and such a fanciful return to the origin can happen only in mythology, not in the real world. The third solution is a polyglot existence necessary in our civilization: It is obviously the more difficult to accomplish simply because it requires an infinite amount of human energy. But it is the solution that transgresses the original meaning the least. Perhaps it is a solitary device, but the search for a perfectly meaningful language can be accomplished only when the one is inhabited by the many: when God and man are one.

Of course multilingualism has an extraordinary capacity to live in many words at once. Besides, scientists have shown that a polyglotic child must activate more brain cells and ultimately acquires a higher IQ than children exposed to a single tongue. Knowledge of many languages also allows one to understand the nuances that distinguish one culture from another. As for translation, I spend a good many hours of my day reading literature removed from its original source. I do so mechanically, to the point where I, like millions of other readers, forget it is a translation I am reading. That, precisely, is the nature of technological communication in our mass culture: a reality where every encounter seems to contain a degree of separation. Encounters today come through sophisticated artifacts— phone, TV, radio, computers; direct human contact is becoming a casualty of modernity. Translations can thus be perceived as metaphors for our reluctant accessibility to dialogue: Our original voice is often replaced by a secondary source. As for interpretation, we are children of Einstein's relativity and pupils of Rashomon, thriving in finding multiple perspectives, multiple truths. Such multiplicity pushes us to a bizarre form of idolatry: Truth, the Truth spelled with a capital *T*, becomes fragmented, departmentalized, broken into numerous pieces. Interpretation gives way to deception. But again, we cannot do without it: I interpret, thus I exist.

To return to my main interest, the bridge where language and religion intertwine, the more I reflect on the subject, the more I am persuaded to believe in a neo-Platonic structure linking the two: First comes the original language, a proto-language—be it silence or music—through which the Almighty communicates with Himself and, at the same time, narrates the history of the universe; second comes a sacred though imperfect tongue—Hebrew for the Jews—a bridge between heaven and earth; and third comes the plurality of languages we use daily to communicate with one another. Hence, the search for an original language can be understood as an impossible journey, an emanation process that craves a return to the Origin of origins through stops in many linguistic spheres. A proto-language, it seems to me, is a corpus in which every word is simultaneously reduced to one meaning and still keeps a dose of poetry; a vehicle of communication in which words contain within themselves the ancestral memory of everything that once was and will ever be; a tongue in all places at once; a set of infinite words impossible to misunderstand—a linguistic temple that reverses, once and for all, the idiomatic fracture that came after the destruction of the Tower of Babel. It is an abstraction made of smoke rings, of course. The closer we want to get to it, the more we burn the energy that enables us to travel in search of the original tongue. We waste it without any revenue. Some would, of course, suggest that the pilgrimage in search of the primal tongue can also be approached as an end in itself, that the object of the search is always in the searcher. But this opinion leads us nowhere, for nothing can replace the original proto-language: Like paradise, its true worth is beyond human reach. We therefore must find satisfaction in dissatisfaction, happiness in multiplicity. As Borges wrote in "The Analytical Language of John Wilkins": "The impossibility of penetrating the divine scheme of the universe cannot dissuade us from outlining human schemes, even though we are aware that they are provisional." Unity, as a result, is but a dream: We shall always aspire to reach it but will inevitably fail to attain it. The human language thrives in alternatives to the unifying dream in translation, in polyglotism, even in Esperanto; but these are all self-consuming forms of confusion. I am reminded of Stéphane Mallarmé's poem equating the soul to a cigar:

> Toute l'âme résumé
> Quand lente nous l'expirons
> Dans plusieurs ronds de fumée
> Abolis en autres ronds
>
> Atteste quelque cigare
> Brulant savamment pour peu
> Que le cendre se sépare
> De son clair blaiser de feu . . .

# ELIAS CANETTI

## *Sephardic Master*

A cerebral, austere observateur, Elias Canetti never quite found his audience, and the reissuing of his memoirs in a single hefty tome, spanning thirty-two years and originally published in English in three installments (1977, 1982, and 1986, respectively), is unlikely to alter such fate. And happily so, I must add, for there is something quite enchanting and not a bit anachronistic in having Canetti for oneself, without the disquiet of a boisterous crowd applauding in the background. He is, perhaps like the Portuguese poet Fernando Pessoa, a writer's writer—or better, a writer's Jewish writer. Or even better: an unparalleled writer's Jewish writer that serves as a kaleidoscope of twentieth-century Jewish European culture. Why share so secret a treasure?

I sometimes wonder what it must have been, in the late 1950s, to read Borges without the whole intellectual apparatus revering him like a demigod, as it began to do just after 1961, when the Argentine, along with Samuel Beckett, was awarded the prestigious Formentor's Prize, turning him ipso facto into a transnational sensation. Canetti, too, was the recipient of high honors, including the Nobel Prize for Literature in 1981, shortly after Saul Bellow and Isaac Bashevis Singer, in a sequence some anti-Semites in the Hispanic world shamelessly called "Stockholm's Jewish triumvirate." And yet, unlike Borges, he remains an invisible giant—in Salman Rushdie's phrase, "famously unknown"— proof that no award, no matter how prestigious, stands in the way of obscurity.

First published in *The Forward*, February 12, 1999.

Bellow and Singer chronicled, through fiction, the perils of Ashkenazic angst; this Sephardic master, instead, is a nonfictionalist whose quest is to explore the wanderings of the intellect—and its wonderings too. His odyssey is one of constant exile, of repeated switching of languages, of an unrequitable longing for an impossible home. He epitomizes, better than any other Jewish litterateur I know of, the silent perils of the modern Diaspora. His Jewishness, and within it his Sephardic roots, placed him in the privileged position of witness and beholder. He never quite became an actor in the European literary stage; instead, he remained a mere reactor, but one capable of explaining for posterity the continent's overall significance in its days of intellectual and moral decline. Indeed, one feels that in Canetti modern European culture found its ultimate keeper—its larger-than-life shamesh.

He was born in Rutschuk, Bulgaria, in 1905. Ladino was his first tongue, but he came of age in England, Vienna, and Paris and, in his last years, lived in London. Fluent also in English and Bulgarian, he wrote in a dry, Goethean high German, a reflection of his education in Zurich and Frankfurt-am-Main. The *weltanschauung* that resulted from the juxtaposition of his studies with his Jewish ancestry endowed him with the type of cosmopolitanism that allowed him to grab European culture by the throat, deciphering its essence with astonishing accuracy. But how German was he really? Well, at least as much as Kafka and Heinrich Heine, two Jews whose status as pariahs made German literature considerably more elastic, if also more xenophobic. Canetti was a pariah too, a sympathetic stranger. While his oeuvre is required reading in today's Germany, his cultural status is that of a hybrid whose comments are a bit like those of an invited guest to a dinner party whose foreignness automatically gives him the permission to criticize and make people uncomfortable without ever bringing them to expel him permanently from their sight.

Some claim Canetti's most accomplished and memorable achievement is *Die Blendung* (1936), which was first translated in English as *The Tower of Babel*, then reissued as *Auto-da-Fe.* Born a classic, it is a quintessential novel, allegorical in its core, about the nightmares of reason and about the way barbarism threatens the foundations of Western civilization. Its protagonist, Peter Kien, is an alienated intellectual navigating a sea of books, meant to symbolize progress. When they burst into flames, Kien is pushed into the outside world, where one misadventure after the next pushes him to the limit of human knowledge and morality. It is a kind of Jewish novel out of fashion today: lengthy, meditative, profound, tackling an entire civilization in its pages.

Canetti does not excel in inventing alternative universes; he is far better at explaining the mendacity of the one in which we are imprisoned. His forte is not fiction but essays and memoir. He authored the philosophical study *Crowds and Power* (1960), *The Voices of Marrakech* (1967), and *The Human Province* (1985), as well as *The Other Process: Kafka's Letters to Felice* (1969), a meditation on Kafka's romantic life. Nonetheless, his towering accomplishment is the three-volume memoir. In it, his style is suave yet enrapturing, his memory and attention to detail simply extraordinary.

*A Tongue Set Free* takes us from Canetti's birth to 1921. It begins with domestic images—his brother's birth, his grandfathers, the festivity of Purim. The most inspired passages are about the precarious health of Canetti's mother and about his father's unexpected death in 1912. No clear explanation was given to him, but someone mentioned to the seven-year-old that he had died after finding out in the newspaper that the Balkan War was about to break and many people— many of his own, perhaps—would die. "These words sank into me as though Father had spoken them personally. I kept them to myself, just as they had been spoken between us, as though they were a dangerous secret." His mother was forced to take up alone the education of the family. The narrative takes them to Manchester, England, where one of Canetti's uncles, whom the boy thoroughly despised, brought the extended family in search of prosperity. Eventually Canetti moved to Vienna in 1913, a place and time in which he comes to terms with his adolescent ghosts and reckons with the impact of World War I on every level of life.

*The Torch in My Ear* covers his experiences in Frankfurt, Vienna, and Berlin between 1921 and 1931. It describes his first marriage to the Sephardic intellectual beauty Veza Calderon, a first-rate fiction writer in her own right. Its most memorable segments cover Canetti's acquaintance with Brecht, Isaac Babel ("he meant more to me than anyone else I met in Berlin"), and especially Karl Kraus. Kraus was famous, among other things, for his 1898 *Eine Krone für Zion,* an anti-Zionist pamphlet that attacked Theodor Herzl and his dream of Jewish repatriation in Palestine. And he was also known as the editor of the controversial magazine *Die Frackel (The Torch).* Thus Canetti's German title: *Die Frakel im Ohr.* The second volume concludes with his descriptions of the first drafts of *Auto-da-Fe,* which he says he originally wanted to title "Human Comedy of Madmen" and, even less appropriately, "Kant Catches Fire." And it describes how Canetti came to be fascinated by the behavior of crowds, a topic for which he has a name among a small circle of sociologists. An open crowd has no leader, he says. By definition, "it has to fall apart, "to disintegrate," to behave like a hungry beast: ruled by instinct, without logic or common sense. "Crowds," he adds, "is what the 20th-century is truly about."

The third installment, which ends in 1937 with the death of Canetti's mother and the arrival of Nazism (he left Austria in 1938, when the Nazis annexed it), is equally hypnotizing. It includes portions on Joyce, Hermann Broch (author of the masterpiece *The Sleepwalkers*), Thomas Mann, Alban Berg, and, most notably, Robert Musil, the author of *The Man without Qualities,* which is so akin to Canetti's artistic endeavors in its pensive, philosophical pursuit of Europe's intellectual defeat. He also talks about the Spanish Civil War and how it made him frequently think of Goya and Quevedo. He was against Generalisimo Franco. But what matters is not his politics, for Canetti, unlike Orwell or Heminwgay, simply looked at the battles from afar. In his case, though, the war in the Iberian peninsula, and the acquaintance with Sonne, a "todesco"—a German Jew—prompted him to revisit the multifaceted Spanish culture and to ponder his own Iberian roots.

All in all, the memoirs are a monumental feat in the way Canetti ponders intellectual and political ideas and balances them with modest anecdotes. Self-definition as a person, but especially as a writer, is Canetti's *leitmotif.* "A writer needs ancestors," he writes. "He must know some of them by name. When he thinks he is going to choke on his own name, which he cannot get rid of, he harks back to ancestors, who bear happy, deathless names of their own. They may smile at his importunity, but they do not rebuff him. They too need others, in their case descendants. They have passed through thousands of hands; no one can hurt them; that's why the have become ancestors, because they have succeeded without a struggle in defending themselves against the weak." The autobiographer is placed at center stage, but he never kidnaps our attention. It is the overall European continent—its exhaustion and its ideological explosions, seen from a Jewish viewpoint—that in the end becomes the true protagonist: Europe as a civilization gone sour, tired of itself, abducted by its most extremist forces.

Brilliantly translated by Joachim Neugroschel and Ralph Manheim, a pair of first-rate language wizards, the volumes are full of scorn and euphoria. Fascism Canetti investigates patiently, as he does Communism, studied less patiently but with equal conviction. His politics are nondoctrinaire; the only side he takes is that of humanism. Hence his silences. Some ideological currents, like Zionism, he simply chooses to ignore. It is as if he is paying tribute to Kraus, and in Canetti's eyes Zionism seems like a mere distraction. And he says nothing about Bundism or other Jewish ideologies, simply because, unlike many Jewish intellectuals of his age, he is not in search of utopia, not looking for ways to escape the present; instead, he is very much a denizen of the time, much like a ship's architect that, when news reach him that his craft is about to sink, chooses to stay on.

But these silences are paradigmatic and ought not be avoided. Canetti's avoidance in his later work of the Holocaust, for instance, and his disinterest in the post-Holocaust Jewish world, can make him look like a romantic hero: isolated, dismal in his engagement with the present. Is this the reason why, I wonder, his readership is ever so small? Because he failed to speak to a living Jewish community? Did his obsession with exile, his views of the Jews as metaphors, stopped him from establishing a connection with the currents that agitated the sixties and onward? Is this, in the end, why Zionism, in its attempt to bring the Jews back into history, so alien to him?

These autobiographical pages are enthralling not just for what they say but also for what they evade. Canetti is the ultimate somnambulist. His is the odyssey of assimilated German, French, and Austro-Hungarian Jewish intellectuals whose ties with the present were ceased, even though many of them witnessed the radical transformations that took placed after World War II. In his shoulders is the weight and pathos of modernity, the tension between the individual and society, the relentless need to record one's own odyssey and, probably most importantly, the urgency with which the Jewish "I" strives to become a center of gravity, a continent's "eye." Susan Sontag once wrote that Canetti "is someone who has felt in a profound way the responsibility of words . . . [and] his work eloquently defends tension, exertion, moral and amoral seriousness." It does, indeed, and with enormous power. As the globe shifts toward distraction and anti-intellectualism, as territorial politics tore apart the Jewish heart, however, this spirited defense is likely to remain, kindly, only for the initiated.

Pop

Culture

# ¡VIVA EL KITSCH!

Kitsch is king in the Hispanic world. Nothing is original and all things are their own parody. I say this not in a condescending tone: Counterfeit is beautiful. The region is hypnotizing in its artificiality; everything in it is bogus: The Roman alphabet is, in and of itself, an extraneous import, and so life must be lived in translation; likewise, democracy, condoms, Aristotle, TV soaps, clocks, blackness, money, violins, Satan, and antibiotics are all foreign idols. No wonder its citizens aren't skilled at producing but at reproducing.

In fact, kitsch, as a concept, must be fully and painstakingly redefined so as to capture its immense possibilities south of the Rio Grande. Clement Greenberg believed it to be a counterpoint to bohemian art. "Where there is an avant-garde," he would argue, "generally we also find a rearguard . . . that thing to which Germans give the wonderful name of *Kitsch*: popular, commercial art and literature with their chromeotypes, magazine covers, illustrations, ads, slick and pulp fiction, Hollywood movies, etc., etc." Walter Benjamin saw it as the automatic attempt to turn a one into a many, of making uniqueness into multiplicity. But these views apply solely to Europe and the United States, where kitsch, "that gigantic apparition," is a mass-made product. In the modern Latin American orbit, though, it encompasses much more: high- and lowbrow culture and middle-brow as well; the masses and the elite; the unique and the duplicated—in short, the entire culture. Everything in the region is

First published as Preface to *The Riddle of Cantinflas: Essays on Hispanic Popular Culture* (Albuquerque, NM: University of New Mexico Press, 1998).

slick, everything a postcard, everything a never-ending et cetera, including, of course, those manifestations striving to be pure and authentic at heart and designed to repel all foreign influences. What is its population without these foreign influences?

All this leads one to conclude that the triumphant entrance of kitsch into history did not come about, as Greenberg falsely believed, with the rapid population growth that affected the industrialized nations in the first third of our century. Nor was it born, as Benjamin misstated in "The Work of Art in the Age of Mechanical Reproduction," when photography became a fashion in France and Germany. Instead, the origins of kitsch are to be found elsewhere; they are a product of the Spanish mediocrity, of its frivolity. Yes, honor to whom honor is due. If Spain can pride itself of any solid contribution to Western civilization, it is precisely that derivativeness, that hand-me-downness practiced from generation to generation light years before the Xerox machine was even invented. Only within its national borders is the art of copying, of imitating, a national sport, and it is apparent in all epochs, from the massively produced chivalry novels that accompanied the Iberian conquistadors in the colonization of the so-called New World to Pedro Almodóvar's fashionable *cursilería.* Kitsch, in Western eyes, carries along a sense of fraudulence, of sin, of imposture, of plagiarism, but not in Spain, where talent must be found in the lack of talent, where fantasy is congenital to the trite and repetitive. What is *Don Quixote* if not first-rate art born from exhaustion and duplication? How to explain the Spanish Golden Age if not by invoking Lope de Vega's 728 "original" *comedias*? What is baroque architecture if not a caricature of previous architectural modes? In fact, I am tempted to date with as much precision as is advisable—and I do so in "Appeal of the False *Quixote*"—the moment when kistch became an inseparable stamp of the Hispanic idiosyncrasy: in 1614, when Avellaneda, trying to beat a turtle-paced Cervantes, appropriated the characters of Don Quixote and Sancho and published the second part of *Don Quixote.* The age of illegitimacy was thus legitimated.

Analogously, the Americas, an outgrowth of Spain, are a sequel, an imitation of an imitation, a plagiarist plagiarizing another plagiarist, Velázquez's *Meninas* within Velázquez's *Meninas*. No wonder Simho and published the second part of onization of the so; no wonder the first modern novel in Spanish America, *The Itching Parrot* by Fernández de Lizardi, was modeled after *El lazarillo de Tormes*; no wonder Cubans are called "the Jews of the Caribbean"; no wonder Benito Juárez is the Mexican Abraham Lincoln; no wonder Buenos Aires is London-on-the-River-Plate; and no wonder Pierre Menard rewrites *Don Quixote*—that is, he doesn't set out to copy it verbatim, but simply to *re*compose it from memory, word by word and comma by comma. To *re*compose, to *re*create, to *re*vive. . . . If Spaniards are semimodels, Latin Americans are hypermodels, countermodels, and antimodels: Frida Kahlo's pure fake becomes a myth; Selena's virginal beauty is a hybrid, an in-between confused with the *Vírgen de Guadalupe*; Subcomandante Marcos is not a freedom-fighter but an actor; Cantinflas is Charlie Chaplin without conscience. Nothing is real but the surreal.

I have been infatuated by this duplicity, by this all-encompassing artificiality, for quite some time. Its possibilities seem to me infinite. If asked to explain the reason behind my obsession, I am tempted to reply that I am myself a double-entendre, a bit Jewish and a bit Hispanic and, lately, a bit American as well, neither here nor there—a faked self. The reply might not be convincing enough, but at least it insinuates what I've said elsewhere: that I live my life possessed by the feeling that others before me have already done the same things I do, that I am but a replica. So why do *I* matter? What are my role and purpose? To call attention to this deception, perhaps, to unveil this trickery only to find out, of course, that I am both the veil and the veiled, the searcher and the object of my search.

# THE LATIN PHALLUS

## A Survey

*Somos el duelo a muerte que se acerca fatal.*

—Julia de Burgos

I envision a brief volume, a history of Latin sexuality through the figure of the phallus, not unlike Michel Foucault and René Magritte's *Ceci n'est pas une pipe:* a compendium of its capricious ups and downs, ins and outs, from the Argentine Pampa to the Rio Grande and the Caribbean. An essay in representation, it would begin with the intimidating genitalia of the sovereigns of courage, Hernán Cortés, Francisco Pizarro, and Spanish explorers like Hernando de Soto and Cabeza de Vaca. It would make abundant display of the often graphic art of the gay awakening of the early 1970s, shameless in its depiction of the male organ. And it would conclude, perhaps, with the ribbing of feminists. Here, for instance, is a poem by Cherríe Moraga, for one of its last pages:

> there is a man in my life
> pale-man born infant
> pliable flesh his body remains
> a remote possibility
> in secret it may know many things
> glossy newsprint female thighs
> spread eagle wings
> in his flying imagination

First published in *Transition* 65 (Spring 1995). Reprinted in *Art and Anger: Essays on Politics and the Imagination* (Albuquerque, NM: University of New Mexico Press, 1996).

soft shoe
he did the soft shoe
in the arch that separated the living
from dining room
miller trombone still turns his heel
and daughter barefoot and never pregnant
around and around and around

soft-tip
penis head he had
a soft-tipped penis that peeked out
accidentally one kitchen cold morning
between zipper stuck and boxer shorts
fresh pressed heat lining those tender white-meat loins

wife at the ironing board:
"what are you doing, jim, what are you doing?"
he nervously stuffed the little bird back
it looked like *Peloncito*
the bald-headed little name
of my *abuelita's pajarito*

*Peloncito*
a word of endearment
never told to the child
father
yellow bird-man
boy

Let me map the ambitions of my little book by starting at the beginning. The Iberian knights that crossed the Atlantic, unlike their Puritan counterparts in the British Colonies, were fortune-driven bachelors. They did not come to settle down. As Cortés wrote to Charles V in his *Cartas de Relación*, the first conquistadors were trash: rough, uneducated people from lowly origins. Their mission was to expand the territorial and symbolic powers of the Spanish crown; their ambition in the new continent was to find gold and pleasure. And pleasure they took in the bare-breasted Indian women, whom they raped at will and then abandoned. A violent eroticism was a fundamental element in the colonization of the Hispanic world, from Macchu Picchu to Chichén Itzá and Uxmal. The primal scene of the clash with the Spaniards is a still-unhealed rape: The phallus, as well as gunpowder, was a crucial weapon used to subdue. Machismo as a cultural style endlessly rehearses this humiliating episode in the history of the Americas, imitating the violent swagger of the Spanish conquerors. (This, despite the Indian legends that Cortés was the owner of a tiny, ridiculous penis.)

The hypocrisy of the Church played a role as well. Although the priesthood bore witness to the rapacious sexuality of the Spanish soldiery, *fingieron demencia,* they pretended to be elsewhere. Simultaneously, they reproduced the medieval hierarchy of the sexes that prevailed in Europe: man as lord and master, woman as servant and reproductive machine. In his insightful book *Demons in the Convent,* the journalist and anthropologist Fernando Benítez eloquently described how the Church in the seventeenth century established an atmosphere of repressed eroticism. The archbishop of Mexico City, Aguiar y Seijas, a demonic man who walked with crutches and nourished a thousand phobias, *detested* women: They were not allowed in his presence. If, in a convent or monastery, a nun walked in front of him, he would ipso facto cover his eyes. Only men were worthy of his sight—men and Christ. In the religious paraphernalia of the Caribbean, Mexico, and South America, Jesus and the many saints appear almost totally unclothed, covering only their private parts with what in Spanish is known as *taparrabo;* whereas the Vírgen de Guadalupe, the Vírgen de la Caridad, the Vírgen del Cobre, and a thousand other incarnations of the Virgin Mary are fully dressed.

In a milieu where eroticism reigns, my volume on the Latin phallus is obviously far from original. In Oscar Hijuelos's Pulitzer prize–winning novel *The Mambo Kings Play Songs of Love* (1989), the male organ plays a crucial, obsessive role. The narrative is a sideboard of sexual roles in the Hispanic world. Nestor and Cesar Castillo, Cuban expatriates and musicians in New York City, personify Don Quixote and Sancho Panza: One is an outgoing idealist, the other an introverted materialist. Throughout Nestor's erotic adventures, Hijuelos refers to the penis as *la cosa:* the thing. Its power is hypnotic, totemic even: When men call on women to undo their trousers, women reach down without looking to unfasten their lover's buttons. The novel's libidinal voyeurism even extends to incestual scenes, like the one in which Delores, Hijuelos's female protagonist, finds herself in touch with her father's sexuality.

> In imitation of her mother in Havana, Delores would cook for her father, making do with what she could find at the market in those days of war rationing. One night she wanted to surprise him. After he had taken to his bed, she made some caramel-

glazed *flan*, cooked up a pot of good coffee, and happily made her way down the narrow hallway with a tray of the quivering *flan*. Pushing open the door, she found her father asleep, naked, and in a state of extreme sexual arousal. Terrified and unable to move, she pretended that he was a statue, though his chest heaved and his lips stirred, as if conversing in a dream. . . . He with his suffering face, it, his penis, enormous. . . . The funny thing was that, despite her fear, Delores wanted to pick up his thing and pull it like a lever; she wanted to lie down beside him and put her hand down there, releasing him from pain. She wanted him to wake up; she didn't want him to wake up. In that moment, which she would always remember, she felt her soul blacken as if she had just committed a terrible sin and condemned herself to the darkest room in hell. She expected to turn around and find the devil himself standing beside her, a smile on his sooty face, saying, "Welcome to America."

For a culture as steeped in sexuality as our own, it is strange that the substance of our masculine identity remains a forbidden topic. We are terrified of exposing the labyrinthine paths of our unexplained desire, of engaging in what the Mexican essayist and poet Octavio Paz once called "the shameful art of *abrirse*"—opening up and losing control, admitting our insecurities, allowing ourselves to be exposed, unprotected, unsafe. We are not Puritans; our bodies are not the problem. It is the complicated, ambiguous pathways of our desire that are too painful to bear. We have adopted the armature of our Spanish conquerors: Hispanic men are machos, dominating figures, rulers, conquistadors—and also, closeted homosexuals. In *The Labyrinth of Solitude*, Paz has been one of the lonely few to criticize male sexuality:

> The macho commits . . . unforeseen acts that produce confusion, horror and destruction. He opens the world; in doing so, he rips and tears it, and this violence provokes a great, sinister laugh. And in its own way, it is just: it reestablished the equilibrium and puts things in their place, by reducing them to dust, to misery, to nothingness.

Unlike men, Hispanic women are indeed forced to open up. And they are made to pay for their openness: They are often accused of impurity and adulteration, sinfulness and infidelity. We inhabitants of the Americas live in a nest of complementing stereotypes: On one side, flamboyant women, provocative, well-built,

sensual, lascivious, with indomitable, even bestial nerve and intensity; on the other, macho men. Both seemingly revolve around the
phallus, an object of intense adoration, the symbol of absolute
power and satisfaction. It is the source of the macho's self-assurance
and control, sexual and psychological, and the envy of the Hispanic
woman. Our names for the penis are legion; besides the *pajarito* of
Cherríe Moraga's boxer-short reverie, it goes by *cornamusa, embu-
tido, flauta, fusta, garrote, lanza, masta, miembro viril, pelón, peloncito,
pene, pinga, plátano, príapo, pudendo, tesoro, tolete, tranca, verga,* and
*zurriago,* among many others.*

Where to begin describing the multiple ramifications of the adoration of the phallus among Hispanics? In the Caribbean, mothers
rub a male baby's penis to relax him, to force him out of a tantrum.
In Mexico the *charros (guasos* in Chile, *gauchos* in Argentina) are legendary rural outlaws, independent and lonely men. Their masculine adventures, clashes with corrupt landowners and politicos, live
on through border ballads, known in the United States–Mexican border as *corridos,* and *payadores,* a type of South American minstrel
who accompanies himself with a guitar. (The celebrated no-budget
film by Robert Rodriguez, *El Mariachi,* is a revision of this cultural
myth.) The Latin man and his penis are at the center of the
Hispanic universe. Ironically, more than one rebellious Hispanic
artist, including Andres Serrano, has equated the Latin penis to the
crucifix. Which helps understand what is perhaps the greatest contradiction in Hispanic male sexuality: our machismo, according to
the dictionary an exaggerated sense of masculinity stressing such
attributes as courage, virility, and domination. Take bullfighting, an
erotic event like no other, supremely parodied in Pedro Almodóvar's
film *Matador.* Where else can the male strike such provocative sexual poses? Carlos Fuentes described the sport in his book *The Buried
Mirror:* "The effrontery of the suit of lights, its tight-hugging
breeches, the flaunting of the male sexual organ, the importance
given to the buttocks, the obviously seductive and self-appraising
stride, the lust for blood and sensation—the bullfight authorizes this
incredible arrogance and sexual exhibitionism." Essentially bestial,
the *corrida de toros* is a quasi-religious ceremony unifying beauty,
sex, and death. The young bullfighter, an idol, is asked to face with
grace and stamina the dark forces of nature symbolized in the bull.
His sword is a phallic instrument. A renaissance knight modeled
after Amadís de Gaula or Tirant Lo Blanc and parodied by Don

---

* See *Léxico Sexual,* by Hernán Rodríguez Castelo (Quito, Equador: Ediciones Libri
Mundi, 1979).

Quixote, he will first subdue and then kill. *Viva el macho!* Blood will be spilled and ecstasies will arrive when the animal lies dead, at which point the bullfighter will take his hat off before a beautiful lady and smile. Man will prevail, the phallus remains all-powerful, and the conqueror will be showered with red flowers.

The Hispanic family encourages a familiar double-standard. Few societies prize female virginity with the conviction that we do. But while virginity is a prerequisite for a woman's safe arrival at the wedding canopy, men are encouraged to fool around, to test the waters, to partake of the pleasures of the flesh. Virgins are *mujeres buenas:* pure, ready to sacrifice their body for the sacred love of a man. Prostitutes, on the other hand, are hedonistic goddesses, *mujeres malas,* safeguards of the male psyche. Like most of my friends, I lost my virginity to a prostitute at the age of thirteen. An older acquaintance was responsible for arranging the "date," when a small group of us would meet an experienced harlot at a whorehouse. It goes without saying that none of the girls in my class were similarly "tutored": They would most likely become women in the arms of someone they loved, or thought they loved. But love, or even the slightest degree of attraction, were not involved in our venture. Losing our virginity was actually a dual mission: to ejaculate inside the hooker, and then, more important, to tell of the entire adventure afterwards. The telling, the story of the *matador* defeating his bull, the conqueror's display of power, was more crucial than the carnal sensation itself. I still remember the dusty art deco furniture and the blank expression of the woman. She was there to make me a man, to help me become an accepted member of society. Did we talk? She asked me to undress staightaway and proceeded to caress me. I was extremely nervous. What if I were unable to prove myself? The whole ceremony lasted twenty minutes, perhaps less. Afterward I concocted a predictable cover, announcing to my friends that the prostitute had been amazed at my prowess, that I had made her *very* happy, that she had been shocked at my chastity.

We told tall tales to compensate for the paucity of our accomplishments. After all, a prostitute is an easy triumph. Even consensual sex is an unworthy challenge for the aspiring macho. Courting women with serenades and flowers, seducing them, undressing and then fucking them, *chingar,* only to turn them out: that's the Hispanic male's hidden dream. *Chingar* signifies the ambiguous excess of macho sexuality. Octavio Paz's exploration of the sense of term concludes that the idea denotes a kind of failure: The active form means to rape, subdue, control, dominate. *Chingar* is what a macho does to women, what the Iberian soldiers did to the native

Indian population, what corrupt politicos do to their electorate. And the irreplaceable weapon in the art of *chingar*, the key to the Hispanic worldview, is *el pito*, the phallus.

Not long ago, while writing on the Chicano Movement of the late sixties, I came across the extraordinary figure of Oscar "Zeta" Acosta, defender of the dispossessed. Born in 1935 in El Paso, Texas, Acosta became a lawyer and activist, well-acquainted with César Chávez, Rodolfo "Corky" González, and other political leaders of the era. An admirer of Henry Miller and Jack Kerouac and a close friend of Hunter S. Thompson, whom he accompanied in his travel to Las Vegas (Acosta is the three-hundred-pound Samoan of *Fear and Loathing in Las Vegas*), Acosta wrote a couple of intriguing novels about the civil rights upheaval in the Southwest: *The Autobiography of a Brown Buffalo,* published in 1972, and *The Revolt of the Cockroach People,* which appeared a year later. Both volumes detail a man's rite of passage from adolescence to boastful machismo. A cover photograph by Annie Leibovitz showed Acosta as a Tennessee Williams–type, a perfectly insecure macho with flexed muscles and spiritual desperation in his eyes: He is in an undershirt and stylish suit pants, fat, the lines in his forehead quite pronounced. He is thirty-nine years old and looks a bit worn out. Besides this picture, nothing is certain about him, except, perhaps, the fact that in the early seventies he went to Mazatlán, a resort area and port on Mexico's Pacific coast, and disappeared without a trace.

The moral of Acosta can be used to understand what lies behind the ostentation and bravado of the macho: a deep-seated inferiority complex. The size and strength of the penis is the index of masculine value, as well as the passport to glorious erotic adventure. Inevitably, then, it is also a boundless source of anxiety.

Acosta is all emblem of the insecure Hispanic male. His machismo could not hide his confusion and lack of self-esteem. He spent his life thinking his penis was too small, which, in his words, automatically turned him into a fag. "Frugality and competition were my parents' lot," he writes, describing his and his brother's sexual education. "The truth of it was [they] conspired to make men out of two innocent Mexican boys. It seems that the sole purpose of childhood was to train boys how to be men. Not men of the future, but *now*. We had to get up early, run home from school, work on weekends, holidays and during vacations, all for the purpose of being men. We were supposed to talk like *un hombre,* walk like a man, act like a man, and think like a man." But Acosta's apprenticeship in masculinity was undermined by the embarrassment of his tiny phallus. He perceived himself as a freak, a virile metastasis.

If it hadn't been for my fatness, I'd probably have been able to do those fancy assed jackknifes and swandives as well as the rest of you. But my mother had me convinced I was obese, ugly as a pig and without any redeeming qualities whatsoever. How then could I run around with just my jockey shorts? V-8's don't hide fat, you know. That's why I finally started wearing boxers. But by then it was too late. Everyone knew I had the smallest prick in the world. With the girls watching and giggling, the guys used to sing my private song to the tune of "Little Bo Peep."

. . . "Oh, where, oh where can my little boy be? Oh, where, oh where can he be? He's so chubby, *pansón,* that he can't move along. Oh, where, oh where can he be?"

Acosta is a unique figure among male Chicano novelists, in that his bitter, honest reflections do nothing to enhance his machismo.

I lost most of my religion the same night I learned about sex from old Vernon. When I saw the white, foamy suds come from under his foreskin, I thought he had wounded himself from yanking on it too hard with those huge farmer hands of his. And when I saw his green eyes fall back into his head, I thought he was having some sort of seizure like I'd seen Toto the village idiot have out in his father's fig orchard after he fucked a chicken.

I didn't much like the sounds of romance the first time I saw jizz. I knew that Vernon was as tough as they came. Nothing frightened or threatened him. He'd cuss right in front of John Hazard, our fag Boy Scout leader as well as Miss Anderson [our teacher]. But when I heard him OOOh and AAAh as the soap suds spit at his chest while we lay on our backs inside the pup tent, I wondered for a second if sex wasn't actually for sissies. I tried to follow his example, but nothing would come out. With him cheering me on, saying, "Harder, man. Pull on that son of a bitch. Faster, faster!" it just made matters worse. The thing went limp before the soap suds came out.

He advised me to try it more often. "Don't worry, man. It'll grow if you work on it."*

* I developed these reflections on Acosta's identity in my book *Bandido* (New York: HarperCollins, 1995).

Taboos die hard, if they ever do. After emigrating to the United States in 1985, my identity changed in drastic ways. I ceased to be Mexican and became Hispanic, and my attitude toward homosexuals underwent a metamorphosis. Still, that transformation took time. Even as homosexuals entered my peer group and became my friends, I was uneasy. At times I wondered whether having homosexual friends would make others doubt my sexual identity. Though I've never had an intimate encounter with another man, I have often wondered what I would feel, how I would respond to a kiss. As José Ortega y Gasset said: *Yo soy yo y mi circunstancia,* I am the embodiment of my culture.

My father had taught me to show affection in public. When departing, he would kiss me without inhibition. But as I became an adolescent, I heard my friends whisper. Was I secretly a deviant? To be a Hispanic man was to hide one's emotions, to keep silent when it came to expressing your heart. We are supposed to swallow our pain and never cry *como una niña,* like girls. Keep a straight face, suck it up—*sé muy macho.* Many Hispanic adolescents still find role models in the confident and aggressively reserved stars of the Golden Age of Mexican film, black-and-white celebrities like Pedro Armendáriz, Jorge Negrete, and Pedro Infante, Hispanic analogues of James Dean and John Wayne. These figures were classic macho: ultra-masculine Emiliano Zapata mustaches, closely cropped dark hair, a mysterious Mona Lisa smile, thin, well-built bodies, and an unconquerable pride symbolized by the ubiquitous pistol. Vulnerability means cowardice. Deformity was not only evidence of weakness but a sign of unreadiness to face the tough world. In spite of his verbal bravura, Cantinflas, the Charlie Chaplin of Spanish-language films like *Ahí está el detalle,* was antimacho: poorly dressed, badmouthed, short, unhandsome, without a gun and hence probably possessed of a tiny phallus.

Among Hispanics, homosexuals are the target of nearly insurmountable animosity. If the Latin phallus is adored in heterosexual relations, it is perceived as wild, diabolic, and uncontrollable for homosexuals. Reinaldo Arenas, the raw Cuban novelist who died of AIDS in New York City in 1990, argued that Latin society comprises five classes of homosexual: the *dog-collar gay,* boisterous and out, constantly being arrested at baths and beaches; the *common gay,* who is sure of his sexual identity but who never takes risks, save to attend a film festival or write an occasional poem; the *closeted gay,* a man with a wife and children and a public profile, who is reduced to sneaking off to the baths without his wedding ring; the *royal,* a man whose closeness to politicians and people of power allows him

Movie posters of *Cantinflas y su prima* and *Ahí está el detalle*

César Chávez in Delano

Mario Vargas Llosa and
Gabriel García Márquez

Subcomandante Marcos and
Rigoberta Menchú

Elias Canetti and Lionel Trilling

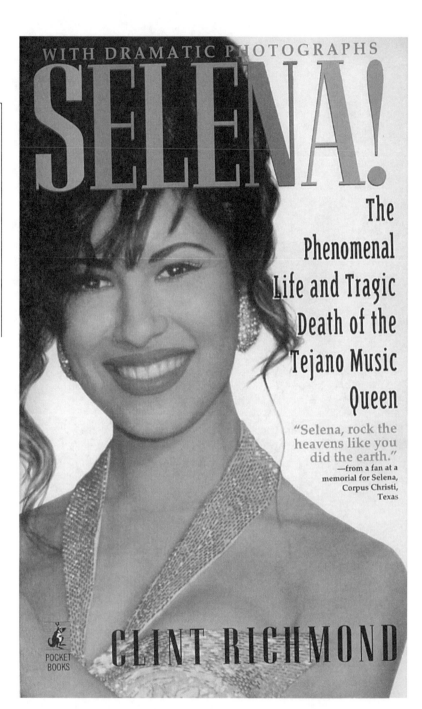

WITH DRAMATIC PHOTOGRAPHS

# SELENA!

The
Phenomenal
Life and Tragic
Death of the
Tejano Music
Queen

"Selena, rock the
heavens like you
did the earth."
—from a fan at a
memorial for Selena,
Corpus Christi,
Texas

CLINT RICHMOND

POCKET
BOOKS

# Vuelta

REVISTA MENSUAL • 25 PESOS

O XXII · JUNIO DE 1998 · NÚMERO 259

## In memoriam Octavio Paz

Walter Benjamin

to be open about his sexual identity, to lead a "scandalous" life, while still holding public office; and finally the *macho*, whose cock-sure bravado is intended to fend off questions about his sexual identity. It goes without saying that most gay men are forced to assume the less public personas.

In his second book, *Days of Obligation*, Richard Rodriguez includes an essay, "Late Victorians," about his own homosexuality and AIDS. He ponders the impact of the epidemic. "We have become accustomed to figures disappearing from our landscape. Does this not lead us to interrogate the landscape?" Very few in the Hispanic world have dared to address the subject: Hispanic gays remain a target of mockery and derision, forced to live on the fringes of society. To be gay is to be a freak, mentally ill, the sort of abnormality José Guadalupe Posada, the celebrated turn-of-the-century Mexican lampooner, often portrayed in his sarcastic cartoons: a creature with legs instead of arms, a dog with four eyes. And yet, homosexuality, a topic few are willing to address in public, is the counterpoint that defines our collective identity. Despite the stigma, homosexuals have been an ubiquitous presence in the Hispanic world, a constant from the Cuban sugar mill to the colonial *misión* from Fidel Castro's cabinet to the literary intelligentsia. And, like St. Augustine's attitude toward the Jews, the established approach toward them follows the maxim: Don't destroy them, let them bear witness of the lawless paths of male eroticism. They are the other side of Hispanic sexuality: a shadow one refuses to acknowledge—a "they" that is really an "us." Again, the language betrays us: the panoptic array of terms for homosexual includes *adamado, adelito, afeminado, ahembrado, amaricado, amujerado, barbalindo, carininfo, cazolero, cocinilla, enerve, gay, homosexual, invertido, lindo, maría, marica, mariposa, ninfo, pisaverde, puto, repipí, sodomita, volteado, zape,* to name only a few.

I recall an occasion in which one of my Mexican publishers, the Colombian director of the extraordinarily powerful house Editorial Planeta, sat with me and a gay friend of mine from Venezuela. In a disgusting display of macho pyrotechnics, the man talked for the better part of an hour about the size of his penis. His shtick was full of degrading references to homosexuals, whom he described variously as kinky, depraved, and perverted. The presence of a self-identified "queer writer" at the table only stimulated his attack. He suggested that the United States was the greatest nation on earth, but that sexual abnormality would ultimately force its decline. Days later my Venezuelan colleague told me that the publisher had made a successful pass at him that very night. They shared a hotel room. This sort of attitude isn't uncommon. The Hispanic macho goes out of his way to keep appearances, to exalt his virility, but he often fails. Sooner or later, his glorious masculinity will be shared in bed with another man.

In the Mexico of the 1970s in which I grew up, common sense had it that machos were the unchaste victims of an unsurpassed inferiority complex. Unchaste victims—impure, yes, but sympathetic characters, and commanding figures. Homosexuals, on the other hand, were considered oversensitive, vulnerable, mentally imbalanced, unproven in the art of daily survival. At school, the boys were constantly made to test their muscular strength. Girls were allowed to cry, to express their emotions, while we *men* were told to remain silent. If to open up was a sign of feminine weakness, to penetrate, *meter*, meant superiority. Sex—fucking—is how we prove our active, male self, subduing our passive, female half. Physical appearance was fundamental to this regime: Obesity and limping were deviations from the norm, and hence effeminate characteristics.

Who is gay among us? It's a secret. We simply don't want to talk about it. Although a few essays have been written about Jorge Luis Borges's repressed homosexuality, the topic is evaded in Emir Rodríguez Monegal's 1978 biography. Borges lived most of his life with his mother and married twice: once, briefly, in his forties, and then to María Kodama a few months before his death in 1986, in order to turn her into the sole head of his estate. His writing is remarkable for its lack of sexuality. When his stories do verge on the intimate, they portray only rape or molestation. Still, the matter is hushed up, the details of a life subordinated to the dense lyricism of an oeuvre. Undoubtedly, concern for the master's reputation can explain some large part of the silence.

Take the case of John Rechy, whose 1963 novel *City of Night*, a book about hustlers, whores, drugs, and urban criminality, garnered him accolades and a reputation as one of the most promising Chicano writers of his generation. Shortly thereafter Rechy's book was categorized as a "gay novel," a stigma that tarred the book for Hispanic readers in the United States. It is only recently, since the onset of the North American gay rights movement, that Rechy's achievement has been reevaluated. And then there's Julio Cortázar, the celebrated Argentinean novelist and short-story writer responsible for *Hopscotch*. In 1983, at the peak of his fame and just a year before his tragic death, he made a trip to Cuba and then New York, there to address the United Nations about the *desaparecidos* in South America. Cortázar was alone, and lonely, as a strange sickness began taking over his body. He lost his appetite, became thinner, became susceptible to colds. After his divorce from Aurora Bernárdez some fifteen years previous, he had been involved with a number of women and men, although he tried desperately to keep his homosexual encounters secret. In the depths of his solitude, he told Luis Harss, he began to lose confidence in his own writing. A symbol of liberation for many Hispanics, Cortázar, so the rumor goes, probably contracted AIDS. He died in Paris, on February 12, 1984, when the epidemic was still largely unrecognized, its details elusive to scientists and never openly discussed. A number of Cortázar's tales deal with homosexuality and lesbianism, including "Blow-Up" "The Ferry, or Another Trip to Venice," and "At Your Service." The last, the story of an elderly servant woman working as a dog-sitter in a wealthy Parisian home, moved a Cortázar specialist to ask him about his own homosexuality. He answered quite impersonally, with a lengthy dissertation on the general subject, a history of homosexuality from the open love of the Greeks to the present-day climate of ostracism and homophobia. "The attitude toward [it]," he suggested, "needs to be a very broad and open one, because the day in which homosexuals don't feel like . . . persecuted animals . . . they'll assume a much more normal way of life and fulfill themselves erotically and sexually without harming anyone and by being happy as much as possible as homosexual males and females." He concluded by applauding the more tolerant atmosphere of select North American and European societies. One might assume that the profound questions of sexuality and repression broached in this discussion would have had severe, productive, repercussions in the critical work on one of the giants of Latin American literature. But Cortázar's gay life, like Borges's, remains a forbidden issue.

Since the 1960s, gay artists in Latin America have worked to put Latin homosexuality on the map. They have devised strategies to name the unnameable and map a symbolic picture of our collective erotic fears. The Argentine Manuel Mujica Láinez's 1962 novel *Bomarzo,* for instance, equates the male organ, and homosexuality in general, with the monstrous. Thanks to him and to many others (José Ceballos Maldonado, José Donoso, Carlos Arcidiácono, Reinaldo Arenas, José Lezama Lima, Richard Rodriguez, Manuel Puig, Virgilio Piñera, Severo Sarduy, Xavier Villaurrutia, Luis Zapata, and Fernando Vallejo), a small window of vulnerability has been created, a space for the interrogation of suffocating, monolithic sex roles. The most significant of these, to my mind, are Puig, Areans, and José Lezama Lima. *Kiss of the Spider Woman,* Puig's most celebrated work, directed for the screen by Héctor Babenco, portrayed a forced male relationship in a unspecified prison in Latin

America. The film made waves from Ciudad Juárez to the Argentine Pampa with its startling conclusion, a kiss between a macho Marxist revolutionary and a gay man, and the suggestion that the characters complemented each other.

Puig is one of the principal characters in the long history of homophobia and gay-bashing in the Hispanic world. In the early 1970s the committee for the prestigious Seix Barral award in Spain selected his first novel, which the filmmaker Néstor Almendros and novelist Juan Goytisolo openly endorsed. But the publisher rejected the recommendation of the selection committee because of Puig's sexual orientation. He was similarly stigmatized in his native country, where the Peronists banned his work, calling it "pornographic propaganda."

Puig died in his mid-fifties in 1990, in Cuernavaca, Mexico, during a bizarre (and suspicious) gall bladder operation. Was it AIDS? Puig chose to keep silent about his impending demise. At the time I was preparing a special issue of *The Review of Contemporary Fiction* about his oeuvre and had been in contact with him. I last saw him at a public reading at the 92nd Street Y in New York City a few months before his death; he looked thin but energetic. There was no mention of an illness. Of course, having been burned so many times before, it was unlikely that he would open up now. Two years after Puig's death, Jaime Manrique, the Colombian author of *Latin Moon in Manhattan* and a close friend of Puig, reconstructed the gay subtext of Puig's life in a moving reminiscence, "Manuel Puig: The Writer as Diva," for *Christopher Street*. After considering the possibility of Puig opening up, *abrirse*, in public, Manrique concluded that whatever honors Puig could still hope for were infinitely more secure with his personal secrets kept hidden. In the end, he had moved back to Cuernavaca with his beloved mother, spending the last months of his life "busy building his first and last home in this world," a fortress closed to strangers, filled with Hollywood memorabilia. Puig's death is emblematic of the fate of the Hispanic gay.

Puig's work was remarkably tame, at least with regard to the representation of the Latin penis; he feared the persecution of the Argentine military, and only ever depicted its image in a short section in the novel *Blood of Required Love*. Like most gays in the Hispanic world, Puig was trapped between his sexual preference and the prejudices of the larger society. And yet, what is distinctive about him and the literary generation that came of age in the wake of the 1960s is the desublimation of the phallus. Puig and other gay writers began a process of *apertura:* They have named names, celebrated and mocked Latin masculinity and the omnipresent phallus.

Reinaldo Arenas is probably the best-known openly gay writer from Latin America. His writings explore Latin sexuality and the phallus with eloquence. His final years, prior to his suicide—years marked by extreme fits of depression, a chronic and abrasive pneumonia, paranoia, and increasing misanthropy—saw him complete a surrealist novel, an autobiography, the last two installments of the *Pentagonía*, a five-volume novelization of the "secret history of Cuba." *Before Night Falls, the* autobiography, is destined to become a classic. It traces Arenas's birth in Holguín in 1943 as well as his rural childhood; his difficult transition to Havana; his friendships with Virgilio Piñera, José Lezama Lima, Lydia Cabrera, and other important Cuban artists and intellectuals; his "youthful loyalty" to Castro's socialist regime and his subsequent disenchantment with the revolution; his betrayal by a family member; the persecution, "re-education," and imprisonment he suffered in Havana's infamous El Morro prison because of his homosexuality; his participation in the 1980 Mariel boatlift; and his bondage experiences in Florida and Manhattan.

Dictated to a tape recorder and then transcribed by friends, *Before Night Falls* is one of the most incendiary, sexually liberating texts ever to come from Latin America. Published posthumously in 1990, shortly after the long-suffering author committed suicide in his New York City apartment, it appeared in English in 1993. Its confessional style and courageous depiction of homosexual life make it a remarkable and haunting book. Its impact on the Spanish-speaking world, including Spain (where it appeared under the prestigious Tusquets imprint), has been enormous. "I think I always had a huge sexual appetite" writes Arenas. "Not only mares, sows, hens, or turkeys, but almost all animals were objects of my sexual passion, including dogs. There was one particular dog who gave me great pleasure. I would hide with him behind the garden tended by my aunts, and would make him suck my cock. The dog got used to it and in time would do it freely."

Guillermo Cabrera Infante, a fellow Cuban, summed up Arenas's career in an obituary published in *El País:* "Three passions ruled the life and death of Reinaldo Arenas: literature (not as game, but as a consuming fire), passive sex, and active politics. Of the three, the dominant passion was, evidently, sex. Not only in his life, but in his work. He was a chronicler of a country ruled not by the already impotent Fidel Castro, but by sex. . . . Blessed with a raw talent that almost reaches genius in his posthumous book, he lived a life whose beginning and end were indeed the same: from the start, one long, sustained sexual act." And indeed, Arenas repeatedly describes his sexual intercourse with animals, family members, children, old people, friends, lovers, and strangers. The volume ends with a personal letter, written shortly before Arenas's death, in which he bids farewell to friends and enemies. "Due to my delicate state of health and to the horrible emotional depression it causes me not to be able to continue writing and struggling for the freedom of Cuba, I am ending my life," Arenas writes. "Persons near to me are not in any way responsible for my decision. There is only one person to hold accountable: Fidel Castro."

The autobiography details his multifarious sexual encounters. He recalls the fashion in which he was abused by his grandfather, his close attachment to his mother, a woman who left Cuba early on in the child's life to make money for the family by working in Florida. What's remarkable is the fact that the book comes out of the Spanish-speaking world, where erotic confessions are few, and seldom related to politics.

> In [Cuba], I think, it is a rare man who has not had sexual relations with another man. Physical desire over-powers whatever feelings of machismo our fathers take upon themselves to instill in us. An example of this is my uncle Rigoberto, the oldest of my uncles, a married, serious man. Sometimes I would go to town with him. I was just about eight years old and we would ride on the same saddle. As soon as we were both on the saddle, he would begin to have an erection. Perhaps in some way my uncle did not want this to happen, but he could not help it. He would put me in place, lift me up and set my butt on his penis, and during that ride, which would take an hour or so, I was bounding on that large penis, riding, as it were, on two animals at the same time. I think eventually Rigoberto would ejaculate. The same thing happened on the way back from town. Both of us, of course, acted as if we were not aware of what was happening. He would whistle or breathe hard while the horse trotted on. When he got back, Carolina, his wife, would welcome him with open arms and a kiss. At the moment we were all very happy.

Arenas's other major work, the *Pentagonia* quintet, is similarly obsessive about sex and politics. Though the text has fascinated critics for some time, it continues to scare lay readers. All exercises in literary experimentation modeled after the French *nouveau roman,* the first three volumes, *Singing from the Well, The Palace of the White Skunks,* and *Farewell to the Sea,* display a fractured narrative and convoluted plot that often make them appear impenetrable. *The Assault*, the fifth installment, is the most accessible. A compelling exercise in science fiction, it is structured as a tribute to Orwell's *1984* and Kafka's *The Castle*. It is narrated by a government torturer, a leader of the so-called Anti-Perversion Brigade, who spends his days visiting concentration camps and prisons looking for the sexual criminals to annihilate. The book's nightmarish landscape is a futuristic Caribbean island deliberately similar to Cuba under Castro's dictatorship. At the heart of the book is the torturer's search for his mother, whom he glimpses from afar but seems unable to approach. He is passionate and inscrutable in his hatred for her, ready to undertake any action that might lead to her destruction. The book opens: "The last time I saw my mother, she was out behind the National People's Lumber Cooperative gathering sticks." Approaching her, the narrator thinks to himself: "This is my chance; I knew I could not waste a second. I ran straight for her, and I would have killed her, too, but the old bitch must have an eye where her asshole ought to be, because before I could get to her and knock her down and kill her, that old woman whirled around to meet me." With macabre echoes of Luis Buñuel, the allegory is not difficult to decipher: Pages into the book, the reader comes to understand that the torturer's mother is Castro himself. As the search for her continues in various "Servo-Perimeters" of the land, Arenas prepares us for a colossal encounter, savage and profane. In the final scene, Arenas's protagonist fearlessly employs his penis one last time: He fucks and then kills his lover, whose identity is dual: his own mother, whom he describes as a cow, and the Resident, as Fidel Castro himself.

With my member throbbingly erect, and my hands on my hips, I stand before her, looking at her. My hatred and my revulsion and my arousal are now beyond words to describe. And then the great cow, naked and horrible, white and stinking, plays her last card; the sly bitch, crossing her ragged claws over her monstrous breasts, looks at me with tears in her eyes and she says *Son*. That is all I can bear to hear. All the derision, all the harassment, all the fear and frustration and blackmail and mockery and contempt that the word contains—it slaps me in the face, and I am stung. My erection swells to enormous proportions, and I begin to step toward her, my phallus aimed dead for its mark, the fetid, stinking hole. And I thrust. As she is penetrated, she gives a long, horrible shriek, and then she collapses. I sense my triumph—I come, and I feel the furious pleasure of discharging myself in her. Howling, she explodes in a blast of bolts, washers, screws, pieces of shrapnel-like tin, gasoline, smoke, semen, shit, and streams of motor oil. Then, at the very instant of my climax, and of her final howl, a sound never heard before washes across the square below us. . . . While the crowd goes on moving through the city, hunting down and destroying to the accompaniment of the music of its own enraged whispering, I tuck the limp mass of my phallus (now at last spent and flaccid) into my overalls. Weary, I make my way unnoticed through the noise and the riot (the crowd in a frenzy of destruction, like children, crying *The Resident is dead, the beast at last is dead!*), and I come to the wall of the city. I walk down to the shore. And I lie down in the sand.

It is the singular achievement of the gay Cuban writer Lezama Lima to have provided an accounting of the Latin phallus equal to its inflated importance in the Hispanic world. Lezama Lima (1912–1976) was the author of *Paradiso,* published in 1966, a book hailed by Julio Cortázar and others as a masterpiece. It is a remarkable text: In the words of the critic Gerald Martin, the text rendered "both classical and Catholic imagery, lovingly but also scandalously, achieving the remarkable double coup of offending both the Catholic Church and the Cuban Revolution through its approach to eroticism in general and homosexuality in particular." Chapter VIII details the promiscuous sexual adventures of young cassanovas Farraluque and Leregas. Leregas's penis, which would swiftly grow from the length of a thimble to "the length of the forearm of a manual laborer," becomes legendary among his classmates:

Unlike Farraluque's, Leregas's sexual organ did not reproduce his face, but his whole body. In his sexual adventures his phallus did not seem to penetrate but to embrace the other body. Eroticism by compression, like a bear cub squeezing a chestnut, that was how his first moans began. The teacher was monotonously reciting the text, and most of his pupils, fifty or sixty in all, were seated facing him, but on the left, to take advantage of a niche-like space, there were two benches lined up at right angles to the rest of the class. Leregas was sitting at the end of the first bench. Since the teacher's platform was about a foot high, only the face of his phallic colossus was visible to him. With calm indifference, Leregas would bring out his penis and testicles, and like a wind eddy that turns into a sand column, at a touch it became a challenge of exceptional size. His row and the rest of the students peered past the teacher's desk to view that tenacious candle, ready to burst out of its highly polished, blood-filled helmet. The class did not blink and its silence deepened, making the lecturer think that the pupils were morosely following the thread of his discursive expression, a spiritless exercise during which the whole class was attracted by the dry phallic splendor of the bumpkin bear cub. When Leregas's member began to deflate, the coughs began, the nervous laughter, the touching of elbows to free themselves from the stupefaction they had experienced. "If you don't keep still, I'm going to send some students out of the room," the little teacher said, vexed at the sudden change from rapt attention to a progressive swirling uproar.

The chapter becomes increasingly daunting as the florid prose continues.

An adolescent with such a thunderous generative attribute was bound to suffer a frightful fate according to the dictates of the Pythian. The spectators in the classroom noted that in referring to the Gulf's currents the teacher would extend his arm in a curve to caress the algaed coasts, the corals, and anemones of the Caribbean. That morning, Leregas's phallic dolmen had gathered those motionless pilgrims around the god terminus as it revealed its priapic extremes, but there was no mockery or rotting smirk. To enhance his sexual tension, he put two octavo books on his member, and they moved like tortoises shot up by the expansive force of a fumarole. It was the reproduction of the Hindu myth about the origin of the world.

The phallus remains an all-consuming image for Hispanic society, whether as the absent, animating presence in the *repressive* culture of machismo or the furtive purpose of the *repressed* culture of homosexuality. It is the representation of masculine desire, a fantastic projection of guilt, shame, and power. Hyperactive bravura and suppressed longing are its twin modalities.

Like its subject, my little text on the Latin phallus has swelled to gargantuan proportions. I now envision an open book, steeped in the infinite richness of reality, a Borgesian volume of volumes incorporating every detail of every life of every man and woman in the Hispanic world, alive and dead—the record of every innocent or incestuous look, every masturbatory fantasy, every kiss, every coitus since 1492 and perhaps even before. The book is already in us and outside us, simultaneously real and imaginary, fatal and prophetic, *abierto* and *cerrado*. As a civilization, we *are* such a history— a living compendium of our baroque sexual behaviors. From Bernal Díaz del Castillo's chronicle of the subjugation of Tenochtitlán to Mario Vargas Llosa's novella *In Praise of the Stepmother,* from Carlos Fuentes's climax in *Christopher Unborn* to José Donoso's *The Obscene Bird of Night* and his untranslated erotic novel *La misteriosa desaparicíon de la Marquesita de Loria,* from Lope de Vega's Golden Age comedies to Sor Juana Inés de La Cruz's superb baroque poetry and Cherríe Moraga's *peloncito,* the tortuous history of our sexuality is the story of the Latin phallus. In a continent where tyranny remains an eternal ghost and democracy (the open society, *la sociedad abierta*) an elusive dream, the phallus is an unmerciful dictator, the totemic figure of our longing.

# CARTOON FREAK

*¡¡¡Splash!!! ¡¡¡Kaboom!!! Ay diosito, y ahora, ¿quién nos salvará?*
—Kalimán: El hombre increíble

Pop art, the highbrows say, is junk. It results, so the argument goes, from the masses wanting to satisfy their spiritual thirst without any sense of refinement. Pure art is the result of an artist's finding an aesthetic way to channel his purposeful alienation from society into an original and authentic creation. But pop art—in German, *kitsch*—is art by imitation: second-rate, derivative, a hand-me-down. It does not come about out of inspiration but is assembled, manufactured, and thus, has no soul to speak of.

The problem with this view, of course, is that it is utterly false, to say nothing of snobbish and supercilious. If everything popular is by definition unworthy and inadequate, then all modernity, from beginning to end, is counterfeit, particularly in the vast regions of the globe where Europe was for endless years the sole provider of so-called legitimate art.

I came of age in Mexico, in the 1970s, surrounded by fast food, American TV sitcoms, cartoons, and Muzak. "Is there a true national art?" asked the intellectuals, distressed by the prevailing "colonial" mentality. The United States is nothing but artificial, they claimed, looking instead to Mexico's rich past. Why, then, I might have retorted, does the country need so much trash to survive? Why is

First published in *Hopscotch: A Cultural Review* 1:4 (Winter 1999–2000). Reprinted as Introduction to *Latino U.S.A: A Cartoon History* (New York: Basic Books, 2000).

*Star Wars* so popular? Furthermore, why is pop art in Mexico—soaps, comic strips, rock music—so deceptive? They would point at muralists Diego Rivera and Frida Kahlo, musicians Carlos Chávez and Silvestre Revueltas, literatteurs Ramón López Velarde, and Alfonso Reyes as models to emulate.

I was overexposed to this "illiteracy," this bastard nature of pop art, which supposedly underlined the abysmal ignorance of the masses. All kitsch is pernicious, but Mexican kitsch is twice as bad, for it is derived from an already derivative product—a Xerox of a Xerox. Nothing in this argument made sense to me. I loved Indiana Jones, ate burritos at Taco Bell, watched episode after episode of *Simplemente María*, listened to Juan Gabriel, and voraciously read the strips El Payo, Kalimán, and *Los supermachos*. My feeling, had I been asked, was that the authenticity of it all was found precisely in its beautiful unoriginality. Pop culture, my instinct told me, was much closer to the nation's collective psyche than anything by Kahlo and Reyes.

Comic strips and cartoons were my favorite pastime. They were known invariably as *los monitos, los comics, las tiras.* I dreamed, from early on, of becoming first a graphic artist and then a filmmaker. I was held spellbound by the union of word and image. A baroque kiosk just a few blocks from my house festively displayed all sorts of comic books. I found in them, and my friends did too, a much-needed dose of adventure, laughter, and satire. Poetic language, Aristotelian unity, intellectual sophistication, these were alien terms to me. What I wanted most was salvation through escape to become a superhero—*a la mexicana*—part mariachi and part Spiderman, to ridicule the ruling political elite, to travel to the Chiapas rainforest by horse with a flamboyant maid by my side. A cheap imagination? Well, perhaps, but vivid nonetheless. TV and comics were not noxious. I found them electrifying.

Mine was not an escapist middle-class mentality, as I have often heard it described. Mexico's population in its entirety, men and women, children and adults, rich and poor, rulers and the populace, also visited the kiosk, delivering the rigorous 3.50 pesos without any misgivings whatsoever. Paul Theroux, in his 1979 travelogue *The Old Patagonian Express*, writes that, arriving in San Luis Potosi, "I went to the plaza and bought a Mexican newspaper. . . . [T]he rest of the [train] passengers bought comic books." The division between haves and have nots is clear, Theroux being among the latter. I can hardly invoke, as I look back, a more egalitarian pastime, one as democratic in its mission. And things have hardly changed since I grew up and since Theroux visited Mexico. Just ask any street ven-

dor to describe who the audience for comics really is: *todo el mundo,*
he will automatically say, just about everybody. A few comics were
imports badly translated into Spanish, but most of the ones I read
were not. They proudly displayed the logo *Hecho en México,* certify-
ing not only that they were written, designed, and produced by
nationals, but that nationals, too, consumed them en masse.

I am aware of the argument, defended most prominently by
Irene Herner, and by Ariel Dorfman with Armand Mattelart in their
book *How to Read Donald Duck,* that, in the so-called Third World,
the comics industry is linked to American imperialism. Walt
Disney's characters, so the litany goes, are hardly about innocence.
Their tainted message is designed "to colonize the minds of children
all over Latin America." Nonsense, I say, *puras tonterías.* Our global
culture is not about exclusion and isolation, but about cosmopolitanism, which, etymologically, derives from the Greek terms *cosmos*
and *polis,* a planetary city.

My strip heroes were definitely locals. Kalimán, among them,
an immensely handsome, intellectually portentous macho, defied
stereotypes. Raised by Tibetan monks, his mission is to ensure the
security of the earth, not just Mexico, through his astonishing
breadth of knowledge and enviable bodily strength. Who ever said
Mexicans are dumb and without role models? Blue-eyed, uncor-
rupted, generous, he was much like Borges's Funes the Memorious:
He spoke all human languages, was a walking encyclopedia, and
even communicated with animals. These attributes were sustained
by daily yoga exercises, meditation, and physical relaxation. Batman
and Superman, Kalimán's role models, in my eyes seemed to pale
when compared to him.

Equally compelling were other superheroes of more indigenous breeds, such as El Zorro and El Payo, the former a mestizo in
nineteenth-century New Mexico, the latter a charro with an
admirable sense of righteousness. Or El Santo, a masked wrestler.
Or Chanoc himself, a Mayan ace raised in Ixtac, on the southern
coast of Mexico, whose portentous swimming habits and expertise
with knives allow him to kill one gigantic animal after another. Or
some more prosaic quadruped, like Paquín and El Chamaco,
Rocambole, Memín and Detective Fisgón, Adelita and Condorito.
Sure, they are all manipulative, repetitive, and predictable. But they
were a source of national pride, too. How many enjoyable school
bus rides did we spend together? How oftern did I hide them inside
a history textbook, trusting they could offer a better lesson in civics.

Unlike elitist art, comics, although not quite anonymous, pay
little attention to ownership. An author's name, with very few

exceptions, is invisible. One of the exceptions is Eduardo del Río, aka Rius, probably the most prolific, versatile, and personal of Mexico's cartoonists. Born in 1935 in Zamora, Michoacán, he went to school in the nation's capital and, before becoming a national figure, he worked in a bar, a bottling plant, a funeral parlor, and as a delivery boy in a firm that distributed Walt Disney's comics. He began working as a cartoonist for various newspapers until, switching to comic strips, he produced *Los supermachos*, a political satire that, in the late 1960s, attacked President Gustavo Díaz Ordaz. It was adapted to theater and made into a film, *Calzonsin Inspector*, by Alfonso Arau, famous as the director of *Like Water for Chocolate*. Rius ran into trouble with the government for his strong Marxist views. He was fired and rehired elsewhere. Eventually he managed to build his own one-man company, which produced another landmark film, *Los agachados.*

Ideology, obviously, is at the core of his art. His characters are social types, archetypes, and stereotypes. His style, displayed in some 2,000 original fouilletons and booklets, most notably *Cuba Libre* and *El amor en los tiempos del Sida*, is not quite what strip readers are used to. Instead of developing a plot, he often explores national and international issues by dropping capsules of commentary that mix information with humor. He pioneered this didactic approach in *Marx for Beginners* and *The Myth of the Virgin of Guadalupe*, which are available in English, too.

(I stopped reading Rius one specific day, when a most anti-Semitic installment of *Los agachados*, endorsing Hitler, reached my hand. I have kept the strip with me, a testament to my disillusion.)

I came to learn that there are more comic strip publishers in Mexico than in any other Latin American country by far, and I had also witnessed the boom of Mexican comics. Individual weekly issues had print runs varying between 300,000 to almost 9 million copies, by all accounts an astronomical number, particularly when compared to the Lilliputian number of books sold by literary figures. For example, books by authors of the stature of Carlos Fuentes often sold fewer than 10,000 copies per title in half a decade. And this huge number of comics didn't include exports to Central or South America and especially to areas of the United States highly populated with Latin Americans: East Los Angeles, Chicago's Pilsen and La Villita, and San Francisco's Mission district. *¡Jijole!*, El Chamaco would say.

The true roots of the strips, these "filthy artifacts," as arrogant intellectuals called them, are much contested in the artistic and academic communities. Some attribute the inspiration to Egyptian hieroglyphics and perhaps to illuminated Medieval manuscripts. Some even claim Aztec codices, ancient writings, and other pre-Columbian images as the true sources of Mexican comics. While I agree some inspiration may have been drawn from the Aztecs and other pre-Columbian societies, I believe that the strips have the exact same inspiration that nurtured the highbrow yet populist art of Rivera and Kahlo—the *retablos*, anonymous paintings that include a written prayer, which were offered by Catholic believers to Jesus Christ and the Virgin de Guadalupe as a token of appreciation for a miracle performed. I also believe the cartoonists drew inspiration from the engravings and penny-dreadfuls (sensationalist writings of crime or violent adventure) of lampoonist José Guadalupe Posada. Posada invented the *calavera*, a skeleton poking fun at death and destiny that, with time, has come to represent for Mexico what Uncle Sam does for the United States.

I remember studying many a calavera with scrupulous eyes. What did I see? Myself? The histrionics of those around me? A perfect mask, no doubt. Masks, indeed, are what Mexican pop culture is all about: faces hidden behind faces. The Mexican shuts himself from the world, wrote Octavio Paz. "In his harsh solitude, which is both barbed and courteous, everything serves him as a defense: silence and words, politeness and disdain, irony and resignation." What Posada did so well, and modern strips continue doing, is to exploit, effortlessly, the smile behind those masks.

This passion for graphic art, for using images as vehicles of communication, is not accidental. It is inherent to Mexican culture, whereas the written word is, in many ways, an imported property. The way the Mexicans have turned words into a communication tool, both in conjunction with graphic images and alone, however, is astonishing.

As I matured, I came to realize the whole Hispanic world was home to millions of comic strips. My cadre of idols grew dramatically. From Posada and Rius, I graduated to Abel Quezada, whose endearing work was featured in *The New Yorker* in the 1980s. I then found my all-time favorite, Quino, the nom de plume of Joaquín Lavado, the Argentine artist responsible for creating the character of Mafalda, a little girl whose sharpness and wisdom make her readers realize how convoluted our modern times are. ("Please stop the world!" she screams in a strip, "I want to get off!") I soon appreciated the deftness and flair with which Fernando Botero, the master Colombian painter, turned cartoons into highbrow art. This led me to realize how fragile the line is between avant-garde and "junk." By the time I settled in the United States, graffiti and the Chicano cartoons and murals in California by Frank Romero and Ester Hernández had become a magnet, for what is street art if not the attempt to return iconography to the masses?

As Hispanics—a large majority of them Mexicans—cross the Rio Grande to become Latinos, they might switch languages, but their joie de vivre remains intact. I myself have always been fascinated by the challenges of capturing the joys, nuances, and multiple dimensions of Latino culture within the context of the English language. Hence, when a phone call from Sheila Friedling, an old friend and editor of an early book of mine, came with the invitation to do a cartoon history of Latinos, I was enthralled. Long-dormant adolescent memories surfaced, and Rius's art flashed into my mind. I also thought of a favorite experimental book I once read, *Fantômas contra los vampiros multinacionales* by Julio Cortázar, and fruitlessly looked for my old copy. Cortázar appropriated the character of the legendary French thief Fantômas, a Robin Hood of sorts, to ruminate, through cartoons, against U.S. imperialism. It surely was not the most inspired performance by the author of *Hopscotch*, but it was unquestionably an endearing try-out. And I reread *Cosmicomics* too, a fin-de-siècle novel by Italo Calvino, inspired by comics inspired by novels. I even asked myself: When did I really become a writer? Was it by reading one too many installments of *Los supermachos* or when I finished *Don Quixote*, fully hypnotized by its magic? The opportunity had arrived to become, finally, a manufacturer of kitsch, while paying tribute to a core aspect of my upbringing that I had cast aside when I focused my professional career on the muses of literature and academia.

In developing the manuscript for *Latino U.S.A.: A Cartoon History*, I consciously sought to combine the solemnity of so-called serious literature and history with the inherently theatrical and humorous nature of the comics. The experience was liberating: As an essayist, I am handcuffed by the abstraction of words, by the merciless need to make a cohesive, persuasive argument with words only. Cartoons and comics present the perfect stage to blend words and images, and engage the reader with their freshness, imagination, caricatures, and fantastical and delightfully irreverent overtones. Naturally thespian in their format, with characters spouting lines against an ever-changing backdrop of realistic and exaggerated settings, cartoons and comics can be more anarchic than a typical drama. My models from the theatrical world were Cervantes and Rius, Pirandello and Chanoc . . . as imagined by Mafalda.

My objective was to represent Hispanic civilization as a fiesta of types, archetypes, and stereotypes. As soon as I began sketching the layout, Posada's calaveras took control of me, as did other cliche figurines: a toucan, displayed regularly in books by Gabriel García Márquez, Isabel Allende, and the like; a beautiful señorita, addressing the exuberant sexuality I grew up with; Cantinflas, a beloved comedian known, paradoxically, as "the Hispanic Charlie Chaplin" (even after Chaplin described himself as "second best to Cantinflas"); a masked wrestler; and so on. By featuring these strips as the narrators and counternarrators of their own history and as actors in an imaginary stage, I avoided using, as much as possible, an official, impartial tone, embracing instead the rhythms of carnival. My "unofficialness" translated itself into what I think is a less Europeanized, more democratic viewpoint. History, of course, is a kaleidoscope where nothing is absolute. The human past and present are far more malleable than the future. This, in short, is my own account, a pastiche of angles I have made my own.

Matching with cartoonist Lalo López Alcaraz was the key relationship that shaped the vision, humor, and form of the book. Ever since I came across his cartoon in *LA Weekly* and read *Pocho*, his satirical Chicano magazine, I realized I had found my artistic soulmate. I was born in Distrito Federal, he in San Diego: Between the two of us, I trust, we are able to capture the perspectives of both south and north of the Rio Grande; also, both of us are fluent in Spanish and English with a fascination with Spanglish, the new integration of these two languages. His strips are about mischief and caprice, poking fun at human nature without compromising historical integrity. I trust his strips and my ideas are complementary echoes, echoooooooes. . . . Everything in them is purposeful imitation.

# SANTA SELENA

*Saint, n. A dead sinner revised and edited.*
—Ambrose Bierce, *The Devil's Dictionary*

During a recent trip to South Texas, a dignified old man told me Selena had died because heaven was desperate for another cherub. He described her to me as "a celestial beauty whose time on earth was spent helping the poor and unattended." In San Antonio, a mother of four has placed Selena's photograph in a special altar in her home, surrounded by candles and flowers, just beneath the image of the Virgin of Guadalupe. "Please, Selena," her prayer goes, "let me remain a virgin . . . just like you." (This despite the fact that, at the time of her death, Selena was married to Chris Pérez, her guitar player.) The collective imagination is stronger than anything reality has to offer: A young lady from Corpus Christi who spends a good portion of her days singing "selenatas" swears she sees the singer's ghost appear on her TV screen every night—after she's switched the set off. And a Spanish teacher I know in Dallas who recently lost her job has begun selling a poem of her own creation, "Adiós mi linda estrella," make money. She sent me a copy of the poem, a tribute to the pop star she considers her angel protector:

First published in *Transition* 70 (Summer 1996). Reprinted in *The Riddle of Cantinflas: Essays on Hispanic Popular Culture* (Albuquerque, NM: University of New Mexico Press, 1998).

Do not cry for me, do not suffer for me
Remember I love you with all my heart
I know if you listen and do as I ask
I will be content because
I have completed my mission here on my beautiful earth and
I can continue to sing to Our Father in Heaven.
Listen, Heaven does not thunder
The sun begins to hide
Our father has given us a new light
Look up to Heaven
The light comes from a divine star
That lights up all of Heaven
It is the Angel Selena
The most beautiful star of the world
and now of Heaven.
Goodbye, my lovely Star.

Welcome to *la frontera,* the painful wound dividing Mexico and the United States, a land of kitsch and missed opportunities where outlandish dreams and work-a-day life intertwine. Encompassing 12 million people, its capital is Tijuana, where *el día de los muertos* is the most popular holiday: an opportunity for the living to spend a wild night carousing in the cemetery at the side of their dearly departed. The flag of the region is red, white, and blue, but at its heart is an eagle devouring a writhing snake. *La frontera* is where NAFTA and Kafka cohabit, where English isn't spoken but broken, and where *yo* becomes *I,* and where *I* becomes *Ay, carajo*—a free zone, autonomous and self-referential, perceived by Mexicans as *el fin del mundo* and by Anglo-Americans as a galaxy of bad taste.

Since her tragic death, Selena has become omnipresent in *la frontera,* the focal point of a collective suffering—a patron saint, of sorts. Tender *señoritas* cannot bring themselves to accept the idea that she is no longer with us. On radio call-in shows, her followers bemoan the injustice of her disappearance. A movie is in the works, several instant biographies have already been published (in Spanish and English), and more are on their way to the printer. Countless imitators mimic her style, her idiosyncratic fashion, her smile: An upcoming national contest in Corpus Christi will soon crown the girl who impersonates Selena most perfectly, who loses herself in Selena's chaste yet sexy persona. In fact, the whole of Lake Jackson, Texas, Selena's hometown, has already become a kind of Graceland: Pilgrims come to weep at her birthplace and to pay homage at the places she graced with her presence: her home, the neighborhood rodeos where she sang at intermission, the arenas where she entertained the masses. Her grave at Seaside Memorial Park is inundated daily with flowers, candles, and mementos, and the cemetery keeper has trouble disposing of the colorful offerings. Amalia González, a radio host in Los Angeles, says Selena had sojourned on earth in order "to unite all creeds and races."

Elvis, John Lennon, Kurt Cobain, and Jerry Garcia . . . roll over: There's a new kid in the pop star firmament, one who gives voice to the silenced and the oppressed. This until-yesterday unknown *tejana*, née Selena Quintanilla Pérez—awarded the Grammy for Best Mexican American Performance for an album titled, ironically, *Selena Live*—has instantly become the unquestioned queen of *mestizo* pop, part wetback and part *gabacha*.

Selena's life may have been tragically short, but death has given her an imposing stature. At 1:05 P.M. on Friday, March 31, 1995, she became immortal: Just short of her twenty-fourth birthday, she ceased to exist as a pop singer of modest means but high ambitions, poised to cross over to a mainstream market, and became not only Madonna's most fearsome competitor (her album *Dreaming of You*, which included a handful of songs in English, sold 175,000 copies in a single day), but also a cult hero, a Hispanic Marilyn Monroe, an object of relentless adoration and adulation. Magically, she has joined Eva Perón in the pantheon of mystical and magical *hispanas*, protectors of the *descamisados*, immaculate personification of eternal love.

How many of us from outside *la frontera* had heard of her before the murder? Not many. But even if we had heard some of her songs on the radio, we could not have fathomed her appeal: Her music is *cursi*—melodramatic, cheesy, overemotional. Tejano rhythms, which Selena was in the process of reinventing, are a jumbled fusion of rock, jazz, pop, and country, seasoned with a hint of rap— an endless addition resulting in a subtraction. She was beginning to master them all when she died. But that's not the point: Her *conjunto* pieces, as well as the mental imbalances of Yolanda Saldívar, the administrator of her fan club and her killer, are only props in a theatrical act in which Selena is the star regardless of her talents. She was a symbol, not a genius.

Selena's father, Abraham Quintanilla, Jr., whose family has been in South Texas for at least a hundred years, forced her to learn Spanish in order to further her career. She debuted at age five with Los Dinos, her father's group. (He was a vocalist.) Less than twenty years later, with a sexy public persona built around a halter top and tight pants, she was worth more than $5 million. Since she passed just as her crossover dreams were beginning to materialize, her legend was never—will never—be forced to confront the conundrum of assimilation: She will go down as a brave, courageous chicana—perhaps ambivalent toward, but never ashamed of, her background. "You'd see her shopping at the mall," people in South Texas say, wistfully. "And you'd see her working at home. A real sweetheart." Some even recalled how accessible she was—*una de nosotros:* Selena never turned up her nose at Mexican popular entertainment, performing in variety shows like *Siempre en Domingo* and the melodramatic soap *Dos mujeres, un camino,* starring Erik Estrada. Small parts, no doubt, but the real *sabor.* Had Selena been visited by the angel of death only a few years later, it would have been a very different story: she would have been an American star, and her tragedy would not serve to highlight the plight of *la frontera.*

Now Selena is ubiquitous: on TV screens and CDs, on book covers and calendars, on velvet slippers and plastic bracelets, on shampoo bottles and make-up advertisements, on designer clothes and *piñatas.* She is a present-day Frida Kahlo: a martyr whose afterlife *en el más allá* promises to be infinitely more resonant than whatever she managed to achieve *en el más acá.* In *la frontera,* she has been made into a heroine, an ethnic mass-market artifact. "Thanks to her *tejanos* are being heard," a disk jockey from Houston told me. "She put us in the news—and on the front page." And so she did: Rosa López was merely a bit of Hispanic seasoning in the O. J. Simpson mix, but Selena has turned *la frontera*—whose children, adopted and otherwise, include film director Robert "El Mariachi" Rodriguez, performance artist Guillermo Gómez-Peña, and novelists Laura Esquivel and Cormac McCarthy—into a banquet of possibilities for the media. The trial and sentencing of Saldívar alone has catapulted Selena to eternity, winning more newspaper columns for Latinos than the Zapatista rebellion. Even Texas Governor George W. Bush, whose knowledge of *tejano* culture is close to nil, was quick enough to declare April 16, 1995—Selena's birthday and Easter Sunday—*el día de Selena.* There's even a motion to put her face on a postage stamp.

Selena's was a life quilted by sheer coincidence but which, studied in retrospect, shows the deliberate design of a well-patterned tapestry. The murder itself (which, strangely, took place on César Chávez's birthday) is already legendary, rivaling the Crucifixion for pathos and histrionics: Saldívar—whose much-lauded punishment is life in prison—comes out of Room 158 of the Corpus Christi Days Inn on Navigation Boulevard with a .38-caliber revolver. Selena stumbles ahead of her, wounded, bleeding, and crying for help. She names her assassin and then dies, in close-up. Cut! Roll the commercial. The next scene takes place minutes later, as Saldívar seals herself in a pickup truck and, holding the pistol to her temple à la O. J., threatens to commit suicide and keeps the police at a standstill for nine and a half hours. Blood, tears, desperation—the recipe lacks not a single ingredient. Saldívar had been a good friend of the singer and her business partner in Selena, Inc., the company that managed the singer's boutiques and beauty salons in Corpus Christi and San Antonio. So what went wrong?

You might find the answer in cyberspace, where a Selena home page on the World Wide Web has kept her *admiradores* up to date since a few weeks after her death. Or simply tune in to *El Show de Cristina*, the Spanish-speaking Oprah Winfrey, which was among the first TV programs to capitalize on Selena's tragedy by devoting several episodes to her family's sorrows. Or you might give up on investigating the logic and become a *selenomaníaco* and start building up your pile of collectibles: nightgowns, hats, purses, money holders, sleepers, umbrellas and a lot more—all sporting her beautiful photograph. Or, if you are ready for a deeper investment, keep in mind the seventy-six-page special issue of *People*, which retailed at $3.95 and now sells for more than two hundred dollars. There is also, of course, the notorious April 17, 1995, issue of the same magazine, which appeared in two different versions: 442,000 copies with Selena on the cover, for sale in Texas, and 3 million issues (featuring the cast of the TV show *Friends*) for the rest of the country. A single copy of *that* Selena issue has auctioned for over $500. My own favorite item is the advertisement for the colorful T-shirt on sale at Selena, Inc. ($10.99), which is marketed as a sign of loyalty: "Tell the world of your love for Selena and her music with one of several full-color designs." One size fits all.

For those inclined to read more about it, an illustrated tribute to *La Virgen Selena* is now available, complete with photos of her grave, third-grade class, and mourning mother, plus a snapshot of the singer and her killer cavorting at a fan club appreciation party at the Desperado's Club in San Antonio during the Tejano Music Awards in 1993. Or you might want to bring home the most complete of Selena's thirteen biographies (at this writing), titled *Selena: Como la Flor* and written by Joe Nick Patoski, a senior editor at *Texas Monthly* and co-author of the bestseller *Stevie Ray Vaughan: Caught in the Crossfire*. Patoski's definitive report on the life of *la reina* will tell you how many hours a day she exercised to keep up her figure, the names of her favorite stores, the shoes she was wearing at the time of her death, and all the skinny you will never find in *The National*

*Enquirer.* The newspaper's anti-Hispanic bias has forced its editors to ignore Selena's story from A to Z.

Never fear: Selena will survive all aggressions, and her apotheosis is not yet complete. That apex will most surely be reached with the release of the Hollywood movie by director Gregory Nava (who brought you *El Norte*, a film about the plight of poor Guatemalan immigrants in *el otro lado*, as well as *La Familia*, a transgenerational melodrama to end all melodramas). From the moment Selena's body hit the hotel floor, a pitched battle has raged over securing the movie rights to her story. (Patoski devotes several pages of his biography to the wrangling.) By all accounts, her father is firmly in command of choosing the screenwriter and, more important, who gets to play his daughter. (He also chooses who gets to play himself; unidentified sources claim that he rejected Edward James Olmos as too ugly). Selena will surely do wonders for Nava's career. She has already granted so many miracles—one more shouldn't be a problem. Victor Villaseñor is next in line for redemption, a Chicano writer known for his *Roots*-esque family epic, *Rain of Gold*, who is under contract to write the "official" companion to the film. Although the second book of his family saga was almost unreadable, it will be hard to go wrong with Selena for inspiration.*

Inspiration is what she is all about. Just when Latinos were convinced no one cared for them, along came Selena. As long as *la frontera* remains a hybrid territory, hidden from the sight of Anglo America and ignored by the Mexican government, people north and south of the Rio Grande will continue to pray to their new Madonna. They have realized that the best way to conquer the mainstream culture of the United States is by media storm, a subversion from within. They are confident that sooner rather than later all *gringos* will make room for Latino extroversion and sentimentality. Sooner, rather than later, *The National Enquirer* will publish a report on her return to earth in a UFO. A new, darker-complected Elvis is here to capture the imagination of a nation: SELENA IS ALIVE.

---

* As it turned out, Olmos did get to play the father and Villaseñor was eliminated as screenwriter. *Selena*, the movie released in 1997, was so saccharine it didn't even have a murder sequence.

# UNMASKING MARCOS

*Tout révolutionnaire finit en oppresseur ou en hérétique.*

—Albert Camus

The Subcomandante Insurgente Marcos, or *El Sup*, as he is known in Mexico. His skin is bleached, whiter than that of his compañeros. He speaks with palpable erudition. The sword *and* the pen: He is a rebel, yes, but also an intellectual, a mind perpetually alert. And like some ranting dissenter, he is always prepared to say *No: No* to five centuries of abuse of the indigenous people of Chiapas and the nearby Quintana Roo in the Yucatán Peninsula. *No* to the sclerotic one-party state that has mortgaged Mexico and her people for generations, and for generations to come.

*No, No,* and *No.*

El Sup is also like Sisyphus, or possibly like Jesus Christ: He bears on his shoulders an impossible burden, the aspirations and demands of an embattled people. He must know, in his heart, that the rock is too heavy, the hill too steep; his efforts will change very little in the way people go about their lives south of the Tortilla Curtain. His real task, the best he can do, is to call attention to the misery of miserable men and women.

He isn't a terrorist but a freedom fighter, and a peaceable one at that. He took up arms because debate is unfruitful in his milieu. He

First published in *Transition* 69 (Spring 1996). Reprinted in *The Riddle of Cantinflas: Essays on Hispanic Popular Culture* (Albuquerque, NM: University of New Mexico Press, 1998).

is a *guerrillero* for the nineties who understands, better than most people, the power of word and image. He uses allegories and anecdotes, old saws and folk tales, to convey his message. Not a politician but a storyteller—an icon knowledgeable in iconography, the new art of war, a pupil of Marshall McLuhan. As he himself once wrote, "My job is to make wars by writing letters."

El Sup is a tragic hero, a Moses without a Promised Land. He stands in a long line of Latin American guerrilla heroes, at once real and mythical, an insurrectionary tradition stretching back nearly half a millennium. Figures like the legendary Enriquillo, who orchestrated an uprising among aborigines in La Española around 1518, about whom Fray Bartolomé de Las Casas writes eloquently in his *Historia de las Indias*. And Enriquillo's children: Emiliano Zapata; Augusto César Sandino, the inspiration for Daniel Ortega and the Sandinistas; Simón Bolívar, the revolutionary strategist who liberated much of South America from Spanish rule and who dreamed in the 1820s of La Gran Colombia, a republic of republics that would serve as a Hispanic mirror to the United States of America; Tupac Amaru, the Peruvian Indian leader of an unsuccessful revolt against the Iberians in 1780, whose example still inspires the Maoists in Peru; Edén Pastora, *Comandante Cero*, an early Sandinista guerrillero turned dissenter; and, of course, Fidel Castro and Ernesto "Ché" Guevara. A robust tradition of revolutionaries, overpopulated by runaway slaves, *indios, subversivos,* muralists, and disenfranchised middle-class intellectuals.

El Sup: newspaper columnists and union organizers credit him for the wake-up call that changed Mexico forever. He had gone to Chiapas in 1983 to politicize people. "We started talking to the communities, who taught us a very important lesson," he told an interviewer. "The democratic organization or social structure of the indigenous communities is very honest, very clear." He fought hard to be accepted, and he was, although his pale skin marked him as an outsider. (Though the preeminent spokesman of the Zapatista movement, he could never aspire to a position greater than subcomandante, as the highest leadership positions are customarily reserved for Indians.) The next ten years were spent mobilizing peasants, reeducating them and being reeducated in turn. The rest, as they say, is history.

And rightly so: after all, on the night of January 1, 1994, just as the so-called North American Free Trade Agreement, NAFTA, among Canada, the United States, and Mexico, was about to go into effect, he stormed onto the stage.

Lightning and thunder followed.

It was a night to remember. As José Juárez, a Chiapas local, described it, "It was on New Year's Eve when President Carlos Salinas de Gortari retired to his chambers thinking he would wake up a North American. Instead he woke up a Guatemalan."

*No*, said the Subcomandante. Mexico isn't ready for the First World. Not yet.

Everywhere people rejoiced. *¡Un milagro!* A miracle! A wonder of wonders! So spoke Bishop Samuel Raúl Ruíz García, the bishop of San Cristóbal, whose role in the Zapatista revolution angered conservatives, but who was endorsed by millions worldwide, turning him into a favorite for the Nobel Peace Price.

With his trademark black skintight mask, El Sup was constantly on television. *Un enmascarado:* Mexicans turned him into a god. Since pre-Columbian times Mexico has been enamored of the mask. A wall between the self and the universe, it serves as a shield and a hiding place. The mask is omnipresent in Mexico: in theaters, on the Day of the Dead, in *lucha libre*, the popular Latin American equivalent of wrestling. And among pop heroes like El Zorro, El Santo the wrestler, and Super Barrio, all defenders of *los miserables*, masked champions whose silent faces embody the faces of millions.

Suddenly, the guerrilla was back in fashion. The "news" that the Hispanic world had entered a new era of democratic transition had been proven wrong. Once again weapons, not ballots, were the order of the day. Within the year, the lost "motorcycle diary" of Ché Guevara was published in Europe and the United States—a record of a twenty-four-year-old Ché's travels on a Norton 500 from Argentina to Chile, Peru, Colombia, and Venezuela. A free-spirited, first-person account unlike any of his "mature" works, it recalled Sal Paradise's hitchhiking in Jack Kerouac's *On the Road*. El Sup had discovered new territory: the revolutionary as easy rider.

El Sup had a rifle, yes, but he hardly used it. His bullets took the form of faxes and e-mails, cluster bombs in the shape of communiqués, and nonstop e-mail midrashim through the Internet. He wrote in a torrent, producing hundreds of texts, quickly disproving Hannah Arendt's claim that "under conditions of tyranny it is far easier to act than to think." In less than twelve months, during sleepless sessions on the word processor in the midst of fighting a war, El Sup generated enough text for a three hundred–page volume. And he sent it out without concern for copyright. His goal was to subvert our conception of intellectual ownership, to make the private public and vice versa.

He was a master at marketing. By presenting himself as a down-to-earth dissenter, a nonconformist, a hipster dressed up as soldier, he made it easy to feel close to him. To fall in love with him, even. In one communiqué, for instance, he addresses the Mexican people:

> Brothers and sisters, we are the product of five hundred years of struggle: first against slavery; then in the insurgent-led war of Independence against Spain; later in the fight to avoid being absorbed by North American expansion; next to proclaim our Constitution and expel the French from our soil; and finally, after the dictatorship of Porfirio Díaz refused to fairly apply the reform laws, in the rebellion where the people created their own leaders. In that rebellion Villa and Zapata emerged— poor men, like us.

In another, he writes to his fellow Zapatistas:

> Our struggle is righteous and true; it is not a response to personal interests, but to the will for freedom of all the Mexican people and the indigenous people in particular. We want justice and we will carry on because hope also lives in our hearts.

And in a letter to President Clinton, El Sup ponders:

> We wonder if the United States Congress and the people of the United States of North America approved this military and economic aid to fight the drug traffic or to murder indigenous people in the Mexican Southeast. Troops, planes, helicopters, radar, communications technology, weapons and military supplies are currently being used not to pursue drug traffickers and the big kingpins of the drug Mafia, but rather to repress the righteous struggle of the people of Mexico and of the indigenous people of Chiapas in the southeast of our country, and to murder innocent men, women, and children.
>
> We don't receive any aid from foreign governments, people, or organizations. We have nothing to do with national or international drug trafficking or terrorism. We organized ourselves of our own volition, because of our enormous needs and problems. We are tired of so many years of deception and death. It is our right to fight for a dignified life. At all times we have abided by the international laws of war and respected the civil population.

Since all the other compañeros of the Zapatista national Liberation Army were more modest, El Sup stole the spotlight. He was unquestionably *la estrella*. And his enigmatic identity began to obsess people. His education, some said, is obviously extensive. He must be a product of the *Distrito Federal*, the Mexico City of the early 1980s.

Was he overwhelmed by the outpouring of public affection? "I won't put much stock in it," he told one interviewer.

> I don't gain anything from it and we're not sure the organizations will, either. I guess I just don't know. About what's going on. I only get an inkling of what's going on when a journalist gets angry because I don't give him an interview. I say, "Since when am I so famous that they give me a hard time about being selective, and the lights, and I don't know what all." That is pure ideology, as they say up there, no? We don't have power struggles or ego problems of any kind.

Being selective: *el discriminador*. But his ego, no doubt, is monumental. He courted attention relentlessly. By 1995, stories circulated that internal struggles within the Zapatistas were growing, fought over El Sup's stardom.

Meanwhile, unmasking El Sup became a sport. Who is he? Where did he come from? I, for one, thought I knew, though not through any feat of journalistic prowess. I haven't been to the Chiapas jungle since the Zapatistas launched their rebellion. And if he is who I think he is, I haven't spoken to him since long before his communiqués began streaming from the Lacandonian rain forest.

The clue to his identity came in early 1995, after Salinas had ceded power to his successor, Ernesto Zedillo Ponce de León, in the aftermath of a series of political assassinations that had rocked the PRI, the governing party. The enemy grew restless. El Sup had become too dangerous. And too popular! He was better known than any politician. He commanded more attention than any of the soap operas on Mexican TV, the opiate of the Mexican masses. Enough was enough. It was time for him to go.

*Desenmascarar*. What the Mexican government performed was an ancient ritual at the heart of the nation's soul: the unmasking. Quetzalcoatl was unmasked by the Spaniards, Sor Juana by the Church, and Pancho Villa by a spy. To unmask can mean to undo, or to destroy, but it can also mean to elevate to a higher status: Every six years, as the country prepares to receive its new president, the head of the PRI literally unveils his successor before everyone's eyes.

In the public eye—El Sup's own terrain—Mexican government revealed his true self: Rafael Sebastián Guillén Vicente, a thirty-seven-year-old former college professor. A revelation, indeed, which El Sup immediately disputed . . . before vanishing into the night. Just like that, he disappeared. Off the TV screens. Out of the spotlight. He became a nonentity: *un espíritu.* Other Zapatistas replaced him in the high command of the Zapatista army.

In Mexico, of course, the government is always wrong; that is, since it promotes itself as the sole owner of the Truth, nobody believes it. And yet, El Sup might well be Guillén. I personally have no trouble equating the two. They sounded the same, right down to their rhetoric—a language I learned at the Xochimilco campus of Mexico City's Universidad Autónoma Metropolitana (UAM), the decidedly radical school where Guillén taught. In discussing his communiqués with several old college friends, we were struck by the similarities between his postmodern tongue and the often hallucinatory verbiage at Xochimilco, full of postscripts and qualifications and references to high and low, from modernist literature and academic Marxism to pop culture. El Sup said his idols were the nationally known "new journalists" Carlos Monsiváis and Elena Poniatowska, whom my whole intellectual generation deeply admired and whose own works trespass intellectual boundaries with glee. When asked to describe the books that influenced him, he would cite the 1970s writing of Octavio Paz, Julio Cortázar, Mario Vargas Llosa, and Gabriel García Márquez, although he would be careful to distance himself from the right-wing politics of Paz and Vargas Llosa.

El Sup mooned journalists with his writings. His speeches, like the authors we studied at UAM, seamlessly mix fiction with reality, becoming masterful self-parodies, texts about texts about texts. In a reply to a letter from the University Student Council of the University Nacional Autónoma de México (UNAM), he writes that with great pleasure the Zapatistas ave received the students' support. He asks them to get organized following the pattern of the Zapististas, and concludes:

> If you accept this invitation, we need you to send some delegates so that, through an intermediary, we can arrange the details. We must organize everything well so that spies from the government don't slip through. And if you make it down, don't worry about it. But keep up the fight over where you are, so that there can be justice for all Mexican people.

That's all, men and women, students of Mexico. We will be expecting a written response from you.

Respectfully,

From the mountains of the Mexican Southeast.

P.S.: El Sup's section: "The repeating post-script."

Another postscript follows, and then more and more.

P.P.S.: As long as we're in the P.S.'s, which of all the "University Student Councils" wrote to us? Because back when I was a stylish young man of 25 . . . there were at least three of them. Did they merge?

P.S. to the P.S. to the P.S.: In the event that you do (whew!) take the Zócalo, don't be selfish. . . . Save me some space where I can at least sell arts and crafts. I may have to choose between being an unemployed "violence professional" and an underemployed one, with underemployment wages (much more marketable that way, under NAFTA, you know).

P.S. to the nth power: These postscripts are really a letter disguised as a postscript (to hide it from the Attorney General's Office and all the rest of the strongmen in dark glasses), and, but of course, it requires neither an answer, nor a sender, nor an addressee (an undeniable advantage of a letter disguised as a postscript).

Nostalgic P.S.: When I was young (Hello, Attorney General's Office. Here comes more data), there used to be a lightly wooded place between the main library, the Facultad de Filosofa y Letras, the Torre de Humanidades, Insurgentes Avenue and the interior circuit of Ciudad Universitaria. We used to call that space, for reasons obvious to the initiates, the "Valley of Passions," and it was visited assiduously by diverse elements of the fauna who populated at 7 P.M. (an hour when those of good conscience drink hot chocolate and the bad ones make themselves hot enough to melt); they came from the humanities, sciences, and other areas (are there others?). At that time, a Cuban (Are you ready, Ambassador Jones? Make a note: more proof of pro-Castro tendencies) who used to give lectures seated in front of piano keys the color of his skin . . . and who called himself Snowball, would repeat over and over, "You can't have a good conscience and a heart. . . ."

Final fortissimo P.S.: Have you noticed how exquisitely cultured and refined these postscripts are? Are they not worthy of the

First World? Don't they call attention to the fact that we "trans-gressors," thanks to NAFTA are striving to be competitive?

"Happy Ending" P.S.: Okay, okay, I'm going. This trip is coming to an end, and the guard, as usual, is still asleep and someone is tired of repeating "Is anybody out there?" and tell myself, "Our country" . . . and what is your answer?

El Sup's unconventional style was a commonplace at UAM in the early eighties. I was a student there at the time, the same time that Guillén, about five years my elder, was teaching. Some of my friends took classes with him, remarking on his sharp intellect and infectious verbosity. Crossing paths with him in hallways and cafeterias, I remember him as bright and articulate.

Well-known as an incubator for Marxist, pro-Cuba, pro-Sandanista activity, UAM's Xochimilco campus had been built by the government in the early 1970s. It included two other campuses in far-flung corners of the city. It was built in an attempt to dilute the massive student population at UNAM, the oldest institution of higher learning in the country.

In her book, *La noche de Tlatelolco*, Poniatowska chronicled the protests of 1968. It was UNAM's student body, some 30,000 strong, who led the protests, which were brutally crushed in the massacre at Tlatelolco Square. El Sup, although not Guillén, was born during that massacre—a ritual birth, an origin in which his whole militant odyssey was prefigured. If the revolution couldn't be won in the nation's capital, he would join the unhappy peasants in Chiapas and Yucatán—he would become an urban exile.

When Xochimilco opened, it immediately superseded UNAM in antigovernment militancy. It became a magnet for subversive artists, would-be guerrilla fighters, and sharp-tongued political thinkers. The place was known for its unorthodox educational methods, and fields of study often lost their boundaries. Professors not only sensitized us to the nation's poverty and injustice, they encouraged us to take action. Friends would take time off to travel to distant rural regions and live with the indigenous people. Most eventually returned, but many didn't—they simply vanished, adopting new identities and new lives.

Injustice, inequality, freedom of speech—we wanted changes. "Down with the one-party system!" We would take advantage of cheap fares and travel to Havana, to become eyewitnesses to the profound transformation that had taken place in a corner of the

Hispanic world. The Sandinistas in Nicaragua captured our attention and love. We admired their courage and identified with intellectuals like Julio Cortázar, Ernesto Cardenal, and Sergio Ramírez, who had put their literary careers on hold to work for the Nicaraguan government, or who had orchestrated international campaigns to support the Sandinista fight. We were excited—and we were blind. Our personal libraries were packed full with Marxist literature. Our writers were busy fashioning a style in which art and politics were inseparable. We disregarded any argument that tried to diminish our utopian expectations.

Indeed, finding bridges between political theory and activism became a sport. Those of us who studied psychology embraced the antipsychiatry movement and were expelled from asylums for allowing patients to go free. I, for one, worked with a metropolitan priest, Padre Chinchachoma, who devoted his ministry to homeless children. He believed that to help the children he needed to live among them, in Mexico City's garbage dumps—foraging with them for food, making and selling drugs for money, and occasionally engaging in acts of vandalism. I read Padre Chinchachoma's books with great admiration. He was my messiah, my Sup before El Sup.

Xochimilco—exciting, contradictory. Our teachers were dissatisfied middle-class Mexican leftists, exiled Argentinean intellectuals, and other Latin American émigrés. Our idols were Ché Guevara, Felix Guattari, Antonio Gramsci, and Herbert Marcuse. Wealthy professors urged us to agitate among peasants in the countryside. And, what's more, we were aware that the government perceived our radicalism, our animosity, as productive.

In fact, it wanted our hatred. Its rationale was clear: If adolescents in the Third World are always full of antigovernment feeling, they should be provided with a secluded space to vent their rage. They'll scream, they'll organize, but as long as they're kept in isolation, nothing will come of it. And so we did, investing our time and energy in countless hopeless insurrectionary projects. But it wasn't a waste of energy. Something great did come out of it: El Sup.

I left Mexico in 1985, but I often look back at my years at UAM as a turning point. Between the pen and the sword, I thought I was wise for choosing the pen. But El Sup was even wiser: He chose both.

My politics and artistic views have changed somewhat. I have become a critic and scholar and have adopted a new language. In the process, I acquired a new mask of my own: I became part Mexican and part North American—at once both and neither.

Evidently, El Sup is also an academic, although a less reticent one. I was the coward, the egotist. He was the hero. We are both bridges—across cultures, across social classes. I chose the library as my habitat, while he made Mexico itself his personal creation.

So what if he is Guillén, and vice versa? Simply that his unmasking has served its purpose: El Sup has faded away from public attention. His once-omnipresent visage now appears infrequently, if at all, a haggard reminder of the still miserable conditions in the South.

Now there's talk of him, El Sup, becoming a leftist candidate in national politics. But history has little room for heroes shifting gears, and even less for legends who undress themselves. Besides, no career is more discredited in Mexico than that of a politician. Better to vanish: only then will his trademark become truly indelible. Or better still: to become a novelist. After all, Latin America is depressing in its politics, but vivid in its imaginings. Viva El Sup, the intangible— a giant of the imagination.

# THE RIDDLE OF CANTINFLAS

*In everything that can be called art there is a quality of redemption.*
—Raymond Chandler

Culture in Mexico is governed by two opposing sides, sharply divided by an open wound: on the one hand, a highbrow, Europeanized elite dreams of inserting the nation's creative talent into a global stream of artistic consciousness; on the other, native art, a hybrid that results from ancient and borrowed elements, is produced by and for the masses. Highbrow: Frida Kahlo; the painters Rufino Tamayo, José Clemente Orozco, Diego Rivera, and David Alfaro Siqueiros; the globe-trotting opera singer Plácido Domingo; even the Russian and Spanish filmmakers Sergei Einsenstein (*¡Que viva México!*) and Luis Buñuel (*Los olvidados*), who greatly influenced the nation's self-understanding through powerful cinematic images. Lowbrow: the popular wrestler El Santo; the *ranchera* movies of the 1930s and 1940s with Pedro Infante, Jorge Negrete, Blanca Estela Pavón, and Lupe Vélez; the arch famous children's songwriter Francisco Gabilondo Soler, aka Cri-Cri; and the romantic balladist Juan Gabriel. Don't worry if you're unable to recognize the latter references: The nation's cultural exports are invariably Westernized products, hardly any proletarian items.

A common belief has it that lowbrow Mexican culture is kitschy. Nothing is further from the truth. The terms *kitsch* and *camp,* which

First published in *Transition* 67 (Fall 1995). Reprinted in *The Riddle of Cantinflas: Essays on Hispanic Popular Culture* (Albuquerque, NM: University of New Mexico Press, 1998).

*Webster's Dictionary* defines as "artwork characterized by sentimental, often pretentious bad taste" and "something so outrageously artificial, affected, inappropriate, or out-of date to be considered amusing," don't even have an equivalent in Spanish; *cursi,* meaning parodic, self-referential, inbred with intentional exaggeration, or perhaps misrepresentation, of human feelings, is the closest in esthetic terminology Spanish gets to them. But American icons like the *Lawrence Welk Show,* Barry Manilow, and the Bee Gees are *cursi;* native art in Mexico, instead, is nothing but *rascuache,* a south-of-the-border colloquialism ignored by the Iberian standardizer, the *Diccionario de la Real Academia Española,* yet often used in Mexico to describe a cultural item of inferior quality and proletarian origin.

*Rascuache* has no English cognate: The Pachuco fashion style in Los Angeles, for example, is *rascuache;* the musician Agustín Lara; the porcelain replicas of smiling clowns and ballerinas known as Lladrós, sold at department stores; imitation of Yves St. Laurent and Ralph Lauren clothing; T-shirts of the music group Menudo; native soda such as Chaparritas and flavored Tehuacán; tamarind and coconut candy; in spite of their global recognition (or perhaps as a result of it), the novelists Laura Esquivel, responsible for *Like Water for Chocolate,* and Paco Ignacio Taibo II, known for dirty-realist thrillers that have Private Detective Héctor Belascoarán Shayne as protagonist, are somewhat *rascuache* as well. While Mexico's highbrow society uses and abuses the term in order to establish a distance, to distinguish itself from cheap, low-born inventiveness, *rascuachismo,* with its trademark of authenticity, is also a source of pride and self-respect among the dispossessed. It is applied by the bourgeoisie to *alguien más*—someone else judged to be outside the demarcations of approved taste and decorum: to be *rascuache* is to be inferior, undeserving. But the lower classes assume its esthetics with a happy smile: A *rascuache* item is truly, unequivocally Mexican and therefore a magnet of self-satisfaction. Throughout the decades, *rascuachismo* has acquired something like a logic of taste, a consistent sensibility which can be crammed into the mold of a system. Avant-garde bourgeois art, even when addressing the most vulgar and tasteless, will by definition never descend to such low esteem. But the ruling class always maintains a kind of "negotiating relationship" with it; it uses it to establish a bridge across economic and social lines, to create an image of the nation's collective psyche, and to benefit the tourist industry.

As proven by the case of the early twentieth-century engraver José Guadalupe Posada, occasionally a proletarian artist can be "saved" from his *rascuache* background through the help of enlightened, upper-class artists. Posada died poor and forgotten and was buried in an anonymous grave in 1913, as the Socialist Revolution was sweeping the country. His lampoons ridiculed Porfirio Díaz's dictatorship (1876–1911) and commemorated holidays and natural disasters. But he would have remained anonymous had Jean Charlot, a French immigrant to Mexico and a friend of muralists Rivera and Orozco, not shown Posada's prints around and written about him in the context of the European style, Cubism. He brought him to international attention, thus redeeming him from the imprisonment of *rascuachismo* and turned him into a veritable artifact of highbrow culture. In other cases, nonetheless, a *rascuache* artist will be used by the intelligentsia to promote a certain "official" vision of the country, only to be dropped when such vision becomes either unnecessary or obstructive. Popular arts and crafts endure and grow because they fulfill certain functions within nationalism and capitalist reproduction, and because they offer a valuable mirror through which to sell an accepted, convenient image of society as a whole. For example, the anthropologist Néstor García Canclini, author of *Transforming Modernity: Popular Culture in Mexico,* has written eloquently on the values of *rascuache* art, folklore, and aboriginal souvenirs for a certain government regime interested in sponsoring the production of export artifacts among the lower classes for purely touristy purposes. They sell and they offer an image of Mexico as intimately connected with its pre-Colombian roots: a nation with a historic past and a non-Western philosophy of life, a civilization thirty splendorous centuries in the making.

The art critic Tomás Ybarra-Frausto, in a stimulating 1990 essay, explains in more detail this attractive concept, *rascuachismo:*

> Propriety and keeping up appearances—*el qué dirán*—are the codes shattered by the attitude of *rascuachismo.* This outsider viewpoint stems from a funky, irreverent stance that debunks convention and spoofs protocol. To be *rascuache* is to posit a bawdy, spunky consciousness, to seek to subvert and turn ruling paradigms upside down. It is a witty, irreverent, and impertinent posture that recodes and moves outside established boundaries.

While pertaining to Mexican culture in general, Ybarra-Frausto's study is centered on the Chicano community of the Southwest, where, to distinguish itself from its Mexican past, it becomes something of an insider's private code. "Very generally," he argues, *"rascuachismo* is an underdog perspective—a view from *los de abajo,* an attitude rooted in resourcefulness and adaptability, yet mindful of stance and style. . . . It presupposes the worldview of the have-nots, but is also a quality exemplified in objects and places (a *rascuache* car or restaurant) and in social comportment (a person who is or acts *rascuache*)." Ybarra-Frausto suggests a random list of *rascuache* items akin to the Mexican-American community: the Royal Chicano Air Force, paintings on velvet, the calaveras of Posada, and the movie by Cheech Marín, *Born in East L.A.* He then distinguishes levels of *medio* and *muy,* low and high *rascuachismo*: Microwave tamales, the comedian Tin Tán, shopping at K-Mart, flour tortillas made with vegetable oil, pretending you are Spanish, and portraits of Emiliano Zapata on velvet slippers (*chanclas*) belong to the first category; to the second, frozen capirotada, flour tortillas made with lard, being bilingual and speaking with an accent in both languages, shopping at J. C. Penney's, portraits of Francisco Villa on velvet *chanclas,* and Cantinflas. Which brings me back to kitsch and camp, two terms implying a sense of parody and self-consciousness never found in *rascuachismo. A rascuache* artifact will not become emblematic of lowbrow Mexicanness until the sophisticated elite, always an alien force, says so—that is, until it is rescued to become a souvenir, a Mexican curiosity in the universal archives of Western civilization.*

Of the whole *rascuache* galaxy in Mexican lowbrow culture, Cantinflas, Ybarra-Frausto's last entry, is of particular interest to me. In spite of his incredibly high profile south of the border, today he is virtually unknown in Europe and the United States, which, I am sure, is directly related to the lack of sympathy with which the Mexican sophisticated elite views him nowadays. Indeed, this most revered Spanish-speaking comedian, admired at first by the middle class and the ruling intelligentsia, aside from the masses, of course, illustrates the never-ending rivalries between high and low culture, between elitist and *rascuache* perspectives in Mexico and the Hispanic hemisphere at large. His fame and decline show what's hot and cold, in and out, south of the border—and why.

Cantinflas, whose real name was Fortino Mario Alonso Moreno Reyes, was the *peladito* par excellence—a lumpen, street-wise itinerant citizen, the master of *mal gusto*—bad taste. He's slightly abusive, often disoriented, never totally happy, in total control of *la peladez,* with an irreverence that at once highlights and eases the tension between upper and lower classes in Mexico. Cantinflas's *rascuachismo*

---

* I explore the issue of *rascuachismo* and Chicano politics in *Bandido* (New York: HarperCollins, 1995).

is also Mexico's. When he first appeared on stage, in the late 1930s, the sophisticated elite championed him as a crystalline expression of the native soil. But by the time he died, at the age of eighty-one, he had become a casualty in the struggle to find an identity that suited the ruling party's desire to be part of the industrialized world. His mannerisms, his simplicity, while still adored by the populace, are today largely ignored by highbrow Mexican culture. Obviously, a drastic change of heart had taken place in the nation's mood.

A symptom of such a change is the fact that, when Cantinflas passed away, on April 20, 1993, he never received an obituary in *Vuelta,* Octavio Paz's literary monthly, probably the best cultural thermometer south of the border by which one can understand the ups and downs of the Latin American literati. The magazine is a sideboard of cosmopolitanism and finesse, a catalogue of bourgeois taste, a promoter of Europeanized ways of thought and conduct. Everybody's favorite rascal, Cantinflas, on the other hand, symbolizes the rough-and-tumble slapdash in poor barrios, the treacherousness of the illiterate, the vitality of the dispossessed, the obscenity of working-class people. By the mid-1990s his appeal had certainly passed, at least for the ruling class. Determined to sell NAFTA, the North American Free Trade Agreement, to Canada and the United States, the Partido Revolucionario Institucional, PRI, led by President Carlos Salinas de Gortari, was interested in selling an altogether different image of Mexico, not as a perfidious and disloyal neighbor but as honest, stable, trustworthy, a country made by a growing, money-oriented middle-class hypnotized by the American Dream.

Cantinflas: an unpleasant face to be hidden. Cantinflas: an arbiter of low taste in the process of eradication. But he was viewed this way only among the wealthy and socially mobile because half a century after the splash he made as the ultimate master of *rascuachismo,* among the poor and dispossessed he still typifies, as least for the masses, Mexico's true heart and soul. It's the ruling class and the intelligentsia that have changed: first love, then rejection. The transformation is not surprising. Others have suffered a similar fate. Cantinflas's early achievements were rapidly capitalized by a segment of the Europeanized Mexican intelligentsia that saw him as the champion of the forfeited, a magnetic representative of the underdogs with a larger-than-life charisma. In 1948, for instance, Tamayo painted his portrait, *Retrato de Cantinflas,* and three years later, Rivera placed him at the center of his 1951 mural in Teatro de los Insurgentes, in Mexico's capital. But around 1968, when the regime of President Gustavo Días Ordaz ordered a massacre of students in

Tlatelolco Square, just as the Olympic Games were about to take place, the country underwent a deep identity crisis. Good-bye to the disoriented *peladito*. No more disjointed, disheveled heroes. It was obvious that the PRI was starting to implement a less *rascuache*, more modernized image of Mexico. The nation was ready to abandon the Third World, to cease looking south to Latin America and begin looking north: to emulate Uncle Sam. The transformation would take place over a period of decades, and, in the end, Cantinflas and other similar lowlife symbols would become a mishap.

As a result of this increasingly incurable allergy to *rascuachismo* and pop art, the intellectual elite has generated almost no bibliography about Cantinflas, neither panoramic nor reflective. The index of Carlos Fuentes's *The Buried Mirror: Reflections on Spain and the New World*, makes no mention of his incomparable contribution to Hispanic humor. Here and there, some marginal references to him are made by others. The poet Salvador Novo, for instance, described his intrepid ascendance in *Nuevas grandeza mexicana*; the playwright Xavier Villaurrutia praised him in the magazine *Hoy*; and Jorge Ibargüengoitia, the comic novelist responsible for *The Dead Girls*, does refer to him in passing in an essay included in his 1991 collection, *Autopsias rápidas*. Perhaps the only serious, thought-provoking interest in Cantinflas can be found in Carlos Monsiváis, a practitioner of New Journalism *à la mexicana* attracted to the cultural manifestations of the underclass. A text of 1988 states: "The smiles and laughter that Cantinflas's performance still generates among Mexican and Latin American audiences are not incidental. . . . What is being applauded? His incoherence is the incoherence of the masses, the aggression that is ignorance among the ruling class, the memorizing joke that is certified to be repeated, time and again, with success." And Monsiváis adds:

> Cantinflas, programmatic mumbling and conditioned reflex. He shows up, he moves, he begins a verbal twist, he puzzles his listener, he makes fun of the knowledge never captured in linguistic chaos . . . and his audience is bamboozled, is entertained and feels happy, finds inspiration in everyone's joy. . . . Cantinflas is a true Son of the People, the idiosyncratic expression that will become our tradition. This powerful asset allows the comedian-impresario to overcome the numerous mistakes of his films and generate permanent admiration through the gag in which there's much talk but nothing is said. What's

humorous in Cantinflas: his image and voice; his comic message; his silhouette. The myth, a function of memory.

The only available biography of Cantinflas is a second-rate, "official" one written in 1994 by Guadalupe Elizalde: *Mario Moreno y Cantinflas . . . rompen el silencio.* Full of innuendoes, repetition, unverified information, typos, and spelling mistakes, its quality encapsulates the comedian's *rascuache* spirit: It confuses and deceives. It details the tense relationship he had with Mario Arturo Moreno, his illegitimate son, and the scandalous suicide of one of Moreno Reyes's lovers, the United States model Marion Roberts. But the biography does succeed in delivering an image of him as an institution: photographs of Cantinflas alongside every single Mexican president, from Días Ordaz to Miguel de la Madrid Hurtado, as well as with Lyndon Johnson and Richard Nixon, invade the volume. It discusses also his liaison with Mexico's Actor's Union, ANDA, which once accused him of mishandling the organization's money and of abusing his fame during a benefit performance for the Red Cross by embezzling donated funds.

But if studies about his life and oeuvre are almost nonexistent, his influence in Hispanic art is far-reaching. His name is invoked everyday on TV, the radio, and in the printed media. His movies are shown everywhere from Ciudad Juárez to Buenos Aires. Performance artists invoke his ghost. Musicians sing to his legend. Take the case of Luis Valdez, the legendary Chicano playwright and funding director of El Teatro Campesino in California and responsible for *Zoot Suit, La Bamba,* and other works. His 1973 epic play *La carpa de los Rascuachis* follows a Cantinflas-like protagonist from his crossing the border into the United States to the subsequent indignities he undergoes. Even if the name Cantinflas is never mentioned, the play is a direct homage, a tribute to this most durable and beloved comedian.

Lewis Jacobs once said of Charlie Chaplin that his importance lay not in what he contributed to film art, but in what he contributed to humanity. Cantinflas had a less universal, if equally ambitious impact: He remains an archetype, a model, a bottomless well of inspiration personifying the plight suffered by a preindustrial Mexico struggling to insert itself in the twentieth century. His adventures allow his audience to understand the transition from a rural to an urban setting many poor, uneducated *campesinos* have been forced to make in Latin America to earn only a few pesos. This means that, in spite of his cultural eclipse among the powerful, Cantinflas is an invaluable map to his nation's psyche, a compass to a *rascuache* esthetic, an invaluable tool to understand the clash between haves and have-nots in his society and culture. Through him we see, hear, and feel the Mexican self better. Posterity refuses to incorporate Moreno Reyes's villainous aspect; it prefers to remember him in an undiscriminating, uninformed, uncritical way—as the one and only *peladito*.

Born on August 12, 1911, in Santa María la Redonda, a poor neighborhood in Mexico City, Moreno Reyes was the son of a mailman, the sixth of thirteen children. A born entertainer, he charmed passers-by with his dancing and rapid-fire jokes and wordplay. As a teenager, he became, by turns, a bullfighter, a shoe-shine boy, a taxi driver, and a successful boxer before joining up with a *carpa,* an itinerant side show that combined circus acrobatics with slapstick comedy from the turn of the century to the advent of mass media in the forties. The *carpa* was a favorite gathering point for the disenfranchised mired in elemental daily struggle. A mixture of clowns, acrobats, and standup comedians, the *carperos* contributed a unique sense of *weltanshauung* to lowbrow culture south of the border: They emphasized rapid corporeal movements interlaced with slapstick action, pratfalls, and verbal virtuosity. Tin Tán, Clavillazo, Mantequilla, and Resortes were all acclaimed comedians in the 1940s and 1950s with a large following. Tin Tán in particular offered a different picture of *lo mexicano.* As John King, the British film and literary critic, argues in his book *Magical Reels,* "[H]is Mexican-American pachuco, the zoot-suited, upwardly mobile con man, could talk and dance his way out of any difficult situation in a mixture of Spanglish idioms and border-music rhythms."

The *pachuco* image had to be modified to suit the popular taste of the time, but the origins of Tin Tán—the border towns such as Ciudad Juárez, the mass migrations (legal and illegal) across the border, the Americanization of Mexican culture—were all to become an irresistible part of the Mexican experience. In *El rey del barrio* (King of the Neighborhood, 1949), his most memorable film, the verbal patter is exhilarating as are the spectacular dance situations with Tongolele (Yolanda Montes).

One night, the story goes, Cantinflas had to stand in for a sick master of ceremonies and made the audience laugh without end. The first thing he did was pee in his pants. Afterward, nervous, virtually out of control, he became incoherent, his sentences tangling one another up, ridiculous. Instead of getting him boosted off the stage, his muddled patter was greeted with applause. Accident became routine.

But the name Cantinflas only came into being when someone in the audience shouted *En la cantina tú inflas!* (You tank up in the cantina! You're drunk!). The words conflated in Moreno Reyes's mind into a name: Cantinflas. It became his nom de guerre and ultimately entered the *Diccionario de la Real Academia Española* as a verb, *cantrinflear,* which means to blather on and on and say nothing; as a noun, *cantinflada,* something done by an adorable clown; and as an adjective, *cantinfleando,* which means dumb. The combination produces the following dog-Latin expression: *Cantinflas cantinflea cantinfladas,* or Cantinflas blathers cantinflanisms.

Cantinfladas are heard everywhere in Mexico. The ear grows so accustomed to them, it quickly ceases to pay attention. An example of an eponymous one is the famous joke about one of Mexico's former presidents, Luis Echeverría Alvarez. In a legendary speech detailing the ruling party's political ideology, he is said to have explained: *No somos de la izquierda, ni de la derecha, sino todo lo contrario*—We are neither of the left, nor of the right, but entirely the opposite.

Cantinflas began as a supporting actor in 1937 and then married Valentina Zubareff (she died in 1966), the daughter of the owner of the *carpa* where he worked. It was she who suggested that Cantinflas appear in advertisements for products made in Mexico. The commercials were a success, so Moreno Reyes decided to found a film company, Posa Films, whose exclusive product would be movies starring Cantinflas. By 1941, the company had a couple of major Latin American hits, and Mario Moreno Reyes was well on his way to becoming a legend. During World War II, he met Miguel M. Delgado, who directed him in one hit after another, films such as the parodies *Romeo y Julieta* (1943) and *Gran Hotel* (1944). During those years, Moreno Reyes shaped the identity of his alter ego. Eventually, his creation would be recognized by visual and spiritual features: a dirty, long-sleeve T-shirt; a rotten tie; baggy, patched pants always covering only half his buttock; a robe used as a belt; old, broken shoes; on his head a hat several sizes small; a sparse mustache and short, uncombed hair. He is the Spanish Golden Age's *pícaro* reincarnated: a scoundrel, a knave. When Cantinflas walks, he seems to be loose in his posture. When Cantinflas talks, he takes his hat off, switches it from one hand to another, and often hits the furniture or a friend with it to accentuate his anger or discomfort. Social mobility is taboo in Mexican society: once indigent, always underprivileged. Since classes are dogmatically rigid and unchangeable, Cantinflas ridicules the abysss between social groups and allows for relaxation and acceptance. He often goes from oppressed to oppressor, but no explosive conclusion is drawn. His movies lack an ideologically charged message inviting the unhappy to rebel. They open a space in which discomfort and complaint are dealt with through healthy laughter. This explains why the Mexican government endorsed Cantinflas when his image was useful: He makes the agitated masses happy; his subversive spirit works on the abstract, never upsetting the status quo. As Jonathan Kandell, a *New York Times* reporter, argues, Cantinflas "was riotously effective at deflating the rich and pompous, the staid and convention. . . . [He transformed the] apprehension of the burgeoning urban poor into laughter."

Mexicans constantly use verbal puzzles that demonstrate the cleverness of the speaker and challenge the wit of the audience. They are akin to *adivinanzas* and *rompecabezas,* riddles and brain-teasers, often obscene, as well as proverbs, unexpected rhymes, humorous naming, folk poetry, and shrewd puns. Through humor the nation handles collective and individual catastrophes and short-comings. Only a few days after Pancho Villa was assassinated, in Hidalgo del Parral, in 1923, thousands of riddles and jokes circulated among the population. The same thing happened following the tragic 1985 earthquake in Mexico City. Whenever a group of Mexicans gets together at a friendly gathering, they invariably spend ten, fif-teen minutes, perhaps longer, cracking jokes about politicians and television stars, food and habits. Such jokes have a linguistic edge personified by Cantinflas. A scene in the film *Ni sangre ni arena* (*Neither Blood Nor Sand,* 1941) exemplifies his linguistic bravado, his verbal virtuosity, and the often insurmountable difficulty in making him available through translation. Cantinflas is selling cigars—in Spanish *puros,* a word also meaning "only" and "pure"—outside a bullfighting arena. "Puros! Puros!" he says. Confusion takes place and he ends up selling tacos as well. "Puros! Tacos! Tacos! Puros!" More confusion takes place and Cantinflas is left without cigars, only with tacos. The humorous sequence concludes as he shouts: "Puros tacos! Tacos! Tacos puros!" Both *tacos* and *puros* have the same shape, except that the former is a symbol of Mexico's lower class, whereas the latter exemplifies the highbrow European aristo-cracy. By mixing them up, the comedian offers a sample of his worldview: social extremes south of the Rio Grande are based on cultural paraphernalia that, when scrambled, loses its power and invites laughter. Replace a rich white man's cigar with a taco and you get an average *mestizo.*

What is remarkable is the fashion in which Cantinflas's *ras-cuachismo* brought world literature to Mexico: His films adapted, or subverted, Shakespeare's *Romeo and Juliet,* Cervantes's *Don Quixote,* and Alexander Dumas's *The Three Musketeers.* As in vaudeville art, a single theme recurs in all of Cantinflas's films (available on VHS from Arkansas Entertainment, without subtitles): the mistaken identity. He is often confused with somebody else: a rich entrepreneur, a hotel bellboy, a corrupt policeman, Don Quixote. Plots circle around comic misunderstanding that allows for linguistic irreverence and pyrotechnics. One enters his universe without esthetic pretension and invariably leaves it with a sense of fulfillment: We have attended an enlightening rendezvous through the twisted behavioral paths of underprivileged Mexicans. He is the ultimate satirist, making fun of the macho husband, the virginal female, the abusive priest, the naive foreigner; but he also promotes the image of Mexicans as lazy, siesta-driven, immoral, and treacherous. By doing it, does he somehow perform a disservice to his people by poking fun at Hispanic mannerisms? He brings forth a sense of relaxation that allows for Mexican culture to cope with its tragedies and digest its shortcomings. Therefore, he proves (if proof was ever needed) that humor, while universal, is indistinctly local: There is nothing more difficult than translating it from one language to another, from one *entourage* to the next. Whenever Cantinflas ignites a hearty laughter, it's usually about something nonnatives would find unappealing, even insensitive. His oral jokes need to be explained, redesigned, and reformulated for foreigners to understand.

From 1939, when his first fifteen-minute-long films, *Siempre listo en las tinieblas* (*Always Ready in Darkness*) and *Jenjibre contra dinamita* (*Ginger against Dynamite*), were distributed, to 1981, when *El barrendero* (*The Garbage Man*), his last movie, was produced, he was the protagonist of a total of forty-seven films. Every single one was a huge box-office success, turning him into a millionaire. His comic talents were appreciated worldwide. Chaplin, for instance, is reported to have said, after watching a Cantinflas movie: "He's the greatest comedian alive . . . far greater than I am!" In Mexico and elsewhere in Hispanic America he was repeatedly the subject of innumerable homages and retrospectives and inspired a celebrated comic strip, many TV cartoons, and a weekly magazine called *Ahí está el detalle*. He was sought by diplomats and artists alike and was the symbol for the 1986 Soccer World Cup. Furthermore, rumors have it that since World War II, nobody else has been the runaway winner in every national presidential election, simply because the electorate knows its vote is ultimately irrelevant in a system plagued by fraud. Thus, Cantinflas becomes a much-beloved *subversivo* through which the population manifests its unhappiness with the undemocratic, repressive spirit it inhabits. A magnetic insurgent figure, Cantinflas is a proud ignoramus and a master in the lack of refinement. Ignorance is his weapon. He hides his illiteracy, stupidity, and lack of knowledge about the importance of science and technology in the modern world by pretending he is a consummate master in just about everything, from quantum mechanics to Shakespeare. In that respect, he symbolizes twentieth-century Mexico's unfulfilled desire to be a contemporary of the rest of humankind.

His authentic talents, visual and verbal, cinematic and linguistic, are also the areas in which his country's art has reached higher distinction: pictorial art and literature. While in politics Mexico has always been unimaginative, the artistic legacy, from the Aztecs to Octavio Paz's 1990 Nobel Prize, is unquestionable. When attempting to find an equivalent in the English-speaking world, the obvious choice might appear to be Charlie Chaplin's wistful Little Tramp. Both use pantomime; both poke fun at social types; both are unredeemed romantics, championing love as the true medicine of the human spirit; both refuse to approach film as a malleable, experimental art. But the similarities between the two are only superficial. Chaplin's creation was essentially a hostile character. His was a socially conscious message, inserted in the tradition of Jewish European liberalism, and his left-wing views often placed him at the center of heated controversies. In the era of silent cinema, which he refused to let go even when talkies were already dominating the market, his career achieved its apex from the 1920s to the 1940s, in films such as *The Gold Rush, Modern Times,* and *The Great Dictator.* Cantinflas's main strength is in speech—his tongue is his main weapon. He twists and turns it; he talks nonsense ad infinitum to confuse and disorient. As critic Rosa Linda Fregoso claims in her 1993 study *The Bronze Screen,* he emerged as the unchallenged master of *cábula,* using "the subversive (and pleasurable) play with language. . . . [He] satirized a rhetorical tendency of Mexican politicians known as *pura palabrería,* the excessive usage of words that said either 'nothing' or very little." He filled the vacuum of his solitude with verbs and adjectives, if only not to feel lonely and alone. While Chaplin's switch to talkies was challenging and ultimately unsuccessful, his mute hero, because of his unspecified background, achieved universality. Cantinflas, on the other hand, spent his energy exploring the intricacies of the Mexican collective self. Consequently, his art was overwhelmingly regional and parochial, and only through that particularity he achieved universality. Cantinflas's true Hollywood equivalents might be the Three Stooges, with their humorous vaudevillian sketches that captivated their audience in the late 1930s; or, even better, the Marx Brothers. Their debut took place in 1929, and as Guadalupe Elizalde claims, in

spite of his miserable English, Cantinflas was their loyal fan.
Groucho's humor is based on funny looks and a caustic sense of
laughter that uses ridiculous statements to philosophize about politics and daily life. W. C. Fields used to call the Marx Brothers "the
only act I could not follow," and many Spanish-speakers often say
the same about Cantinflas. While he uses (and abuses) sighs, shrugs,
and grimaces, language is his strength—his aggressive weapon, his
defense mechanism, his true forte, the crucial expression of his convoluted self. He conjugates verbs erroneously, invents adjectives
and adverbs, and consistently fails to complete his sentences. In
short, he reinvents the Spanish language, makes an idiosyncratic
hybrid, a Mexican jargon, a *rascuache* code. Indeed, his verbal
pyrotechnia is at its best when Cantinflas talks to the educated: He
takes detours, repeats sentences, gets lost, starts all over again. The
message is clear: In Mexico, high- and lowbrow cultures live misunderstanding each other; they misrepresent, misquote, deceive, distort,
and slant each other. The following transcription, representative
of his convoluted style, comes from an interview published in the
newspaper *Excélsior* on October 20, 1938:

> Vamos por partes: ¿Usted me pregunta que cuál ha sido mi
> mejor interpretación? ¿Y yo le tengo que responder que . . . ?
> ¿Qué le tengo que responder? ¿O usted me responde? Bueno,
> pero ¿qué relajo es éste? A ver, otra vez: usted quiere que le
> diga cuál ha sido, es y será, a través del devenir histórico-
> materialista-dialéctico, la mejor de mis interpretaciones
> proletarias. Y yo creo que hasta cierto punto, y si no, de
> todos modos, porque usted sabe que, al cabo y que, y como
> quiera que, la mejor de todas mis interpretaciones ha sido
> la interpretación racional y exacta del Universo conforme
> al artículo tercero. . . . ¿Qué? ¿Eso no . . . ? ¿Bueno, pues
> usted de qué habla?

An inevitably raw, insufficient translation. The reader should
known that in Spanish, *interpretación* means simultaneously "performance" and "interpretation":

> Let's see: You're asking me which has been my best interpre-
> tations [i.e., performance]? And I have to answer that . . . ?
> What do I have to answer? Or is it you who should answer?
> OK, but what mess is this? Again, let's see: you want me
> to tell you which has been, is and will be, throughout
> historical-materialistic-dialectical, the best of my proletarian

interpretations. And I believe that up to a certain point, and if not, in any case, because as you know, notwithstanding, and in spite of all, the best of my interpretations has been the rational and exact interpretation of the Universe, according to article 3. . . . What? It isn't true . . . ? OK, so what are you talking about?

Not long ago, during a one-day tribute at Lincoln Center's Walter Reade Theater, I had *Ahí está el detalle* (*That's the Deal*), his most famous movie, shown as part of a retrospective on modern Mexican cinema. The response was intriguing. Whereas the rest of the films, a product of contemporary artists, attracted a cosmopolitan, intellectually sophisticated audience, Cantinflas brought a large number of lower-class *hispanos* anxious to recapture a certain sight, a charming laughter of a native culture left behind. It was impossible to get a subtitled copy, which forced us to use simultaneous translation. Richard Peña, the Harvard-educated executive director of the New York Film Festival and a native Spanish-speaker of Puerto Rican background, took upon himself the impossible task of translating the comedian. Seeing him after the show was saddening: He was empty of all energy, humorless, completely mute. To understand his plight, imagine for a minute doing a simultaneous translation of Woody Allen into Hebrew or German while retaining its New York sense of Jewish comedy.

In the 1940s the Mexican film industry underwent a tremendous transformation. From small studio productions to blockbusters, movies were delivered at an amazing speed and had a successful running throughout Hispanic America. Jorge Negrete, María Félix, Dolores del Río, and Pedro Infante populated the screen with peasant heroes, ignorant and naive in the ways of the industrial world. As John King puts it: "The success of Mexican cinema in the forties was due to a series of circumstances: the added commercial opportunities offered by the war, the emergence of a number of important directors and cinematographers and the consolidation of a star system resting on proven formulae." Cantinflas, in spite of his *rascuachismo,* worked with internationally renowned figures in Mexico: the Russian émigré Acady Boytler, a pupil of the theater director Konstantin Stanislawsky; the musician Silvestre Revueltas; the filmmaker Chano Urueta; the screenwriters Salvador Novo and Pepe Martínez de la Vega; and the cinematographers Jack Draper, Alex Phillips, and Gabriel Figueroa.

Figueroa is of special importance. His work always leaned toward exteriors or sequences of the countryside. Together with

Emilio "El Indio" Fernández, responsible for the movies *Flor Silvestre* and *María Candelaria,* he inaugurated a black-and-white esthetic view of Mexican lowlife, particularly the peasantry. He worked with John Ford and John Huston. His liaison to Cantinflas is another intriguing connection between high- and lowbrow art. Figueroa photographed a total of seven films of his, including *Los tres mosqueteros* (*The Three Musketeers,* 1942), *Un día con el diablo* (*A Day with the Devil,* 1945), and *El bombero atómico* (*The Atomic Fireman,* 1950). Their work together marks the time in which Cantinflas was not only adored by the masses, but highly respected by the middle class and the intellectual elite. He personified Mexican street wisdom. "In my view," Figueroa wrote in a 1990 autobiographical essay, "Mexican cinema has excelled above all in the dramatic genre, and in the antics of Cantinflas. Mario Moreno's early performances were brilliant, a marvelous portrayal of the Mexican *peladito.*" The 1930s, when Cantinflas began his acting career, were a period of intense search for the clues to the nation's psyche. In 1934, Samuel Ramos, a philosophy professor at Universidad Nacional Autónoma de México, inspired by Sigmund Freud's and Alfred Adler's theories, published his influential *Profile of Man and Culture in Mexico,* a collection of interrelated essays in which he analyzed the personality of *el pelado,* as well as the urban and the bourgeois Mexican. Ramos believed Mexico was incapacitated for progress, owing to a paralyzing inferiority complex. The best way to examine the nation's soul, he argued, is through *el pelado mexicano.* He describes him as "less than proletarian and in the eyes of intellectual, a primitive. . . . [His] explosions are verbal and his lexicon is nasty and aggressive."

> We shouldn't be deceived by appearances. The pelado is neither a strong person nor a brave man. The physiognomy he exhibits is false. It's a camouflage to deceive him from those that interact with him. One could indeed establish that, the stronger and braver he behaves, the bigger the weakness he is trying to hide. . . . He lives with continual fear of being discovered, doubting himself.

Other thinkers afterward, including Octavio Paz in *The Labyrinth of Solitude* and Roger Bartra in *The Melancholy Cage,* have expanded this argument. Although unmentioned, the early Cantinflas is always in these writers' (and their readers') minds: a rogue, a cunning devil, an awkward citizen, a parasite. He incarnates the chaos of modern Mexican life. Can he put aside his complexes to work toward progress? Not quite: His convoluted self will always make him walk on the edge of an abyss, neither falling down nor moving away to safety. Cantinflas's Mexico: a mirror of confusion.

By the next decade, the Mexican film industry had pretty much exhausted its talents, but it was precisely in 1950 when a Spanish émigré, Luis Buñuel, produced a most astonishing film, one that would reeavaulate the whole era *Los olvidados,* a study of orphans in Mexico City pushed to a low life in crime. Buñuel was already in his late forties; the film established him, a Surrealist *enfant terrible,* as an international figure. Astonishing in numerous ways, it retains an intriguing link with Cantinflas, its cast of astute rascals openly emulating him, which, in the end, results in a masterful metamorphosis of *rascuachismo* into highbrow culture and in one more cultural theft by the haves of the have-nots. *Los olvidados* is Cantinflas for the politically sensitive, which helps explain why Cantinflas's vicissitudes beyond continental borders, particularly in the United States and Europe, are almost nonexistent. In 1956, already a monumental hero south of the Rio Grande, he was cast as Passepartout, opposite to David Niven, Buster Keaton, Frank Sinatra, and Marlene Dietrich, in *Around the World in Eighty Days* (directed by Michael Anderson). But the multistellar Hollywood movie was a total disaster. Soon after, George Sidney directed him in *Pepe* (1960). The cast included Shirley Jones, Edward G. Robinson, Zsa-Zsa Gabor, Janet Leigh, Jack Lemmon, and Kim Novak. But again, the success was limited. Although Cantinflas made the cover of *Life en español,* in Mexico and elsewhere in the Southern Hemisphere he was sharply criticized. His performances, people argued, were a death stroke to his comic capabilities. Vulgarity was his nature, why escape it? I must agree: What's remarkable about him is found in the humorous situation in the legendary *Ahí está el detalle,* where he acts as his own lawyer against a prosecutor ready to put him behind bars for a crime he didn't commit.

In his mature years, he was famous for his wealth. He had witnessed the modernization of his own country and had played a crucial role as therapeutic instrument and as millionaire. At the time of his death his personal fortune was estimated at $25 million. He loved luxury, owning five mansions, the one in Mexico City containing an art gallery, a swimming pool, a jai alai fronton, a theater, a barber shop, and a beauty parlor. His private jet flew him to his thousand-acre ranch, La Purísima, where he practiced his favorite hobby, bullfighting. He was a philanthropist and each year distributed $175,000 to the homeless waiting outside his door on his birthday. He built apartment houses in the Granjas neighborhood in his nation's capital and sold them to the poor for a fraction of their worth. His high-ranking contacts in the ruling party, and he himself, often went out of their way to assure his audience that Moreno Reyes's fortune had nothing to do with drug trafficking and corruption. In *Cantinflas: Aguila o Sol*, a commemorative illustrated volume published by the government's Consejo Nacional para la Cultura y las Artes in 1993, shortly after his death, critic Carlos Bonfil time and again portrays him as an honest, self-made man, a humble, dignified Mexican—an image the state, for obvious reasons, is obsessed with safeguarding. In old age, however, Moreno Reyes was known to have close links to members of Mexico's drug cartel and to corrupt union leaders. Several million Mexicans attended his funeral (¡El rey ha muerto!). As time went by, Cantinflas, his creation and theirs as well, had become an immobile feature in the Mexican landscape. Like Superman and Little Orphan Annie, he never aged: Hs features were exactly the same from the 1940s to the 1980s. (Moreno Reyes did gain considerable weight, but his movies never addressed this transformation.) It became obvious, at least to the ruling class, that Cantinflas could not continue as the idol of the Mexican poor simply because he had switched classes, becoming immensely rich. Rich and obese. Indeed, the whole country had grown in size: From 1938 to the early 1980s, Mexico underwent drastic changes—a massive overpopulation, growing political corruption, social injustice, the institutionalization of authority, and a student massacre. In his movies Moreno Reyes hardly addressed this metamorphosis. His Mexico was ahistorical, immutable. His protagonist was static, uninvolved, apolitical. Occasionally he does ridicule an adolescent for wearing long hair or a union leader is brought to justice for incompetence, but nothing more serious or dangerous. The total government support he enjoyed early in his career translated into his own complacent silence: laughter without criticism, suffering sublimated into comedy.

By the early 1960s his aesthetic contribution—his championing of *rascuachismo*—had been accomplished and what followed was mere repetition: Cantinflas imitating himself in movie after movie. The status quo grew accustomed to him. His verbal usage, his civil subversion, his tasteless self, his cheap attitude were antielitist, antiprogress, perhaps even anti-Mexican, but never against the establishment: comedy without meanness, mass appeal without aggression. Unlike Chaplin, he never exhibited any form of leftism. In fact, his canonization probably was a result of his apolitical stand: ridicule, but not aggression. So when Mexico needed to revamp its collective identity, when it looked northbound to sell another image of itself to the world, Cantinflas's *rascuachismo* was put aside: It became useless—an obstacle. Technology and education, not apathy and confusion, were now in the nation's agenda; consumerism and political stability were the accepted values, not improvisation and anarchy.

His life cycle is better understood as one realizes that when Mario Moreno Reyes entered the national scene, during the hypernationalistic period of President Lázaro Cárdenas, from 1934 to 1940, the government was preoccupied with selling an image of a peasant country in search of its pre-Columbian roots. Cárdenas expropriated foreign-held properties and oil companies, distributed land to *campesinos,* and instituted social reform to benefit Indians and Mexican workers. Cantinflas at the time was an irreplaceable expression of *lo mexicano.* But as the nation south of the Rio Grande moves into the twenty-first century looking northward instead of southward in search of economic, social, and political stability, another image of the country's collective spirit has emerged: enchanted with modern technology, in an eternal shopping spree, enchanted with its media image, and dressed up like the rest of Western civilization. While Cárdenas, before he was elected Mexico's president, was a general in the revolution of Pancho Villa and Emiliano Zapata, a leader in touch with the masses, contemporary presidents and their cabinet members, particularly under Carlos Salinas de Gortari's and current President Ernesto Zedillo Ponce de León's regimes are Ivy League–educated, English-speaking dealmakers. Cárdenas has ceased to be a role model; the new inspirations are magnates and neoconservatives north of the Rio Grande, known for fortune and stability, not populist visions. And thus, Cantinflas's art, if not always remarkable in filmmaking terms, but at least always authentic, has lost the favor of the sophisticate elite, which I guess only serves to highlight the utilitarianism of the highbrow Mexican culture.

But culture is a composite, a united effort, a mosaic—the production and reproduction of symbols and motifs by upper and lower levels of society. If anything, the esthetics of *rascuachismo* highlight the enmity, the tension between rich and poor in Mexico, between Europeanized and native viewpoints. Cantinflas might be too harsh, too confronting, too conflicted an image for the bourgeoisie to accent: Unwillingly, he denounces his own and everyone else's laziness, his intellectual confusion, his immature strategies to deal with modernity. Overall, he promotes a negative stereotype of *el mexicano* and might nurture fear and uncertainty toward Mexico among foreigners and "potential investors" that somehow manage to understand his verbal agitation. It's a matter of fashion, of course: To reject him, to deny his importance is to ignore the tattered, shattered, broken world of proletarian Mexico, perpetually ruptured, yet constantly stitched together and proud of itself. To discard Cantinflas, to portray him as a ruffian or parasite is to neglect one of the two halves of the Mexican self.

4

Southern

Exposure

# RIGOBERTA MENCHÚ

---

## Truth or Dare

Rigoberta Menchú is a disgraced angel. That, in brief, is the thesis of David Stoll's inflammatory volume, much discussed in the international press in the past couple of months. Menchú is the Indian activist from Guatemala on whom the Nobel Committee in Norway bestowed its Peace Prize in 1992, to mark the quincentennial of Columbus's arrival in the Americas. The award was for her campaign on behalf of Central American Indians. In fact, while Menchú enjoyed a considerable reputation in the world at large, to a large extent thanks to her bestselling autobiography, *I, Rigoberta Menchú* (1983), she was then little known in her own country. Stoll, a professor of anthropology at Middlebury College, Vermont, has been pursuing Menchú for more than a decade, ever since, in the course of his doctoral dissertation at Stanford University, he began interviewing Guatemalan peasants in, among other places, Menchú's home town, Chimel, Uspantán, and discovered that segments of her autobiography were gross falsifications. At first, Stoll decided, wisely no doubt, to put his research on hold; Guatemala was still submerged in almost three decades of bloody civil war; peace negotiations between the government and the Guatemalan National Revolutionary Union, an umbrella organization of four guerrilla groups, had begun in 1991, but an agreement, sponsored by the United Nations, would not be signed for five more years. If Menchú's character was attacked in the interim, the life of even

---

First published in *Times Literary Supplement* 5012 (April 23, 1999).

more innocent people would be in jeopardy. But as Guatemala settled gradually into an uncomfortable democracy after 1996, Stoll's silence gave way to a shriek.

And a loud shriek it is. To be fair, his accusations are far milder than what one commentator after another, from Eduardo Galeano to Manuel Vázquez Montalbán and the *New York Times* reporter Larry Rohter, have encouraged the public to believe. In fact, they constitute a small fraction of his 336 pages, the rest of which Stoll devotes to building up the context in which the falsifications ought to be read; and, perhaps more appropriately, to constructing a defense against the attacks he foresees as likely to descend on him. The main plot of *I, Rigoberta Menchú*, Stoll confides, is essentially true, and truthful too are most of its details. What is questionable are a handful of passages and the narrative perspective under which they are delivered. The factors behind the death of Menchú's brother Petrocinio, for instance: Stoll does not deny his murder, but asserts that Menchú's version is an invention in several ways; Menchú cannot have been an eyewitness, as her autobiography suggests she was. In addition, Vicente Menchú, the activist's father, is said to have died during a protest in 1980 at the Spanish Embassy in Guatemala City, but the fire in which he died was not started by the military, as the revolutionaries claimed. Stoll calls attention to the role the insurgent Guatemalan guerrillas played vis-à-vis the indigenous population: It is wrong, he argues, to portray the military as the sole tormentor of civilians, when the rebels were equally (if not more) ruthless. For decades, the Menchú family has been ensnared in tribal rivalries, and its victims are not always the martyrs the activist makes them out to be. "The tragedies that befall [them]," Stoll writes, "are undeniable. How these were understood by the revolutionary movement, its foreign supporters, and human rights activists is another matter."

Stoll scrutinizes almost every sentence in Menchú's memoir, setting her words against archive material and the voice of many participants on both sides of the battlefield. He also interviews Elisabeth Burgos-Debray, the Venezuelan-born anthropologist and former wife of Régis Debray, who has long been seen as the crucial stepping-stone in Menchú's ascent to global fame. It was in 1982, barely two years after her father's death, when Menchú visited Paris from her Mexican exile. Her role was to speak out, in her traditional Indian costume and precarious Spanish, in favor of the revolutionary front in Guatemala. Burgos-Debray personified the circuitous paths of the Latin American Left: When very young, she fought against the Pérez-Jiménez dictatorship in her native country, joined the Communist Party, traveled with her husband Debray, in 1966, to Cuba, where she went into military training hoping to join Che Guevara in his quest to ignite "two, three, or many Vietnams," subsequently moved to Chile to support Salvador Allende, and finally settled in France. At the request of a magazine, Burgos-Debray interviewed Menchú, first for a couple of hours, then, since the Guatemalan was in no hurry, for a whole week. The anthropologist then transcribed and edited the tapes, turning them into a full-length book. Menchú and Elisabeth Burgos (now divorced) are no longer on speaking terms. The activist, feeling the pressure of Stoll's investigations, has publicly denounced their liaison. "That is not my book," Menchú announced in 1997 to the newspaper *El Periódico*. "It is a book by Elizabeth Burgos. . . . [It] does not belong to me morally, politically, or economically." The anthropologist, on the other hand, is clear about her role in the shaping of Menchú's name: "If I had wanted to do it as a professional publication, with my questions included, I could have done so," Burgos reiterates, "but this was not my objective."

■ ■ ■

Menchú's ambivalence is half-hearted. This is understandable: The book remains her primary outlet; it appeared at the right time and place, just as Latin America as a whole was moving full swing into its neoliberalist mood, its armed struggle tarnished as a viable strategy. (In 1998, Menchú produced a sequel: *Crossing Borders: An Autobiography*, edited by Ann Wright, published by Verso.) Still, the issue is whom to believe. Strictly speaking, *I, Rigoberta Menchú* is not a standard autobiography, but what has come to be known as a *testimonio*. Academics refer to it as "a document" delivered from the viewpoint of a colonial subject, whose voice is Westernized by means of a sophisticated, ideologically motivated transcriber. No matter how Menchú's words are read, they are a case of mediated confession—or better, "a translated life." Who is to be blamed for its inaccuracies? Since its appearance, various questions have been asked: How on earth, one wonders, did an illiterate Indian woman reach such a degree of intellectual refinement, her account filled with metaphors and metonyms, and even epigraphs from the Bible and the other Guatemalan Nobel Prize winner, the novelist Miguel Angel Asturias? Burgos acknowledges her input as editor, but her red pen was not too intrusive; she even played some of the tapes to Stoll to show him what a powerful voice Menchú already owned.

She claims: "[Rigoberta's] Spanish was very basic. She translated from her own language [in her head]. . . . Yes, I corrected verb tenses and noun genders, as otherwise it would not have made sense. . . . [Her] narrative was anything but chronological. It had to be put in order. And the passages about culture I elicited had to be inserted into the narrative of her life." Burgos sent the transcribed manuscript to Menchú's organization. Menchú herself returned it with a letter asking Burgos to delete three little passages and the epigraphs at the beginning of each chapter. The former disappeared, but not the latter.

In Oslo, the Nobel Committee, aware of the scandal, is not revoking Menchú's award. In fact, it continues to endorse her, arguing that it is her activism, and not her career as an author, which brought her the laurel. Sadly though, the political reverberations following Stoll's intervention have begun to take effect, especially in Guatemala, where a right-wing campaign to discredit Menchú is in full flight, combining with an attempt to refurbish the military's opprobrious image. At the center of the Menchú scandal is the fallibility of truth, and, as such, it brings to mind the denunciation of Holocaust memoirs, such as Binjamin Wilkomirski's *Fragments* and Salomón Isacovici's *Man of Ashes*. In and of themselves, these examples offer the gamut of troublesome eyewitness accounts. Wilkomirski, a classical musician in Switzerland who recovered his childhood memories by means of psychoanalysis, is accused of fabricating most of his concentration-camp odyssey. Memory, in his case, is unreliable. On the other hand, Isacovici, a survivor in Ecuador, delivered his chronicle through interviews with an ex-Jesuit priest, Juan Manuel Rodríguez, who, in turn, transcribed and "novelized" them, soon after claiming the book was really his and not Isacovici's. Isacovici himself died in 1998 and thus cannot deny the charges. Menchú's case falls somewhere between Wilkomirski and Isacovici: Her voice is translated, but she personally read and approved her account before it reached the printer. Is her whole message to be distrusted? No, argues Stoll. "[She] is a legitimate Mayan voice." But her integrity is nevertheless in question, particularly since at the heart of *I, Rigoberta Menchú* is her attempt to present her odyssey as an archetype, one encapsulating those of all Guatemalan Indians. Those who would deny the Holocaust have used controversial memoirs by survivors. And the same approach is heard in Guatemala today. Is the undeniable misery of the Central American native population less relevant because Menchú lied?

But Menchú's case is more complex, simply because truth is a most shrouded institution in the Americas. The continent is built on falsifications:* Columbus's description of his voyages to Spain's Catholic kings is a masterful exercise in self-deception; the record of chroniclers and missionaries is single-sided; and the eyewitness accounts by Indians are mere adaptations appropriated by sophisticated minds. The fact that Spanish and Portuguese are the region's official languages already announces the degree to which the whole civilization is translated. Menchú, no doubt, ought to be held accountable for "her" *testimonio*, but it must not be forgotten that the region from which it springs is a machine of counterfeit. By unmasking a myth-making Guatemalan Indian, Stoll, a fact-obsessed, Stanford-trained anthropologist, embarked on a journey into the abyss between south and north. His book is not really about Rigoberta Menchú per se, but about what she has been turned into by the West: a symbol of victimhood. Foreigners, especially the U.S. academy, use and abuse her: For some, she is a symbol of oppression and regression, and even her lying should be excused; while for others, she has been used as a weapon to vilify the status quo, and her self-aggrandizing lies should be denounced. And behind Rigoberta Menchú's public persona, a lonely person strived to remain in touch with her roots. David Stoll himself, uneasy in the role of victimizer, has succeeded in making her more human.

---

* I develop these themes in my introduction to *Facundo: Civilization and Barbarism*, by Domingo F. Sarmiento (New York: Penguin Classics, 1998).

# VUELTA

## A Succinct Appraisal

Literary supplements and journals of opinion have always played a major role in the shaping of Hispanic culture. They have served as gathering points to catalyze transnational artistic moods, crystallize current political opinions, and promote intellectual trends that would otherwise never reach the largest segment of the population. They also function as ideological galaxies in which secondary voices endlessly rotate around an imperious dictatorial figure, making them temples of adoration and sacrifice in which to pay tribute to a *caudillo* and, simultaneously, from which to orchestrate fanciful battles to debunk the enemy. By the same token, their autocratic editors use them as springboards for their own personal and artistic purposes.

The prestigious Cuban magazine *Orígenes* launched an aesthetic renewal promoting seriousness and artistic commitment regardless of political affiliation. Initiated by high-caliber figures such as Virgilio Piñera and Cintio Vitier and controlled by José Lezama Lima, the periodical, active between 1944 and 1956, while mapping out Cuban culture, pretty much behaved as a centralized, undemocratic, self-generating system. Similarly, José Ortega y Gasset's long-running *Revista de Occidente,* interested in natural and human sciences, as well as in literature and pictorial art, from 1923 on promoted German philosophy (Oswald Spengler, Max Scheler, Ludwig Klages) in the Iberian peninsula and throughout Latin America. The magazine served Ortega y Gasset as a springboard to project his own ideas and

First published in *Salmagundi* 108 (Fall 1995). Reprinted in *Art and Anger: Essays on Politics and the Imagination* (Albuquerque, NM: University of New Mexico Press, 1996).

make them extremely influential. And *Sur,* the Buenos Aires monthly founded by Victoria Ocampo, where Borges published his most enduring and dazzling essays and stories, for decades exerted an incredible influence on Argentine culture, welcoming Europeanized literary fashions and accusing pro-Soviet, pro-aboriginal writers of obscurantism.

As a result of the insularity and peculiar metabolism of the Hispanic intelligentsia, commanding journals of this stature can only flourish in cosmopolitan centers like Buenos Aires, Havana, Mexico City, Madrid, and Barcelona. But their impact reaches far beyond urban and national borders, as is the case of *Vuelta,* a monthly magazine of enormous influence, controlled by a small group of writers. Since its troublesome birth, in 1976, it has gravitated around the colossal figure of Octavio Paz, the Mexican poet and essayist of imposing power. Published in a southern suburb of Mexico City and sold in major Spanish-speaking capitals, as well as in select bookstores throughout Europe and the United States, its handsome, refined pages regularly feature works by an international cast of contributors, from Milan Kundera and Daniel Bell to Susan Sontag and Hans Magnus Ensenzberger, from Leszek Kolakowski to George Steiner, from Irving Howe to Joseph Brodsky, from Derek Walcott to Charles Tomlinson. But they also include a vast number of Spanish-speaking counterparts (Mario Vargas Llosa, Jorge Edwards, Javier Marías, Guillermo Cabrera Infante, Fernando Savater, et al.), thus promoting the Bolivarian view of the hemisphere and the Iberian peninsula as a rich mosaic of dreams and ideas. Paz's primary interests, coloring the journal from the beginning, are politics and literature, both separate and together. An average of eight of the twelve monthly issues contain a text written by him. The topics: his own life, the 1994 *campesino* uprising in Chiapas, the Berlin Wall, the pictorial art of Wolfgang Paalen, Sor Juana Inés de la Cruz's intricate intellectual universe, Anglo-Saxon poetry, and so on. Or he'll publish a new poem or a translation of Chinese, French, or English classics. His writing is invariably lucid and insightful. A renaissance *homme de lettres* in full command of a vast array of knowledge, Paz, through powerful arguments, allows the reader to see the world anew.*

---

* A number of studies on literary magazines in Latin America have appeared recently, but unfortunately none devoted to *Vuelta*. See John King's *Sur: A Study of the Argentine Literary Journal and Its Role in the Development of a Culture, 1931–1970* (Cambridge: Cambridge University Press, 1986); and Jesús J. Barquet's *Consagración de La Habana: La peculiaridades del grupo Orígenes en el proceso cultural cubano* (Miami, Fla.: University of Miami–North South Center, 1992).

Allergic to any form of dogmatism and isolationism, he champions a view of Hispanic culture as deeply rooted in its pre-Columbian past but fully devoted to inserting itself in the banquet of Western civilization. Not surprisingly, *Vuelta* has served to open up Mexican literature to outside forces and to promote Pan-Americanism among the region's intelligentsia. Much like its predecessor *Sur,* its implicit dream has always been to become a sideboard of Latin America's collective search for democracy and against dictatorship, *un lugar abierto,* an "open place," and a site of intellectual and artistic convocation, as evidence that the Hispanics are not part of the so-called Second or Third World but, in Paz's own words, "contemporaries of the rest of humankind." But the magazine and its environment aren't without major contradictions, and the content of its pages cannot but reflect the fractured Mexican literary scene, divided, since the early days of our century, into opposing crowds unified by a political stand and dancing around a leading luminary. Indeed, others before Paz have functioned as the nation's literary *caudillos,* including Alfonso Reyes, an essayist and Hellenistic scholar once described by Borges as "the greatest prose writer in Spanish in any era."

In spite of its universalistic, antiprovincial stand, *Vuelta* is more receptive than projective. At least a third of the essays and reviews in every issue are translations from European and U.S. contributors. As for its original Latin American material, aside from Paz's own, very infrequently does it get translated and reprinted elsewhere. In an environment long known for pirating text from international periodicals, the magazine is a pioneer in fulfilling its copyright obligations: It regularly requests permission to reprint articles from, say, *The New York Review of Books* and *Nouvelle Revue Française,* and, unlike its competitors in Mexico and elsewhere in the Hispanic world, it pays its monetary dues. But its honesty doesn't compensate for its dependence on other languages and cultures. *Vuelta* always takes considerably more than what it gives. That is, although Paz's hope is to bring the Hispanic intelligentsia to Western civilization, it often looks the other way around.

As any living organism, the monthly is always in constant change. It consistently reflects Paz's rotating political beliefs. In its almost twenty years of life, it has crystallized his anti-Communism and his animosity toward the Mexican government in 1976 (he used to address it "the philanthropic ogre"), his subsequent partnership with top national politicians of the ruling Partido Revolucionario Institucional, and his current concern with the country's fragile civil and financial stability. Overall, what unifies the magazine's pages is a passive, dilettantish philosophy: To observe, to contemplate, to reflect and meditate seem to be *Vuelta's* uniform attitude, never to act, to participate actively in order to change the way things are. Its young staff (the average age is thirty-five) isn't known for encouraging hard-writing journalism or debate about national and continental affairs; instead, it often sponsors discursive literary essays about abstract aesthetic issues and literary subjects, which assume a high level of sophistication among readers. Rather than debating the crisis of confidence of Mexico's population in its untrustworthy politicians and its repressive government system, for example, it sponsored global conferences on transcendental subjects such as "the experience of freedom," inviting international specialists. This contradiction ends up delivering a portrait of the periodical as uninvolved in local issues, isolated and inhabiting a self-contained bubble.

Of course one could argue that just because *Vuelta's* offices are south of the Rio Grande, the magazine is not obligated to reflect solely on national and Third World issues. After all, the Latin American intelligentsia, like all others, is allowed a dose of dilettantism. Besides, it isn't the first to turn its back to regional problems: Ortega y Gasset and Victoria Ocampo often endorsed similar platforms in *Revista de Occidente* and *Sur.* Paz's pages no doubt fulfill an escapist function, vis-à-vis other Mexican monthlies (*Epoca, Proceso, Nexos*), where hard-writing journalism and antigovernment views are often expressed. Whenever its editorial policy does opt for a more active involvement in local affairs, it comes as a result of Mexico undergoing a deep crisis, like the one in 1982 involving the nationalization of the bank industry, or else every six years, as presidential elections are held. Recently, for example, as the nation lacked confidence in its politicians and in reaction to the assassinations of Luis Donaldo Colosio and Ernesto Ruíz Massieu, the magazine reevaluated its principles and took a more decisive, participatory attitude. And during the decisive 1994 presidential elections in which Ernesto Zedillo Ponce de León was declared winner, it published occasional news analysis and opinion pieces on Mexico's need for democracy. It also included a special supplement, "Chiapas: Days of Challenge," dealing with the Ejército Zapatista de Liberación Nacional. But if previous outbursts of commitment are any sign, this editorial direction is likely to fade away the moment the crisis is resolved.

Paz's old-time co-editor and right hand, Enrique Krauze, is an iconoclastic historian interested in revolutionary heroes and in Mexico's monolithic political structure. While concerned with national and international matters, he is careful enough to have a cordial relationship with Mexico's government. It's a well-known fact that while the country has undergone an abrupt modernization process since the end of World War II, it has also experienced impossible corruption, guerrilla warfare, and urban unrest, and Latin America in general has been torn apart by foreign invasions and military coups. But readers browsing through *Vuelta*'s past issues would know very little about it. In a region where leftist intellectuals are in the pay of petty tyrants, the journal often discusses diplomatic issues in an obnoxiously abstract philosophical fashion. Krauze's pieces approach long-dead historical personalities like Humboldt, Hernán Cortés, Cuauhtémoc, Emiliano Zapata, Porfirio Díaz, and Pancho Villa with a critical eye, but his comments on present-day government matters, unless a crisis makes them urgent and unavoidable, are comparatively shy and without edge. Rather than inviting opposing parties to discuss their differences, the magazine frequently preaches universal values.

On the other hand, *Vuelta* ought to be commended for its independent spirit—and here again, its pages mirror the contradictions of its environment. Since the paper industry is government-run, and because a considerable segment of the advertisement of every single Mexican periodical comes from state institutions, freedom and integrity of opinion are often at stake. With a circulation of 15,000, it depends on national and international subscriptions as well as publicity, but only some 30 percent of its ads come from the government. Nevertheless, private corporations such as Televisa, a television consortium, the largest in the southern hemisphere, with close ties to the ruling party, is a strong advertising supporter, and in the eyes of the average Mexico reader, that amounts to having one's hands handcuffed. In the past, whenever periodicals have proven too critical of the state, the government has threatened to interrupt their ads and boycott paper supplies. But *Vuelta*, in spite of its condescending politics and as a result of its financial autonomy, has not been involved in a head-on confrontation with the authorities.

That is, aside from its very conception. Its birth was the result of a brutal government takeover. Its predecessor was a magazine called *Plural*, published under the aegis of *Excélsior*, one of Mexico's leading dailies. At Paz's return in 1971 from a long stay abroad, Julio Scherer García, then the newspaper's editor-in-chief and a Paz acquaintance, invited him to take charge of a publishing project devoted to literature and debate. Paz had finished his tenure as ambassador in India with a resignation used to protest the student massacre in Tlatelolco Square, made by President Gustavo Díaz Ordaz's regime, to control the population's growing unhappiness with corruption and rapid modernization. The student revolt coincided with uproars in Paris, Czechoslovakia, and Berkeley, among other places, and threatened to jeopardize Mexico's international reputation at a time when the Olympic Games were about to take place in the country. The Tlatelolco incident angered many intellectuals and was a turning point in their dubious, long-standing liaison with the State. Like Carlos Fuentes in Paris, Paz quit his diplomatic job as a sign of solidarity. He spent time at U.S. and European universities, and his return to his native home plagued him with doubts and uncertainty. Scherer's invitation was an excellent opportunity to air out his anger, to discuss critically the prospects of Mexico's democracy, and, more than anything, to open up the nation's culture to international influences. Although accepting the offer meant giving up, in part at least, his most precious treasures (time and solitude), it was also a chance to solidify his position as dean of Mexican letters. He envisioned a publication with a universalistic standpoint, pro-debate, against any form of tyranny, appealing to an ideal ethical standard, much like *Sur* (where Paz began contributing in 1938) and *Nouvelle Revue Française*, a publication that conceived literature "as a self-sufficient world—neither apart, nor in front of other worlds—but never at their service." Its name, *Plural,* was its banner.

Paz had more than enough experience dealing with literary magazines. In his adolescence, between 1931 and 1943, he had edited the exciting and short-lived *Barandal, Cuadernos del Valle de México,* and *El Hijo Pródigo,* through which he had introduced dozens of foreign voices into Mexican circles and where he had forged his essayistic style. Later, after a brief incubating period, he helped to make *Plural* into an exquisite periodical. It had high editorial standards and its contributors did indeed inject a refreshing new life into Mexican letters. Paz quickly invited a number of major figures to write and promoted Mexico as a meeting point for discussing critical thought and inspiring good writing. As time went by, however, *Excélsior* as a whole came to be recognized as a focus of antigovernment feeling. Moreover, its views often clashed with Paz's. Expectedly, in July 1976, angry with its staff and having exhausted other venues to quiet the criticism targeted at him at home and abroad, Luis Echeverría Alvarez, then Mexico's president, ordered the army to intervene. The newspaper's offices were taken over, its employees dismissed. The scandal turned out to have positive consequences. While both the newspaper and *Plural* continued under new stewardship, Scherer and Paz, each supported by private funds, launched separate monthly magazines: *Proceso,* edited by the former, was devoted to "accurate, honest journalism that is ready to denounce corruption wherever it might be found"; Paz, on the other hand, orchestrated a reorganization of his editorial staff and began *Vuelta.* He was sixty-two—a totem, a T. S. Eliot–like figure in Hispanic American letters. Anything he touched he quickly turned into gold.

Eventually, like *Les Temps Modems* in its relation to Jean-Paul Sartre, *Vuelta,* even more than *Plural,* came to be known as Paz's instrument of cultural control—his extremity, a permanent source of congratulation, a compass signaling the many influences of his fascinating mind. From its first issue its editorial principles were clear: to leave behind any form of provincialism, to reflect on international events from a philosophical perspective. In its first issue, Paz argued that *Vuelta* was not a beginning but, as its words imply in Spanish, "a return." In 1981, in a commemorative essay on its fifth anniversary, he described the magazine as borne out of a desire to oppose state power and Marxism as an ideological doctrine. He reinstated the magazine's utopian objective to create a platform where one could simultaneously find the writer's imagination and modern critical thinking. But Paz's democratic wishes could not fight against the well-known, essentially dictatorial facet of his personality. Consequently, the magazine never includes a correspondence section where ideas can be freely exchanged and left-wing writers such as Gabriel García Márquez, Julio Cortázar, José Agustín, and Paco Ignacio Taibo II, although their books might be reviewed, are generally excluded from its content. Paradoxically, dogmatism isn't only attacked but practiced in its pages: Views differing from Paz's and the staff are pushed aside and ridiculed, never debated. As a result, readers interested in the whole spectrum of contemporary trends in Latin American thought and literature hardly get a comprehensive, uncensored view. *Vuelta* routinely ignores Hispanic pulp fiction, and either looks down at or handles with unusual care the work of regional celebrities with whom Paz is at odds, personally and politically—particularly his nemesis, Fuentes.

To read its pages is to suppose that most people in Mexico, and for that matter in the whole Southern Hemisphere, are comfortably tolerant of diverse views, not much concerned with local politics, highly literate, and metaphysically driven, which is far from true in a nation where 75 percent of the population live in poverty and 49 percent are still illiterate. This helps explains why, as counterpoint to *Vuelta,* left-wing Mexican intellectuals launched *Nexos,* a monthly, currently edited by the well-known journalist Miguel Aguilar Camín, skeptical of abstract cosmopolitanism, devoted to *realpolitik* and trendy literary movements. Unlike those of Argentina and Cuba, the Mexican intelligentsia is polarized, zealously moving around these two major periodicals, which often waste their energy discrediting the enemy.

To understand why throughout Latin America the journal is largely considered today a conservative publication, one needs to follow Paz's own ideological journey, from the Spanish Civil War to the fall of the Berlin Wall. At first a fervent supporter of Socialism and an enthusiast of Castro's Cuban Revolution, he grew disappointed in the late 1960s with naive utopian thought and turned against the Havana regime when he learned of its alignment with the Soviet Union. At a time when the Latin American Left was still stuck in its dogmatic Stalinism, he denounced the Gulag, supported Aleksandr Solzhenitsyn, and in the pages of *Plural* was in favor of democratic change, not abrupt revolutions. His intellectual development, and that of *Vuelta,* pushed him more to the center: He declared himself in favor of an open market of ideas in the Hispanic world and, while still viewing dictatorship as the region's major evil, he grew more complacent with the ruling party. By 1984, his seventieth birthday, and then again a decade later, in 1994, his eightieth, were jointly celebrated, with great fanfare, with TV programs, conferences, and museum exhibits, by the ruling party and by Televisa. Paz was seen by a large segment of Mexico's population as disconnected from the nation's new artistic, antiestablishment trends, as a close friend of the status quo and as an ally of the United States, his magazine as a reactionary organ of Mexico's intellectual right. Anybody critical of Paz as *caudillo* was either excluded from or viciously attacked in *Vuelta,* as was the case of José Emilio Pacheco, an internationally renowned poet targeted as an enemy by some of Paz's supporters. And yet, when Pacheco's house in Mexico City was the target of a shoot-out, Paz's journal quickly published a manifesto denouncing the violence.

Although each issue, when compared to similar periodicals in the United States, sells a small number of copies, its impact on Latin American intellectual life cannot be minimized. Young writers dream of having manuscripts accepted and their books reviewed. By the late 1980s the ownership opened an ultimately ill-fated branch in Buenos Aires, called *Vuelta Sudamericana,* and it also expanded to the book business, launching, in 1987, Editorial Vuelta, a publishing house largely devoted to translations and to promoting the oeuvre of its contributors. Its efforts were crowned in 1993, when Paz and his staff were awarded Spain's Príncipe the Asturias Prize for their major contribution of the development of Hispanic culture.

It's a known secret that Paz, already in his eighties, often found at home alone writing or abroad lecturing, only occasionally comes to the offices of *Vuelta*. Whatever business he conducts, he does it mainly by phone. And yet, his shadow casts an incredible challenge to the magazine's future. To be honest, dilettantism in Latin America has always had a healthy life, particularly since the late nineteenth century, when the so-called *Modernistas*, led by José Martí and Rubén Darío, championed a literature obsessed with French Symbolism and Parnassianism. Indeed, Paz's magazine is an embodiment of the Hispanic intellectual contradiction between commitment and withdrawal: It supports an image of the intellectual as a creature devoted to producing high-quality writing, concerned with world affairs, but too individualistic to participate in making history. So make no mistake about it: Issue after issue, *Vuelta* is indeed a pleasure to read: It's carefully edited, and most of its contributors, native Spanish writers and otherwise, are consummate stylists. But it's also a temple of adoration with Paz in its supreme altar and a map to his intricate, extraordinary mind.*

---

* The last issue of *Vuelta* (XXII, 259), a tribute to Paz shortly after his death, was published in June 1998. Krauze closed it and soon after debuted with his own magazine, *Letras Libres*. The move, it struck me, was an attempt to free himself from Paz's ghost.

# OCTAVIO PAZ

## *Farewell to a Renaissance Man*

*We do not know where death awaits us, so let us wait for it every-where. To practice death is to practice freedom.*

—Montaigne

"There is no sense in pursuing a literary career under the impression that one is operating a bombing-plane," Edmund Wilson once said. The life of the mind doesn't kill enemies. Instead, it builds bridges between who we are and who we think we should be. The duty of the intellectual is to serve as a compass, a road map.

More than anyone else today, Octavio Paz, the essayist and poet who died of cancer in April 1998 at the age of eighty-four, was committed to that duty. He was the quintessential surveyor, a Dante's Virgil, a Renaissance man. His complete oeuvre—some 150 titles, which he himself edited into more than a dozen hefty volumes—is a blueprint, an atlas to this most turbulent century, which approaches its dusk with the same rancor that permeated its dawn. Our self-deprecating dreams, the evil that we do, our insatiable search for happiness amid incessant technological improvements, the value we place on the word, written and oral—all were explored by Paz's peripatetic pen, for he was a genuine polymath, a redis-coverer, a believer in reason and dreams and poetic invention as our only salvation.

He would surely have preferred to be remembered as a poet, but his prose is a better metronome for our times. I, at least, consider it

First published in *Hopscotch: A Cultural Review* 1:1 (1999).

an apex. Often deep in the night, when everything else feels banal, I open *The Bow and the Lyre*, Paz's meditation on poetry and poetic revelation, and am quickly hypnotized by it. *The Traps of Faith*, his magisterial biography of Sor Juana Inés de la Cruz, takes one through colonial Mexico on a hallucinatory journey almost as mystical in its effect as Sor Juana's own *First Dream.*\* And Paz's study of eroticism, *The Double Flame*, is as thought-provoking as his reflections on the shortcomings of translation. Indeed, it would be impossible for me to name my favorite of his books. What seems easy instead is to recognize the vision that unifies them, a vision made of endless communicating vessels. Each time I read him, I am convinced that every human act has a purpose.

Paz's essays gained him acolytes and enemies the world over; they invariably turned him into a cause célèbre. His convictions were clear even when they were unappealing. He believed in literature not as a business but as an act of faith. It never mattered to him how many copies his books sold, and many sold poorly. *Leaves of Grass*, he enjoyed remembering, was at first utterly ignored by Walt Whitman's contemporaries, to the point that he himself had to write anonymous reviews of it. Paz will never be a bestseller on the scale of Stephen King, but his influence on our culture and his endurance are infinitely wider. With erudition and stamina he turned his attention to every aspect of life, from jokes to the paintings of Diego Velásquez, from VCRs to Subcomandante Marcos. His style was terse, crystalline, never short of enthralling. By the time he had won the Nobel Prize in Literature, in 1990, he was considered a giant. He was equally at ease discussing T. S. Eliot and the role of poetry in the modern age, Buddhism in India, the Aztec empire, Japanese haiku, the balkanization of the former Soviet Union, and the modernity of Latin America.

In an era of obnoxious specialists who know more about less, Paz's cosmopolitanism, his capacious eye, made him a rara avis. In fact, he ought to be credited, along with Jorge Luis Borges, with opening up the Hispanic mind and making it savvier and more discerning. Consequently, Latin America is less provincial, less obscure and awkward, and more modern. Paz once argued that it became a contemporary of the rest of the world only after World War II. Not only Hispanics but the entire globe's population is more connected, thanks to him.

It was not always easy to empathize with him. His self-congratulatory personality became more evident in his old age,

---

\* See my Introduction to *Poems, Protest and a Dream*, by Sor Juana. Translated by Margaret Sayers Peden. (New York: Penguin Classics, 1997).

and so did his stubbornness. His political odyssey took him from communism to utopianism and ultimately to a center-right revisionism. He had participated in the Spanish Civil War and befriended Pablo Neruda, whose Stalinism he had quickly found repellent. In 1958–59 he had sympathized with Fidel Castro's revolution in Cuba, and a decade later he had endorsed student upheavals Prague, Berkeley, and Paris and denounced Mexico's ruling party for the massacre in Tlatelolco Square. But old age turned Paz into a conservative. In his last decade the Mexican government anointed him the nation's official man of letters, manipulating his reputation and making him an unattractive commodity. The young in the Hispanic world no longer identified with him, for he had come to personify Albert Camus's famous dictum, "All revolutionaries end either as oppressors or heretics." On the public stage Paz championed democracy, but in private he was infuriatingly dictatorial. In short, Paz the rebel had become Paz the despot. Not surprisingly, many intellectuals in Mexico felt enormous relief when his death was announced by President Ernesto Zedillo. "God has died," one of them scornfully uttered to a TV camera.

Paz died in Distrito Federal, his home and headquarters, where his telescope looked outward while his microscope looked inward. The metropolis is the scenario of his best poetry. During his lifetime Mexico City underwent tremendous change: From a semibucolic locale it grew into an uncontrollable mammoth in which 28 million were besieged by traffic jams and pollution. While environmental decline seldom occupied him, Paz's effort to turn Mexico City into a multifaceted center of enlightenment and civilization is startling. His influence was the kind exercised not by a civic administrator but by an effulgent fashion model. With his magazines *Plural* and *Vuelta,* his dilettantism, his incessant political commentaries, and his love of museums, he made the city far more livable. Without him, it somehow feels—momentarily, at least—depleted of hope. Scores of other intellectuals and artists make their home in Distrito Federal, but Paz was its brain, its centripetal force, what William H. Gass has called "the heart of the heart."

The shadow Paz cast over Mexico's intelligentsia was overwhelming. I confess to having often thought, during his last years, how liberating a world without him could be. I had emulated his teachings, but I had come to think of him, particularly in the 1980s, as a "philanthropic ogre"—the very expression he had used to describe Mexico's government in the 1960s—a benign yet suffocating presence, a know-it-all and do-it-all. Envy probably played a part in my attitude toward him, but so did the need to go beyond him, to experience a universe without Big Brother. But now that he is dead, the world feels suddenly empty of role models to me. (Coincidentally, Paz died just a few weeks before Alfred Kazin, the Jewish American literary critic responsible for the classic *On Native Grounds.* One year younger than Paz, Kazin was also an original, another majestic intellectual whose work, though less panoramic and pathfinding, I cherish.)

Ours is a most puzzling age. It is often difficult to know what to do, but Paz was sure that, as Edmund Wilson also said, "a conviction that is genuine will always come through—that is, if one's work is sound." Would it be fatalistic to describe Paz as the last intellectual? No doubt his demise symbolizes the end of an era, in which the writer truly mattered. As we move into the next millennium, intellectuals must reconfigure their place in society. They must reinvent themselves from A to Z. Words have been replaced by images, and opinions are frighteningly volatile. We all may be less provincial today than a century ago, but truth and certitude have become casualties. Nowadays, to build bridges across the chambers of the mind, across cultures, one needs not only to write but to perform, for the only real bombing-planes are on the Internet.

So many visionaries have their paths cut short by the accidents of nature. Paz was lucky to live so long. And he lived with death as his obsession: individual death, spiritual death, cosmic death—the death of the mind's eye and the soul's I. In life, the invocation of death was liberating to him, and he experienced that liberation with passion, for passion is our best weapon in the battle against nothingness, even though nothingness in the end prevails.

# TRANSLATION AND IDENTITY

*The original is unfaithful to the translation.*

—Jorge Luis Borges, "On *Vatek*, by William Beckford"

I

Translation, its delicious traps, its labyrinthine losses, was at the birth of the Americas, and I am often struck by the fact that to this day, the role language played during their conquest is often minimized, if not simply overlooked. There's little doubt that without the "interpreters," as Hernán Cortés referred to them, an enterprise of such magnitude would have been utterly impossible. Although *la conquista* was a military endeavor encompassing social, political, and historical consequences, it was also, and primarily, a verbal occupation, an unbalanced polyglot encounter. More than a hundred different dialects spoken from the Yucatán peninsula to modern-day California were reduced to silence, and Spanish became the ubiquitous vehicle of communication, the language of business, government, and credo. Through persistence and persuasion, Cortés and Pizarro, to name only the most representative warriors, took control of the powerful Aztec and Inca empires. Cortés, for one, was astute enough to convince their unprepared, naive monarchs, Moctezuma II and Cuauthémoc, that he indeed was Quetzalcóatl, the Plumed Serpent, a bearded god the Aztec calendar had been

---

Published in enlarged form as Introduction to *Prospero's Mirror* (Willimantic, Conn.: Curbstone Press, 1998).

prophesying as a triumphant sign for the coming of a new age. But to make themselves understood, he and his Spanish knights were constantly on the lookout for a very special type of soldier: the translator, capable of using words as weapons, reading not only the enemy's messages but its mind as well; someone who, in modern terms, would be not only perfectly multilingual but, more important, a cultural analyst able to explain one culture, one *weltanschauung* to another. Only by enlisting a "word wizard" were they able to achieve their goals; translators needed to be true loyalists, part of the invader's army, at once supporters and promoters who would eventually have a share of the gain and make victory their own.

These reflections recently came to mind during a pleasant afternoon reading sacred Nahuatl poetry. Indeed, although I don't purport to be a specialist in pre-Columbian literature, my interest in the ancient cultures of the Americas has produced ongoing readings and book collecting, and I was happily wandering through the work of Daniel G. Brinton, the first American ever to translate from the Nahuatl into English, when I was struck by the obvious: the difficulty of making the pre-Columbian people accessible to modern readers. Their poetry, an expression of their vision of time, their dreams and frustrations, has changed countless times in front of our very eyes; they are what we want them to be; and what one commentator believed they were is light-years away from the views of others. In spite of many generous scientific discoveries, dating back to the early nineteenth century, about Macchu Picchu, Tenochtitlán, and other ruined population centers, the pre-Columbians are nothing but our own image reflected in a distorted mirror: the observer observing himself in others. From the moment it clashed with European culture to our fin de siècle, Nahuatl civilization was betrayed and misrepresented, then renewed and reinvented, by innumerable interpreters. More than five hundred years after their tragic subjugation, their worldview remains a puzzle—alien, exotic, unclear to us—the product of adventurous scholars (mostly Mexicans) unmasking a certain facet, contradicting a predecessor, searching for lost sources. And although since World War II the new discoveries have been nothing but outstanding, the added collective efforts are still incomplete; they certainly don't present a fair, comprehensive view simply because the Nahuatl civilization was almost erased by the European invaders. Finding clues to its identity is a challenge worthy of a superhuman detective.

All this signals the impotence of translation, the act of bridging out by means of language. Obviously, finding such useful "bridges," such vital entities, has proven to be an incredibly difficult task. For purposes of argumentation, let me focus on Cortés's conquest of Mexico. Bernal Díaz del Castillo, in his chronicle of the conquest of Tenochtitlán, recounts how, around 1517, two Mayans, Melchorejo and Julianillo, were captured in the Yucatán peninsula by Capt. Francisco Hernández de Córdoba. In spite of their shyness and introversion, which we would probably interpret today as a lack of desire to cooperate, they were forced to become interpreters. In keeping with their new role, they were treated better than other prisoners of war. After traveling to Cuba to answer the questions of a governor anxious to know if their land had any gold mines, and thus passing the crucial test of a tête-à-tête with the highest authority, Melchorejo and Julianillo were asked to dress up and behave like Europeans. They were given their own hamlet in Santiago; they were required to attend mass and were indoctrinated in the ways of the Church, and they were taught as much oral Spanish as they could digest. But in spite of the intense training, their patrons remained suspicious of the Indians' ultimate motives and service, mainly because, as Díaz del Castillo puts it, Melchorejo and Julianillo were incapable of looking one in the eyes. They had an obnoxious way of looking down to the floor, not as a sign of respect, but to evade contact. And, just as expected, when the interpreters traveled to Cozumel with the expedition of Juan de Grijalba, it was clear to many that the Spanish message was only being partially conveyed to the natives, if only because, after a friendly exchange, the enemy didn't show up for the next agreed-upon meeting. The Spaniards, needless to say, were very worried.

We know very little about Melchorejo and Julianillo. Unlike the military heroes of the time, these translators are but a footnote in history, their words overshadowed by the weaponry of those interested in action, in wealth, in fame, not in communication and understanding. Even if their skills were indeed questionable, they deserve some sort of acknowledgment; instead, their fate, I'm afraid, is the one commonly granted to translators: oblivion. While their death is actually recorded by Díaz del Castillo, it is done only in passing, without much fanfare; they have no monuments and their memory is never celebrated. Julianillo apparently died either of sadness or as a victim of one of the many epidemics decimating the native population at the time. Melchorejo, on the other hand, had a more heroic, if also more tragic, death. He changed sides around 1519, when he understood that Cortés's real intentions were disastrous. Rather than delivering his translation in a cold, straightforward, objective manner, after the crucial battle in Tabasco, he took off his European costume, regained his Indian identity, and ran to his people to explain what he knew. But his was not a happy welcome: After listening to what he had to say, the Tabascans killed him in revenge for his many lies, his betrayal, and his hypocrisy.

No doubt the most distinguished bridge between languages and cultures during the conquest of Mexico, at least the one mythologized since early on, was a woman whose name is as evasive as her biography, but one who, we know for sure, acted as an interpreter wholeheartedly and with very few reservations. Known as Marina, Malina, Malinalli, Malintzin, and Malinche, she was at once a translator, Cortés's concubine, and an endeared presence among the Spanish army—Latin America's counterpart to Pocahontas. Some historians believe she was born in a small town some forty kilometers from Coatzacoalcos, was sold as merchandise after her father's death, and became Cortés's mistress (she mothered one of his sons, Martín Cortés) after he stole her from a high-ranking official. Cortés himself mentions her often in his *Cartas de Relación,* and so does Díaz del Castillo in his chronicle. Whereas Melchorejo and Julianillo remain in shadow, Malinche is famous: Her stature inspires and infuriates, so much so that Mexicans apply the term *malinchista* to a person who sells his country to foreign forces for his own sake. Malinche knew the value of sleeping with the powerful commander of the Spanish army. She was fluent in many native dialects and quickly picked up the rules of Spanish; above all, she understood the role of translator as loyalist and charlatan. Aside from interpreting, her function was to advance her lover's military purposes. Her words were intimately linked to her body: One couldn't function without the other; the message and her personal beliefs were deeply intertwined. In short, Malinche personifies the translator as concubine. Scorned for years, Mexicans today perceive her as the true mother of the nation, the woman who used her body to betray her people, who incorporated European manners into her repertoire while incubating the mestizo race.

Malinche, of course, was never an impartial, objective interpreter; far from our modern view of what literary translators are called to do, she wasn't looking for aesthetic beauty, for honest communication across cultures. Her role was purely strategic: She misled and deceived her peers and ultimately helped dismantle the Aztec empire. She used words as artillery to unveil the secrets of the Aztec mind and thus helped Cortés and his men appreciate the real strength of their enemy. But it would be a mistake to assume that her role as word wizard was something new and alien to the Nahuatl and other autochthonous people. Interpreters such as she must have prevailed in Mexico between the late fourteenth and early sixteenth centuries. In order to interact, to do business, the many pre-Columbian cultures that populated Mesoamerica before 1492 were surely in need of interpreters. While a true *lingua franca* did not exist, dialects were considered more or less important depending on the force their speakers exerted. Thus the Nahuatls, the Mayans, the Otomis, and other groups were somehow acquainted with the business of adapting their words for those lacking knowledge of their tongue. Yet all this can be an understatement if one fails to realize that, once aligned with the Spaniards, translators such as Malinche were involved in a sophisticated form of deception. They could see the military advantage the invaders had over the natives; they were witnesses to a catastrophe of immense proportions; and yet, more often than not their personal interests had more weight than the suffering of their people. It's the classical portrait of the Latin American scoundrel: Once in power, the Spaniards granted them high esteem and celebrated them as heroes. And while these translators (mostly aborigines) are obviously not to be blamed for the dynamite the Europeans fired against the native population, they certainly played a crucial role in their tragic disappearance. Since the Nahuatl conceived the idea of preserving one's past only through oral tradition (an advance alphabet was still in the making when the Spaniards arrived), European chroniclers—liberal friars and priests devoted to saving what was being demolished—could not do enough to rescue aboriginal culture from being eclipsed. Their own capacity to understand native culture was limited, linguistically and psychologically. Consequently, what we have left today is but a minuscule slice of ancient native Mexican civilization. Add to this the fact that since 1523 other so-called interpreters have obscured the lens through which we could have begun to appreciate Nahuatl culture. Proselytes found Christian imagery in ancient manuscripts, for example, destroying and revamping old texts. To understand the implications of the conquest in Mexico, imagine who we would be today if only a twelfth of *The Divine Comedy* was all that was available from ancient and medieval Europe—and not in Italian but in a language totally forbidden to us.

## II

As a result, the corpus of pre-Columbian literature available today is quite small. For argument's sake, take Nahuatl poetry again as an example: What we have are no more than twenty sacred hymns, collected by Fray Bernardino de Sahagún; songs scattered in several annals and testimonies; the manuscript of *Cantares mexicanos y otros opúsculos,* collected by an anonymous priest and kept at

Universidad Nacional Autónoma de México; and the manuscript of *Romances de los señores de la Nueva Esapaña,* housed at the University of Texas at Austin. Most of what we know about the Nahuatl people is a result of the intense scholarly studies of Angel María Garibay and Miguel León Portilla. The lack of familiarity with the original culture makes the translation process unfair and problematic: Translations are first done into Spanish, and then into other European languages. A few exceptions occur: Eduard Seler, for example, has worked directly in German. Daniel G. Brinton was the first ever to bring Nahuatl poetry out from obscurity in his books *Rig Ved Americanus* and *Ancient Nahuatl Poetry,* both published in Philadelphia at the end of the nineteenth century and translated directly into English. Brinton's work was based on the manuscript of *Cantares de los mexicanos,* which, as he stated from the outset, was an incomplete transcription by one Abbé de Bourbourg, signaling, once again, the innumerable abuses to which this type of material has been exposed. How much or how little of the final work was a product of Brinton's own making has been a subject of speculation. León Portilla, Seler, and Garibay have found his translations loyal, if extravagant. Brinton's anthropological obsession to compare the Nahuatl civilization to ancient India also puts him in trouble. But more than anything else, his erratic English makes for a questionable, if interesting, version. Still, Brinton's work is amazing in that it needed no intermediary language. León Portilla himself has recently published a collection of his own, *Fifteen Poets of the Aztec World,* where he translates into English material he anthologized in 1967 and subsequently expanded on at least five occasions. This collection is immensely more reliable than Brinton's; his technique, yet again, employed Spanish as the bridge language.

Correlating Brinton's work with León Portilla's can be a frustrating act. More than a hundred years of research and analysis run from the pages of one into the other. Brinton had only a segment of the Nahuatl legacy in front of him; he had no predecessors to map his route; and more important, he was unable to individualize poets because other historical sources were still unknown. And yet, in spite of his many shortcomings, his Victorian English translations ought to be acknowledged because he happily inaugurated a tradition that is slowly expanding. His task as interpreter, perhaps unconsciously, was an attempt to undo what Julianillo, Melchorejo, and Malinche had helped to achieve: the closing of the Nahuatl mind. But one should approach the texts cautiously once one is past the initial sense of joy felt in coming for the first time face-to-face with a universe long gone. I cannot but encourage the reader to consult *Fifteen*

*Poets of the Aztec World,* which identifies individual poets and comments historically and literally on themes and motifs: flowers, life as a dream, the cravings of the heart, the death of a monarch, the passing of time, and so on. The effort to establish a link between the two translations will not be meaningless and will somehow help reduce the endless chain of misinterpretations that has victimized Nahuatl literature. The work of Garibay and León Portilla has done much to disclose what translators and interpretors during the colonical period and afterward had actively misinterpreted.

Nowadays we thankfully have volumes such as J. Richard Andrews's *Introduction to Classical Nahuatl,* which begin to unveil the Nahuatl language and worldview for us. We are beginning to learn, for example, to what extent the Nahuatl people were devoted to contemplation and the role poetry played in society. We have also been able to penetrate the oeuvre of a handful of Nahuatl poets, most important King Netzahualcóytotl (1401–1472) and Aquiauhtzin de Ayapanco (circa 1430–1490). Diego Durán, in his *Historia de las Indias,* describes the Nahuatl poet as playing a crucial role among the elite: Rulers were constantly surrounded by singers and dancers, and rhymes were taught to children in school. Concerts, sometimes from early morning to nightfall, were performed in front of a large audience, and beloved poets, accompanied by melodious instruments, were asked to perform in public. If the importance of music, lyrics, and dance in modern Mexican villages is any sign, Durán's words must be true: People rejoice in fiestas and use poetry to recount individual or collective anecdotes and happenings. Sahagún, Clavigero, and Torquemada explained that Nahuatl poetry was divided into historical and fictitious plots. But Garibay and León Portilla have taken us much farther: They explored the fiesta as ritual, analyzed the sacred hymns known as *Teocuícatl,* and made available what León Portilla calls *la visión de los vencidos,* the Indian accounts and eyewitness testimony of the conquest. After Brinton opened the door, they expanded our horizon.

But Brinton and his successors are as much interpreters as they are translators, bridges in the tradition of Melchorejo, Julianillo, and Malinche. Brinton's language of reception, English, allowed him to open up, in his own terms, the pre-Columbian mind to Western civilization. Similarly, Cortés's and Pizarro's translators, albeit reluctantly, had made accessible to Europeans their own personal interpretation of the Americas by means of explaining in a rudimentary Spanish their non-Western linguistic codes. The overall result is nothing but a global misapprehension; one could even say delusion. A sense of this verbal maze can be captured in full the moment one realizes that Hispanics and Brazilians today communicate in a language that is theirs only by imposition. The fact that they talk, the fact that they read and write in Spanish and Portuguese, already carries a degree of falsification. In order to insert themselves into Western culture, they have appropriated, or have been appropriated by, a communication vehicle that wasn't theirs in the first place. In short, as a result of its colonial history, Latin America, to paraphrase Robert Frost, is what is lost in translation. It is also what is lost in interpretation.

Literature, more specifically the art of fiction, is the magnifying glass that more clearly exposes the abyss between reality and language, world and word. Why have the region's artists and writers been so imaginative and its politicians so unimaginative? The answer, perhaps, is that in the eyes of foreigners, the colorful, exotic, or, to use the fashionable term *magical,* reality south of the Rio Grande has always been a field of dreams. We might not know much about the pre-Columbian civilizations, but what is clear from the historical artifacts we have inherited (hieroglyphics, codices, vessels, and architectural wonders) is that they had a florid fantasy life. André Breton once described Latin America as "a Surrealist Continent," a land where chaos and the unknown, the instinctual and the unconscious, prevail—a land, clearly, essentially un-Western. Others have added layers to his concept, describing it as "marvelous." But the Cuban musicologist and *homme de lettres* Alejo Carpentier, in his famous 1949 prologue to *The Kingdom of This World,* tried to reverse Breton's concept. After a trip to Haiti, he argued that Latin America was the perfect stage of *lo real maravilloso,* where the triteness of Europe was left behind, where the search for an imaginary utopia is mixed with astonishing surprises, where the world is always in a stage of unfinishedness. He realized during his journey

> that the presence and authority of the real marvelous was not a privilege to Haiti but the patrimony of all the Americas, where, for example, a census of cosmogonies is still to be established. The real marvelous is found at each step in the lives of the men who inscribed dates on the history of the Continent and who left behind names still borne by the living: from the seekers after the Fountain of Youth or the golden city of Manoa to certain rebels of the early times or certain modern heroes of our wars of independence, those of such mythological stature as Colonel Juana Azurduy.

And yet, to make "the real marvelous" accessible to internal and external observers requires its translation to bring it to a "standard" code of communication. When the Mexican thinker José Joaquín

Fernández de Lizardi plots *The Itching Parrot,* when the Chilean poet Pablo Neruda shapes his masterpiece *Canto general,* when the Guatemalan Miguel Angel Asturias delivers *El Señor Presidente,* when the Brazilian mulatto Joaquim Maria Machado de Assis writes his *Epitaph for a Small Winner,* and when Isabel Allende gives the final touches to *The House of the Spirits,* the appropiation of a nonnative language has been completed to deliver a view of this side of the Atlantic to international readers, the very same readers educated by Ovid, Dante, Cervantes, and Shakespeare. The images might be original, but not so the verbal code. In fact, we can even talk about a form of linguistic cannibalism: In order to be members of Western civilization, Latin Americans need to be initiated into, and then are forced to perfect, the language of the invader. Cannibalism, as a metaphor of the struggle to at once define and translate oneself to the rest of the world, is certainly not a new idea. In runs throughout the chronology of the whole hemisphere, acquiring different masks, being called by different names, depending on the context. In Brazil, for instance, Oswald de Andrade, while stationed in Paris in the 1920s with his wife, painter Tarsila do Amaral, awoke to the possibilities of the so-called primitive art of his own country as a source of inspiration. And some years after returning home in 1923, he published the *Manifesto Antropófago.* Its central message, in the words of critic Edward LucieSmith, was that "Brazilian artists must devour outside influences, digest them thoroughly and turn them into something new"; in other words, to use the verbs and punctuation, the manners and excesses of Europeans ad nauseam until a refreshing view, a distinctive Brazilian approach to the universe, can be recognized. Translation as anthropophagy.

All this makes any translation from Spanish into English, or for that matter any other European language, an attempt at removing what was already once removed. Translation in this metaphorical sense is ubiquitous in the so-called Third World. Colonialism has colored the aborigines culture. Foreign invaders have imposed their *weltanshauung* in numerous ways, especially through culture and religion. But these two can only be assimilated through language. Today Latin America is the perfect case study of a verbal hodgepodge. Spanish and Portuguese are the prevailing languages in the region, behind which many others palpitate. If what Malinche conveyed to Cortés is already a falsification, a deformation, an interpretation, her words, or what she purportedly said, once they are translated from Spanish into another tongue, take the listener even farther away from the original source. By this I'm not suggesting, at least not in concrete terms, that whenever he writes, García Márquez, or any of the other Latin American literati before or after him, is, in essence, translating himself. His native vocabulary is his by subject of inheritance: He was born into, and raised in, Quevedo's language; and for that simple reason it's his as much as it's Quevedo's. One cannot forget, obviously, that, as a product of endless transformations, Spanish itself is a hybrid, a sum of parts, an addition. Its roots can be found in vulgar Latin, in Arabic, in Castilian and other Romance tongues of the Middle Ages and Renaissance. Besides, like all other languages, Spanish is the property and product of its speakers, no matter who they have been and where they have lived. This means that García Márquez, by virtue of history, is as much its owner as any Spaniard today. And yet, Aracataca, where the Colombian was born in 1928, was a landscape where pre-Columbian languages and dialects were used. That is, its usage necessarily implies the eclipse of other grammatical structures, subdued by external forces.

Furthermore, when the Spanish knights and Catholic proselytes arrived, they didn't only bring their physical presence but also, and more important, a whole set of values and traditions, which include, among a vast array of offerings, the novel and verse poem as we know them. In order for *One Hundred Years of Solitude* to be written in the mid-1960s, its author needed to be immersed, in one form or another, in the European novelistic tradition: He had to know what the novel as cultural artifact is about, its purposes and limitations. He obviously had to be acquainted with at least a small number of early practitioners. For García Márquez to revolutionize the genre, he first was required to be familiar with it. He was first required to impregnate himself in its European style and language. When writing it, he unconsciously, one could even say inadvertently, cannibalized a foreign artistic vessel and, even if it was his from his very birth on, he also appropriated an outside tongue.

What kind of collective identity emerges from this act of losing and regaining oneself in translation? A complex question. Since Cortés and Pizarro, the continent has been inhabited by a conflicted view of itself. Where does it belong: to the Iberian peninsula or to the native Aztec, Inca, Quechua, Olmec, Mayan, and other pre-Columbian worldviews? Spanish, no doubt, is spoken without the discomfort of knowing it is a borrowed language. And yet, the whole region lives in a permanent state of nostalgia, of longing for a past that is long gone but could perhaps be rescued, relived, renourished. Identity, then, is a schism, a division, a wound—a sense that, in the translation process, the original and the copy will never match.

# TWO PERUVIANS

*To abandon one's life for a dream is to know its true worth.*
                                                    —Montaigne

At what precise moment did Peru fuck itself up? Mario Vargas Llosa posed the query in his 1969 novel *Conversation in the Cathedral*, a multilayered narrative about Peru's haves and have-nots, and the query runs through public discourse on Peru at home and abroad. There is no easy answer, of course. Was it during the disastrous war with Chile in 1879, which threw a roadblock before the country's economic progress? Was it after the tyrannical two-part regime of President Augusto B. Leguía (1908–1912, 1919–1930), a national patriarch who promoted economic development in the interest of the small wealthy minority? Or during the dictatorship of General Manuel Odría (1948–1956)? Did it happen when Fernando Balaúnde Terry, a moderate reformer and a populist, became president in a 1963 democratic election, only to be deposed five years later by a military junta headed by General Juan Alvarado Velasco? When the same Balaúnde Terry returned in the early 1980s to govern as a Conservative? Or was it when Alan García, a highly popular Social Democrat, came to office in 1985 and refused to pay Peru's foreign debt to the International Monetary Fund?

Whatever date one might settle on, the devastation now seems incurable, as if apocalypse has already taken place. Massive

First published in *Transition* 61 (Fall 1993). Reprinted in *Art and Anger: Essays on Politics and the Imagination* (Albuquerque, NM: University of New Mexico Press, 1996).

emigration, a useless, overgrown bureaucracy, a decade-long guerrilla insurrection with tentacles that seem to be everywhere and head-quartered nowhere—all this has turned the banana republic, comprising a narrow strip of 500,000 square miles, into the dead zone of the Pacific coast.

For many, life has come to seem unbearable, the future elusive. During the 1980s, Peru's skyrocketing inflation was as unpredictable as the lottery. While the GNP maintained a downward spiral, dynamite explosions and the assassinations of civilians and diplomats became part of the texture of everyday life—and they still are. With a population of some 24 million (50 percent Indian, 37 percent mestizo, and 13 percent white) concentrated in Lima, a megalopolis holding a third of the citizenship, Peru today is South America's time bomb. As its inefficient, bankrupt government flounders, ideological fundamentalists are at the brink of seizing power. If, in the Hispanic hemisphere, Fidel Castro's Cuba represents order under repression, contemporary Peru presents the mirror image of regression through chaos. Confusion, anomie, lawlessness—the present is in shambles.

Politically fractured and socially disfigured, today the nation is divided into two essentially opposed ideological projects, facing off belligerently: one identified with the principles and traditions of our fin-de-siècle Western way of life, the other attached to Marxism-Leninism and to the glories of the Inca empire—especially its last hero, Atahualpa, who was captured and killed by the conquistador Francisco Pizarro. Progress versus dogmatism, civilization versus barbarism—a bloody, all-too-common contest south of the Rio Grande.

Inasmuch as Peruvian society is led more by passion than by reason, its multitudes clamor to be guided by a single mind. What they seek is not the direction of enlightened logic, but the personified will of a common dream, a common fear, a common desire to avenge collective injury. Their enthusiasm has been divided between two prominent figures, who together represent the spiritual cleavage of contemporary Peru.

On stage left stands Carlos Abimael Guzmán Reynoso, alias Presidente Gonzalo, the obese, bearded, psoriasis-suffering mastermind of the guerrilla movement Sendero Luminoso, or Shining Path. Guzmán: a man who claims his five to seven thousand kamikaze followers have been preparing the one true path to a political paradise on earth. Guzmán: a man who, since his capture on September 12, 1992, and his uneffected death sentence a month later, has been ill, depressed, and rapidly losing weight as prisoner no. 1509, living out his days in solitary confinement—first in San Lorenzo, also known as El Frontón, an island prison off the Pacific coast, then in a specially constructed underground cell in Callao, where he is to spend the rest of his existence.

On stage right stands Mario Vargas Llosa, a tall, handsome, and elegantly dressed novelist and presidential candidate, who first achieved international esteem in 1963 with his debut novel *The Time of the Hero*. Vargas Llosa: a man who has come to personify Peru's Europeanized oligarchy and whom many see as the nation's link to reason and enlightenment.

So there you have it: a man of action and a man of letters—a sword and a pen. One a merciless ideological agitator, the other a refined prose stylist and a dilettante; one a dialectical materialist captivated by Mao Zedong and the Chinese Cultural Revolution, the other an idealist and epicure whose literary imagination inclines toward Faulkner and Flaubert (among his favorite books are *Light in August* and *Madame Bovary*). Guzmán and Vargas Llosa, perfect strangers, have become twin emblems of Peru's search for a solution to its sorrowful reality.

Fate had them born two years apart in the very same southern state, Arequipa: Guzmán on December 4, 1934, Vargas Llosa on March 28, 1936. It is a state that shares its name with its capital, Peru's second largest city, founded by the Spaniards in 1540 not far from Lake Titicaca, and home to scores of romantic poets and revolutionaries. Guzmán and Vargas Llosa came from different social classes, lower-middle and upper-middle, respectively, with no record of a tête-à-tête; and yet, as Vargas Llosa has acknowledged, it's not impossible that as children they saw each other at a bus stop or as passers-by in Arequipa's downtown commercial district.

Both are members of a distinguished Peruvian generation commonly referred to in intellectual circles as *la generación del '50*, which also includes the writers Julio Ramón Ribeyro, Sebastián Salazar Bondy, José Miguel Oviedo, and José María Arguedas; the painter Fernando de Szyszlo; and the politician Hector Cornejo Chávez. Torn between a heartfelt patriotism and an adversarial relation to the status quo, between sympathy toward the aboriginal minority and an allegiance to global modernization, this generation, with Guzmán and Vargas Llosa representing its polar extremes, has had an enormous impact on Peru's recent history.

In spite of the families' different financial condition, the two men went to branches of La Salle, a prestigious Catholic school, Guzmán in Arequipa and Vargas Llosa in Cochabamba, Bolivia, where the boy and his mother—separated from her husband and seeking help after a troubled marriage—had moved in 1937, when

Mario's grandfather was named consul. Each was an only child (the novelist had two stepbrothers) and has the personality of one. Each grew up in the absence of a paternal figure (Vargas Llosa met his father at age ten); each was marked by a traumatic encounter with urban life in his early adolescence.

Born out of wedlock to a mother who is said to have twice attempted an abortion, Guzmán as a boy is remembered by teachers and classmates as a hardworking, unusually dedicated student. Rejected by his biological father, a small-time businessman in the provinces, he was educated by his mother until she died when he was twelve. Only then did his father take him back, pledging to continue his education. In the La Salle secondary school, Guzmán discovered a passion for political philosophy; he and a group of friends founded a club to analyze capitalism's discontents and to study the connections between metaphysics and militancy, between Marxism and Hegel's dialectics.

Arequipa—from *Ari quepay,* meaning "Yes, stay around" in Quechua (alongside Spanish, Peru's other official tongue)—was a remarkable setting for an incubating activist. A shadow box of Peru's economic contradictions, the city was in turmoil during the 1950s, stricken by successive labor strikes and organized unrest that would be imprinted forever in Guzmán's memory. Indeed, his conviction that violence was the only road toward secular redemption dates back to his early twenties. As a pariah—an illegitimate child welcomed by neither parent—he grew convinced that the ills afflicting the society he knew reflected a larger inequality that was rooted in the Spanish conquest during the sixteenth century and perpetuated by foreign powers who had continued to subjugate his countrymen.

Vargas Llosa returned to Peru at the age of nine, at first living with his mother in the northern coastal town of Piura near the border with Ecuador (the setting of his second novel, *The Green House*), then, after his parents reconciled, moving to Lima in 1946. The transition from small town to big city was difficult and his personal encounter with the troubled capital quite shocking. "Piura was a wonderful town," he would later on write, "full of happenings that sparked the imagination. There was La Magachería, a district of huts made of reeds and mud, where the best taverns were found, as well as La Gallinacera, the district between the river and the canal." Lima, on the other hand, was unappealing: "I hated the metropolis from the beginning because of the unhappiness I felt there."

When he was fourteen, his father sent him to the Leoncio Prado Military School, a rigid educational institution portrayed in his first novel. "My father, who had found out I was writing poems, feared for my future . . . and for my 'manhood.'" The army environment, his father believed, would be an antidote to these perilous tendencies. Vargas Llosa spent two years, 1950–1952, as a boarding student at the school, which he later described as "a microcosm of Peruvian society." He then returned once more to Piura, where his work began appearing in newspapers and where, at the age of seventeen, he finished his first of many plays, a naturalistic drama titled *The Flight of the Inca*.

Half persuaded by his father's view of poetry as an unmanly and unremunerative vocation, he entered the San Marcos University to study law, an established and safe career. Even so, his passion for literature remained unvanquished. In 1958 he won a prize for a short story from the *Revue Française*, and his award was a fully paid trip to Paris, where he was able to retread the footsteps of his beloved idols, Victor Hugo and Flaubert, and to try to befriend Jean-Paul Sartre and Albert Camus (he only met the latter, briefly). On his return to Peru, he visited the Amazon jungle, a theater of colors and animality he would put at center stage in his literary universe. But the allure of the indigenous would not suffice for him. Unable to satisfy his cosmopolitanism at home, he again returned to Europe—Spain this time—and enrolled in graduate studies at Madrid's Universidad Central.

During the 1950s, General Odría's corrupt, brutal, and oppressive dictatorship suffused everything Peruvian. Barbarism—often state-sponsored barbarism—reigned. Guzmán, who, like Vargas Llosa, would become a law student, lived in Arequipa at the time. He entered the University of San Agustín immediately after his high school graduation. By then he had no trouble identifying with victims.

The nation's independence had been achieved in 1821, thanks to generals José de San Martín and Simón Bolívar, and to the defeat of Spain in the battles of Ayacucho and Junín. But once European control was gone, Peru remained sharply divided between the wealthy aristocracy, mostly Creoles, and the poverty-ridden Indian majority. Where was the justice in that? But Guzmán's commitment to the oppressed was not without hope. He imagined a utopian future in which natives would rule in an equal fashion, a universe where whites would have no role to play unless they gave up their undeserved privileges.

Ambitious and spirited, he simultaneously registered in two academic fields, law and philosophy, and would write two theses, one about the democratic bourgeois state and the other on Kant's theory of space. Judging from these texts and from the manifestos and communiqués he would publish later on in *El Diario*, the Shining

Path's official party publication, Guzmán's writing skills were always mediocre. His long paragraphs are tortured by what seems to be a convoluted train of thinking. His prose is unpolished, tending toward a sermonic drone. And yet his large number of acolytes bear witness to his powers of absolute persuasion. Besides, his lack of verbal panache would in the end matter little: The loaded gun, not the embellished word, would become Guzmán's most effective weapon. Even from his student days, politics monopolized his attention. Deepening cynicism about the possibilities of peaceful parliamentary socialism turned a Social Democrat into a fervent Marxist-Leninist, one who views Peru's government as a Satan on earth.

Guzmán left Arequipa in 1962. He had been teaching at San Agustín for a while but was soon hired away by the University of San Cristcratóbal of Huamange in the south-central city of Ayacucho. Famous for its nickel, gold, and silver mines, and as a historic site of victory by General Antonio José de Sucre aginst the Spanish army, this Peruvian city, with a population of 27,000 in the mid-1960s, was driven by a radical economic divide between upper and lower classes. Guzmán's experience in Ayacucho heightened his awareness of the inequality under which a large segment of the Peruvian population labored.

"My greatest and deepest impression was to meet and discover the Ayacucho peasants," Guzmán would state during the fifteen-day interrogation that ensued upon his September 1992 arrest. "Their reality shook my eyes and mind. . . . They endure an oppressive semifeudal burden. I saw people working as slaves on ranches." Outraged by what he had witnessed, he decided to organize a national student assembly and began studying Mao Zedong in depth. He then traveled to China, in 1965 and 1967, to fully submerge himself in Communist affairs and to witness firsthand the agitations of the Cultural Revolution—a campaign set forth by Chairman Mao to revitalize the popular fervor toward Marxism and to renew his nation's basic public institutions. First in China and then in Albania, Guzmán met top-level Marxist leaders and was able to solidify overseas contacts and reaffirm his ideological allegiances.

There was no turning back. Having seen the Red Guards, allied with the army, attacked so-called bourgeois elements in intellectual and artistic circles and the bureaucracy, Guzmán was convinced that a similar state of affairs needed to be organized at home. "Honor and glory to the Peruvian people!"—the throaty cry would resound for almost three decades. He would recruit and indoctrinate the young and the poor, preparing them to fight the aggressor within, imperialism's fifth columnists who were ready to do anything to dismantle the country's dignity. Peru's salvation, it was clear to him, lay in the establishment of a Communist regime similar to that of Mao's China. Presumably in an effort to "naturalize" Maoist thought, Guzmán, on his return to Ayacucho, gave his full attention to the work of José Carlos Mariátegui—Peru's original socialist commentator, nicknamed Amauta after a handful of Inca teachers and philosophers—drawing clear parallels between his beliefs and Mao's. And so it was that Mariátegui came to play a crucial role in the shaping of Shining Path. One can only speculate whether he would have been pleased by this. Born in 1894 in Moquegua, Mariátequi was a self-educated man who was unable to finish primary school for lack of money but who, at the age of nineteen, was already a respected journalist for the Lima newspaper *La Prensa*. He had been strongly influenced by Georges Sorel's thinking and came to believe the only solution to Peru's problems was a process of revolution. During his twenties he met and became friends with Victor Raúl Haya de la Torre (1895–1979), a young activist who would found a political organization known by the name of Alianza Popular Revolucionaria Americana, or APRA (later on Alan García's party), and would have become Peru's elected president in 1962 had a military coup not prevented him from taking office.

Like his effusive follower, Abimael Guzmán, Mariátegui traveled abroad—to Spain, to Italy (where he met Antonio Gramsci and Benedetto Croce), to Germany. On his return he finished a number of books, many of them composed of essays and reviews published in newspapers and weekly magazines, including his famous 1928 title *Seven Interpretative Essays on Peruvian Reality*. Paying special attention to the forgotten Inca population, the book offers a Marxist analysis of the country's most urgent social, economic, and political problems, showing how the nation's infrastructure is conditioned by colonial and semifeudal elements. Breaking with Haya de la Torre and the APRA, Mariátegui went on to create the Partido Socialista del Perú, or PSP, which enthusiastically joined the Communist International Movement and was later redefined as Partido Comunista del Perú, or PCP.

Although Mariátegui died at the age of thirty-six, the party grew steadily until the early 1960s, when a few global controversies—including debates over the "true value" of Castro's revolution in Cuba, the Sino-Soviet split, and Khrushchev's denunciation of Stalin—caused the party to fragment. By 1975, it had been divided into some twenty different organizations, with two factions retaining most of the power: a pro-Soviet group favoring a peaceful transition to Communism through reform and a pro-Maoist one that promoted change through violence. For a while those members leaning toward Mao called themselves Partido Comunista del Perú-Bandera Roja, or Red Flag.

After a few more internal quarrels, yet another faction was born in 1970: the Partido Comunista Peruano por el Sendero Luminoso de Mariátegui, PCP-SL, or Shining Path. Its leader was Abimael Guzmán, a man who, having invested a considerable part of the 1960s in internal political struggles, was now emerging as a key figure in leftist politics. Not for him the temporizing of some of his comrades. He was convinced that conditions for radical revolution were already present in Peru—the only things needed were a date and a cathartic explosion.

Meanwhile, all through the next decade, Vargas Llosa was in the process of becoming, in the eyes of Europe and the United States, the nation's most prominent citizen—Peru's favorite son, but stationed, like a diplomat, in Europe—intelligent, outspoken, sexy, and cosmopolitan. A litterateur, a sophisticated op-ed commentator, and a very articulate keynote speaker, he had championed democracy in international forums (after an ill-fated flirtation with Castro's 1959 revolution) and was known for his stylish novels and plays, which were frequently set in Piura, Lima, and Arequipa. For his works, he was recipient of a number of prestigious awards, including the Biblioteca Breve Prize, the Rómulo Gallegos, the Premio de la Crítica, and the PEN-Faulkner Award; he was also a regular contender for the Nobel Prize. When Carmen Balcells, a very capable Barcelona literary agent, took him as client (she also represents Gabriel García Márquez, Isabel Allende, and other writers from the so-called Latin American literary boom), his name was immediately established in the international literary arena.

While Shining Path was being created, Vargas Llosa was finishing a doctorate from the Universidad Central, for which he submitted a voluminous dissertation (over a thousand manuscript pages) called "García Márquez: History of a Deicide." Published in book form in 1971 but never reprinted or translated into any other language, this study of the life, times, and artistic contribution of the Colombian author of One Hundred Years of Solitude provided the Peruvian an opportunity to elaborate his own theory of the "total novel," one seeking to encompass through narrative art a comprehensive social reality: it would parse the various segments of society, every nuance of their hopes, dream, and sorrows. Inspired by Balzac's epigram, "Il faut avoir fouillé toute la vie sociale pour être un vrai romancier, vu que le roman est l'histoire privée des nations," Vargas Llosa had put this idea to work in his first three novels and took it even further in his encyclopedic *The War of the End of the World*, a title generally used as a divider between the writer's creative periods. Some 560 pages long in its 1981 Spanish original, the novel is a rewriting of a Brazilian classic, Euclides Da Cunha's *Os Sertões*, known in English as *Rebellion in the Backlands*. A combination of biography, journalism, documentary history, and narrative fiction considered by many "the Bible of Brazilian nationalism," Da Cunha's magnum opus is about an 1886 uprising in Canudos, an old cattle ranch on the banks of the Vasa-Barris River, laid low by the type of poverty that inhabits Latin American shantytowns. Critics are sharply divided regarding the actual value of Vargas Llosa's work, originally commissioned as a screenplay by a Brazilian filmmaker: while some consider it too ambitious to hold the reader's attention, others, including me, regard the book as an outstanding piece of fiction—the tribute of a twentieth-century Hispanic writer to his precursor. But whatever the final assessment might be, a consensus holds this to be the author's last novel of real distinction, at least for now; his aesthetic standards having been impoverished by the high demands of stardom. At the apex of his career, Vargas Llosa has had trouble focusing his attention on the type of meganarratives he had trained his audience to expect. His literary work since *The War of the End of the World* has been reduced to slim transitional novels, what Graham Greene used to call "entertainments"—works with more looks than substance. It was in the late 1970s that he had matured and recognized his true voice—in just the years that Guzmán's lasting impact was about to begin.

Guzmán began suffering health problems in 1972. In June of that year, he asked for a leave of absence from the University of San Cristóbal to get a complete medical checkup at a hospital in Lima, followed by another series of doctor's appointments in subsequent months. His psoriasis, which specialists diagnosed as chronic and believed would deteriorate rapidly in Ayacucho because of its high altitude, had become a real impediment. What Guzmán needed was a place at sea level, like Lima or La Cantuba. Around that time he got a scholarship to finish "Mariátegui's Philosophy," a seminal study in which he displayed his commitment to his idol and one of the last intellectual projects he accomplished in Ayacucho—with the exception, of course, of masterminding Shining Path's secret birth.

He resigned from his academic job in 1976. Until then he had used colleagues and students to spread his gospel. But now an inner calling assured him a different strategy was needed in order to destabilize Peru's status quo. He had been living the divided life of Mr. Verloc in Conrad's *The Secret Agent:* In a world of fatuous civil servants and corrupt policemen, he dreamed of becoming a chilling terrorist and began organizing an underground guerrilla army. Vargas Llosa's egotism, his globetrotting ways, held absolutely no appeal for Guzmán. Peru had to be transformed from within, and Guzmán cared little if foreigners saw his Maoist utopia as an anarchic killing field of utter madness, despair, and desolation. Paradise on earth could wait no longer.

And so he disappeared from the public eye. He became a ghost, a mythical figure—an abstract entity. No one knew his whereabouts: His presence could be felt everywhere, but physically he was a shadow, a wraith. While Guzmán was never an invalid, his skin disease had a direct impact on his politics. And accompanied by a susceptibility to migraines, quick changes of mood, and a sense of vulnerability expressed in impatience and easy anger, it made him a more tyrannical figure. Because of his psoriasis, he had to restructure Shining Path to control its actions from a habitat benign to his health; otherwise he would have had to interrupt his strategy to "descend" to a place where he could recover in peace. (Interestingly, the legendary Argentine guerrilla Ernesto "Che" Guevara, whom Guzmán often ridiculed to show how tenderness can destroy a life, suffered frequent asthma attacks that impeded his will to fight.) Thus Shining Paths' *incahuas*—literally "the Inca's House," a term used by Haya de la Torre to describe a clandestine party's secret headquarters—had to be adapted to its leader's physical disabilities.

In any event, Guzmán spent his days and nights plotting the first terrorist attack. It took place in 1980, when a group of student sympathizers set fire to the ballot boxes in the remote Andean village of Chuschi. Although it looked like a peripheral incident of violence, the horror had begun. Guzmán's ultimate goal was to establish a People's Republic of the New Democracy in Peru: a greater good in the name of which any sort of mayhem and brutality would ultimately be justified. In conventions and meetings, he sermonized about the "troublesome" contradictions of Peruvian reality and would read out loud passages by Mao as well as segments of Washington Irving's now forgotten *Life of Mahomet* (to demonstrate "how when men are unified by a common cause, they act together hand-in-hand") and Shakespeare's *Macbeth* ("to show how treason can poison the human mind").

Vargas Llosa was overseas at the time. With residences in London and Barcelona he would spend most of his time across the Atlantic and would make only an occasional trip home to reinvigorate his professional and family ties, to keep his "Peruvian persona" alive. He had unsuccessfully tried to return to live there several years before but quickly gave up the idea; "I left Europe and didn't live in my country again for any length of time until 1974," he later recounted. "I was twenty-two when I left and thirty-eight when I returned. In many ways, I was a totally different person when I came back. . . . Peru is for me a kind of incurable disease, and my feeling for her is intense, bitter, and full of the violence that characterizes passion." But a year later he again crossed the ocean to Europe. (He has spent comparatively little time in the United States, first in 1968 at Washington State University and later at academic institutions like Syracuse and Princeton.) Named president of PEN Club International, he enjoyed the glittering lifestyle of a successful *homme des lettres* that only Europe can offer. He was constantly interviewed by journalists and asked to comment on world affairs, appearing in academic congresses, and dined by diplomats. He also tried his luck as a film director and wrote a number of dramatic plays. His emerging profile had less to do with sober intellect than with a sparkling, perhaps irresponsible wit; in middle age, he seemed more the *enfant terrible* than elder statesman.

As Guzmán's *El Diario* and other Peruvian periodicals have insisted, frivolity in Vargas Llosa was always a synonym for indiscretion. A case in point is his 1977 novel *Aunt Julia and the Script Writer,* which became a long-running television miniseries and was turned into a Hollywood-style movie (retitled *Tune in Tomorrow* and set in New Orleans, starring Peter Falk, Barbara Hershey, and Keanu Reeves). The novel tells two parallel stories, that of Varguitas, a young promising writer in Lima who works for a radio station in the 1950s, and Pedro Camacho, the scriptwriter who is responsible for popular radio soap operas adored by a large Peruvian audience. As Varguitas gets more fascinated with Camacho's fantasy, his personal life unravels in a humorous fashion: He falls in love with his aunt Julia and, in spite of the family's opposition, he marries her in a secret ceremony. Based on the writer's real-life liaison with Julia Urquidi Illanes, a Bolivian and the force behind Vargas Llosa's early success, whom he married in 1955 at age nineteen (she was twenty-nine), the novel created a scandal. When Urquidi read it she is said to have exploded in fury: Truth had been distorted, her privacy destroyed, her reputation ruined (the press called her "a seducer of minors").

Indiscretion generates more indiscretion, says Blaise Pascal in his *Pensées.* In revenge Urquidi wrote *Varguitas' Silence,* a confession published in La Paz, Bolivia, in 1983; in it she sets the record straight, basing her arguments on actual letters and portraying Vargas Llosa as "a paranoiac daydreamer." The polemic, not unlike another one launched by an article in the *New York Times Magazine* where the novelist ridiculed one of his sons for his Rastafarian tastes, is relevant only insofar as it illustrates a facet of the writer's flamboyant personality: his rashness.

Frivolity and guerrilla warfare—the pen and the sword. While Vargas Llosa continued to receive international applause, Guzmán's nightmarish methods of indoctrination and terror shook the Peruvian population. After killing adults and children alike, Shining Path would cut out their eyes and tongues, hang their bodies from trees, and set entire villages on fire. The targets, although varied, were rarely indiscriminate: the attack would single out peasants who refused to join the guerrillas' ranks, eyewitnesses, and innocents whose death could send a message to the Lima government. The army responded with equal harshness. Among contemporary guerrilla movements, the Shining Path is comparable only to Pol Pot's Khmer Rouge. And yet, as Tina Rosenberg has pointed out, the 27,000 deaths in Peru since 1980 have not been perpetrated solely by Guzmán's squads: The brutal and incredibly inept Peruvian military has contributed more than its share.

Shining Path's paraphernalia is borrowed from Communist parties in Spain, Italy, and what used to be the Soviet Union. But if the music of its anthems and marches is inauthentic, the wording is original:

Communist Party, conduct us to a new life,
Make doubt and fear vanish like smoke;
We have the strength, the Future is ours.
Communism is a goal and will be a reality.

And this:

And people listen carefully
When returning from a day's work;
It's Gonzalo! sings the fire,
Gonzalo means armed struggle.

Gonzalo! the masses roar
and the Andes tremble
expressing ardent passion,
Sure and well-aimed faith.

Sonia Goldenberg, author of *Report on the Unknown Peru,* reports that Guzmán's movement has tentacles beyond regional borders that portray him and the Shining Path as the only hope for an egalitarian future for Peru. Its major organization, the Committee to Support the Revolution in Peru, paints graffiti and hangs posters in urban centers worldwide and places ads in mainstream periodicals (in the United States, it gets the support of the Revolutionary Communist Party, which distributes Maoist literature from Atlanta to Honolulu) to condemn massacres of political prisoners and oppose foreign military intervention.

Latin America has a long-standing tradition of writers who involve themselves in political affairs. Perhaps the first, and certainly among the best known, is Domingo Faustino Sarmiento, a nineteenth-century Argentine intellectual heavily influenced by the novels of James Fenimore Cooper and Benjamin Franklin's *Autobiography*, who wrote the groundbreaking *Facundo: Civilization and Barbarism* in 1845 (it was translated into English twenty-three years later by Mrs. Horace Mann). The book was part biography, part novel, part nonfictional account of Juan Facundo Quiroga, a gaucho leader, and its political impact was tremendous. Sarmiento became his country's most important citizen, and when he ran for president after a life in exile, the vote easily placed him in office (1868–1874). Many have followed his path, including Ernesto Cardenal, Alejo Carpentier, Octavio Paz, and Carlos Fuentes— authors who, at one point or another in their literary careers, became ministers of culture, ambassadors, and cultural attachés in Europe and the Far East.

Since his beginnings as a writer, Vargas Llosa had been vocal about political issues: he had written about the Arab-Israeli conflict, the Irish Republican Army, and Castro's ideology, among other topics. But until 1987, he never succumbed to the temptation to enter politics, although such a temptation was present. In fact, he refused the invitations by Fernando Belaúnde Terry, during his return to presidential power in the early 1980s, to become ambassador in London and Washington, minister of education, minister of foreign relations, and, finally, to fill the office of prime minister. Vargas Llosa constantly rejected the offers—with one exception: He did accept the unpaid, month-long appointment to head the commission investigating a 1982 massacre of eight journalists in Uchuraccay, a remote region of the Andes, after which he published a report, translated into English as "Inquest in the Andes." "A big mistake," he would later on say. "I was mercilessly attacked and slandered for months by the press" for accepting the appointment. A temporary job, it had seemed, apparently nothing of great importance. He was dead wrong, of course. Whatever his misgivings, though, politics was not a side interest for him; it constantly occupied his thoughts. So when he officially entered politics a few years later, what surprised people was only how long it had taken.

In July 1987, by his own account (published in *Granta* and expanded into a 538-page memoir published in book form by Seix Barral in Barcelona in 1993) he was in Punta Sal, a resort in the far north of Peru, when he heard Alan García's annual speech to Congress on the radio. García had been in office for two years and was having a difficult time controlling the insatiable beast of the nation's foreign debt. In the past, García had had a confrontation with the International Monetary Fund and the World Bank because he refused to continue paying huge amounts of the foreign debt. His policies, although immensely popular, didn't fit in Vargas Llosa's own vision of how Peru could be rebuilt. In the speech, the president announced what others like Salvador Allende in Chile, José López Portillo in Mexico, and Siles Suazo in Bolivia had done: the nationalization of the country's banks. An uproar followed. The strategy was clear—to target the monetary institutions as responsible for Peru's inflation and deeply rooted poverty. This was not an unexpected move, one might add. During the 1970s, still enchanted with Castro's Communism, Latin American politicians saw capitalism and the United States as evil forces that had only compounded the region's difficulties. By contrast, they understood the role of the state to be omniscient and benign, what Octavio Paz called "the philanthropic ogre." Since only a small segment of the population was affluent and controlled the nation's wealth, the solution was to mobilize the government to counterbalance social and economic inequalities. And before that, in 1938, Lázaro Cárdenas, then Mexico's president and, like Alan García, hugely popular, struck at rich American oil companies by declaring the mineral resources the sole property of the Mexican people. Suddeny, a vast foreign industry lost its ground and was declared illegal. Cárdenas—who was father of today's opposition leader Cuauhtémoc Cárdenas, the founder and head of the National Democratic Front—appealed to the masses for immediate support. He invited peasants and blue-collar workers to donate money, jewelry, goods, and other valuable possessions—anything to help compensate the owners who had been stripped of their companies. Alan García's plan wasn't very different.

Vargas Llosa had found him power hungry and immature. They had met for an interview that lasted an hour and a half at the government's palace in Lima. According to the writer's account, they talked about a number of topics, including Shining Path's attack on the palace with handmade bazookas. It was clear the politician was hoping to get the backing of the writer. But after their dialogue, the novelist appeared on television to state that instead of voting for García in the coming elections, he had chosen to support the candidate of the Christian Popular Party, Luis Bedoya Reyes. And in a move that infuriated the president even more, the novelist published an open letter in June 1986 in which he blamed García for the massacre of Shining Path rioters in three prisons.

The story behind the massacre was a widespread topic of conversation among Peruvians. By the mid-1980s, Shining Path had branches everywhere in the highlands—most prominently in Ayacucho, Junín, Cerro de Pasco, Apurímac, and Huancavelica. And though the vigor of the insurgency seemed undiminished by it, many Guzmán followers had been captured. They populated Peru's prisons under miserable conditions yet remained loyal to the cause. So much so that on June 18, 1986, an uprising in three Lima jails took place: Lurigancho, Santa Bárbara, and El Frontón. After taking seven policemen hostage, the prisoners demanded better health facilities and the unification of Shining Path followers in a single building. Frustrated by the ineptness of his own forces, President Alan García ended the mutiny by sending the military to quell the insurrection. After soldiers assaulted the three prisons with heavy artillery, close to 250 inmates were killed—at Lurigancho, for instance, nobody survived, and El Frontón lay in ruins after the incident. The action shocked the public and the international uproar was tremendous. García's own political credibility was just one of the casualties.

After listening to Alan García's address on the radio, Vargas Llosa wrote an article on August 2, 1987, for the newspaper *El Comercio* in which he talked of the perils of a totalitarian Peru and declared his opposition to the president's policy. A day later, together with intellectuals, artists, and highly regarded professionals like painter Fernando de Szyszlo and architect Freddy Cooper, he joined a group that drafted a manifesto calling for more democratic freedom for citizens and less dictatorial power for the state. Those two days transformed him forever. Suddenly, Vargas Llosa found himself in the spotlight: He was the most famous, and vocal, antagonist to Alan García's plan. And on August 21 he gave a speech in the Plaza San Martín, the first in which he faced his new persona: Vargas Llosa, politician.

It was also the start of a new freedom movement, Libertad, which grew very quickly and is now registered as an official Peruvian party. The movement actually had its origins in Fernando de Szyszlo's studio in September 1987. (Vargas Llosa used one of his paintings as inspiration in his erotic novel *In Praise of the*

*Stepmother.*) As the writer himself put it, in its birth this new party had as its greatest goal "to attract young people and show them that the real revolution for a country like ours would be one that replaced arbitrariness with the rule of law, and convince them that liberal reform could make Peru a prosperous modern country."

Before the presidential campaign, Vargas Llosa was said to be nurturing five projects: a theatrical piece set in the Lima of the 1950s about an old Quixote who tries to save the colonial-era balconies that are threatened by demolition; a novel set in the Andes; an essay on Victor Hugo's *Les Misérables;* a play about a change-of-gender surgical operation and its humorous consequences in the friendship of two men, former schoolmates, who meet at the Savoy Hotel in London; and a novel about Flora Tristán, a Franco-Peruvian revolutionary. Since politics dominated his days, none of these projects would be accomplished.

As candidate, the novelist made an early alliance, called Frente Democrático, with the Popular Action Party of Fernando Balaúnde, as well as with the Christian Popular Party. The campaign did not go as smoothly as he had hoped, however, and in the middle of it, feeling suffocated and regretful, he quit and fled to Spain. It seemed he had had second thoughts about the wisdom of running for office—mainly because he and his wife Patricia had received constant death threats, some by Alan García's supporters, but also because his dream to change Peru's economic and social course seemed an impossible one. And while he eventually doubled back and returned to campaigning, the harm was done. (Alvaro, one of his three children, was his press officer. He later wrote a campaign memoir, *The Devil on Campaign,* where his father's inner life is well described.) The country suffered from an incurable disease, Vargas Llosa believed: corruption and incompetence. His life had changed, he wrote in his memoir: "I had ceased to be private. Until I left Peru . . . after the second round of voting for the presidency, I lost the privacy that I had always guarded jealously."

In spite of Vargas Llosa's goodwill and heavy publicity apparatus organized by the reputable U.S. agency of Sawyer Miller (which also advised Corazón Aquino on her campaign for the presidency of the Philippines), the decisive winner of the presidential election was Alberto K. Fujimori, a fifty-one-year-old Peruvian of Japanese descent, who had been an unknown agronomy professor and headed La Molina's Agronomist University. The outcome came as a surprise to almost everybody, including world leaders such as U.S. President George Bush and Britain's Prime Minister Margaret Thatcher. Interestingly enough, Abimael Guzmán did not regard the two with the same degree of antipathy. El Chinito—the little Chinaman, a nickname given to Fujimori in spite of his Japanese ancestry—was a rival he wanted dead; the novelist, on the other hand, while symbolizing European intervention and the hierarchy of those Western values Presidente Gonzalo thoroughly dislikes, was treated less aggressively in 1990 and thereafter by *El Diario*. Its editorials, as the Peruvian journalist Gustavo Gorriti Ellenbogen has found, portrayed Vargas Llosa in a more benign fashion—even as "a man of wisdom." He certainly isn't seen as a friend, but neither is he seen as "a pig, a brute and tyrannical type" personified by Fujimori. The curious distinction the Shining Path drew between the two might have to do with ethnicity. Since Guzmán is known to express contempt for anything foreign, he perceived Fujimori, raised in popular Lima neighborhoods in an "un-Peruvian" Japanese household, as an image of external intervention. By contrast, Vargas Llosa is the embodiment of patriotism turned bourgeois. A lesser sin, apparently.

In retrospect, Vargas Llosa says that only three speeches he wrote made him proud: the one prepared in the garden of a friend's house—without the intrusive presence of bodyguards, reporters, and telephones—that launched his candidacy in the Plaza de Armas of Arequipa on June 4, 1989; the one that closed it in the Paseo de la República in Lima the next year; and the address he gave at the Libertad headquarters as soon as it became known he had lost the election. "Democracy," he said in that final occasion, "is driven by the electoral process, and in elections that are victories and defeats. But the work that had been done by the members of Libertad cannot be judged in this way. I know, I am certain, that Peru too will come to know and acknowledge this. That the seeds that we have sown together during these two and a half years will continue to germinate and finally produce those fruits that we desire for Peru: the fruits of modernity, justice, prosperity, peace and *libertad*."

Once again he was wrong. At one point in the campaign, in a public debate, Fujimori said to Vargas Llosa, "It seems that you would like to make Peru a Switzerland, Doctor." In truth, the novelist *had* hoped to turn his into a country of cultured, prosperous, and free people, without poverty or unemployment or illiteracy, and certainly without an army. Quite the opposite happened. During his first few months as president, Fujimori borrowed from Vargas Llosa the shock-treatment therapy that was now renamed "Fujishock"—a package of neoliberal reform measures the novelist-candidate had proposed to help remedy Peru's financial insolvency. The national situation swiftly worsened. If before the election 7 million

Peruvians were under the poverty level, in 1993 the number increased to 12 million; a cholera epidemic left thousands dead throughout the country and spread to South and Central America; the incidence of tuberculosis grew to the highest in the region.

Once Fujimori came to office, moreover, Shining Path made a commitment to intensify its attacks in the provinces and in Lima. With Vargas Llosa in Europe and thus out of the picture, the struggle between Guzmán and the government was fearfully relentless. Peruvians began to talk of their country as ruled by two presidents: El Chinito and Presidente Gonzalo. Which one could outrule his opponent? On April 5, 1992, Fujimori struck what is now called *autogolpe,* a self-coup in which he closed down Congress, announced the complete reconstruction of the legal system, purged elderly judges, and suspended individual liberties. For decades Peru had been plagued with corruption, he claimed, and a drastic restructuring was urgently needed. Vargas Llosa was in Berlin's Wissenchafts Kolleg at the time, finishing that narrative inspired by his presidential campaign *El pez en el agua.* In fact, since his defeat to Fujimori he has returned to Peru just twice—to attend the marriage of his daughter Morgana and to make Libertad an official Peruvian party. Although he wrote op-ed articles deploring the *autogolpe* for *El País* in Spain and the *New York Times,* by and large he has become a dilettante, his best and most comfortable role.

Vargas Llosa's book-length memoir is a compelling exercise in self-deception. Constructed in such a way that two separate narratives find a common message only in the last page, the volume's odd-numbered chapters recall the novelist's childhood and adolescence, the dogmatic paternal figure he reencountered in 1946–1947, his education and early readings, his marriage to Tía Julia, up until his departure for Europe in 1958. Even-numbered chapters, on the other hand, detail every aspect of the presidential campaign and end in 1990, when Vargas Llosa leaves Peru once more, to fully devote himself to writing.

A few elements in the book are puzzling—above all first the author's messianism. Throughout the narrative, Vargas Llosa is convinced he and he alone is the savior, the redeemer of Peru's national sickness, his ideas a prescription from heaven. He uses a disproportionate amount of space to rage at and vilify his enemies, who, by definition, are corrupt, inefficient, nearsighted, or simply stupid. He attacks attachés, confidants, and even onetime partners like Hernando de Soto, an economist and the author of *The Other Path,* a 1989 international bestseller about the "informal" black marketeers who work outside the law in Lima, which had a foreword by

Vargas Llosa that he now regrets having written. But Vargas Llosa's analysis is also marked by welcome insights. In one section, he studies the behavior of Peruvian artists and writers, what Gramsci called "organic intellectuals," to conclude convincingly that one of the most dramatic features of underdeveloped countries is the way in which the Left persuades the educated to adopt socialist gestures to hide their mediocrity and their personal frustration.

What's unforgivable in *El pez en el agua* is that, in such a compulsive account of the Peruvian cosmos, Vargas Llosa only mentions Guzmán in passing—and that only in the nine-page-long epilogue. His presence as an emblematic national figure is never acknowledged, his dangerous power never studied. There's only one explanation for this omission: In spite of his political involvements, Vargas Llosa remains essentially disconnected from Peru's inner soul, a stranger in a strange land. In fact, he lost the election precisely because he was seen as a member of the oligarchy, a member of the ruling class. Presidente Gonzalo, on the other hand, has deeply transformed the way things are conceived and perceived in Peru. For all his many atrocious crimes, he is considered to speak for a segment of the population which, even if small, directly affects the nation's present. Such irony makes one think of an analysis offered by Alfredo Bryce Echenique, author of the masterpiece *A World for Julius*, Peru's second-most important novelist, and once a student of Vargas Llosa, who has been living in Europe since 1972. In an article called "Peru: Our Daily Violence," published in the Spanish magazine *Claves*, he argues that the two selves, the Westernized and the *cholo*, divided across racial lines, have always existed by ignoring each other—the less they interact the better, and if they are doomed, it is simply because they refuse to face each other.

Fujimori's lucky day was September 12, 1992, when the members of the Dirección Nacional Contra el Terrorismo, or DINCOTE, finally captured Abimael Guzmán, with minimum fuss, in a house that functioned as a modern dance studio located in a quiet Lima neighborhood. (His closest allies are women, and one of them, Maritza Garrido Lecca, was once a ballerina.) Although Peru's embattled constitution prohibits the death penalty, Fujimori, after shutting down Congress, has openly declared his will to make Guzmán an exception by placing him on death row. This wasn't the first time Presidente Gonzalo had been arrested. Gorriti Ellenbogen's *Sendero: History of Peru's Millenary War* details how the police captured him in January 1979, linking him to a number of well-publicized strikes. He was taken to the State Security offices and interrogated by high authorities. Ironically, though, he was released after confessing to having a Marxist-Leninist ideology but "not to [being] Shining Path's commander-in-chief." Considered by his followers the Fourth Sword of Marxism (Marx, Lenin, and Mao are the other three), Abimael Guzmán is now Latin America's most famous prisoner.

Is he still a threat? Peru is inhabited by other guerrilla groups, including Victor Polay's Tupac Amaru Revolutionary Movement (MRTA), which began action in 1984 and is considerably smaller than Shining Path. Unlike Guzmán, the MRTA followers revere Che Guevara and have links to Cuba. But Presidente Gonzalo dismisses the group and its idol as a supporting cast, a bourgeois extremity of the nation's government. The Shining Path is another story. As Tina Rosenberg argues, Shining Path, which controls a "liberated territory" in Peru's jungle, has broken most of the rules of guerrilla warfare, of urban and rural subversion, and has left international intelligence services thoroughly perplexed. Since Guzmán's imprisonment, bombs and assassinations have not ceased. On the contrary, a seemingly headless Shining Path seemed to be launching a counterattack, a wave of revenge for its leaders's arrest.

Fujimori's decline is imminent: His tyranny, the fourth such regime in Peru's twentieth-century history, will sooner or later bring more uncertainty. This semifeudal, quasi-modern Banana Republic is torn apart: Vargas Llosa's Westernized supporters are in a face-off against Guzmán's reactionary militarism. And so the question returns, as it does time and again: At what precise moment did Peru fuck itself up?

Or should one say that the nation was always divided—that it was defective from birth? Wandering around the globe in a self-imposed exile, the novelist continues to write, his sharp pen explicating, or perhaps distorting, Peru's impossible dilemma. Carlos Abimael Guzmán Reynoso, alias Presidente Gonzalo, caged in an underground cell and metamorphosed into a media artifact, has in turn become a living martyr, a monument, his Shining Path certain to have a role in the country's future. If Peru eventually becomes South America's Iran, complete with a fanatical ayatollah ready to cut international ties, Marxist-Leninist ideology will sweep the nation like a tide crashing upon a sand castle. By then the white European minority will long be gone, of course, replaced by mythical Inca heroes. Mao Zedong in Macondo: Market economy and democracy alike stand to be a casualties of ideological absolutism. Guzmán and Vargas Llosa: two aspects of the country's identity, their lives mapping out the forking paths to Peru's future.

# CALVERT CASEY

## Renegade Artist

*What every author hopes to receive from posterity—a hope usually
disappointed—is justice.*

—W. H. Auden

It has become a commonplace to embrace renegade artists as symbols of our modern condition. Our first response is to ignore them, to deprive their work of any serious consideration. But no sooner do they fall completely into the abyss of oblivion than our omission becomes apparent. So we change our mind to embrace them profusely and obsessively, as if regretting a terrible sin. Poe, for instance, the master of the macabre, was at first so forgotten that his grave had no tombstone for twenty-six years. When he finally got one, only Whitman attended the ceremony. How ironic, then, that no other American writer today, with the probable exception of Poe's nemesis, Henry James, commands so much public and critical attention. How jarring that after his contemporaries time and again denied his genius, he is today a commodity in textbooks and a magnet to bring the young to good literature. Or take Kafka. His shadowy self, his sense of alienation, of break from the rules of social behavior, made him a pariah, an eternally unhappy person whose work during his lifetime failed to command any thoughtful response from publishers and readers. He even asked his best friend, Max Brod, to burn his entire oeuvre after his death. But we

First published as Introduction to *Calvert Casey: The Collected Stories* (Durham, N.C.: Duke University Press, 1998).

revere Kafka now. We turn him into an idolized rebel because that allows us to recriminate against Western culture, against its mechanisms to normalize individuals, from which all of us like to think we are somewhat disconnected. Kafka and Poe figure as oversensitive and painful creatures inhabiting the margins, individuals suffering from physical and psychological sicknesses we see as nightmarish. "I would prefer not to," cries Bartleby, Melville's famous eccentric, a motto well suited for all renegade artists, scapegoats of a society that doesn't quite know how to react to them. So it sings to them in chorus: Ah sufferers! Ah humanity!

Calvert Casey, an unsettling Cuban, belongs to the same type of artist: the rambler and rebel who prefers not to. Through his shyness and silence, through his perception of reality as a smoke screen behind which Truth is hidden, he dreamed of remembrance, of leaving behind a legacy endorsed by future generations. One nurtures paternal feelings toward one's work, Casey once wrote, hoping it would be safe and protected for the ages. But for too long already, since his suicide in Rome in 1969, his work has remained unfairly trapped in oblivion. Unfairly, I say, because some of Casey's short stories, such as "The Visitors" and "Piazza Margana," are incomparable, of the type that deeply disturbs our conventional views of life. Like "The Building of the Great Wall of China," like "The Pit and the Pendulum," they have a fugitive quality. Every single one of them is less about a character participating in a well-defined plot than about a mood and a state of mind. Casey's testament was to explore, through prose the other side of things, that "feeling of irreality" that constantly haunts us.

His presence, by most accounts, was "pallid," i.e., subtle, unfelt by many, as if this renegade artist, this troubled soul, needed to apologize for his actions. And he did apologize, repeatedly. Proof is the instance just before taking his suicidal overdose of sleeping pills, when, already inconsolably depressed, Casey drafted a letter to the Italian police deploring the inconvenience of being found in such a distasteful state. An inconvenience? Or when he agonized about being followed all over Europe by Fidel Castro's secret police, who he believed had orders to annihilate him. Was he paranoid? Was he yet another Cold War schizophrenic, constantly looking back in case someone followed him? His tomb, like Poe's at first, remains unknown. Worse, after his untimely death, an Italian news reporter found in his apartment statues of fornicating Indian gods and pornographic postcards and immediately branded him as a sodomite, a monster of the perverse—this in spite of his attempt, evident in his "Notes on Pornography," to extricate the vicious from the erotic, the superficial from the esoteric. Thus, in death Casey quickly enhanced the anathema that had surrounded him like an unwelcome shroud all his life. He lived and died in a permanent state of eclipse, a larva frozen in time.

Periodically, however, someone somewhere will try to revive him. Literati of a high caliber all tried their luck: Italo Calvino, Vicente Molina Foix, María Zambrano, Luis Goytisolo, Guillermo Cabrera Infante. These hopeful attempts have surely kept Casey's legacy alive. He remains a well-kept secret, a martyr on the road to beatification. But he never quite makes it there, in part because he was a true nomad from a no-man's-land, a visionary from nowhere and everywhere. He made his reputation in Spanish, though he switched tongues with such vehemence, from English to Spanish, from Spanish to English and Italian, that he belongs to no single language and to all at once. And while he found real solace only in Havana, his odyssey pulled him from Istanbul to New York, from England to India to Italy, to the point that no locality was ever truly his. In other words, Casey was the freakish nonconformist we all nurture within, an Irishman from the United States dancing to syncopated Caribbean rhythms, crushed by his own sexual and political identity, always in search of the elusive word and world he could call his own. Is his "I would prefer not to" destined to find a wider audience? Will posterity ever grant him the justice he deserves? Or are we to be disappointed?

To some degree, Casey's close friend, Cabrera Infante, is most responsible for keeping him around, for not letting oblivion triumph decisively over memory. His excellent essay "Who Killed Calvert Casey?" written in 1980, did much to generate a halo of supreme mystery around him. "A decade after his death," wrote Cabrera Infante, "Calvert resuscitates, rises from the dead and from underneath the bookish stone stretches out his bony hand that holds up a few pages to let us know what true literature is, visible in that writing that is his winning pawn: his prose is a communicating vessel: on the reverse is life; on the obverse, death. Calvert Casey lives and dies in each reading and his texts are a Moebius strip of reading: finite, infinite." Known among friends as La Calvita, Cálver, or simply as Cal, he produced a prose that is allergic to the baroque linguistic vices and devices ubiquitous in the Havana of the 1950s. His style has a queerness to it that makes it unique but difficult to grasp. The best way to define it, I suppose, is simply to say that it seems wrapped in a thin, white veil. We want to caress Casey's sentences but can't. They are removed, intangible. They are for us but not fully ours. He left us with only a small number of fictional tales, a very small number: seventeen original stories in total, all of them with one exception remarkably short, collected in a couple of volumes: *El regreso,* first published in 1962 in Havana, expanded a year later and enlarged again in 1967, when a Spanish edition by Seix Barral appeared in Barcelona; and *Notas de un simulador,* which appeared in 1969, shortly before Casey's death. Dead at forty-five, Casey seems to have been at the brink of artistic maturity but not quite there. While he tried his luck at a novel in progress—*Gianni, Gianni,* which he announced time and again and seemed to be working on toward the end, with "Piazza Margana" as one of its segments— he either never managed to finish it or simply destroyed it after it was almost completed. What he did generate, apparently with some hesitation, was a novella, "The Master of Life and Death." His personality, obviously, was suitable for the condensed and meteoric, as if he could make himself offer only snapshots of his plight, never a sustained account. Throughout his life, he also published a number of essays in periodicals, for the most part Cuban but also Mexican, many of which were gathered in 1964 in *Memorias de una isla.* They fail to capture us because Casey was not a thinker but a dreamer. He did not master a strategy to develop and critique ideas. Instead, he was adept at turning words into windows to the heart. Each of his stories is an exploration of the act of survival of the weakest in the margins of society. They all read like segments of a fractured novel and an autobiographical one at that, for Casey understood literature as a key to unlock his troubled soul. This explains why the same type of protagonist, a Gregor Samsa *à la cubana,* parades throughout his oeuvre, always bargaining with a small set of motifs. At the brink of maturity but incapable of grasping it—that, to me, is how Casey's legacy ought to be described. How much richer would we have been had he lived a few more years? And yet, his immaturity seems enough. It has weight and power.

Fate was never on Casey's side. In fact, death in many ways was a more suitable alternative than more years of suffering. He suffered from inexplicable periodic pains. Also, not only was he quiet and introspective, but he had a way of vacillating existentially, to make his presence unnoticeable. This hesitation was enhanced by his stuttering, of course, a birth handicap that became his trademark in Havana and was obviously connected to his timid temperament and introverted spirit. And one could also explain his recurrent pains as connected to his verbal impediment, for stuttering remains a most mysterious malady, connected, since the Enlightenment, to an imbalance of forces in the body. At any rate, Casey's nondescript behind-the-curtains style has its counterpart in his legendary stuttering. Luis Agüero, who met him during a *tertulia* in the offices of the weekly *Lunes de Revolución,* under the editorship of Cabrera Infante, once described him as "wearing thick glasses and dressing like a post-office employee." When he was nervous, Agüero adds, his stuttering would make his cheeks red as blood. In the shallow waters of conversation, Cabrera Infante himself claims, Casey would unexpectedly fall, "tripping over the least prominent words, like a rock on his oral road even if it were only an oral cobblestone." Antón Arrufat, another friend, to whom *El regreso* is dedicated, claimed Casey choked on the words he could not swallow.

No matter how we see it, a stuttering writer is an extraordinary metaphor for modernity. Words were both his tool and his trap. He made them his, but they betrayed him. For Casey, stuttering was a way to negotiate between silence and statement, between death and literature. Only in "Homecoming," his most personal story, does a character actually suffer from a language impediment, but throughout all his pages characters tremble and stagger. In fact, each of Casey's tales, I'm convinced, stutters: Each stumbles and bobbles and gets lost in its own verbal labyrinth. The reader invariably finishes the tales exhausted, with a feeling of inconclusion. What are they really about? What do they say? And what do they seek? What is it that words conceal? Their characters are constantly disconnected from their surroundings, as in "The Execution," a tale, with a quotation from the Song of Solomon 1:12, somehow reminiscent of Camus's *The Stranger,* in which a man is imprisoned for a crime he never committed and is taken to his death without uttering a word of complaint. This attitude is symptomatic: Loners abound in Casey's universe, loners without self-esteem, tormented by a vast galaxy of aunts: A young man prepares the burial of a baby who is his relative; a misfit returns to a park bench hoping to establish human connections that seem ill fated from the beginning; a disoriented adolescent imagines being introduced to his manhood by a prostitute but never realizes his fantasy; an outcast is hypnotized by a group of homeless people who make him feel accepted; a gay man is bewitched by his lover's blood. Hypnosis, fantasy, enchantment: In all these stories, words are only an excuse; they seduce and deceive.

Casey was born in Baltimore, Maryland, in 1924. He was thrown by birth into a verbally mixed habitat, for his father was American and his mother Cuban. Conflicting biographical reports abound: Apparently, he grew up in Havana but in 1948 he moved back to the United States. However, when his first published story appeared, he identified himself as having lived and gone to school "in his native Cuba" until 1946. A deliberate mistake? Elsewhere he added that he had worked in Canada and Switzerland until 1950, when he had been a translator for the United Nations, first in New York City and then in Rome. This sense of dislocation, of an itinerant life, permeated his worldview: Home was nowhere and everywhere—neither in space nor in words. Baltimore doesn't figure at all in his memory, nor does Paris or the metropolises of other countries he went through: France, Mexico, Czechoslovakia, and Haiti. New York City is mentioned but dispassionately: It is too cold, too impersonal, too aggressive. Only in two cities did Casey feel comfortable: Havana and Rome, Rome and Havana—undeclared mirrors of each other. He would live in Havana but die in Rome or vice versa. Once in the mid-1950s, wandering in Europe without a goal, he experienced an eerie insight. "One morning in Rome," he wrote later,

> in a Rome impoverished by the first postwar years, I had a curious vision that might have lasted a few seconds but that I remember quite clearly. The heat was intense. In a café in Corso Umberto I was drinking some liquid that would allow me to continue walking. A noisy crowd, mostly populated by brown faces, descended through the wide Via Barbieri, leaving behind the ivory sculpture with images of dolphins. The sound of people getting onto a bus, their little scenes of violence turned into little scenes of laughter, the intense life of a city curiously cosmopolitan and provincial had the virtue of pushing time back. That city wasn't Rome anymore but another remote city, Havana. The similarities were painful: the ivory sculpture was the old Neptune exiled in a Vedado park after presiding over the dealings of many generations in mornings such as this one. On the arcades I had crossed moments before, I saw a crowd descending in the *portales* of the Calzada de la Reina. The balconies were the same cement balconies of the old avenue where I first contemplated the great spectacles of this world. The emotion this vision produced in me carried along an infinite panic. (I recalled the panic elephants feel when death is near and they are far from the place where they were born.) I was terribly far from Havana. Perhaps I had forever lost the paradise (and also hell) of my first vision. My voluntary exile ended that morning. I had to return to the scene of discovery, where everything is given and nothing is in need of explanation.

When seen from beginning to end, Casey's fate is made only of arrivals and departures. Havana, the scene of discovery, as authentic a habitat as he would ever find, made him believe his homelessness was temporary. It also convinced him that Spanish, his mother's tongue, was his true household. His first story, "The Walk," had been written in English. It was published in the *New Mexico Quarterly* in 1954–1955 and was awarded a prize by Doubleday in New York. But his "homecoming" is signaled in multiple ways: He himself translated "The Walk" into Spanish (or, I should say, rewrote it) as "El paseo" for inclusion in the first edition of his debut collection of stories, *El regreso,* published in 1962 by Ediciones R in Cuba; and as early as 1955, at age thirty-two, he began sending material from the United States to the magazine *Ciclón*. Eventually, he switched to Spanish, and the fall of the Batista regime and the incident in Sierra Maestra inspired him, in the early 1960s, to relocate to Cuba. This metamorphosis, this heartfelt homecoming, is minutely and movingly described in his 1960 essay "Memorias de una isla," as well as in the story "Homecoming." In the latter, an idealistic young Cuban, exhausted by the "feeling of irreality," by the loneliness of New York, returns to the land of his origins. The autobiographical ingredient cannot be a coincidence: Like Casey, the protagonist is guilt-ridden, insecure, lonely, bookish, prematurely bald, and a stutterer. But the story is imbued with prophecy, for his hope quickly turns into hopelessness. Like Joseph K., he is suddenly and inexplicably arrested. In prison he is tortured and, toward the end, he falls off a cliff as he staggers along the place where his torturers have dumped him. More than anything, "Homecoming" is about guilt: By returning to his homeland he dreams of freeing himself from the guilt that possesses him, but the guilt might not bring him to his end, since his death is inflicted on him with complete indifference to his integration into Cuban society.

The resemblance to Casey's own pilgrimage is astounding: He spent only a bit over half a decade in Havana and then left the island, deserting it in 1965 while on a lecture trip to Budapest. The cycle went in reverse: He first resettled in Geneva, working once again as a translator for the United Nations, but eventually he returned to the Via Barbieri and the café of Corso Umberto, relocating in Rome. He continued to live in Spanish but readopted English as his artistic tongue. In the latter he wrote *Gianni, Gianni.* Switching landscapes and languages is a shocking act of self-transformation: By giving up one habitat and code and embracing another, a person undergoes a deep sense of loss and resurrection. For Casey, however, the loss is not a beginning but an end; in him the homecoming carried along its counterpoint: His departure was a return, and his return brought a sense of closure—*la huida y el regreso.*

Casey's Cuban period was incredibly prolific: Not only did he quickly move up in the intellectual hierarchy, but he published two books and more than two dozen "occasional" pieces—essays and reviews—on Edward Albee, Pedro Juan Soto, Juan Carlos Onetti, and René Marqués, among other authors and topics, originally commissioned by *Lunes de Revolución* and other weeklies of equal quality, a handful of which were collected in 1964 in the volume *Memorias de una isla;* but this period was also marked by a deep ambivalence, as is his whole life. Upon his arrival, he first worked in a department store. Later he became drama critic of Havana's evening daily, *Pueblo.* He frequented a small circle of friends, among them Agüero, Virgilio Piñera, Cabrera Infante, Arrufat, Oscar Hurtado, Lisando Otero, Humberto Arenal, Miriam Acevedo, Juan Arcocha, Pablo Armando Fernández, and Heberto Padilla. When *Lunes de Revolución* was closed by the government because its staff was considered politically dangerous and sexually promiscuous, Casey worked in the Casa de las Américas, directing the Colección Latinoamericana book series. He was, to be sure, a supporter of Castro's Revolution, not always openly enthusiastic about its drastic changes, but convinced, no doubt, that Socialism was the only road to a better tomorrow.

However, this enthusiasm soon turned to disappointment. Toward the end of that period, in 1964, he came across Italo Calvino, who at the time was a judge for the Casa de las Américas prize and was reading manuscripts. Their relationship is illustrative of his state of mind. As it turns out, Casey gave Calvino and his Argentine wife Chiquita a tour of *La Habana vieja* and of the city's cemeteries and churches. "At that time," Calvino wrote later, "he still had high hopes for the Revolution: not to abandon the besieged island, he adapted himself to its miserable life with a tranquil and ironic understatement. One needed to go beyond the layers of his reserve and humor to understand how hard it must have been for a man like him, with his graceful physical appearance and renal colic, the experience of joining the 'volunteer brigades' sent to *la zafra* in order to increase sugar production." But Casey had a moral standard unlike those around him, which left Calvino impressed. Everyone made use of the black market to satisfy basic needs, but not Casey. He ate only what the official food ration allowed, and his clothing was reduced to a pair of rotten pants. "That man," Calvino further remarked, "so friendly and courteous, who had opted for Cuba because it was his mother's country, but could have equally chosen his original *yanqui* citizenship, lived the Revolution as a moral experience, both individually and collectively, stuck to his endurance, never asking for benefits or having wrong illusions." And yet Casey described Cuba's "new life" to Calvino as "overcast with thunder."

And his Italian friend was impressed—so impressed that at his return to Rome he commissioned the Italian translation of *El regreso,* which Einaudi published in 1966. Did Calvino, himself part Cuban, understand that Casey wouldn't last long on the island? Assuredly, for *Il ritorno* eventually persuaded Casey to return to Rome. Havana had a future, but not for him. His circle of friends was already ostracized and, what's worse, his sexual preferences obviously turned him into a pariah.

Casey's sexuality might have been nonbelligerent, but it certainly wasn't tenuous. He was open about it and discussed it, in sonorous privacy, with friends like Piñera, Severo Sarduy, and José Lezama Lima. Cabrera Infante tells a revealing episode. One day while walking the Havana streets that join the Parque Central to the Plaza de Alvear, Casey, Cabrera Infante, and Cabrera's wife Miriam Gómez pass along the Asturian Center, with its iron grilled and paving stones. Inside is a magnificent staircase: "'Do you see that staircase?' asks Calvert, obliging us to look and see once more the familiar steps of the palace, all marble, wide above and opening up even wider below, with balustrades that become stony volutes at its end, coruscating conches." Casey says:

> OK, I have to make a confession to you. More a confidence, really. . . . The desire, the dream of my life is to go down that staircase. . . . But I want to go down it wearing a flowing crinoline, laced and low-cut, my shoulders bare, my breasts bursting out all over. The sleeves will have to be short to show off my perfect arms. On my long beautiful neck a pearl necklace catches the light, and I wear ruby ear-studs like a drop of blood on my lobe. Also, perhaps a diadem, if it is not very burdensome, of precious stones. My sleek blond hair will fall in romantic locks on my naked shoulders. Have I already told you that my shoulders are naked? You'll see my round shoulders and my splendid back. I would be made up to perfection: arched brows, violet eyes, red garnet lips and touches of rouge, very light, a highlight and nothing more, since my complexion will be translucid. Then decked out like that, I will go down the staircase, step by step, slowly, like a queen, all the lights on my descent. . . . What do you think?"

And what do *we* think? Casey's transvestite fantasies had doom written all over them. He tried all sorts of subterfuges, even marriage, but to no avail, for sooner rather than later, the regime ostracized him. His homosexuality, along with his political disenchantment, pushed him to the limit. Unlike others, he was lucky for, although out of public favor, at no point was he ever imprisoned, as other gays were, nor was he sent to a labor camp designed for *los indeseables.* Exile was Casey's only option and to exile he went. By then most of his oeuvre had been written, including the various stories, "In Partenza" and "Polonaise Brillante," for instance, dealing tacitly—and tactfully—with gays under repressive political systems. *Un cobarde,* a coward? Perhaps, but so were Boris Pasternak and Isaac Babel. Still, in an age such as ours, obsessed with difference, we should be careful not to overinflate Casey's gay identity. He is unlike Reinaldo Arenas in his "civilized" quietness. And even Lezama Lima's erotic totemism seems too explosive for Casey. No, his style was subdued, closer to Piñera's than to anyone else's. His sexual ambivalence (he had gay and straight love affairs) manifests itself in the ubiquitous theme of sexual disenchantment that permeates his work. Carnal encounters are forced on characters, who invariably end up dissatisfied. What is preferable, Casey seems to suggest in stories like "Goodbye . . . and Thanks for Everything," is the creation of an imaginary lover, the best means of escape through love. Fantasy, in short, is the only hope, even the sort of vampire-like fantasy in "Piazza Margana."

Imaginary lovers, imaginary homelands. . . . Once in exile, Casey's artistic spark greatly diminished. A state of paranoia overwhelmed him. He feared *El líder máximo.* He was convinced Cuba's secret police was about to capture him. When the translator and editor J. M. Cohen invited him to be part of an anthology published by Penguin in England called *Writers of Fidel's Cuba,* he declined unless the title were changed. His overall objective was to keep as low a profile as possible—or even lower. The truth is that he wanted to vanish altoge-ther, to cease being Calvert Casey, to be reborn under another identity. As a result, not only did he stop writing for periodicals but he almost ordered Seix Barral not to publish the Spanish editions of *El regreso* and *Notas de un simulador,* which were under contract, for fear of attracting too much attention. And so he became a ghost, a Cold War monstrosity, victimized by the general state of fear that made the life of Cuban exiles in Europe utterly unbearable. He traveled to places like New Delhi, Czechoslovakia, London; he used Krakow as the setting of "Polonaise Brillante"; he met Gianni, an Italian gigolo who became his raison d'être. What he never stopped was his enormous outpouring of correspondence to friends (Cabrera Infante, Arrufat, Piñera), some of which has begun appearing in Cuba and elsewhere but still awaits serious consideration. Typically, in a June 24, 1967 letter to Arrufat, Casey describes the terrible nostalgia that invades him in his exile from Cuba, but he also celebrates Rome as the sole medicine that can cure his longing. He applauds his addressee's completion of a novel and talks about a translation he has just completed of H. P. Lovecraft, "who kept me sleepless in Geneva out of sheer terror," he writes. After two or three lines, he adds:

> I reread this letter. With its fury and apocalypses and its essential incomprehension [one could say it is] the letter of a defeated man. I assure you it isn't. While translating Lovecraft (who can be a horrible writer) I had this vision of human life: we are bubbles that suddenly puff, but if we make puff or paff when we vanish it really doesn't matter, and if we don't vanish it also doesn't matter. . . . Will we see each other again? In fact, we have never ceased to see each other, and if we accept that matter is eternal then we were always one, and if going a bit further you can tolerate my pantheism . . . you will understand that we are one and the same, that any separation or difference is only a form of illusion."

This correspondence is all about death, but then again, so is his entire oeuvre. Death is always on the way, zigzagging his characters—death and its double, the enervating heaviness of life. What is the capacity to die, Casey's idol, José Martí, once claimed in Mexico, but the capacity to organize? In "Potosí," anthologized in *Nuevos cuentistas cubanos,* for instance, designed as a tale of *lo fantástico* with its surprise ending and set in a cemetery, the unnamed narrator wanders around reading inscriptions on tombs—in Chinese, Spanish, and Hebrew. (What the narrator calls Poles in the story are really Jews, and thus Polish is Hebrew.) And in "The Sun" he records the reaction of six characters to a nuclear holocaust two hours and fifteen minutes before the hydrogen bomb is set off.

All this makes Casey Kafkaesque. He shows an affinity for prostitutes and the indigent, as if only in the underworld, the realm of the wicked, could he find his calling. His vision entails an inescapable feeling of alienation, of remoteness that is very much the product of modernity and came to him as a result of his peripatetic journeying, for in essence Casey was nothing but a loose cannon. Curiously, *Memorias de una isla* includes essays on both Martí and Kafka: In Martí, an icon in Castro's regime, Casey cherished the romantic hero obsessed with death, his own and the abstract nothingness of Kierkegaard; and in Kafka, denounced as "an abomination" by Soviet Communism, he also sees his own reflection: an artist of the unreal and nightmarish, isolated from society, alone and lonely. Casey oscillated between the two: He glorified Martí's political commitment but knew deep inside that he himself was anything but romantic, and he treasured Kafka as a symbol of modern pain and wrote about necrophilia, which in his stories goes hand in hand with occultism. One of his most memorable literary performances, and a favorite of mine, is "The Visitors," often ranked by critics among the best Cuban stories ever written. As is usual, we enter a universe of aunts and relatives linked to one another not solely by blood but by inexplicable forces, but we see it through the eyes of a lonely young man. The link between this world and the next is explored through a series of spiritualistic sessions in which the dead punish the living and vice versa. This is a tale of longing and fear, though not a horror story. What is life if not a punishment for sins we are irremediably forced to perform?

During his last couple of years, Casey befriended new people and reencountered old acquaintances: the philosopher María Zambrano and the critic Vicente Molina Foix of Spain, Sarduy in France, Cabrera Infante in England, Calvino in Italy. But in spite of himself, he was truly a defeated man. Mysticism had been an alternative. Sarduy saw his name inscribed in the *Tibetan Book of the Dead*. His nervous suffering and itinerant existential jogging map his slow disintegration. Was he too fragile? Was modernity too heavy a burden on him? When did his character give in to the cruelty of everyday life? What is unquestionable is that a tepid depression kept him *in partenza*. Altogether, this last phase looks like a descent, but Zambrano preferred to describe it as an elevation—an ascent to symbolism. Obscurity and pain surrounded Casey as he began to emanate a halo of light. After a fervent romance, Gianni abandoned him. Love was gone, and so was meaning. Already in the Havana of the mid-1960s, he had talked to people about suicide. "Only through suffering," he told Arrufat, "does our life acquire its true meaning." But how much suffering can a pallid renegade artist handle? In the final count, Casey did have a bitter doom, but he also had his rewards. Not many wandering authors have been able to relocate themselves in another habitat, geographical and verbal, and in the end awake such stubborn admiration among their peers. Not many have inspired in their land of choice magnetic poems such as the following one by José Triana, written in 1969 at the news of Casey's death, of which this is John H. R. Polt's translation:

Like smoke he comes toward you, like
a buzzing will-o'-the-wisp
that runs you over and rips you up.
What arms and legs and wings!
You see him slipping along, more like a sleepwalker
or disoriented perhaps by the shadows,
through crickets jubilant in their madness.
He's probably coming from Istanbul,
from some solitary wrung-out river;
though they say that by Saracen hands,
back in the age of Titus, he perished.
You can make him out among the swallows
with his tenacious lips and shoes.
A monk would send you messages from him
when spring was dreaming wildly
of charcoal, shouts, and salamanders.
In your own adolescent dreams you may
have had an inkling of his biting eyes,
and more than once on dirty steps you thought
you saw him fornicating, drunk.
Someone said they'd seen him in some tribe
choking the autumn's arrows
and that the Sultan of Persia had retained him
among the dwarf attendants of his harem.

We need not speak his name, and we do need to.
What's left of him is still about,
and all disasters find their way into the cabala.
Dawn shifts the shadows, memories
are little drops and stones that importune
the vast house of the abyss.

Ah, falling shadows, falling shadows!
Beneath the water you can see his body.

# GABRIEL GARCÍA MÁRQUEZ

## The Master of Aracataca

*The invention of a nation in a phrase . . .*
> —Wallace Stevens

*For God's sake!—quick!—quick! put me to sleep—or, quick!—*
*waken me!—quick!—I say to you that I am dead!*
> —Edgar Allan Poe

Honor to whom honor is due: Gabriel García Márquez, whose labyrinthine imagination has enchanted millions worldwide since 1967, when his masterpiece *One Hundred Years of Solitude* was first published in Buenos Aires, has reinvented Latin America. Macondo, his fictional coastal town in the Caribbean, has become such a landmark—its geography and inhabitants constantly invoked by teachers, politicians, and tourist agents—that it is hard to believe it is a sheer fabrication.

What makes this south-of-the-border Yoknapatawpha irresistible is the idiosyncracy of its inhabitants, who often defy the rules and principles of Western civilization. As V. S. Pritchett once argued, the Colombian novelist "is a master of a spoken prose that passes unmoved from scenes of animal disgust and horror to the lyrical evocation, opening up vistas of imagined or real sights which may be gentle or barbarous." A parade of both gentleness and barbarity,

First published in *Michigan Quarterly* XXXIV, 2 (Spring 1995). Reprinted in *Art and Anger: Essays on Politics and the Imagination* (Albuquerque, NM: University of New Mexico Press, 1996).

Macondo makes beauty of chaos. García Márquez's fictional topos makes Latin America's ancient battle between the forces of progress and those of regression, between civilization and anarchy, look like a mere theatrical prop—an adjuvant to art.

John Updike put it simply: García Márquez dreams perfect dreams for us. But not always, we must qualify—in fact, quite rarely. For the radiant glare of his finest work has obscured the dismal truth: García Márquez's literary career is curiously disappointing. Aside from his masterpiece, his writing often seems uneven, repetitive, obsessively overwritten, forced: cynical in ways even this master of the cycle never intended.

Perhaps it couldn't have been otherwise. So arrestingly powerful is his magnum opus that all beside it looks pallid. I shall never forget the suggestion of a celebrated Uruguayan colleague, who argued at a writer's conference that, after 1967, García Márquez's annus mirabilis, it would have been best had he mysteriously vanished, become prematurely posthumous. This was an unfair, strange, even villainous thought, no doubt, but one that spoke to the curiously monotonous nature of the Colombian's art.

Whatever the lapses of his pen, however, there can be no doubt as to his stature. Alongside Miguel de Cervantes, he is considered today the premier Hispanic writer, *Don Quixote of La Mancha* and *One Hundred Years of Solitude* being the most durable and widely read bestsellers in the Spanish-speaking world, with billions of copies in print and translations into every imaginable language. Who would have thought that this obscure journalist of *El Espectador* in Bogotá (a city he considers "the ugliest in the world"), an admirer of Graham Greene, Virginia Woolf, and William Faulkner, could end up traveling to Stockholm in 1982 to receive the Nobel Prize for Literature—and this on the basis of a single genealogical narrative?

Indeed, critics such as Irving Howe, Tzvetan Todorov, and Emir Rodríguez Monegal claim García Márquez has helped renew the novel as a literary genre. And so he has. After the earlier legacy of the high modernists had almost reduced the form to a philosophical battlefield where, it sometimes seemed, only pessimistic insights were worth writing about, he has imbued prose fiction with a sense of wonder and joy that is both critically and popularly acclaimed around the world. John Leonard believes you emerge from the Colombian's marvelous universe "as if from a dream, the mind on fire. A dark, ageless figure at the hearth, part historian, part haruspex, in a voice by turns angelic and maniacal, first lulls to sleep your grip on a manageable reality, then locks you into legend and myth." Alfred Kazin compared his masterpiece to *Moby Dick* and Mario

Vargas Llosa calls his ex-friend "a total novelist"—able to encapsulate, through words, the complexities of our vast universe. It's hard to imagine a modern voice with more echoes.

But aside from the memorable Buendía saga—its intricate structure destined to remain a much-envied model of creative intelligence—will readers ever witness another achievement of this order? Can García Márquez ever stop imitating, even plagiarizing, himself as he has frequently done since the mid-1970s? Is the sense of déjà-vu conveyed by his post-1967 titles a normal reaction to the decades-long accumulation of his literary talent, the audience always sensing an inevitable return to the same set of metaphors, once fresh and now trite? Or is it that any writer at any given time, Shakespeare aside, is capable of handling only a limited number of ideas and images and that the Colombian has used and abused them all? Can *One Hundred Years of Solitude* leave room for another *coup de maître?*

It could be argued, of course, that García Márquez, more than many, has earned the right to repeat himself. Since *Leafstorm,* a novella he began at age nineteen (later collected with a handful of stories and printed in English in 1972), a dozen volumes by the Colombian have become available in the United States. (Spanish editions of his books include some twenty different titles, including volumes of journalistic pieces and screenplays.) Prolific as he is, his settings, from Macondo to a fictionalized Magdalena River, inhabit a region only about fifty miles square; very rarely does he place a story line elsewhere—say in Mexico, Chile, or Europe. His characters share provincial values in a universe where memory and modernity are antagonists; García Márquez specializes in making the so-called Third World look exotic and anachronistic, in touch with nature and its own roots. His exuberant, grandiloquent style, however, reveals a writer who spends his life creating one sublime book—a book of books whose pages reflect all things at all times, the sort of conceit to which Walt Whitman was devoted.

What's most puzzling, to my mind at least, is that, in spite of his dazzling international esteem, García Márquez remains a literary subject in search of a biographer. While discussions of his work exist in profusion, his intellectual odyssey remains in shadow, as does his carefully guarded private life. We don't even know for sure in what year he was born. In 1971 Vargas Llosa published an ambitious and voluminous literary study of him, *History of a Deicide,* the first seventy pages of which gave the most accurate profile of García Márquez up to that time; but political differences between the Peruvian and the Colombian kept the volume out of print and unavailable, and today the document seems hopelessly dated. In 1983, a volume of conversations with his long-time friend Plinio Apuleyo Mendoza, shedding light on his intellectual anxieties, came out in England. Otherwise, what little is known about this man remains scattered in interviews (with William Kennedy, with Ernesto González Bermejo, with Harley D. Oberhelman, and with some thirty others) and reviews in literary journals and yellowing newspaper pages.

To complicate matters further, García Márquez, a sly humorist, often enjoys deceiving interviewers by revamping his own life story, giving out confusing information and spinning anecdotes and gossip to evade answers. Unfortunately, nothing remotely resembling a true literary biography, à la Leon Edel's *Henry James* or Carlos Baker's *Ernest Hemingway,* is available, while only a few scholarly volumes on the writer's life and work have been published by scholarly imprints, including essay collections put out by the University of Texas Press and G. K. Hall. Thanks to the Colombian's loquacious tendency to embellish the past, even the circumstances surrounding the composition of *One Hundred Years of Solitude* remain shrouded by myth. Ever since 1967, it would seem, García Márquez has been busy fabricating his own eternity. A biographer is needed to bring perspective to his story, at once to render his aspired heroism in human scale and to render his routine existence in the form of narrative art. For the biographer's craft, at its best, is one that at once reduces and magnifies its subject, discovering the ordinariness within the art, but also making art of that very ordinariness.

A serious consideration of García Márquez's ups and downs would probably divide his years into five parts. The first part, 1928–1954, includes his birth and childhood years in Aracataca, his adolescence in Bogotá, his early stories, his years in Cartagena as a law student and journalist, and his writing for Bogota's newspaper *El Espectador.* The second part, 1955–1966, takes us from his first published novel, *Leafstorm*—encompassing the influences of Joseph Conrad, Faulkner, Hemingway, Graham Greene, and John Dos Passos on his work; Colombia's political upheaval in the mid-1950s; and his travels to Paris and marriage to Mercedes Barcha—to the publication of his celebrated novella *No One Writes to the Colonel.* The third part, 1967–1972, includes the origin, impact, and contribution of García Márquez's magnum opus, *One Hundred Years of Solitude;* the writer's friendship with famous Latin American intellectuals like Julio Cortázar, Alvaro Mutis, Mario Vargas Llosa, and Carlos Fuentes; his permanent residence in Mexico City and Cuba;

and his increasing international stardom. The fourth part, 1973–1982, spans the years between his stunning success and his reception of the Nobel Prize for Literature, just after the publication of *Chronicle of a Death Foretold*. And the fifth part, from 1983 onward, begins with García Márquez's second major work, *Love in the Time of Cholera*, and includes his mature political views and friendship with Fidel Castro, his semibiographical account of Simón Bolívar's last days in *The General in His Labyrinth*, his fight against cancer, the shaping of his "European" short stories in the collection *Strange Pilgrims*, his physical and creative decline, and his own attempt to write an all-encompassing memoir.

Yet what the neatness of this or any other schematism leaves out are the ambiguities that attend the pivotal events of his life, especially his formative years and the period in which he wrote *One Hundred Years of Solitude*. So I want to indicate, however sketchily, the difficulties of examining the intricate relation between his life and craft, if only to help point the way toward the route future biographers might follow.

The very first mystery to address is his elusive date of origin. According to some accounts, Gabriel García Márquez—or simply Gabo, as his friends like to call him—was born on March 6, 1928, in Aracataca, a small forgotten town on Colombia's Caribbean coast, but a lack of official documents makes it hard to confirm this information. The writer himself claims he is not sure of the precise birth year, and his father, Gabriel Eligio García, known as Dr. García by friends and acquaintances, maintains that it was 1927, before a famous banana workers' strike that agitated the entire region. What is certain is that he came to this world a couple of decades after his country, once part of a region called New Granada, which included Panama and most of Venezuela, had undergone the far-reaching and thoroughly exhaustive War of a Thousand Days (1899–1902), which resulted in the deaths of more than 100,000 people.

He was an opinionated, intelligent, highly imaginative boy. Legends and myths, ubiquitous in his childhood, are the stuff Latin America's collective past is made of, a region where History is malleable—always adjusted to the needs of the regime in power. During García Márquez's early years, numerous stories about brave army men still circulated, including one about the liberal Colonel Rafael Uribe Uribe—a model for Aureliano Buendía, one of the main protagonists of *One Hundred Years of Solitude*—who had lost a total of thirty-six battles and still remained quite popular. The colonel's pair of identical last names recalls the endogamous marriages that plague the Buendías chronology, where cousins marry each other and have children with pig tails. Indeed, what García Márquez did was to transmute the fictions that surrounded him into literature: His originality is based on the artful redeployment of the flamboyant creations that inhabit Hispanic America's popular imagination. Everything he saw and heard was eventually recorded in his early literary works, given its most crystalline shape in his 1967 masterpiece, and then revamped in subsequent works.

Throughout the nineteenth century, Colombia, which became a republic in 1886, has been filled with political unrest; partisan division along conservative-centrist and liberal-federalist lines would not infrequently erupt into civil war. After the War of a Thousand Days, when the conservatives emerged victorious, the regime of General Rafael Reyes (1904–1910) ushered in a boom of banana plantations along the Magdalena River, the place where *The General in His Labyrinth* and other titles are set. Many foreign companies settled down in the region, including the United Fruit Company, which had three thousand employees in 1908, more than a fourth of the whole banana work force.

Flush with newfound prosperity, Aracataca was a place where, it was remarked, prostitutes danced *cumbias* at the side of arrogant tycoons. "With the banana boom," the writer would later recollect, "people from all over the world began to arrive at Aracataca and it was very strange because in this little town in Colombia's Atlantic coast, for a moment all languages were spoken." A couple of decades later, with the growth and expansion of organized unions from Mexico to Argentina, and after the creation of Colombia's Socialist Revolutionary Party, a bloody massacre took place in Ciénaga. The army used machine guns to disperse striking banana laborers near a train station. Hundreds died, perhaps thousands. The event was retold through stories and folksongs time and again while García Márquez was still young. It took hold in his memory and would eventually make for a powerful scene in *One Hundred Years of Solitude:* scores of bodies of United Fruit toilers lie motionless on the battlefield after an unsuccessful strike and are then piled in a train. The next day, nobody in Macondo acknowledges the tragedy and many even insist that it never happened.

Dr. García, the novelist's father, had a total of fifteen children, three the result of extramarital affairs. One of these three, a daughter, was raised by his wife, Luisa Santiaga Márquez Iguarán, much in the way Ursula Iguarán, the matron at the heart of Macondo, takes upon herself the raising of the vast bastard descendents of Colonel Aureliano Buendía. Gabriel was oldest of the legitimate branch, most of whom share his left-wing politics, although a few of his siblings, like their dad, are *gordos,* or conservatives. As García Márquez has said in public statements, *Love in the Time of Cholera,* his 1986 romance in which an old couple reunites after persistent passion and decades of separation, is based on his parents' relationship. Before getting married, Dr. García was a telegrapher. (Indeed, telegraphs and other forms of pre–World War II wire communication are ubiquitous in his son's oeuvre.) After strong opposition from Luisa Santiaga's family—her parents, probably the most aristocratic couple in Aracataca, were first cousins—they married, and Dr. García and his wife left their then only son Gabriel to the care of the child's paternal grandparents because the father wanted to improve his economic situation. The newlywed couple lived in numerous towns throughout the Caribbean coast. Dr. García eventually received a degree in homeopathic medicine in Barranquilla. Afterward, while studying for four years at the medical school of the Universidad de Cartagena, he became a pharmacist.

After ten years of separation, Gabriel was reunited with his parents, and during 1939–1950, the family, already numerous, settled in Sucre, a port town in Bolívar Province, a place where several of his novels would be set, including *No One Writes to the Colonel.* But soon they had to move again because another doctor had settled in the same town and taken most of Dr. García's clientele. Around 1951 (some say it was 1950), the family moved to Cartagena, where the father, in spite of his unfinished course in clinical medicine, finally received an M.D. and maintained his own practice for decades. Luisa Santiaga, the novelist's mother, a spirited, strong-willed woman with a liberal upbringing—her father, Nicolás Márquez Iguarán, an army man, fought on General Rafael Uribe Uribe's side—is said to have been quite intuitive. She won the lottery several times based on information she claimed to have gotten in dreams.

In interviews and autobiographical pieces, García Márquez has said that his first eight years of life were the most crucial and memorable. At twelve months of age, when his parents left Aracataca, he went to live in his grandparents' home, a place, he says, full of ghosts. In Luis Harss's volume of narrative portraits *Into the Mainstream,* the novelist describes his new tutors as superstitious and impressionable people.

> In every corner [of the house] there were skeletons and memories, and after six in the evening you didn't dare leave your room. It was a world of fantastic terror [in which] there were coded conversations. . . . There was an empty room where Aunt Petra had died. And another one where Uncle

Lázaro passed away. Thus, at night you couldn't walk because there were more people dead than alive. I remember [an] episode well, one that captures the atmosphere of the house. I had an aunt. . . . She was very active: she was doing something else at home all the time and one day she sat down to sew a shroud. I then asked her: "Why are you sewing a shroud?" "Because I'm going to die, my boy," she answered. When she finished sewing her shroud, she lay down and died.

In 1969, a Bogotá journalist who traveled to Aracataca discovered that García Márquez's childhood house was being devoured by ants and covered with dust. Just like the Buendiá mansion, and, for that matter, all of Macondo, it was condemned to perish.

Death, a common, banal fact in Latin America, was a preoccupation of the novelist. Aunt Petra's end and others sharply more violent color his work: Colonels agonizing before firing squads, corpses found in a huge palace, a killing solved by a private eye. Memory, in García Márquez's view, is synonymous with redemption: To remember is to overcome, to defeat the forces of evil. Lust, illusion, corruption, and the recalcitrance of barbarism are also at the core of his work. These themes, openly or otherwise, are frequently intertwined with another pressing subject: a sharp critique of institutionalized religion. His attack on the Catholic Church is not surprising when one considers the fact that García Márquez completed primary and high school in a private Jesuit institution in Zipaquirá, near Bogotá, a place where his mother's liberal views and his own frequently clashed with institutional dogmas. Priests and clerical acolytes are often portrayed by him as distant, corrupt, ill-informed, or simply lazy. In the story "Tuesday's Siesta," a woman and her daughter arrive in a small town to pay last respects to Carlos Centeno, the woman's only son, who became a thief in order to support the family. The response she gets from the local priest is not only cold but offensive: He refuses to help her; when he finally agrees to give her the keys to the cemetery, it is only after asking her for charity.

Such a jaundiced view of matters ecclesiastical is, of course, unsurprising from a leftist. And yet García Márquez, it should be made clear, does not attack God or human spirituality; his target is the clerical hierarchy. In his universe the Almighty is alive and well and, one senses, possessed of literary talents. After all, couldn't *One Hundred Years of Solitude* be read as a daring rewriting of the Bible? Floods, prophesies, sin and condemnation, epic wars and the abuse of power, hero worship and romance—the elements are all there, and so are the theological and teleological undertones. Both the Bible and the Colombian's masterpiece intertwine the individual and the collective in a concrete, urgent fashion with images that seem tangible, real.

Indeed, García Márquez's imagination, since early on, has been graphic: Scenes, however surrealistic, always have an incredible immediacy. This fact is important when one considers García Márquez's life-long passion for the movies. He is founder and executive director of Cuba's Film Institute in Havana, to which he often donates the profits of his films. His interest in the silver screen dates back to when he worked for Mexico's J. Walter Thompson advertising agency. He wrote commercials and was enchanted with the filmmaking process. "To write for the movies," the Colombian once reflected, "one needs great humility. That distinguishes it from the literary endeavor. While the novelist sitting at the typewriter is totally free and in control, the screenwriter is only a piece in a complex machinery and thus the target of contradictory special interests." Aside from his youthful work as a film reviewer for newspapers in Barranquilla and Bogotá, his numerous film projects began when he collaborated with Carlos Fuentes and others in adapting Juan Rulfo's *El gallo de oro*, and include such titles as *Time to Die*, directed by Arturo Ripstein; *Patty My Love*; Alberto Isaac's *No Thieves in This Town*; and Rulfo's *Pedro Páramo*. Later he would also shape the screenplays of *Difficult Loves*, a series made for Spanish TV, as well as *Chronicle of a Death Foretold* and *Eréndira*. Nor can I forbear mention of *Clandestine in Chile: The Adventures of Miguel Littín*, a journalistic piece on his friend the filmmaker Littín and his secretive journey to Augusto Pinochet's Chile in the mid-1980s. (After the downfall of Salvador Allende, García Márquez publicly swore he would not write again until Pinochet gave up power. As it turns out, the dictator had more endurance than the author.)

Many of his adaptations and screenplays originated in short stories and vice versa; a few, in prose form, are collected in *Strange Pilgrims*, conceived as "mere entertainments," to use Graham Greene's fashionable term, and unified by the common theme of investigating the lives of Latin Americans transplanted to Europe—the New World inhabiting the Old. One of them is "The Summer of Miss Forbes," directed by Jaime Humberto Hermosillo, about a German nanny who, in taking care of a pair of childern in Sicily, kills herself in a apocalyptic act of unresolved sexual passion; another is "I Only Came to Use the Phone," about a young wife mistaken as a lunatic and imprisoned in a psychiatric home.

But García Márquez's vivid imagination reaches beyond the screen. Consider the extraordinary metafictional imagery in *One Hundred Years of Solitude*. In the last few pages, Aureliano Babilonia, the last in the Buendía lineage, whose first member is found tied to a tree and whose last is eaten by ants, discovers the lost manuscripts of the gypsy Melquíades. Like *Hamlet*'s play-within-a-play and Cervantes's novel-within-a-novel, García Márquez introduces a text that can be read "as if it had been written in Spanish," in which the very novel the reader holds in hand is included. What follows is Gregory Rabassa's superb translation:

It was the history of the family, written by Melquíades, down to the most trivial details, one hundred years ahead of time. He had written it in Sanskrit, which was his mother tongue, and he had encoded the even lines in the private cipher of the Emperor Augustus and the odd ones in the Lacedemonian military code. The final protection, which Aureliano had begun to glimpse when he let himself be confused by the love of Amaranta Ursula, was based on the fact that Melquíalades had not put events in the order of man's conventional time, but had concentrated a century of daily episodes in such a way that they coexisted in one instant.

It's a passage that recalls Borges's tale "The Aleph," in which the Argentine narrator discovers, hidden in a Buenos Aires basement, a magical object capable of turning past, present, and future into one single unifying moment. But García Márquez's passage, although intertwining spiritual elements, also has a concrete, visual, cinematographic texture: the act of reading, the sudden discovery of death, the past as a bewitchment. Perhaps that's why García Márquez has stated he will never sell the movie rights to *One Hundred Years of Solitude,* for the novel is already a film. By contrast, Isabel Allende's 1982 bestselling genealogical novel *The House of the Spirits*—a novel that suspiciously resembles the Colombian's masterpiece and could almost be considered a trivialization of his trademark style—is, after a highly competitive auction, being directed by the Danish filmmaker Bille August, a concession to the imposing ways of mass culture.

Of course, one could argue that although *Don Quixote* has been adapted to the screen time and again, its sheer literary force remains intact, as enchanting as when first written half a millennium ago. Could Anthony Hopkins play the role of Aureliano Buendía and Vanessa Redgrave that of Ursula Iguarán on location somewhere in the Amazon? Can actual vistas of the jungle do justice to García Márquez's colorful, baroque style? Most devoted fans hope it will never happen, but sooner or later they are likely to be betrayed. It won't matter, though. In keeping with the metaphysical transmutation any literary classic undergoes with time, the book's mesmerizing biblical images are somehow already no longer the property of the author but of language and tradition.

To return to his formative years, García Márquez was still twenty years old in 1948 when another tragic clash between conservative and liberal parties took place, again costing hundreds of thousands of lives. On April 9, Jorge Eliécer Gaitán, ex-mayor of Bogotá and the Liberal Party's populist presidential candidate, who had defended the workers in the strike of 1928, was assassinated. The event, known as *el bogotazo,* inaugurated a decade-long period generally referred to by Colombians as *la violencia,* chaos and disorder prevailing in rural areas. The year before, García Márquez had enrolled as a law student at the National University, and it was around that time that he met Plinio Apuleyo Mendoza, a strong supporter of his talent, whom he would reencounter in Paris in the late 1950s. At age nineteen, García Márquez wrote, in the fashion of Maupassant's "Le Horla," his first short story, to my knowledge still untranslated into English, "La ter- cera resignación" ("The Third Resignation"), published in *El Espectador.* The violence that surrounded him at the time left a pro- found scar. The National University was temporarily closed, and he had to move to Cartagena, where his family had resettled. He entered the local university and, in order to support himself, began his career as a journalist in *El Universal.*

Not much else is known about his beginnings, making the job of a biographer all the more urgent: to dig—to recover, uncover, and discover; to trace lost steps on the map of the subject's existence. Why did García Márquez select law as a profession? Why not a medi- cal career, like the novelist's father, Dr. García? (The doctors in his plots are, in the Flaubertian manner, always representatives of sci- ence and modernity.) The relationship between oral storytelling and literature is at the core of his craft. When did he decide to sit down and write? Was he politically active as a student? Did he per- ceive literature as an instrument to educate and enlighten the masses and to further a process of social revaluation and recon- struction? (This view of literature's purpose is in fashion at the time and was later debated by Jean-Paul Sartre and Albert Camus in a controversy with far-reaching effects in Latin America during the late 1950s and early 1960s.) Did he have any direct confrontations with the government and the armed forces, a rite of passage deci- sive for most intellectuals in the region?

What is sure is that around 1948 he began reading Faulkner, a turning point in his career. Literature would become his sole passion. His goal now was to build an architecturally perfect, fictional universe that most of his ghosts and fears could inhabit, a mirror of the reality that daily overwhelmed him. Faulkner immediately became his secret personal tutor. For Faulkner had, in one novel after another, devoted all his creative energy to investigating the historical wounds of the Deep South—and those wounds are not unlike Latin America's: the acceptance of collective defeat and the adjustment to external colonizing forces and the phantoms of history. At the same time, Faulkner's fictional constellation seemed autonomous and self-sufficient. Besides, his introspective, experimental, Rashomon-like style appealed greatly to the Colombian fabulist.

He started by reading *A Rose for Emily,* which had recently been published in a poor Spanish translation. (García Márquez's English is weak.) Based on a July 1949 newspaper review by the author, critics like Jacques Gilard and Raymond L. Williams claim it was the Colombian's first encounter with the southern U.S. writer, an interest that would evolve into a lifelong fascination. Today, out of saturation perhaps, the Colombian claims he is no longer able to read good old Faulkner. Still, the encounter with the Yoknapatawpha saga changed his view of literature forever. "When I first read [him]," he would later say, "I thought: I must become a writer." A similar Faulknerian impact, by the way, transformed the Uruguayan Juan Carlos Onetti and the Peruvian Vargas Llosa, to name only a few Latin Americans with a Faulkernian drive. More than a decade later, around 1961, García Márquez, married and with a son (he has two, one of them a writer in his own right), traveled by bus from New York to Mexico through the Deep South "in homage to Faulkner." Segregation reigned, and the family encountered signs that read "No Dogs and Mexicans Allowed" and were frequently not allowed to stay at hotels.

Two other U.S. authors commanded an overwhelming influence across the Rio Grande in the 1950s: Hemingway and John Dos Passos. With respect to the latter, one can point to García Márquez's interest in cruel realism; but it was the former who truly influenced him by teaching precision, objectivity, and directness in style. Literature and journalism, he understood, were brothers. Indeed, as was the case with the author of *The Sun Also Rises,* the impact of the Colombian's journalistic writing on his future artistic development was enormous. He learned to write in short, clear sentences. But unlike Hemingway, who claimed journalism could kill a writer's career, García Márquez not only saw the trade as essential in the shaping of a novelist's style but also needed it as a source of income until book royalties began to come in, well into his forties.

In 1952 he began writing for *El Heraldo* in Barranquilla and became part of the so-called Barranquilla Group, a gathering of intellectuals who read and discussed Hemingway, Virginia Woolf, Faulkner, Erskine Caldwell, and Dos Passos. (The group included two aspiring writers who would eventually leave a mark on Colombian letters, although never with the impact of García Márquez: Alvaro Cepeda Samudio and Germán Vargas.) Already in his mid-twenties, García Márquez began to take himself seriously as a writer. He was constantly publishing short stories in newspapers and magazines, and even finished a first novel, *La casa*, which Buenos Aires's Losada, the prestigious imprint responsible for the works of the River Plate luminaries Borges and Adolfo Bioy Casares, rejected after one of its editors told García Márquez he had no talent as a writer and should devote himself to something else. The novel, known today as *La hojarasca*, has an unquestionably Faulknerian style: Its plot is told from three different viewpoints—that of a father, his daughter, and his grandchild—and circles around the funeral of a doctor who had been hated by everybody in town and who, at the end of his life, had become a recluse. As William Kennedy has argued, the protagonist's personality recalls Rev. Gail Hightower of *Light in August.*

It is an interesting fact about the world of letters into which García Márquez emerged that, with very few exceptions, Colombian literature was, and remains, largely undistinguished. When García Márquez was born, José Eustasio Rivera, author of the country's heretofore most famous work, *The Vortex*, was dying. Besides his, few names are worthy of notice: Jorge Isaac, author of the best-seller *María;* the *modernista* poet José Asunción Silva; the eccentric Porfirio Barba Jacob; Eduardo Caballero Calderón, author of *The Noble Savage;* and that's about all. Recently, however, another name has emerged: Alvaro Mutis, who, as it turns out, is a key figure in García Márquez's artistic progress. He invited García Márquez to return from Cartagena to Bogotá to write for *El Espectador,* and, after his acceptance, they became good friends. In the early 1960s, García Márquez sent Mutis, who was in a Mexican prison, two of his short stories, which his friend in turn showed to the journalist Elena Poniatowska. Later, after a few mishaps, she and Mutis managed to convince the Universidad Veracruzana Press to publish them, along-side other tales, as *Big Mama's Funerals,* for which the author got an advance of a thousand pesos. Published in 1962, the book's first printing of 2,000 copies took years to sell.

As a belated expression of deeply felt gratitude, García Márquez dedicated *The General in His Labyrinth* to Mutis, for having given "me the idea for writing this book." The novel, to my mind one of the writer's most sophisticated and accomplished, studies the last few days of Simón Bolívar, who, on December 10, 1930, soon after he dictated his last will and testament and a physician had insisted that he confess and receive the sacraments, said: "What does this mean? . . . Can I be so ill that you talk to me of wills and confessions? . . . How will I ever get out of this labyrinth!" In the section "My Thanks," García Márquez writes:

> For years I listened to Alvaro Mutis discussing his plan to write about Simón Bolívar's final voyagealong the Magdalena River. When he published "El último rostro" ["The Last Face"], a fragment of the projected book, the story seemed so ripe, and its style and tone so polished, that I expected to read it in its complete form very soon afterwards. Nevertheless, two years later I had the impression that he had regarded it to oblivion, as so many writers do with our best-loved dreams, and only then did I dare ask for his permission to write it myself. It was a direct hit after a ten-year ambush.

The Bolívar novel, rather poorly received in the United States because of its abundance of historical data and a period setting that many Anglo-Saxons found unappealing, created a huge controversy in South America. There Venezuelan and Colombian politicians attacked it as "profane," claiming García Márquez was defaming the larger-than-life reputation of a historical figure who, during the nineteenth century, struggled to unite the vast Hispanic world. But Mutis, the author's ideal reader, is known to be very fond of the book. That alone made García Márquez happy.

While working for *El Espectador,* García Márquez wrote a series of fourteen semijournalistic pieces, composed in the first-person voice of a twenty-two-year-old mariner, that chronicled the episode of a shipwreck in which eight crew members were left alone at sea. Only one, Luis Alejandro Velasco, survived, and he became a national hero. According to the official version, bad weather had caused the tragedy, but when assigned to investigate the details, the novelist discovered the boat was carrying *contrabando*—smuggled items: television sets, refrigerators, and laundry machines brought from the United States. Dictator Rojas Pinilla had allowed only progovernment newspapers to cover the event. Although the Velasco celebration had diminished by the time García Márquez published his articles, they became a public sensation and an embarrassment to the government in power. A Barcelona publishing house reprinted the serial in book form in 1970 as *The Story of a Shipwrecked Sailor,* a volume that, had readers never seen the Colombian's name on the cover, would frankly have passed without pomp and glory as a forgettable and poorly structured report.

The year 1955 was among the most decisive in the novelist's life. When he was twenty-seven, a small Bogotá house, Ediciones Sipa, finally decided to publish his first novel under the title *La hojarasca.* Reports of the early critical and commercial reaction are ambiguous, and García Márquez has only added to the uncertainty. In an interview, he claimed it sold some 30,000 copies, but some sources, including Vargas Llosa in *History of a Deicide,* claim it elicited very small interest and passed largely unnoticed.

An indication of the book's poor reception was the writer's reaction: As often happens to South American first-time novelists, García Márquez felt depressed and swore never to write again. Ironically, this wasn't another of his histrionic gestures. His trust in literature actually diminished as he became increasingly conscious of his personal needs in the future: He would have to support himself and a family, and writing novels didn't seem like a money-making venture, at least not at the time. Fortunately, fate managed to stimulate him by other means. That same year he was awarded a prize by Bogotá's Association of Artists and Writers for his story "Un día después del Sábado" ("A Day after Saturday"), and while the amount of money he received was small, his name and photograph circulated in newspapers. To add to the excitement, his editor at *El Espectador* had earlier decided to send him to Geneva as a foreign correspondent. He would leave his native town for Europe, where the literary careers of those from south of the Rio Grande have always been forged.

Things in Colombia changed drastically the moment he left. The overall reach of *la violencia* was omnipresent, and soon the military regime of Gustavo Rojas Pinilla, a merciless *caudillo,* closed down *El Espectador.* The old battle between federalists and centralists took a high toll, and nobody was immune from the violence. García Márquez arrived in Europe excited to be an independent young man in a strange and glamorous place, and ready to seize the opportunity to perfect his craft as a novelist. But now, suddenly, he was left out in the cold. He had been staying at Hôtel de Flandre in the Latin Quarter, where he waited for a check from the newspaper to come in the mail. For obvious reasons, none arrived. In time he would owe the management some 123,000 francs. Since he was on good terms with the hotel administration, he was allowed to stay for a little while, in spite of some clients' complaints of his typing after midnight. He then managed to travel to Rome, where he participated as a student at the Centro Sperimentale di Cinematografia—where Manuel Puig would later enroll—and finally moved to Paris. The legends about his Parisian stay conform to the stereotype of the down-and-out litterateur: He had a hard time making ends meet, and in one instance was seen collecting empty bottles 'at garbage cans to exchange for extra centimes to buy food.

And yet the European years proved to be very fruitful, in part because he finished *No One Writes to the Colonel* and *In Evil Hour,* published, respectively, in Medellín by Aguirre Editor in 1961 and in Madrid by Talleres de Gráficas Luis Pérez the year after. These titles, together with *Big Mama's Funeral,* form a unified whole. "I tried to put in them everything I knew," he said later. But after a painful artistic struggle, he gave up the encyclopedic approach to narrative: "It was too much accumulation." He thus cut sections, expanded chapters, and turned ideas into short stories. (Robert Coover believes the conflict between "the realistic" and" the fantastic" is never adequately worked out in these works.) Away from Latin America, his imagination had begun to metamorphosize his past, his native culture, into the stuff of myth. Distance distorted the actual size and value of things, misforming them into pieces of a personal puzzle. Through literature, he could revisit the ghosts of his grandparents' home. He could re-create the violence he had witnessed by invoking plots where brave military soldiers are forgotten by their army peers. Years later, when a journalist asked him to summarize the region's idiosyncratic nature, he answered with the following tale set in a small rural town in Colombia: At around ten o'clock, two men parked a truck outside a boarding school and said, "We've come to pick up the furniture." No one knew if they were supposed to come, but the principal allowed them in, the furniture was placed in the truck, and the two men left. "Only later people found out they were thieves."

García Márquez returned to South America in 1956. He made a quick stop in Colombia to marry Mercedes Barcha, then moved to Caracas, Venezuela, where he worked for *Momentos* and *Elite.* Together with Apuleyo Mendoza, García Márquez traveled back and forth through Eastern Europe and the Soviet Union in 1957 and produced a report in ten installments, more anecdotal than political, for the magazines *Elite* in Venezuela and *Cromos* in Bogotá, under the general title of *Noventa días en la cortina de hierro* (*Ninety Days on Tour through the Eastern Block*). Among other places, he visited East Germany, Czechoslovakia, Poland, and Russia.

Upon his return, he went to London to learn English, then to Venezuela, and finally to Mexico. At thirty-one, he was enchanted by the Cuban Revolution and began working for Cuba's press agency, Prensa Latina, a job he performed for two years. He was stationed in New York to cover the United Nations General Assembly, but after a while his relationship with the news agency deteriorated and he quit. García Márquez's role in modern politics is evident in his left-wing views, his solid friendship with Fidel Castro, and his defense of Latin America. "I have firm political beliefs," he once told Luis Harss, "but my views of literature change with every digestion." In his Nobel acceptance speech to the Swedish Academy in 1982, he said: "Latin America neither wants, nor has any reason, to be a pawn without a will of its own; nor is it merely wishful thinking that its quest for independence and originality should become a Western aspiration." Often he has acted as intermediary between human rights commissions and the Havana regime, as in the celebrated Heberto Padilla affair, in which a Cuban poet, imprisoned for betraying his country's national security, was freed after many pleas from, among others, Susan Sontag and Robert Silver, editor of *The New York Review of Books,* thanks in part to García Márquez, who persuaded a reluctant Castro to let him go.

Some have criticized García Márquez for at once being a devoted Fidelista and having two mansions, one in Havana and the other in Mexico City, in the exclusive southern San Angel section. Don't his material circumstances contradict his ideological beliefs? García Márquez turns to another subject every time the question is asked. But this apparent tension between lifestyle and politics is prevalent among famous Latin American intellectuals of the 1970s: To act as the voice of people, to attack the government, to promulgate left-wing views has never required that one's daily domestic life be reduced to the bare essentials. It's an irony that becomes all the more evident among exiled scholars and writers who for decades have portrayed the United States as an imperialist aggressor but who, when the time comes to escape from a repressive regime, avail themselves of the safe haven offered by the U.S. academy: a comfortable salary at a college or university. García Márquez, in many ways, epitomitzes this outrageous behavior. While he never stayed at an American campus for a long period of time because of immigration problems with the Immigration and Naturalization Service, he is a symbol of lavish lifestyle and anachronistic Franciscan principles: the revolutionary struggle amid champagne glasses.

After his stay in New York, García Márquez settled in Mexico and was largely inactive as a writer, devoting himself exclusively to gestating Macondo in his own mind. His novella *In Evil Hour* had won an obscure prize, sponsored by Esso in Colombia. Through an ambassador, he was sent word that the award would be his if he agreed to eliminate a couple of "nasty" words: "prophylactic" and "masturbate." In reply, he agreed to censor only one, whichever the ambassador wished. The transcript was sent to Spain to be printed, and a copy editor, to make the style Iberian, changed the wording of his sentences. When García Márquez saw the final product, he was furious. In the Mexican edition of 1966 and the one he considered "official," he added an author's note stating that the text had been restored to its original form.

The mythical Macondo acquired its structure in the stories of *Big Mama's Funerals*. Critics mistakenly claim *No One Writes to the Colonel* and *In Evil Hour* take place in it, when, in fact, as George R. McMurray has shown, their setting is a town, probably Sucre, farther inland in the coastal region. In their exuberant *Dictionary of Imaginary Places*, Alberto Manguel and Gianni Guadalupi describe Macondo "as a Colombian village founded in ancient times by José Arcadio Buendía, whose boundless imagination always stretched farther than the inventiveness of nature." Its apex occurs between 1915 and 1918, during the height of the banana plantations. Toward the east, as Manguel and Guadalupi have mapped it, the town is protected by a high and forbidding range of hills and, toward the south, by marshes covered with a kind of vegetable soup. Toward the west the marshes give way to a large body of water in which cetaceans of delicate skin, with the face and torso of a woman, lure sailors with their firm and tempting breasts. To the north, many days' march away through a dangerous jungle, lies the sea. Among Macondo's most notable events is the unusual insomnia epidemic that strikes the entire population: The most terrible effect isn't the impossibility of sleep—because the body does not tire either—but the gradual loss of memory. When a sick person becomes accustomed to staying awake, memories of his childhood start to vanish, followed by names and concepts of things. With self-reflecting mirrors and all, the novel's self-reflecting ending is simply remarkable:

Macondo was already a fearful whirlwind of dust rubble being spun about by the wrath of the biblical hurricane when Aureliano shipped eleven pages so as not to lose time with facts he knew only too well, and he began to decipher the instant that he was living, deciphering it as he lived it, prophesying himself in the act of deciphering the last page of the parchments, as if he were looking into a speaking mirror. Then he skipped again to anticipate the predictions and ascertain the date and circumstances of his death. Before reaching the final line, however, he had already understood that he would never leave that room, for it was foreseen that the city of mirrors would be wiped out by the wind and exiled from the memory of men at the precise moment when Aureliano Babilonia would finish deciphering the parchments, and that everything written on them was unrepeatable since time immemorial and forever more, because race condemned to one hundred years of solitude did not have a second opportunity on earth.

The legend behind the final shaping of Macondo has come to be referred to, by García Márquez and others who know him, simply as "the miracle." It took place in 1965, on the road from Mexico City to Acapulco in the family's Opel. Suddenly, as the writer puts it, the entire first chapter appeared to him, and he immediately felt he was prepared to write the rest of the story. Afterward he told an Argentine friend that if he had had a tape recorder in the car, he would have dictated the chapter right then and there. Instead of continuing on to Acapulco, he decided to turn around and seclude himself completely for a year. He asked Mercedes, his wife, not to interrupt him for any reason, especially where bills were concerned, and indeed she protected him fully. When the novel was finished, the García Márquezes were $12,000 in debt; to tide themselves over, Mercedes had asked their friends for loans (according to Vargas Llosa, it was around $10,000). Soon rumors of the book's qualities began to circulate: Carlos Fuentes and Julio Cortázar, who had read pieces of the manuscript before it was finished, were so excited they praised it highly in articles and reviews. And so, by the time *One Hundred Years of Solitude* was published in May 1967 by Editorial Sudamericana, it ignited the literary world, and García Márquez, at thirty-nine, became an instant international celebrity. The first edition sold out in a few days, and the novel sold half a million copies in three and a half years, a huge sum for any Spanish book anywhere in the Hispanic world. He immediately began to receive honorary degrees and prizes: the Rómulo Gallegos award; the Prix du Meilleur Livre Etranger in France; the Italian Chianchiano Prize; the Neustadt Prize by the magazine *Book Abroad* (now *World Literature Today*); the National Book Award to Gregory Rabassa for the English translation; and, a bit more than a decade later, the Nobel Prize. (Five Latin Americans have now received it: before him, Gabriela Mistral, Pablo Neruda, and Miguel Angel Asturias; after, Octavio Paz.)

Does someone capable of creating a book of such caliber have a second such opportunity on earth? Having set the standard sky-high, he has written nothing since 1967 that seems fully satisfying. While some maintain that a bad García Márquez is extraordinary by other people's standards, it is clear that the Colombian has always been haunted by his masterpiece's overwhelming success. His method of writing has also changed over the decades. He can spend long seasons without putting a word on paper, and then, during creative periods, write eight to ten pages each day from sunrise to noon. His paragraphs are extremely polished, the opposite of André Breton's idea of automatic writing, which Jack Kerouac and the Beat Generation took to an extreme. The dialogue is infrequent but crisp and full of parables and metaphors. In the age of mechanical type-writers and liquid corrector, he claims to have rewritten *No One Writes to the Colonel* a total of nine times. "I had the impression I was writing it in French," he once said, as if after so many rewritings his native tongue had become alien to him, and pure technique ended up shaping the book. He took a similar approach with future books, until the late 1970s, when he bought a word processor. Considered by many his second best title—a distant second, though—*Love in the Time of Cholera* was published in 1985. It is a romance of sorts (according to Salman Rushdie, "a masterful revamping of the genre") encapsulating the affair of García Márquez's parents from their youth to their eighties. Written with the help of a computer, the book retains his typically labyrinthine paths of fantasy, but the texture seems a bit removed, less immediate than that in *One Hundred Years of Solitude.* The protagonists are Fermina Daza, who is married to Doctor Juvenal Urbino de la Calle, and Florentino Ariza, who has a crush on her that lasts, in one of the novelist's typical phrases, "fifty three years, seven months, and eleven days." Many biograph-ical elements are included: the telegraph, a Flaubertian doctor who functions as a voice of reason, a critique of religion, and an unre-lenting love beyond all odds.

A succession of repetitive, structurally overdone narratives has steadily issued from the Colombian's pen since 1967. Predictably, their reception nevertheless has been enthusiastic, as if anything produced by García Márquez, no matter the quality, is to be applauded. The truth is, his magnum opus had satisfied and engrossed so many readers that each new narrative became leg-endary even before it could reach the bookstores.

The novelist's lifelong interest in continental history is apparent in his 1975 experimental novel *Autumn of the Patriarch,* a favorite of such postcolonial critics as Edward Said but, to my mind, too allegorical, too boring. The book was also a disappointment to those expecting another installment of the Buendía saga. One of about a half a dozen Latin American narratives about dictators (others include Alejo Carpentier's *Reasons of State,* Augusto Roa Bastos's *I, the Supreme,* Tomás Eloy Martínez's *The Perón Nobel,* and Miguel Angel Asturias's *El Señor Presidente*), the novel deals with a tyrant's relentless desire to accumulate power and narrates his obsessive love affair with Manuela Sanchez, the status of "civil sanctity" given to his ailing mother, and his final demise. Already close to his hundredth birthday, he marries Nazareno Leticia and has a child with her, only to find mother and child assassinated, their bodies ripped apart by dogs at a public plaza. Contrary to common belief, García Márquez did not base the story and its protagonist solely on Gustuvo Rojas Pinilla and his military regime in Colombia but also on the Venezuelan *caudillo* Juan Vicente Gómez. "My intention," he once said, "was always to make a synthesis of all the Latin American dictators, but especially those from the Carribbean."

Another unbalanced text is *Chronicle of a Death Foretold,* published in 1981, shortly before the announcement of the Nobel Prize. Built as a detective story in reverse, it describes the assassination of Santiago Nasar, accused of deflowering Angela Vicario, who is hence unable to marry Bayardo San Román. Everybody in town knows Nasar will be killed, but nobody does a thing. The story is told from the point of view of a journalist, a chronicler who years later returns to the place to unveil the truth. As Raymond L. Williams has shown, the novella is based on real events reported by *El Día* in Bogotá in 1981:

> In the municipality of Sucre . . . the elders still remember with horror the rainy morning of January 22, 1951, in which a young man . . . Cayetano Gentile Chimento, twenty-two years old, medical student at the Javeriana University in Bogotá and heir of the town's largest fortune, fell butchered by machete, innocent victim of a confused duel of honor, and without knowing for sure why he was dying. Cayetano was killed by Víctor and Joaquín Chica Salas, whose sister Margarita, married the previous day with Miguel Reyes Palencia and returned to her family by her husband the same night of the marriage, accused Cayetano of being the author of the disgrace that had prevented her being a virgin at her marriage.

García Márquez re-creates the events by mixing sex and exoticism, and filtering it all through the surreal prism of his imagination. According to William H. Gass, the novel is not told but pieced together like a jigsaw. The result, although entertaining, is another minor work in the novelist's corpus.

In some ways a remarkably ordinary man by all accounts, the Colombian is, and will always be, an object of rumors. According to Roger Straus, when to celebrate the centennial of the world's most important awards, the Nobel committee decided to invite every awardee from around the globe (paying handsomely for everybody's room and board), García Márquez alone refused the invitation—unless he received a payment of $10,000, which was not forthcoming. But perhaps the most convoluted of the legends surrounding him is his friendship with Mario Vargas Llosa. They met in Caracas and moved together to Bogotá and Lima, where they participated in a symposium on the novel (published as *The Latin American Novel: A Dialogue* [1968]). Alongside José Donoso, Fuentes, and Cortázar, they are part of the so-called Latin American boom of the 1960s. The Peruvian, of course, wrote the previously mentioned *History of a Deicide,* a 667-page literary study of the Colombian's life and oeuvre, submitted originally as a doctoral dissertation at Madrid's Universidad Central. They shared a room in Mexico's capital, but then, some time in the 1970s, a fight erupted at Cine Lido, in which Vargas Llosa punched García Márquez for circulating tales about an (unconfirmed) extramarital affair with a Nordic model. Since then, they have not spoken to each other. Others claim it was their politics that created a rupture: After the 1959 Cuban Revolution, Vargas Llosa, like Octavio Paz, slowly grew disenchanted with Fidel Castro's worldview and soon became an enemy, his ideology today being center-right.

As the leading voice of the Latin American narrative boom of the 1960s, García Márquez is the decisive force and influence behind Salman Rushdie, Anton Shammas, Isabel Allende, Oscar Hijuelos, Laura Esquivel, and scores of other writers who came to prominence from the 1970s onward. His craft so uniquely mixes magic, hyperrealism, and exotic dreamlike images that one could thank him for having finally put Latin America, long a forgotten part of the world, back on the map. Of course, by the same token, one could also accuse the Colombian of having distorted the hemisphere's reality by reducing it to a theater of clairvoyant prostitutes, opinionated matrons, and corrupt generals. He turned Latin America into a distraction—a chimera, a magical creation.

Today, unfortunately, his decline is not only creative but physical. Around 1991 news began to circulate that García Márquez was sick with cancer. In spite of his reclusiveness, the Associated Press announced a serious medical operation in Colombia. How serious the illness was is anybody's guess. In fact, when *Strange Pilgrims,* an unremarkable compilation of tales written from 1974 on, appeared a year later, people talked about a hidden desire on his part to sum up, to leave the desk clean. His next project, his American editor claims, is a memoir. Although in photographs and public appearances the writer looks healthy, what is unquestionable is his exhaustion. Since *Love in the Time of Cholera* and perhaps even before, he has not seemed at the peak of his power; his creativity seems diminished by an exhausted imagination.

And yet, anybody ready to count him out makes a big mistake. In early 1994, for instance, in a renewed display of stamina, he published a short novel: *Del amor y otros demonios.* Set on the Caribbean coast during the colonial period, it describes a passionate affair, under the shadow of the Church, between a young girl, Sierva María de Todos los Angeles, a saint adored for her many miracles but who supposedly was possessed by the devil, and her exorcist. While García Márquez's story is engaging and well-crafted, it ultimately becomes a showcase of his recent excesses: an overly compressed style that creates a sense of suffocation in the reader, a plot that seems flat, and a lack of spontaneity in the prose that ends up undermining any kind of suspense.

The rumor that he is writing a memoir, which he once claimed in an *El País* interview, would be structured theatrically and not chronologically, raises the expectation of his turning his personal odyssey into literature; and it is obvious that the Colombian himself understands now the imminence of his fate. The closeness of death provides an opportunity for him to wrap up and reshape reminiscences, to translate the past into a historical record. He is ready to consummate his act of fabricating his own heroic destiny by stamping his signature on everything he did and did not do, or preferred never to have done. But most importantly, he, the person and the persona, knows he has already entered the pantheon of literary giants and wants full control, in death as in life, of everything that has to do with his life and craft. The Hispanic world keeps a double standard regarding biographies and autobiographies. As is the way with confessional genres, they do what Hispanic society otherwise wholeheartedly discourages: to make public what is private, to forsake intimacy for extroversion. And yet, the extraordinary attention that the narrative boom of the 1960s received has persuaded many to control memory, to stop cultural thieves from dismantling the mythical aura with which experiences were lived: José Donoso has written a personal recollection of the boom years, originally published in English in *TriQuarterty;* Heberto Padilla did his part in *Self-Portrait of the Other;* in 1993, Mario

Vargas Llosa wrote *The Fish in the Water,* a self-serving study of his first twenty-two years, including a detailed recollection of his campaign as a presidential candidate in 1990; Borges, in collaboration with Norman Thomas Di Giovanni, wrote his "Autobiographical Essay" for the *New Yorker,* and Reinaldo Arenas, the talented Cuban exile who died in New York City, denounced every one of his enemies in *Before Night Fall.* As a fiesta of intellectual rebirth, the 1960s and 1970s in Latin America are emerging as one of the most exciting periods in the regions cultural history. And García Márquez's authoritative voice is probably destined to become the chronicle against which everything else is to be judged. Yet biographical accounts revisiting the period, in Spanish or for that matter any language, are almost nonexistent: Emir Rodríguez Monegal wrote *Jorge Luis Borges: A Literary Biography* for Dutton in 1978, but that's about it. While Norman Mailer, a lover of scandals, has already been written about in several biographies, official and unauthorized—as have Paul Bowles, Saul Bellow, and J. D. Salinger—south of the Rio Grande, little, if anything, has been written about Julio Cortázar, an experimentalist who wrote "Blow-Up" and died in 1984, Manuel Puig, and Juan Rulfo, not to mention Fuentes, Vargas Llosa, and, of course, the creator of Macondo himself.

Physical or creative decadence aside, *One Hundred Years of Solitude,* which, in John Barth's words, is "as impressive a novel as has been written so far in the second half of our century and one of the splendid specimens of that splendid genre," will no doubt remain resplendent with prestige. Its existence alone more than justifies the Colombian's days and nights. John Leonard once wrote that "with a single bound García Márquez leaps onto the stage with Günter Grass and Vladimir Nabokov, his appetite as enormous as his imagination, his fatalism greater than either." If it weren't for this larger-than-life novel, Latin America's prominence on the literary map would be much diminished. And if he has often failed to live up to the supernal standards he set himself, that achievement alone ought to keep García Márquez on the bookshelves of humankind for a long time to come. Redemption through a single artistic stroke, the overcoming of death through memory: What else can a writer desire?

Stories

# XEROX MAN

My share in the explosive case of the so-called "Xerox Man," as the New York tabloids delighted in describing Reuben Staflovitch shortly after his well-publicized arrest and as the *Harper's Magazine* profile reiterated, is too small: It amounts to only fifteen minutes of conversation, of which, unfortunately, I have an all-too-loose recollection.

I first heard of him at Foxy Copies, a small photocopy shop right next to the prewar apartment building where I spent some of my best Manhattan years. Its owner was a generous man in his mid-fifties by the name of Morris. Morris attended his customers with a kind of courtesy and unpretentiousness out of fashion in the city at the time.

I used to visit Foxy Copies almost daily as my duties required material to be Xeroxed and faxed at a regular basis. I refused to have my home invaded by technological equipment, so Morris, for a nonastronomical fee, did the job for me.

He always received me with open arms. If time permitted, he would invite me to shmooze for a little while at his desk behind one of the big photocopy machines. We would discuss the latest Yankee game or that week's Washington scandal. He would then process my documents as if they were his own. He had read one of my pieces once in a trade magazine and prided himself on having what he called "a distinguished list of clients," in which he included me. "You will make me famous one day," he often said.

Aired in BBC Radio 4 London, April 10, 1999. First published in *AGNI* 51 (Spring 2000).

In one of our conversations I asked Morris, out of sheer nuisance, if he ever felt curiosity about his customers and the stuff they photo-copied.

"Why should I?" he answered quickly, but then lowered his defenses: "You want me to really answer your question? Then come with me," and we walked together toward a back room with a huge closet, which Morris opened right away. In front of me I saw a stack of disorganized paper.

"In Brooklyn," he said, "an old teacher of mine used to like strange words. When I bought Foxy Copies one of these words came back to me: Paralipomena. It means remnants that still have some value. What you see here are piles of Xeroxes clients leave behind or throw away."

The sight reminded me of a *genizah*, the annex in every syna-gogue, usually behind the arc, where old prayer books accumulate. Disposable Jewish books cannot be thrown away because they might contain the name of God, which can fall into the wrong hands and be desecrated. So these books are stored until the *genizah* gets too crowded, at which point someone, usually an elder, buries the books in the backyard.

"A *genizah* of sorts, isn't it?" I said. "Yes," Morris answered, "except that a special company comes once every three months or so to pick this stuff up. I hate not to see it properly recycled."

I browsed through the Xeroxes.

"Trash, really," Morris said. "Most of it is in plain English. Except for the remains left behind by Mr. Staflovitch," and as he uttered the name, he pointed to a lower pile. I looked at it closely and its pages appeared to me to be in ancient Semitic languages.

Morris didn't like to talk about his clients but deep inside all New Yorkers are indiscreet and he was too. So he told me that Reuben Staflovitch—yes, as I recall, he used the complete name for the first time at that point—was by far the most taciturn. He described him as well built, of average height, always dressed with a black suit, white shirt, and unpolished moccasins, with an unruly beard and his trademark sky-blue Humphrey Bogart hat. "He comes in with a black doctor's bag about once every two to three weeks," Morris added, "usually at closing time, around 6:30 P.M. He asks to have a Xerox machine all for himself. With extreme meticulousness, he proceeds to take out from the doctor's bag an antiquarian vol-ume, which takes him between thirty and forty minutes to photo-copy. Then he restores it to the doctor's bag, wraps the Xeroxed material in plastic, pays at the cashier, and leaves. Few words are uttered, no human contact is made. He leaves in the exact same way as he arrives: in absolute silence."

I remember talking with Morris about other topics that day but Staflovitch was the only one that truly captured my imagination. "You know," Morris continued, "it is amazing to watch him do his job. His photocopying is flawless; not a single page is wasted. But just after he finishes, he puts his fingers into the pile and takes out a single copy—only one—and throws it away. Why he does this I have no idea. I never dared to ask. But I save the excluded page out of pity."

I extracted the top page in Staflovitch's pile from the closet. "Can I take it with me?"

"You bet," Morris replied.

That night, in my solitude, I deciphered it: it came from a Latin translation of Maimonides's *Guide for the Perplexed*.

■  ■  ■

Not long afterward, while on Broadway, I saw Staflovitch himself. Morris's description was impeccable. Except for the Humphrey Bogart hat, he looked as unemblematic as I had imagined him: a nondescript orthodox Jew just like the ones on Delancey Street. He walked quickly and nervously, with his doctor's bag on his right side. A hunch made me follow him. He headed uptown toward the 96th Street subway station but continued for many more blocks— almost thirty—until he reached the doorsteps of the Jewish Theological Seminary, where, crossing the ironed gate, he disappeared from sight. I waited for a few minutes and saw him reappear, walk uptown again, this time to Columbus Avenue, and disappear once and for all into an apartment building. "This must be his home . . . ," I told myself. I felt anguished, though, wishing that I had come face-to-face with him. I was puzzled by his mysterious identity: Was he married? Did he live alone? How did he support himself? And why did he copy old books so religiously?

When I next saw Morris, I mentioned my pursuit. "I'm feeling guilty now," he confessed. "You might be after a man with no soul."

■  ■  ■

My fifteen-minute conversations with Staflovitch occurred about a month later, as I was leaving Columbia University after a day of heavy teaching. He was entering the subway station of 116th Street. By chance the two of us descended the staircase together. I turned around pretending to be dumbstruck by the coincidence and said: "I've seen you before, haven't I? Aren't you a Foxy Copies customer?"

His reply was evasive. "Well, not really. I don't like the neighborhood. . . . I mean, why? Have you seen me at the shop?"

I instantaneously noticed his heavy Hispanic accent, which the media, especially the TV, later picked on.

"Are you from Argentina?"

"Why do you care?"

"Well, I am a Mexican Jew myself . . ."

"Really? I didn't know there were any. Or else . . ."

Wanting clearly to avoid me, Staflovitch took out a token and went through the turnstile. I didn't have one myself, so I had to stand on a queue, which delayed me. But I caught up with him after I descended to the train tracks. He was as close to the end of the platform as possible. The train was slow in coming and I wasn't intimidated by his reluctance to speak, so I approached him again. "I see you're in the business of Xeroxing old documents. . . ."

"How do you know?"

I don't remember the exact exchange that followed but in the next few minutes Staflovitch explained to me the sum total of his theological views, the same ones expounded to various reporters after he got caught. What I do remember is feeling a sudden, absolute torrent of ideas descending on me without mercy. Something along the lines that the world in which we live—or better: in which we've been forced to live—is a Xerox of a lost original. Nothing in it is authentic; everything is a copy of a copy. He also said that we're governed by sheer randomness and that God is a madman with no interest in authenticity.

I think I asked him what had brought him to Manhattan, to which he replied: "This is the capital of the twentieth century. Jewish memory is stored in this city. But the way it has been stored is offensive and inhuman and needs to be corrected right away. . . ." The word inhuman stuck in my mind. Staflovitch had clearly emphasized it, as if wanting me to flavor its meaning for a long time.

"I have a mission," he concluded. "To serve as a conduit in the production of a masterpiece that shall truly reflect the inextricable ways of God's mind."

"You're an Upper West Sider, aren't you?" I asked him. "The other day I saw you at the premises of the Jewish Theological Seminary."

But by that point he had no more patience left and began to shriek: "I don't want to talk to you. . . . Leave me alone. Nothing to say, I've nothing to say."

I took a step back and just then, by a bizarre synchronicity, the local train arrived. As I entered it, I saw Staflovich turn around and move in the opposite direction, toward the station's exit.

■ ■ ■

A week later the tabloid headlines read "Copycat Nightmare" and "Xerox Man: An Authentic Thief" and the *New York Times* carried the scandalous news about Staflovitch on its front page. He had been put under arrest on charges of robbery and destruction of a large array of invaluable Jewish rare books.

Apparently he had managed to steal, by means of extremely clever devices, some three hundred precious volumes—among them editions of Bahya ibn Paquda's *Sefer Hobot ha-Lebabot* and a generous portion of the Babylonian Talmud, an inscribed version of Spinoza's *Tractatus Philosophico-Politicus* published in Amsterdam and an illuminated *Haggadah* printed in Egypt—all from private collections at renowned universities such as Yale, Yeshiva, Columbia, and Princeton. His sole objective, so the reporters claimed at first, was to possess the rarest of Judaica, only to destroy the items in the most dramatic of ways: by burning them at dawn inside tin garbage cans along Riverside Park. But he only destroyed the literature after photocopying it in full. "Mr. Staflovitch is a Xerox freak," an officer was quoted as saying. "Replicas are his sole objects of adoration."

His personal odyssey slowly emerged. He had been raised in Buenos Aires in a strict orthodox environment. At the time of his arrest his father was a famous Hasidic rabbi in Jerusalem with whom he had had frequent clashes, mainly dealing with the nature of God and the role of the Jews in the secular world. In his adolescence Staflovitch became convinced that the ownership of antique Jewish books by nonorthodox institutions was a wrong in desperate need of correction. But his obsession had less to do with a transferal of ownership than with a sophisticated theory of chaos, which he picked up while at Berkeley in a brief stint of rebellion in the early 1980s. "Disorder for him is the true order," the prison psychologist said, and added: "Ironically, he ceased to move among orthodox Jews long ago. He is convinced God doesn't actually rule the universe, he simply lets it move in a free-for-all cadence. And humans, in emulation of the divinity, ought to replicate that cadence."

When the police inspected his Columbus Avenue apartment, it found large boxes containing photocopies. These boxes had not been catalogued either by title or by number; they were simply dumped haphazardly, although the photocopies themselves were never actually mixed.

Staflovitch's case prompted a heated debate on issues of copyright and library borrowing systems. It also generated animosity against orthodox Jews unwilling to be part of modernity.

"Remarkable as it is," Morris told me when I saw him at Foxy Copies after the hoopla quieted down somewhat, "the police never came to me. I assume Staflovitch, in order to avoid suspicion, must have enlisted the services of various photocopy shops. I surely never saw him Xerox more than a dozen books out of the three hundred hidden in his apartment."

Morris and I continued to talk about his most famous client, but the more I reflected on the entire affair, the less I felt close to its essence. I regularly visualized Staflovitch in his prison cell, alone but not lonely, wondering to himself what had been done to his copy collection.

It wasn't until the *Harper's Magazine* profile appeared, a couple of months later, that a more complete picture emerged—in my eyes, at least. Its author was the only one allowed to interview Staflovitch in person on a couple of occasions and he unearthed bits of information about his past no one else had reckoned with. For instance, his Argentine roots and his New York connection. "I hated my orthodox Jewish education in Buenos Aires," Staflovitch told him. "Everything in it was derivative. The Spanish-speaking Americas are pure imitation. They strive to be like Europe, like the United States, but never will be. . . ." And about New York, he said:

> I supported myself with the bequest I got after my mother's death. I always thought this city to be the one closest to God, not because it is more authentic—which it isn't, obviously— but because no other metropolis in the globe comes even close in the amount of photocopying done regularly. Millions and millions of copies are made daily in Manhattan. But every- thing else—architecture, the arts, literature—is an imitation too, albeit a concealed one. Unlike the Americas, New York doesn't strive to be like any other place. It simply mimics itself. Therein its true originality.

Toward the end of the profile, the author allows Staflovitch a candid moment as he asks him about "his mission," and reading this portion, I suddenly remembered that it was about his mission that he talked to me most eloquently at the subway station.

"Did the police ever notice that the Xerox boxes in my apartment are all incomplete?" he wonders. "Have they checked each package to see that they are all missing a single page . . . ?"

"Did you eliminate that single page?" he is asked.

"Yes, of course. I did it to leave behind a clearer, more convincing picture of our universe, always striving toward completion but never actually attaining it."

"And what did you do with those missing pages?"

"Ah, therein the secret. . . . My dream was to serve as a conduit in the production of a masterpiece that shall truly reflect the inextricable ways of God's mind: a random book, arbitrarily made of pages of other books. But this is a doomed, unattainable task, of course, and thus I left these extricated pages in the trash bins of the photocopy shops I frequented."

When I read this line, I immediately thought of Morris's *genizah* and about how Staflovitch's mission was not about replicating but about creating. I quickly ran downstairs to Foxy Copies. Morris surely must have been the only savvy shop owner to rescue the removed copies. I still had the page of Maimonides with me but I desperately wanted to put my hands on the remaining pile, to study them, to grasp the chaos about which Staflovitch spoke so highly. "Paralipomena: This is the legacy the Xerox Man has left me with," I told myself.

Morris wasn't around but one of his employees told me, as I explained my purpose, that the recycling company had come to clear the back-room closet just a couple of days before.

# THE ONE-HANDED PIANIST

*for Danilo Kiš*

As she woke up yesterday, she knew God was in the kitchen. It was one of those indescribable insights that would take possession of her, and which, somehow or other, she had gotten used to shaking off. Her intuition told her, indeed, that this time God was there to be found. That if she were to get out of bed to look for him she would find Him. Not in human form, though. She would sense His presence in a scent, in the strong scent of a pine tree. Should she get up? How many times would she wake up in pain and later realize that the pain didn't actually exist? How many times had her own insights lied to her? At least now her bedclothes were protecting her. To go or not to go. She couldn't decide. Sure, she could go downstairs and verify that it was all a hoax, that such a smell didn't exist. Or, she could remain in bed.

"God doesn't exist." Esdras said that God doesn't exist. At least not the omnipotent, merciless God of violent religions, the Almighty that gives and takes away without any explanation. "There's another one," he affirmed, "that exists in objects, in details, in the things that no one pays attention to. For example, the smell of an olive tree. . . ." And Malvina had been waiting for weeks, perhaps even months, for Him to appear. Her God.

First published in *TriQuarterly* 91 (Fall 1994). Reprinted in *The One-Handed Pianist and Other Stories* (Albuquerque, NM: University of New Mexico Press, 1996). Translated by Harry Morales.

She knew the feeling of waking up and knowing that He was reachable in the kitchen. It was a rainy morning in October, months before the accident involving her mother and stepfather, Esdras. She was alone, as always. Was there ever a time when she hadn't been? She knew God was waiting for her, that He would be there until she met Him face-to-face. It was 4:30 in the morning, or close to it. The noise the raindrops were making on the window frames was scaring Malvina—poor thing!, a young woman like her, so alone in such an empty house. She turned on the lights and remained silent. She couldn't decide what to do then, either. She didn't want to go downstairs in vain, nor did she want to miss a chance.

She missed it because she was careless. It had taken her too long to put on her robe and slippers, and by the time she reached the kitchen, it was already too late. The only thing she smelled was the strong scent of dishwashing liquid. She was furious. . . . It should never happen again.

■　■　■

Malvina was a stutterer and had difficulty concealing the problem. She would trip over syllables that contained *t*'s and *r*'s, *c*'s and *r*'s, or *p*'s and *r*'s. She couldn't pronounce words like "t-t-triangle," "c-c-r-redit," "c-c-crater," or "p-p-procreation." Everyone laughed at her and she felt ridiculed, embarrassed, inadequate, and hated to talk because, even though she didn't intend to, she always came across one of those tricky words that announced her verbal disability.

Every six months or so, she would hear another theory explaining her defect. She would hear them from specialists and doctors she visited. One of them attributed the problem to the fact that in the mother's uterus, a genetic code had decided that Malvina's embryo was going to be left-handed and at the last minute there had been a change, a hesitation. Why? One of Nature's mysteries, perhaps. In any event, the result was her slowness in communicating. But only to talk, not to sing. Because when Malvina sang she never stuttered. She sang without impediments, as if music injected a supreme power into her syllables.

Another doctor confirmed the stuttering as a minor, insignificant handicap. That's the word he used, "insignificant." It's a defect many babies are born with, even though their mothers aren't aware of it. He said it was possible to correct the condition through intensive therapy sessions and exercise and recommended a teacher who would improve Malvina's public speaking, with whom Malvina began private classes the following week that put her in a terrible mood. The therapist would force her to take a deep breath every time she began to stumble with a difficult word and made her think about the grammatical and syntactic structure of sentences. One of her requirements was that Malvina buy a thesaurus and read it every night before going to sleep. Whenever she would come across words that contained *t*'s and *r*'s, *p*'s and *r*'s, or *c*'s and *r*'s, she would have to memorize an alternative for each. This way, when speaking, she could avoid difficult words.

Malvina took speech classes for three or four years. Her mother forced her to, even if she hated them. She hated to talk, she hated to memorize new vocabulary. She only liked to converse with herself inward. When it was necessary to interact with others, she did it by playing music on a Yamaha piano her father had bought for her when she was a little girl and which she loved. As soon as the speech teacher would leave, Malvina would lock herself in the room to study melodies. An uncle had given her an instruction manual to help her learn how to move her fingers on the piano keys. Pieces by Bartok, Chopin, and Beethoven were her refuge.

Everything changed with the accident, a horrible experience that left her defeated. She could remember (how could she not) each and every detail of that fateful July morning when Esdras and her mother packed their suitcases and got into the car. They were going to take a ten-day vacation near a swimming pool in Tapabalazo. Her mother never liked to leave her daughter alone, regardless of her age. They were very close, and had been ever since her husband, Malvina's father, deserted them. But the young woman didn't like Tapabalazo because there were people with whom she had to be sociable. Esdras, whom she adored, tried to convince her to go, but it was to no avail. Malvina preferred to stay home. She felt without the urge to do anything. She had graduated from high school two weeks before and had been playing piano day and night ever since. Her Yamaha piano had been exchanged for a grand Steinway and Malvina dreamed of becoming a concert pianist.

The news of the accident was unbearable. Esdras's car had lost control, slid, and crashed into a brick wall. Her mother died instantly and Esdras barely made it to an ambulance. It was too much for her to handle. Malvina felt all the world was crashing down upon her. What would she do, alone and isolated, without anyone to keep her company? Her stuttering had resulted in an impenetrable introversion. She loved them. They were her only contact with the world. How would she go on living now? Alone, and no one's daughter. Brave and decisive, she eventually decided to discontinue the speech classes. If she stood out like she wanted to, it would be as a pianist. People would talk to her and she would reply with music . . . *her* music.

Strange physiological symptoms began to emerge. Malvina would wake up with an intense pain in her left ovary, as if someone had pulled on it while she was sleeping—an intermittent pain that made her cry. She went to a doctor for a check-up, but nothing was found. The pain stopped for a few days after she took some aspirins, but returned with the same intensity—as if someone was hurting her on the inside with a screwdriver.

Next, it wasn't her ovary but her left eardrum. Or her left leg, or her left lung . . . always on her left side. Malvina would scream and doubled up in tears. Esdras, who had been fond of Zen and oriental philosophy, had many books in his library that dealt with the mind/body duality. Malvina found one about the counterbalance of opposites. It was written by a Hindu shaman and it said if our fragile internal balance is broken, complications set in: troubling dreams, anxiety, lack of appetite, and pain in the left side of the body. Malvina, then, was sick, one side of her was heavier than the other. The solution, according to the author, consisted of a series of gymnastic exercises like crawling around in circles on all fours. Even though they looked comical, she still tried these and other exercises. She tried them all.

■ ■ ■

Exactly two years later the worst anatomical fracture occurred.

It either happened while she was walking to the bank or returning from the market, Malvina couldn't quite remember. Suddenly and without warning, she felt she was losing one of her hands, the left one. First she had it, then she didn't. The first thing she did was calm down and try not to pay too much attention to the entire incident. Fear could take possession of her, which was dangerous and could contribute to worsening her condition. Malvina took a deep breath. She didn't look around her because she thought people would be making fun of her. Her, a lonely young woman, staring at her hand and at other people in the middle of the sidewalk, how ridiculous! They might think she was still in high school, an immature and incomplete woman—a lunatic.

She walked a few blocks feeling nervous until she stopped at a corner, near a pharmacy. Then, once again, she took a deep breath. With her right hand she felt around for the hand that was missing. Malvina could see it. She pinched it but it didn't hurt. She caressed it. Her right hand had feeling, but the left didn't. She then concluded she had actually lost her left hand and what she was seeing was an optical illusion. The terror that came over her is indescribable. During that time she had been scheduled to give performances in the Haucóyotl Auditorium and the Palace of Fine Arts. She would have to cancel them and live with the disgrace of being a one-handed pianist.

The left hand, *her* hand, returned a few days later. It was there, as much a part of her body as any other organ. Malvina canceled only one of the concerts and performed the rest. But the agony of knowing that it could happen again didn't leave her in peace. What if she lost sense of her hand while playing Bach in public? How could she excuse herself knowing the hand would be there but not really? She was terrified. She would wake up early in the morning thinking she had an insufferable pain in her uterus and a few minutes later realize it was only her imagination. Or she would dream she was being cut vertically in half. Malvina and Malvina's ghost.

The feeling she had on that rainy October morning when she felt sure God (the smell of pine trees) was in the kitchen was only the most recent evidence of those frightening pockets of anguish. And tomorrow, not tonight but tomorrow, she would get another identical feeling. She would wake up early in the morning and slowly put on her robe and slippers. With her nostrils wide open, she would walk down the stairs to the kitchen, longing to find, once and for all, the redeeming smell. But it would be a false alarm, of course. A smell of God? Malvina would see her own left hand on the kitchen table and start to cry uncontrollably. She would then lower her eyes, hoping the authentic hand, *her* hand, would be in its place. But no. She would swallow her saliva, sigh, and approach the table to touch her left hand with her right one. The entire incident would make her laugh . . . quite a bit, as her tears would dry on her cheeks. Only then would Malvina begin to give off a foul smell of pine t-t-trees.

# A HEAVEN WITHOUT CROWS

21, V, 1924
Kierling Sanatorium
Klosterneuberg

Dear Max,*

Thanks for having come ten days ago to visit this old invalid who's about to say goodbye. Just a few miles from Vienna and already I feel I'm in the Other World. I have tuberculosis in the larynx, I know, though the doctors persist in offering other diagnoses, incredible beyond belief. Why won't anyone dare to talk honestly to a dying man? Death is the issue and still they're vague, evasive. Dr. Tschiassny tells me that my throat is looking much better but I don't believe him; I can't even swallow solid food any more, so I live on lemonade, beer, wine, and water. They apply ice packs to my throat on a regular basis. I've also been given medicated lozenges and Demropon which, till now, has been ineffective in treating my cough.

---

First published in *Michigan Quarterly* XXXII, 3 (Summer 1993). Reprinted in *The One-Handed Pianist and Other Stories* (Albuquerque, NM: University of New Mexico Press, 1996). Translated by David Unger.

* I feel great anguish when I consider Franz Kafka's request that his friend Max Brod burn his writings. What could have motivated the writer to insist that his artistic production be destroyed? Perhaps his profound antinomic nature, though that only seems to me half the truth. I have searched in vain through the back alleys of his writings, as well as by reading biographies. I offer, therefore, my own explanation, at once sensible and farfetched, contained in this letter never sent to Brod, composed two weeks before the Czech writer died.

I admit that if it weren't for Dr. Klopstock from Budapest—"the madman," as you refer to him—who I met that frigid February in 1921, I wouldn't even be writing to you now. He takes good care of me, though at times I suspect he's at bottom a hypocrite. He has promised to inject me with sedatives when the pain becomes unbearable; we'll see what happens. Yes, I know there's a vial of camphor ready for me in the medicine chest. Dora Diamant, my dear Dora, trusts him implicitly and that pleases me. They take turns sitting at my side when I can't stay alone. I'm extremely grateful, though I tell them there's no reason to prolong the agony. Guess what? Yesterday late at night an owl perched right outside my window. The bird of death!

You've seen me: 103 pounds fully dressed. I've lost my voice and can only be heard if I whisper—which isn't so bad coming from me. They've suggested that Dora end my treatment and take me home, but she refuses. I'm completely in favor! Dying in a hospital is too impersonal. Furthermore, all this is very expensive—as if one has to pay taxes to a sultan before checking out. Soon I'll get some money from Otto Pick and Prager Presse for the "Josephine" story; also, Die Schmiede owes me a check. If they're sent to you, pass them on to Dora to pay the bills.

When you visited me, we could barely communicate. You claim I was too absorbed, as if hiding a secret, and that my gestures were strange. We talked about my October 22, 1922, request, in which I expressed my final wishes regarding my writings. Since you could make yourself understood and I couldn't I would like to clarify again what I meant: I'll also mention an astonishing and sad development which, I'm afraid, will perhaps disturb our friendship. On the same day of your visit I got the unpleasant news that Dora's father, after consulting with a rabbi, had rejected our wish to marry. But that's another story.

Of all my writings, you know that the only ones of value are *The Trial,* "The Stoker," "The Metamorphosis," "In the Penal Colony," "A Country Doctor," and "A Hunger Artist." (You can save the few remaining copies of *Meditations* since I don't want to give anyone the work of eliminating them—still, none of its stories can be reprinted.) When I say these writings have value, I don't mean to imply they should be reprinted or saved for posterity; on the contrary, my deepest wish would be for them to disappear completely from sight. But everything else in newspapers, magazines, papers, manuscripts, letters—barring nothing—should be retrieved from the people who have them and burned, preferably without being read. I can't stop you from reading them, but I wouldn't like it; in no way should anyone other than you set eyes upon them.

You asked me: Why destroy writings that are already part of humanity? I apologize for not having known how to answer. At first I thought of telling you it was an impulse, an inexplicable premonition. But I understand what you are saying: What is art if not an attempt to transcend death? Isn't art the trace which remains when we are no longer on this earth? That's why I thought of saying that nothing imperfect should survive and what I've written is imperfect, even though I have spent many nights wide awake changing a defective phrase here or there or looking for the right touch of humor. That which is imperfect causes in me great embarrassment. Many times we've discussed Flaubert and his "irritating"—this is your word, dear friend—meticulousness. Doesn't he state in his letters to Turgenev and to his dearly beloved Louise Colet that he spent months, even years, looking for the ideal word, revising a single page over and over? And what is the right word? No one knows. Or better: Only God knows.

Now more than ever I understand my hesitancy regarding my Jewish heritage. I yearn for the immemorial time when a library consisted of just the Whole Book, the one that transcribes Suffering, Truth, and the Law. My father Herrmann is true to his religion though he partakes of its rituals mechanically and without question. His severe, authoritarian manner instills terror. It's difficult for me to get close to him and I suppose K.'s indecision and incapacity in *The Castle* is inspired by him. My idea of God is of a distant warden in a state of alertness, always ready to punish. Is this the same God who wrote the Book of Books? If so, he must've written it in a burst of rage, taking pleasure in the dreadfulness of his creations.

Now I feel I've mocked my father. Fresh in my mind is the letter I wrote him when you and I were in Schelesin. Remember? I had to tell him about my endless yearning for childhood and the suffering I endured under his implacable yoke. I'm sure the death of the two babies my mother bore after I was born was traumatic; truth is they, not I, deserved to live. I have a clear memory in mind: I was a young boy and, on a night like so many others, I was whining, begging for water. It wasn't only that I was thirsty, I also wanted to enjoy myself. Suddenly my father came in, dragged me out of bed and took me to the balcony. He left me there locked up till I grew calm. That was his style—intolerant and demanding. The event left me scarred. From that day on, I dream about a huge man, a judge who comes to pull me out of my bedroom and condemns me. What I leave behind in my writings is a variation on that dream—a handful of complaints which lack the least bit of interest—the view of a conflicted person. Is there any hope in a kingdom where cats chase after a mouse? Yes, but not for the mouse.

For many years this has been my view: Nevertheless, today I feel its hypocrisy and inconsistency. My father always wanted to see me as a successful son, which makes me wonder: Does God perceive us as we are? I'm sure he does. Any other way, then, would be our fault. The weakened and tense relationship with my father is more my fault than his. I take pleasure in playing the role of Jesus Christ—the martyr who suffers for others. Deep down I am an actor specializing in submissive characters. An actor who knows how to create something out of his own being. Is my father truly so severe and authoritarian? Perhaps. Valli, Ottla, and Elli (the latter to a lesser extent) also complain about his character, though they have the benefit of being females. To a larger degree, my father is just like my uncles Philip, Heinrich, and Ludwig, at times even more sensitive than they. Tell me then why aren't any of my cousins—Otto, Oskar, Victor, and the others—afraid? Because I am an impostor who has invented a dark reality. Because I've made a career out of being a victim.

How embarrassing for me to reveal to you at age forty-one my hateful comedy. Did you suspect it already? Of course. Why haven't I burned my own writings? The answer is not cowardice but rather because I'm a person weakened by vanity. Deep inside I know very well you too won't set them ablaze; on the contrary, they're useful to you since your own novels fill you with uncertainty. To achieve a kind of immortality, my books would depend on my own immolation, on creating a legend; one would have to read them in the light of all the errors of a poor crucified Jew who detested himself so much. Is there a more fascinating creature than the one who first describes a detestable world and then censures himself?

Now I'm getting to the heart of this letter. Years ago, during the time when I forced myself to learn Hebrew, I met in Studl's boarding house Julie Wohryzek, a beautiful, if a bit foolish, girl. You know the story very well—I've recounted it to you many times, but not its outcome. Her father was a cobbler who also carried out a few administrative tasks in the synagogue. She was neither Jew nor gentile, German nor otherwise. She had a light-hearted spirit; every time we were together, she was laughing. She had been engaged, but her fiancé died in the war. Julie reminded me of Grete Bloch, the woman with whom I had an unhappy romance unbeknownst to my fiancée Felice. I felt both desire and anxiety with Julie.

Winter brought us together in an old-fashioned room that smelled of ammonia. We were there for a month and a half. Our intimacy, with its implied sexuality, frightened me. Julie did not want to get married and from the start she denied any interest in procreation. We were both happy with the relationship; nevertheless, I saw her change in this respect, till she began to yearn for children: She said that being pregnant is "a privilege no woman should renounce." Our first separation was in March of 1919. We reunited in April in Prague and our intimacy grew even more intense. We became engaged and rented an apartment in Wrschowitz. My parents, of course, were against this. Around this time we received copies of "The Penal Colony" from Kurt Wolff Verlag. I remember how with enthusiasm I gave my father one copy. As soon as he saw it, he snuffed my happiness and said with scorn, "Put it on my desk!" I felt humiliated. A little later, when I announced in the living room our betrothal, they created a scene. My father insinuated that Julie was a common Prague girl—you could tell by her dress and her manners—and my mother agreed without saying a word. All this filled me with doubt, and days later we lost our lease. I decided then to break this—my third—engagement. We separated; Julie, who was twenty-eight years old, was deeply hurt and moved to another city. We separated for a second time, promising to continue writing to each other but didn't. I never heard from her again.

Till a few weeks ago, when I received an airmail letter mailed to my parents' home with no return address. She gave me the astonishing news that my son Zdenek Saul Kafka Wohryzek was four years old. She told me he's a chubby boy with brown eyes and he lost his first tooth in November. He has a scar on his chin from when he tripped in school, hitting his head against a sharp metal edge. His mother added that in a few weeks the two of them would be heading off to America. She didn't say a thing about a reconciliation.

Did this unsettle me? I gasped for breath and lost my balance. When no one was looking, I burnt the letter. Yes, burned it up. What else could I do? You know very well I could never be a father; to have children is to begin a journey toward redemption, and salvation is not for me but for my nullity. Since then I've tried unsuccessfully to put the incident behind me. Furthermore, I'm possessed by an old saying which I repeat day and night till I am worn out. Do you remember it? It's the one about all the crows boasting that just a single crow could destroy the heavens, which proves nothing since the heavens are nothing more than the negation of crows. I mentioned this to a German doctor who periodically reexamines me and he smiled, realizing that Kavka means "crow" in Czech.

Wait, there's more. There's a prostitute here among the sanatorium patients and I sit with her on the terraza to take some sun. She's a fortune-teller, and one day she wanted to read my future. She took hold of my right hand and opened it. When she saw the lines on my palm, she became suddenly silent, unable to hold back a cry of sorrow. She then assured me that though my own future was dark, my son was in good hands. My heart began to race. I told her I had no offspring but she explained that my son was in excellent health and soon would be arriving in New York. She added that the immigration authorities wouldn't let him enter and he would sail throughout the Caribbean until he reached a port where they spoke Spanish named Veri Crucci or Bara Crutz. And what did his future hold? He would be a merchant. He would begin selling knives and would end up with a successful paint business with a number of stores. A businessman, like his grandfather Herrmann. The former prostitute also said that during his adolescence he would search for me. He would visit my grave in Prague and would reclaim from you, Max, the rights to my books, but that you would ignore him.

Do you know how I felt? Covered with muck, full of filth. (Exactly what I felt when I finished *The Trial*). Dora, to whom I'll never be married, spent the next night at my side. She'll tell you I slept poorly and it's true, I had an awful nightmare. I dreamt that someone was washing my corpse with a soft and oily soap; he wrapped it in a white shroud and chopped it in a thousand pieces with a butcher knife. After he placed the pieces in a hole, I saw you, my parents and brothers, and a policeman writing the following words in stone: Evil does not exist, you have crossed the threshold, everything is fine.

I have the feeling my whole life has been a lie. As if I tried for years to go through a door and not succeeded because the lock seemed impenetrable though it really wasn't.

I have a pain in my chest. . . . Will we see each other again? If Zdenek seeks you out, please open the door. Please tell him that I was an actor and executioner.

Franz

# BLIMUNDA

*for L. H.*

Greco lived in Heinlopo, a major commercial shrimp fishing port, and was the owner of several boats, each of them containing two large, strong nets. He would contract day laborers who would leave at dawn to go fishing and would return in the late afternoon to gather and deposit shrimps into small barrels and later clean the nets. Greco had a daughter named Blimunda. Because she was beautiful and intelligent, Blimunda managed to convince her father to enroll her in a convent in Huatusco City. She spent seven years there, educating herself and becoming a young lady. By the time she left the convent, she had earned such a reputation that every handsome man in Heinlopo desired her. As a result, Greco quickly arranged for her to marry Lafcadio Reyes, the son of an associate of his. Blimunda learned to love Lafcadio, living together for another seven years, and eventually having a son. But when their son was three or four years old, Blimunda caught pneumonia and died.

On the night of Blimunda's wake, her son ran into the room where all of the mourners were congregating and said: "Something strange is happening near the nets, behind the house. Mother is there, watching." Everyone thought the boy was talking nonsense. But they all ran out of the room anyway and saw that Blimunda's

First published in *AGNI* 48 (Fall 1998). Reprinted in *The Best Fantasy and Horror 1999*, edited by Terri Windling and Ellen Datlow (New York: St. Martin's Press, 1999). Translated by Harry Morales.

ghost was actually pinned up against an old, cracked wall. She was wearing a beautiful white tunic and her eyes were pointedly fixed on an indiscriminate spot on the ground.

The mourners became frightened. Blimunda's body was resting, shrouded, in a coffin inside the house, but her spirit was outside, entranced and pensive. Greco, who was already an old man at the time, much against his own will, tried to drive it away with a stick. He was unsuccessful and the ghost continued to show no fear. The neighbors, stirred by the news, arrived at the wall and couldn't believe what they saw: one neighbor threw rocks at it, which passed right through Blimunda, while someone else had a crucifix out and was courageously using it as a shield while muttering commands at it to go away, like one does to an evil force.

The next day the body was buried in a cemetery fifteen kilometers away into the mainland, in the Valle del Conejo. The townspeople thought that by moving the body away from Heinlopo and burying it far away, they would solve the problem. But no, Blimunda's spirit remained pinned up against the wall, watching.

There were two reactions in town: Out of fear, most of Greco's neighbors left Heinlopo and headed for the capital. They argued that her ghost would bring others. To them, once a place had been possessed, it would remain satanic forever. The second reaction came from Blimunda's relatives and friends, who treated her naturally. Even though they wouldn't come too close because they noticed her spirit seemed somewhat nervous, they would go shrimp fishing just the same, without a care in the world, mindful that a ghost can be allowed to generate fear but it shouldn't take away one's livelihood.

In the meantime, all the remaining neighborhood children—Blimunda and Lafcadio's son amongst them—would cry whenever they saw the ghost, no matter how many times they were exposed to it. But nothing changed: It continued to be pinned up against the wall, day and night, with her eyes fixed on the ground.

Cabalists, magicians, therapists, and priests arrived in Heinlopo, followed by two politicians from Paranagua, who had decided to come when they learned that mass fear was motivating the townspeople to slowly desert the beaches of Heinlopo. That's also when Plinio, Blimunda's cousin, made it home. He immediately met with Lafcadio, who told him about what had happened. When he learned after an absence of many years that his dear childhood companion had died, his heart started beating fast.

So he went to have a tête-à-tête with the ghost. Blimunda seemed young, serene, and her hair was flowing freely, her white tunic absorbing the light of the sun and the moon. Even then her fixed eyes projected her intelligence.

"What did she say before she died?" Plinio asked later.

"Nothing, really," replied Lafcadio.

Actually, she had mumbled a few syllables, but her fever and chills had drowned them out.

"She appears nervous to me," Plinio added.

He went to her house and then up to her bedroom where he noticed that Lafcadio had removed all the tools, clothing, photographs, and household goods which reminded him of Blimunda, thereby erasing her from his life. He looked all over the room, from top to bottom, and then later searched the other rooms and closets. He was looking for something, but didn't know what. During his search he came across old postcards, a pair of pajamas that Uncle Baltazar had worn during his stay in Texas, old fishing nets which weren't used anymore, trophies, and decorated medals. The search was in vain.

As Plinio was leaving the house that night, he noticed something strange: Blimunda's ghost wasn't where it always was. The wall was bare, and a radiance remained in the area. Suddenly, he turned around and noticed one of the boats was missing. He looked out at the sea and saw that Blimunda's ghost had thrown the oars overboard and was sitting in the boat, looking at him from somewhere in the open sea.

"What are you waiting for?" he shouted at it.

Although she was far away, Plinio could see her smiling. But no answer came.

A storm was threatening from high above. He continued to observe the ghost for a while, then later returned to Lafcadio's house and went to sleep.

The next morning, he saw Blimunda's ghost again, pinned up against the wall with her eyes fixed at a right angle with the ground. Her radiance had now disappeared and she could hardly be seen. A nonbeliever would certainly not have been able to confirm that there was actually a ghost there, floating in the corner, near the fishing nets. But her shining, relaxed smile made her a pleasant entity to behold.

Plinio walked up to the ghost and intuitively started to scratch the wall and dig into the ground with his foot. Although his hands were hurting, he could see her smooth, clear smile in the background. He felt good: He was doing something right. After much digging in the ground, he finally reached bottom and found a chest hidden in the dirt. A treasure. When he looked up and noticed

Blimunda's ghost trembling, he got scared and decided to bury the chest again. Because after all, he knew that such secrets should not be revealed during the day. Plinio then took off his shirt and pants and went swimming in the sea. He swam for three hours or more and afterward went home to sleep.

He woke up at midnight, feeling sleepless. He got up and without knowing why, went to Lafcadio's room and said good-bye. His uncle hardly seemed to notice, though. He did the same with Blimunda's son, then returned to his room, packed his clothes, made his way to the room housing the fishing nets and left the house with the ghost walking directly behind him.

Plinio cast his bags aside near the peeling wall and proceeded to dig up the chest. He opened it up and saw that it contained a notebook, a wristwatch with a crown that was disintegrating from old age, an amulet, and two letters.

"Go in peace," he said to Blimunda. "No one will read the contents of these letters or this notebook . . . except me."

The ghost opened its mouth as if wanting to say something but nothing came out.

Plinio read the material: beautiful, genuine correspondence and a diary of an impossible and passionate love. When he finished, he saw the ghost at the beach, waiting for him in a launch. Plinio walked toward it and climbed into the boat.

They sailed away—nowhere in particular, just far, far away. While sailing, he lit a match and burned the material. He deposited the ashes in the chest, locked it, and threw it into the sea. He noticed how the ghost's shadow started to submerge and then finally sink into the sea, its bubbles hypnotizing him. Blimunda, finally at rest, had disappeared.

Plinio then sailed back to Heinlopo in order to tell Greco the news and summon the townspeople back home.

# THREE NIGHTMARES

To remember Betzi is to invoke three nightmares, with their interludes. None of them give enough details about our relationship, I know. Perhaps they even hide its significance. The truth is that I don't understand details either. Living with Betzi was a way of functioning for me. While we were together, her kisses and caresses would awaken delightful feelings. I would turn over my realm if I could prolong them. But then came the shower of disagreements. We shouted at each other, cursed at each other, contradicted each other, and everything turned into chaos. I stopped understanding. Today I'm cured of the caresses, but not of the dreams.

It all started when I irresponsibly lost my wedding ring. It was a plain gold ring. We had bought it at a small, cramped downtown jewelry store. I couldn't remember when and where I misplaced it. In the office? During lunch? I looked for it until I was exhausted and returned home feeling ashamed, with the intention of explaining to Betzi what had happened. She was furious and let out a scream as big as the world. I apologized. What could I do? While I did promise to look for it better, I never thought the incident could have such connotations. Well, the first nightmare occurred the following night, after an exciting game of poker. Several friends of mine and I had gathered together at home. We bought whiskey, tequila, and appetizers that the maid improved with cheese, onions, and dip. We

First published in *The Literary Review* 39, 1 (Fall 1995). Reprinted in *The One-Handed Pianist and Other Stories* (Albuquerque, NM: University of New Mexico Press, 1996). Translated by Harry Morales.

drank quite a bit. It was after midnight. Betzi had arrived home late from the office and in a bad mood. She seemed to have springs in her face and a grumpy, stony grimace. The alcohol was starting to go to my head. I was dizzy and had the vague sensation that I was drowning in a fish tank. Packs of cards would go. Come back. Noise. The piercing rattling of two bottles that would shatter. Cigarette smoke. I wanted to vomit and, excusing myself, ran to the bathroom and locked myself in for fifteen minutes. For exactly fifteen minutes I threw up my stomach. The lightbulb over the mirror hurt my eyes. I felt chills. Betzi was shouting at me, saying, "Are you all right, Messeguer?" "Yes," I replied, feeling embarrassed. (Now that I think about it, I know that Betzi controlled me like a witch.) Later on she knocked on the door. I opened it; she looked at me and ran into the dining room where my friends were. "Someone go to the drug store," she said. "I need a bottle of milk of magnesia for Messeguer. . . ." How embarrassing! Getting drunk is one of the hardest challenges a man can undergo . . . and I had failed. How long had it been since I last drank? Long enough to lose my resistance . . . to become a child again. To be honest, I would have wanted to vomit my discomfort at Betzi. A shower wouldn't have done me any harm, but I didn't even manage to open the faucet. I waited for Betzi to come and cure me. I later came out of the bathroom and collapsed on the sofa. My friends disappeared. Had the game ended? In my cotton-filled eardrums the voices sounded like squeaking rats, like rusty locks. That was when I had the nightmare that woke me in a single bound. Hours had gone by. Betzi was in the bedroom. I walked up the stairs. The room was dark. Depressed, I slipped into bed between the sheets. "Very quiet, aren't you?" she stammered. My heart trembled. "Arrhythmia," I replied. "My lungs hurt. My heart beats too fast. It was those appetizers that the maid served. They provoked a horrible nightmare." She turned the lamp on. "Talk to me," she said. I resisted. "Relax . . . now, now . . . ," she said, soothing me. "You're nervous. You lost your rhythm. What happened?" Then I told her the sequence of the dream: I was in a grayish room, with very high walls, frozen. Actually, it wasn't a room but a warehouse. Or a refrigerator. One of those old refrigerators that smell damp because the owner forgot to clean it. I felt I was suffocating. I looked for some window or door, an area in which I could breathe. Nothing. Why was I encased in that box? In the center of the box there was a wooden bench. Should I sit down? I walked around in circles, without direction, like a madman. I walked around the bench. Suddenly, a uniformed guard, wearing gloves, a helmet with a visor, and boots, appeared at the corner. His pupils followed the outline of my heels, the joints of my knees. One, two . . . One, two . . . One, two . . . Absurd situation. One, two . . . One, two . . . I would approach him, but he would back away. Surely he was prohibited to mingle with the prisoners. With gloves on, his hands held up his belt . . . or perhaps his belt held up his hands. He had a hairy, curved mustache. "Listen," I told him. But he would ignore me. Nearby, I discovered a briefcase. It was inexpensive, conventional, and Italian-made, with a greenish-yellow band on the side. Surely it hadn't been there before. I was intrigued by its contents. But before I even had the chance to approach it, an abominable monster, a strange medusa, sprang out of its interior. Transparent, it had a dozen tentacles on each side of its body and wore jewelry. Pearls and rings with diamonds, hindu gems and rubies were hanging from its nose, ears, and long hair. But it wasn't hair that flourished on its head: It was cables, miles of multicolored cables of different calibre. A moldy, rotten, and ridiculous-looking sight. Its long, blackish eyelashes were surrounded by electric bulbs. It was a mechanical medusa that vomited (like me in the bathroom), not stomach residue, but semen. It spit semen when it spoke while its tentacles oscillated happily, to and fro, contracting like worms. "Benito Messeguer, we've decided on your sentence." He was saying my name, which implied that he knew who I was. "You have one week to present three letters of recommendation." Three letters? Why? Addressed to whom? "Messeguer, think about what I'm saying. This isn't a joke. Your life is in danger. You lost that ring and deserve the worst punishments. We want to help you. We want you to bring those letters. Through those letters we can prove that you deserve to go on living interminably . . . to continue being Benito Messeguer. . . . Understand?" No, I didn't understand. I hadn't even realized the connection between the refrigerator and the ring. "This is a nightmare. Do you know what a nightmare is? We receive reports of bad behavior. You're just like everyone else, Messeguer, and then some. We won't allow serious depravity. Would you like to continue being Benito Messeguer? Very well then . . . , commit yourself!" I was confused. What were they blaming me of? "It's advisable that you not be too clever. People like you deserve to be in the sewers, crawling like reptiles. We're going to give you a little pat on the rear." I was looking at the guard out of the corner of my eye, who until then had been daydreaming and who now, obligingly, applauded his bosses' words. "I warn you, Messeguer, refusing won't do you any good. We have spies placed in strategic areas. They're following your every move. They know what your mind knows." I felt dizzy and replied: "I don't plan to cooperate." The medusa was becoming furious. "Messeguer, please! Know that by not cooperating, you'll be helping us even more. Remember: three letters of recommendation in one week. Come now, my friend, wake up. The week has just begun."

Betzi burst out laughing. She was making fun of me and her smile was terrifying. "They'll kill you," she announced. "You don't even know under what pretext you should ask for those letters of recommendation. You're screwed, Messeguer!" And as she said this, tears of laughter trickled down her face. "But . . . in case they do kill you," she then said with dignity, "make sure they do it in the most delicate way possible." "What are you talking about?" I asked. "Have you gone crazy? You seem to be spying for them." And Betzi continued: "That's your punishment for having lost the ring." The discussion and Betzi were both proving to be detestable. Still, she gave herself the luxury of finishing, by saying: "What a pity, Benito! You would be better off dead." I felt an unprecedented rage. "Shut up," I said. "Shut up. You're going to destroy me. You're a witch. Please, leave me alone." I left the room, slamming the door behind me. I wanted to kill her.

In the days that followed I found myself driving away ghosts that perch themselves on my knees and shadows that attack me. (I know ghosts don't exist, that's why I would drive them away.) I felt like brutalizing someone, like losing control. There exist resistant men who know how to love . . . and others who are weaker, and dwarfish, who are trapped by passion. My love for Betzi was the trustworthy mirror of my inabilities and fears. Similar were the days that went by during which she acted more and more strangely. She would get up from eating breakfast without giving me my customary goodbye kiss. And she would get into her heavy fox fur coat and would put perfume on while she frowned, loathsome—yes, ignoring me. Hurt and very sad, I would lock myself in the bathroom for more than fifteen minutes and wouldn't come out even if the telephone rang. Or I would shave for hours. I even stopped going to work. If they would call from the office, I wouldn't come to the phone. And what if the maid was a spy?, I would ask myself. Everything was in a state of confusion. At noon, Betzi would also call. She would ask if the gas tank was full or if the bed clothes were being aired out . . . and only at the end, when she was about to hang up, would she ask about me. One time I answered her phone call, saying: "Why didn't you say goodbye?" She replied with whatever stupidity, and then again I said: "What do you think they'll do to me, Betzi, if I don't turn in those letters of recommendation?" "Messeguer, you're an imbecile," she replied, and then she cut me off. She had called me an imbecile.

My mind started to plan requests, think of relatives or close friends from whom I could ask for letters of recommendation. I had to look for someone who knew me well, who had confidence in me. I thought about my poker friends, my boss at the office, my brother. And what was I going to tell them? They would think that I had lost my mind. (Had I?) What do you need to prove, Messeguer? they would ask.

One morning I got on the route number 5 bus, the same bus that would take me to the office every morning. It was horrible. The passengers were watching me. They looked like spies who were working for the medusa. A little girl kept looking at my hands, while her mother had her attention focused on my zipper. (For a moment I thought it was open, but no.) Another individual wearing a silly tie was bending his mouth downward. He felt sorry for me. Even the bus driver, when I went to pay him, waved away the change. He avoided touching me. "Go away!" I shouted, without holding myself back any longer. An old woman tried to help me, but I pushed her. I got off the bus and stumbled into a concrete median. I had a headache and I was exhausted. I returned home and the maid had to open the door for me because I couldn't find the key. She looked at me with fearful eyes. It's funny: Hanging from a handle in her right hand was a suitcase. I could have sworn that it was the medusa's briefcase. "Ms. Betzi called," she said. "She's had to leave for Rochester. It's a *ternational* conference." I deduced that *ternational* meant international. Ternational: The word sounded nice. Betzi was a fashion designer. She designed winter dresses, belts, and shoes. Her professional commitments would call for her to travel frequently, go away. I understood the message. I understood that international conferences could be improvised. What was the maid doing with that suitcase? "Where did you get it," I asked her. "She'll be in Rochester for two days. Said the lady who owned an inn. . . ." She mechanically repeated the same phrase. "That's not what I asked you," I said. "Where did you get that suitcase?" "Which suitcase?" she replied. The maid's hands were empty. I had been dreaming. My throat was dry. "What's the matter, Mr. Messeguer?" she asked. I had been a normal guy until the day before yesterday, and now I was lowering my guard. A bit later I took two aspirin. I also took an antibiotic capsule remaining in the medicine chest and lay down to sleep.

My brother called that afternoon. "Benito, why aren't you at the office?" he said. "As a favor, I need a letter of recommendation from you," I told him. "I'm ceasing to be who I am," and I disclosed my critical moments, the hallucinations. "You've lost your mind, dear. It's Betzi, she's bewitching you." I got on the defensive: "No, she's innocent. It's the mid-life crisis. I'm afraid. . . ." "Stop worrying. Separate yourself from that woman, I know what I'm telling you.

You've never been so frail. You had a reputation for being responsible. Stop worrying! People die of typhoid, cancer . . . but never from having had a nightmare . . . and even less, from owing three letters of recommendation." He laughed. The conversation was encouraging. One word echoed in my mind: *frail . . . frail*. I hung up the receiver and immediately felt better. It's the convalescence of my soul, I thought. I should recover. Your brother is right: You're afraid of Betzi. She's bewitched you. That innermost dissatisfaction is creating this sequence of apparitions. . . . You should alleviate your anxiety.

Another three days went by without Betzi, without controlling my patience, without logic. Three absurd days. I kept looking for the ring. I cleaned the office, and the basement of the house—where I had repaired a pruning hook, looking for the damned ring. And I had a few classified ads placed in the newspaper *Excélsior*. Nothing. That's when I decided to buy another ring. It's necessary, I told myself. Its importance hid powerful secrets. Replacing it would return some lost happiness to me. I went to the same downtown jewelry store and explained to the salesman exactly what I wanted: a plain ring, not luxurious, although made of gold, to replace the previous one. Although they had discontinued the style, they could match it by request. The replacement would be more expensive and they couldn't assure me it was going to be identical. "However . . . nothing is identical," said the salesman. "Things look like themselves." Yes, there would be a similarity, but it would also have its own qualities. After much talk, I accepted. It would be ready in two weeks: the gold would be melted down, and the original mold would have to be found. That would take several days. They would have to work very carefully. No, my urgency was too great. He should have it ready by the end of the week, the date of the second nightmare. The salesman said that he would try, though he couldn't promise. This was enough reason to make me happy. I returned home. There was no news from Betzi, not even a telegram. I thought about the possibility of having been deceived for years during my marriage. While she provoked this emotional crisis, she surely had another man inserted between her legs. All women are bitches, I thought. They're all witches. I wanted to get revenge, to avenge myself somehow. I walked around in the bedroom, went up the stairs, down, and walked around in circles like a madman.

■  ■  ■

The seventh day arrived and the jewelry store didn't have the ring ready. I was exhausted. Even so, I did everything possible not to fall asleep. No, I didn't want to. I resisted, but in the end . . . I dropped off. In front of me was the same refrigerator. The same guard with the belt holding up his hands. The same visor. I was sitting on that bench. In the farthest corner was the briefcase radiating heat. Hours would go by . . . and nothing. Surely they've forgotten about me, I thought. They must be busy reading other letters of recommendation . . . or dreaming them. Suddenly the guard approached me: "Congratulations. We know that you haven't obtained a single letter." Why was he congratulating me? Immediately the transparent medusa appeared out of the briefcase. Its cables were coiled and dirty with grease. It looked like a bubbling sea sponge. "Stop worrying," it was telling me. "Luckily, we've found your ring. You left it here." What? That's impossible. "I misplaced it two or three days before coming here. You couldn't have found it." "Don't be clever, Messeguer. If I tell you we found the ring . . . it's because we found the ring. Look at it." He extended one of its tentacles, showing me the ring amongst so much other jewelry. "Take it, Messeguer, and be attentive. It would displease us very much if we had to judge you again," it was saying while it gave it to me. I slipped it onto the knuckle of my left pinkie finger. "Be happy!" said the medusa, in conclusion. "This nightmare has also ended."

What? I woke up drenched in sweat. I had been used like a puppet. I had never lost the ring, nor did I ever have it. Everything was in a state of confusion. I examined my hand, and there it was. What a surprise! My heart was beating at a wicked pace. Suddenly, I fell asleep again, thus allowing the final nightmare to begin. The following was its sequence: I'm on a shadowy street, standing feverishly under the light of a lamppost, and smoking. I'm wearing a gray suit and preparing to go to the movies. I know that they're showing the film *Shanghai Express* with Marlene Dietrich one or two blocks away. I arrive at the ticket booth and find a beautiful, robust woman there. She's lost her ticket. I want to help her but my shyness impedes me. Immediately she asks me: "Could you lend me some money? I want to go in." I agree to. (She looked like Betzi, but no, it wasn't her.) I give her the money, she pays, and then turns her back on me. "How rude!" I think. Eventually, I stop concerning myself about it. Then I too go in without even looking at her. Later, I unintentionally discover her buying a box of popcorn. I wait. I see that she quietly enters the auditorium and looks for an orchestra seat. Indiscreetly, I follow her and sit down next to her. Good, perfect move, Messeguer. Out of the corner of my eye I look at her tremendous breasts, her slender body. As soon as the film begins the lights go out. I try to concentrate. But I can't. I keep my attention on her. I feel uncomfortable, embarrassed. More out of an obligation to instinct than to conscience, I put my hand on her knee. She wears nylon stockings that make her thin legs smooth. I wait. I know that from one moment to the next she would slap me. My hand is stiff. Sweaty. God, the slap doesn't arrive. What joy! But the hand starts to sweat. I see myself forced to remove it and pull a handkerchief out of my pocket to dry it. Flirting, in the meantime, she tidies up her dress and erotically pulls on the strap of her bra. I'm aroused. I suppose that she too felt desire. Quickly I remember that I'm married to Betzi. Shit! Once again I place my hand on her knee and I let it slide. Fascinated, nervous, she lifts her buttock upwards and gets comfortable. She's asking me for more. . . . I know it. And I'll give her more. I gently bring my hand up to her thighs and oh, what a surprise!, I realize that underneath her slip, amongst those very confused, protective ligaments . . . she wasn't wearing any underwear. I started breathing faster.

The bald-headed man sitting in the orchestra seat in front of us suspected something. He knows that we're not watching the film. He turns around to make sure that everything is all right. No. He turns around because he's jealous of me. He wants to snatch *my* woman away from me. I place my hand across my face because I don't want him to see me. She's probably his wife, I think. No, if she was his wife they would be sitting next to each other. I place my hand on her knee again and quickly find her private part. I find that savage jungle that fills me with passion. I become insane. I try to trap her. Meanwhile, she acts as if nothing was happening, not even batting an eyelid. Hey, this frolicking is nice! I keep fondling her. I should suggest that we go to a hotel or ask her out to dinner. I remove my hand and I quickly discover . . . oh, no! . . . I discover that once again I've lost my ring. Impossible, it's a trick. I'm an idiot. "Lady, I lost my ring," I tell her. She doesn't react. I return to the scene of passion. I introduce my hand again, and then bend down to look. Nothing, not a trace of the damned ring. I insert one of my hands completely, then the other hand. It's a very large, deep, and bottomless hole—a wintry cave. I look up and she's still watching Marlene Dietrich. Shit! What a mess I've gotten myself into. Determined, I bend down once more. Both of my hands and then my head go inside. I'm afraid the bald-headed man could report me. Quiet, Messeguer, do it carefully. I insert my feet and then my entire body. I completely enter that abyss, and it is totally dark. I light a match. It's impossible that the ring could have vanished. I illuminate the area from one side to the other with the lit match. Nothing. My God! I have the feeling that the medusa is going to appear soon. I start walking. I walk. I hear deep voices in the distance. Perhaps they're sounds coming from the film. A jelly-like liq-uid, having dripped onto the floor, makes it difficult for me to walk. My breathing is awkward. And what if I wanted to return? Yes, I want to return. I want to return but I'm lost. I've lost myself. I scream. I tell myself: Scream Messeguer, louder . . . louder. "Give me back my ring." I hope that the bald-headed man can come to save me. Nothing. My hands are sweating. Suddenly I see a couple. I get closer and discover that it's . . . Betzi—accompanied by some stranger. Sure, her deception was obvious. My brother was right. I hear her say something about Rochester even though I can barely decipher the syllables. I soon discover that the stranger standing beside her is wearing my ring on the pinky finger of his left hand. Betzi then says something more about the trip. Yes, they should know the way back perfectly. Would it be indiscreet to ask them to return my ring? "Hey, friend," I tell him slyly, "you're wearing my ring." I look at his face. It's impossible . . . the person who is accompanying Betzi is me.

That was the last time we saw each other.

# INDEX

342

*Index*